Comparative Literature and
Comparative Cultural Studies

Comparative Cultural Studies
Steven Tötösy de Zepetnek, Series Editor

Comparative Cultural Studies is a contextual approach in the study of culture in all of its products and processes. The framework is built on tenets of the discipline of comparative literature and cultural studies and on notions borrowed from a range of thought such as (radical) constructivism, communication theories, systems theories, and literary and culture theory. In comparative cultural studies focus is on theory and method as well as application and where attention is on the how rather than on the what. Colleagues interested in publishing in the series are invited to contact the editor, Steven Tötösy, at <clcweb@purdue.edu>.

1. Comparative Central European Culture. Ed. Steven Tötösy de Zepetnek. 2002. 190 pages, bibliography, index. ISBN 1-55753-240-0.

2. Comparative Literature and Comparative Cultural Studies. Ed. Steven Tötösy de Zepetnek. 2002. 356 pages, bibliograpy, index. ISBN 1-55753-290-7.

Comparative Literature and Comparative Cultural Studies

Edited by
Steven Tötösy de Zepetnek

Purdue University Press
West Lafayette, Indiana

Printed in the United States of America

Library of Congress Cataloging-in-Publication Data

Comparative literature and comparative cultural studies / edited by Steven
Tötösy de Zepetnek.
    p. cm.—(Comparative cultural studies)
Includes bibliographical references and index.
   ISBN 1-55753-288-5 (ebook)—ISBN 1-55753-290-7 (pbk. : alk. paper)
   1. Literature, Comparative Cultural Studies. I. Tötösy de Zepetnek,
Steven, 1950- II. Series.
   PN863 .C584 2002
   809—dc21

                        2002012984

Contents

Preface

This collection of papers is the second volume of Books in Comparative Cultural Studies, a new series of books published by Purdue University Press. The new series follows the aims and objectives of and work published in *CLCWeb: Comparative Literature and Culture: A WWWeb Journal*, also published by Purdue at <http://clcwebjournal.lib.purdue.edu/>. The journal's aims and objectives include the publishing of new work in comparative literature, cultural studies, and comparative cultural studies, the maintenance of an online *Library* with extensive and selected bibliographies, an international directory of scholars in the field, pertinent web links, and the operation of a moderated listserv for news and announcements. Both the journal and the new series are built on principal notions of comparative literature and cultural studies and where work with contextual approaches is encouraged. *CLCWeb* is a peer-reviewed quarterly published online only; however, Purdue publishes an annual of the journal with selected articles of the year's work. The present volume is the first annual of the journal, a hard-copy edition of the journal published in the Purdue series of Books in Comparative Cultural Studies. The theme of the journal's first annual in hard copy is *Comparative Literature and Comparative Cultural Studies*, selected from articles published in volumes 1999 and 2000 of the journal. The selection of papers for the present volume is with focus on theories and histories of comparative literature and the emerging field of comparative cultural studies; presented in alphabetical order by authors, the papers are as follows.

Kwaku Asante-Darko, in "Language and Culture in African Postcolonial Literature," offers both conceptual basis and empirical evidence in support of the fact that critical issues concerning protest, authenticity, and hybridity in

African post-colonial literature have often been heavily laden with nationalist and leftist ideological encumbrances, which tended to advocate the rejection of Western standards of aesthetics. One of the literary ramifications of nationalist/anti-colonial mobilization was a racially based aesthetics which saw even the new product of literary hybridity born of cultural exchange as a mark of Western imposition and servile imitation by Africa in their literary endeavor. Asante-Darko exposes the hollowness of the hostile racial militancy of the works of Frantz Fanon and Ngugi by assessing their salient arguments from the point of view of the themes, the methodology, the language choice, and the stratagem of African literary discourse. He explains that all these aspects contain a duality born of the reconcilability of African literary aspirations on one-hand, and Western standards on the other. Asante-Darko demonstrates that the African literary and cultural past cannot be reconstituted but only reclaimed and that the linguistic, thematic, and aesthetic hybridity this presupposes must be embraced to give African literature the freedom it needs to contribute its full quota to the universality of literature.

Hendrik Birus, in "The Goethean Concept of World Literature and Comparative Literature," presents a new reading and understanding of Goethe's famous dictum: "National literature does not mean much at present, it is time for the era of world literature and everybody must endeavor to accelerate this epoch" (Eckermann 198, 31 January 1827). According to Birus, this dictum is not to be taken at face value today and argues that Goethe's concept of world literature ought to be understood in the sense that today it is not the replacement of national literatures by world literature we encounter; rather, it is the rapid blossoming of a multitude of European and non-European literatures and the simultaneous emergence of a world literature—mostly in English translations—as two aspects of one and the same process. The understanding of this dialectic, Birus argues, ought to be one of the main targets of comparative literature today.

Amiya Dev, in "Comparative Literature in India," bases his discussion on the fact that India has many languages and literatures thus representing an a priori situation and conditions of diversity. He therefore argues that to speak of an Indian literature in the singular is problematic. Nonetheless, Dev also observes that to speak of Indian literature in the plural is equally problematic. Such a characterization, he urges, either overlooks or obscures manifest interrelations and affinities. His article compares the unity and the diversity thesis, and identifies the relationship between Indian commonality and differences as the prime site of comparative literature in India. He surveys the current scholarly and intellectual positions on unity and diversity and looks into the poststructuralist doubt of homogenization of differences in the name of unity. Dev also examines the search for common denominators and a possible pattern of togetherness and Dev underlines location and located inter-Indian reception as an aspect of interliterariness. It is t/here Dev perceives Indian literature, that is, not as a fixed or determinate entity but as an ongoing and interliterary process: Indian language and literature ever in the re/making.

Marián Gálik, in his article, "Interliterariness as a Concept in Comparative Literature," observes that the concept of interliterariness has a relative short history and limited application owing to geo-political reasons. He traces the history of the concept and cites instances of its use within the Central European scholarship of comparative literature. Dionýz Ďurišin is identified as the most prominent exponent of the concept and Gálik locates the question of interliterariness within the context of its potential applications. The concept of interliterariness is defended as both a guiding and unifying principle in so far as it is irreducible, relative, and encompassing. Interliterariness provides the universal concept of literature and the study of literature with an ontological grounding and epistemological justification. Literatures may therefore be compared and understood via a historical process and with respect to a systematic series of related literary facts across cultural boundaries, movements, and moments. Literature thereby remains an interliterary global community, one characterized by trans/formations. Consequently, the system(at)ic study of any given literature(s) should trans/form itself accordingly.

Ernst Grabovszki in "The Impact of Globalization and the New Media on the Notion of World Literature," discusses aspects of communication and scholarship in the humanities in the context of social processes resulting from globalization and the impact of new media. The author suggests that the process of communication, the processes of creativity, and the study of literature and the changes these areas are now experiencing owing to the impact of globalization and new media should be studied contextually, from a systemic and empirical point of view. Further, the article is an exposition of changes we observe with regard to the traditional model of literary communication contrasted with the new possibilities offered by the internet and the world wide web. Grabovszki's discussion includes his views on how this new situation results in new possibilities as well as requirements authors, distributors, and readers of literature today have to cope with.

Jan Walsh Hokenson, in "The Culture of the Context: Comparative Literature Past and Future," poses a series of interrogatives around the question of what comparatists have learned about, in Mario J. Valdés's words, "literature in the context of the culture it represents." Hokenson argues that in theoretical terms, culture has become the new vessel for the old wine of sources and influences, and that global and intercultural contexts change the analytical categories for comparatists in the coming millennium. If comparative literature is to survive, it must regain the panoptic view, and if it is to thrive as an academic discipline, it will have to realize its historical aim of embracing all literature, notably of the East as well as the West. She proposes that comparatists clarify the credentials of the discipline, as historically rooted in the analysis of cross-cultural contexts, so that comparative literature may assume its logical role as premier mode of critical study in the coming era of an emergent global poetics.

Marko Juvan, in his article, "On Literariness: From Post-Structuralism to Systems Theory," argues that the question of literariness concerns the very identity and social existence of not only literature per se but of literary theory as a discipline. A literary theorist is not only an observer of literature; he/she is also a participant who is engaged in constructing both the notion and the practice of literature as well as the study of literature. Literariness is neither an invariant cluster of "objectively" distinctive properties of all texts that are deemed literary nor is it merely a social, scholarly, and/or educational function. Rather, it can be defined as the effect of a text in the context of the system of culture, which is only possible on the basis of paradigms and conventions derived from the literary canon itself.

Karl S.Y. Kao, in "Comparative Literature and the Ideology of Metaphor, East and West," offers a comparative reading of the ideological function of metaphor within Eastern and Western thinking. Nietzsche is recognized as the earliest serious challenger to the concepts of meaning and truth within the West, whilst Derrida and de Man are discussed with respect to their conception that figurality is inherent within—and integral to—Western philosophical and literary discourse. Parallel to this conception of conceptuality is the Eastern view of language and literature. Kao notes that the Western opposition between logic and rhetoric is not inherent within—or integral to—Eastern thought. He examines various rhetorical figures within Eastern philosophy and literature and a contrasting between affective (expressive; East) and mimetic (representational; West) is urged and interrogated. Eastern thought may be distinguished by an awareness of the problematical status of the conceptuality of thought. Despite this awareness, parallel problems threaten to emerge—whilst the West has tried to inaugurate a distinction between metaphor and concept, the East has tended to subsume them. On the one hand, we encounter a problematical distinction between meaning and truth; on the other hand, we encounter a problematic equivocation.

Krištof Jacek Kozak, in "Comparative Literature in Slovenia," provides a historical overview of the practice of theory in the discipline of comparative literature in the intellectual and educational environment of a "minor" culture in Europe. Despite its small size and relative low profile, Slovenia is taken as an exemplar within comparative literature scholarship. Kozak observes that the development of comparative literature in Slovenia may be characterized by an attempt to both arbitrate and mediate between distinct poles. On the one hand, Slovenian scholarship has felt the need to secure or determine itself in accordance with its own interests and concerns. On the other hand, it has recognized the need to be in accord with various movements and determinations across national borders. This situation is primarily mediated via the accounts of Janko Kos, a prominent scholar of the field. Via Kos, Kozak traces the origins of comparative literature to various theoretical movements and counter movements and while a methodological pluralism has emerged, there is resistance to an "anything goes" approach in Kos' thought as well as by Slovenian comparatists in general. This situation is highlighted by the occurrence of recurrent issues, questions, and problems, and the article converges around movements between distinct legacies and poles.

Manuela Mourão, in "Comparative Literature in the United States," offers a historical overview of debates about comparative literature as a discipline from the early years of its institutionalization in the United States until the present. Mourão summarizes the most pointed—and anxious—interventions of prominent scholars in the field and discusses the permanent sense of crisis that has been a characteristic of the discipline. Further, Mourão links the permanent anxiety of the discipline with the prescriptive tendencies that have continued to endure until the present. She then looks at the debates that followed the controversial "Bernheimer Report" of 1993, discusses briefly the development of the field since then, and points out specific ways in which comparatists have continued to push the discipline forward despite decades of self-conscious scrutiny and anxiety.

Jola Škulj, in "Comparative Literature and Cultural Identity," proposes a framework inspired by Mikhail Bakhtin's work. Škulj argues that the validity of cultural identity cannot be an equivalent to the measure of originality of an inherent national subjectivity in it. Such an idea of identity concept, quite acceptable in the nineteenth century, is insufficient to the views in literary studies today. From the standpoint of comparative literature, cultural identity exists only through its own deconstruction and permanent multiplication of several cultural relations. The identity principle of individual cultures is in fact established through the principle of otherness or—to use Bakhtin's terminology—through the principle of dialogism. As any individuality, cultural identity is a meeting point of several cross-cultural implications. It is of a complex plurivocal character, open to its own changes in order to preserve its own being in a new context of interests. Škulj argues that cultural identity is an intertext expressed in many instances in and via culture texts including literature. Thus, permanently re-interpreted, cultural identity refers to the field of research of cross-cultural interactions and such a concept of cultural identity pre-eminently belongs to an expanded field of comparative studies as comparative cultural studies.

Slobodan Sucur, in "Theory, Period Styles, and Comparative Literature as Discipline," attempts to answer the following question: can a rapprochement be brought about between various, often antagonistic, literary-theoretical views and the concept of comparative literature itself, which requires accord, consensus, agreement, etc., for it to function as a concrete body and discipline? Sucur attempts dealing with this question in three parts of the paper: First, he establishes a relationship/link between the theoretical discord of today (humanism, formalism, deconstruction, etc.) and the high theorizing which began during the Jena-Berlin phase of Romanticism (Shelling, Hegel, F. Schlegel, etc.); secondly, he attempts linking the origin of comparative literature with later Romanticism (Virgil Nemoianu's idea of the Biedermeier) in order to account for some inconsistencies between ideas of "theory" on the one hand, and "discipline" on the other; and thirdly, he speculates on whether or not "literary history"—an idea often neglected now—can be the bridge where literary theory meets up with comparative literature as a disciplinary endeavor, that is, in the act of writing a comparative literary history.

Peter Swirski, in "Popular and Highbrow Literature: A Comparative View," discusses the role and status of popular fiction in contemporary culture. Starting with the basic question, "Who needs popular fiction?," he surveys select sociological evidence and prevailing aesthetic arguments in order to take stock of the ways in which highbrow literature and popular fiction relate to each other. He begins with statistical and socio-economic data which casts different lights on many myths prevailing in scholarship as well as in general social and cultural discourse, such as the death of the novel, the alleged decline of the reading public, and the role of paperback publishing and commercial pressures in shaping literary production. In the second part of the paper, Swirski examines persistent aesthetic arguments used to deride and attack popular literature. Both parts of the paper extended arguments for a greater literary democracy, reflected in his recommendations for a critical response to popular fiction more compatible with its actual socio-aesthetic status.

Antony Tatlow, in "Comparative Literature as Textual Anthropology," proposes textual anthropology as a critic's approach in the comparative study of literature. If anthropology is "behavioral hermeneutics" (Geertz) with the implication of self-reflexivity, the anthropologist will be disposed to fashion in the object of attention what is neglected and that can therefore be described as the unconscious of his/her own culture. In an application of his framework, Tatlow relates totemic and utopian thought through the use of animal signs. In his paper, Tatlow shows how cultural demands both fashion the ethnographer-critic and select the perspectives he/she must transcend. As auto-anthropologist, the artist "invents," instead of "describing," the Other. Tatlow discusses in his application of textual anthropology in comparative literature Gauguin and Brecht and shows how Lévi-Strauss enables us to understand Brecht's response to Daoism and Buddhism as energized by the repressions in what we call the social or cultural unconscious.

William H. Thornton, in his article, "Analyzing East/West Power Politics in Comparative Cultural Studies," acknowledges culture as a central force on the geopolitical map and undertakes at once to preserve the strategic potency of political realism and to move beyond the "billiard ball" externality of both neo- and traditional realisms. Although Huntington and Fukuyama are taken seriously on the question of East/West power politics, Thornton develops a world view by grounding balance-of-power politics in national and local (not just civilizational) social reality. Further, Thornton argues against external democratic teleologies both Huntington and Fukuyama have imposed on the cultural Other. The thrust of Thornton's argumentation goes beyond the monolithic fallacies of political modernism, namely, political realism on the one hand and today's "reverse domino" globalization on the other. Once political realism takes this postmodern turn, it confronts the agonistic realities that killed the New World Order in its infancy. Although Huntington's notion of the clash of civilizations also confronted these grim realities, it did so in terms of a negative and retreatist realism. For Thornton, in the post-Cold War world that Huntington well describes but declines to fully engage, any effective realism must temper cultural agonistics with Bakhtinian cultural dialogics.

Steven Tötösy, in "From Comparative Literature Today Toward Comparative Cultural Studies," proposes a merger of tenets and postulates found in the disciplines of comparative literature and cultural studies. The framework of a comparative cultural studies is conceived as an approach containing at this point three main areas of theoretical content: 1) to study literature (text and/or literary system) comparatively with and in the context of culture and the discipline of cultural studies; 2) in cultural studies itself to study literature with borrowed elements (theories and methods) from comparative literature; and 3) to study culture and its composite parts and aspects in the mode of the proposed comparative cultural studies approach instead of the currently reigning single-language approach dealing with a topic with regard to its nature and problematics in one culture only. At the same time, comparative cultural studies would implicitly and explicitly disrupt the established hierarchy of cultural products and production similarly to the disruption cultural studies itself has performed. The suggestion is to pluralize and parallel-ize the study of culture without hierarchization. The paper contains brief descriptions of recent volumes in comparative literature across the globe and closes with a ten-point draft proposal of how to do comparative cultural studies.

Xiaoyi Zhou and Q. S. Tong, in their co-authored article, "Comparative Literature in China," present an intellectual and institutional history of the discipline in China in the context of global comparativism. According to Zhou and Tong, main features of the history of comparative literature in China include the fact that as an academic discipline and a mode of intellectual inquiry imported to China from the West in the early twentieth century, the discpline has always been a priori strategically political and the proposition that the development of comparative literature in China is closely related to the formation of China's literary modernity includes the parallel issue of national identity. Further, Zhou and Tong argue that built upon the politics of national identity construction and the development of modernity, Chinese comparatists tend to remain traditional and adhere, up to recent times, to scholarly practices of traditional comparative literature. Thus, the said ideological background determines some of the concerns Chinese scholars in their analysis of Chinese-foreign cultural relationships inquire into and the authors present the argument that this situation produce scholarship of lesser rigor. Ultimately, Zhou and Tong argue for a redirection of Chinese comparative literature into a more culture-oriented and less traditional comparative literature in China, similar to the situation of the discipline in the West.

For further work in comparative literature and comparative cultural studies, the volume includes "Toward Comparative Cultural Studies: A Selected Bibliography of Comparative Literature and Cultural Studies (Theories, Methods, Histories, 1835 to 2002)," compiled by Steven Tötösy, Steven Aoun, and Wendy C. Nielsen.

Readers now and future decide the merits of the volume and thought within; however, the compiler and organizer of the volume proposes that the papers in the volume present innovative thought for the development of the discipline of comparative literature and that scholars in the humanities would take up the challenge to consider a "merger" of comparative literature with cultural studies. . . .

Steven Tötösy de Zepetnek
Winchester at Boston, December 2001

Language and Culture in African Postcolonial Literature

Kwaku Asante-Darko

Post-colonial literature is a synthesis of protest and imitation. It blends revolt and conciliation. This duality permeates its stratagem, its style, and its themes in a manner that is not always readily perceptible to critics. This has practical didactic implications for the contemporary literary endeavor in Africa. The central concern of this article is to assess the extent to which African protest literature seems to have imitated European and colonial literary discourse in matters such as thematic concerns, aesthetics, and methodology. The relationship of imitation, exchange, and hybridity is presented with the view to highlighting the thematic, methodological, and aesthetic differences between some aspects of African literature on one hand and the Western literary tradition on the other.

The African colonial experience has dominated the origin and nature of contemporary African protest literature and rendered it opposed to Western standards of aesthetics. This Manichean perception must have been a reaction to Horace's position, "O imitatores, servum pecus!" Imitators are a servile race. The rejection was reinforced by the general impression that Africa needed to evolve a literature that will not be an imitation of the literary norms of Europe. It is therefore not surprising that authors of protest literature advocated a literary endeavor, whose style, language, aesthetic standards and concerns were required to be different from those of the colonizing powers who were seen as having subjugated them and undervalued every aspect of their lives. The desire for originality was thus to become the prerequisite for authentic African literature, which would explore Africa's past, buttress its present, and advocate a hopeful future. Wauthier observed that: "The hero of the African novel is nearly always black, and if by chance he is white as in Le Regard du roi by Camara Laye, the action at least is situated in Africa and the story deals with African mentality. The poet, for his part, sings of the African woman and the land of Africa, or denounces colonialism" (Wauthier 1966, 24). It is from this perspective that Negritude came to be seen as an aggressive anti-racist condemnation of white supremacy. A closer look at the strands that went into weaving the fabric of this Negritude protest literature, however, reveals that in executing its work of protest, Negritude imitated some of the objectives and methods of the very racism it kicked against. It is worthy of note that in doing this, there is a move to the imitation of some of the salient methods of the colonial enterprise: The written word which colonialism had introduced to many parts of hitherto unlettered corners of the continent of Africa. The wide range of transformation occasioned by this attests not only to the necessity of literacy but also to the flexibility and pragmatism of African peoples when it comes to adapting to new exigencies. Jacques Chevrier explains the nature and impact of this novelty when he notes that: "A une civilisation de l'oralité se substitue donc progressivement une civilisation de l'écriture don't l'émergence est attestée par l'apparition d'une littérature négro-africaine en langue française. Cette littérature, don't les premières manifestations remontent à 1921, s'est affirmée dans les années qui ont précédé l'accession à l'indépendance des États africains et elle s'est déployée dans plusieurs directions" (Chevrier 1984, 25).

It must be noted, however that the social change introduced by this literary change was not completely imbibed as Chevrier seems to suggest here. To the rejection of the European literary style was added a measure of mistrust, however sullen, the mistrust of the entire European way of life. Michael Dei-Anang in a poem entitled "Whither Bound Africa" disputed the adoption or imitation of European civilization in the following words: "Forward! To what? / To the reeking round Of medieval crimes, / Where the greedy hawks/ O Aryan stock / Prey with bombs and guns / On men of lesser breed?" (Dei-Anang 18–19). The ravages of the Second World War thus become a symbol of European cultural indecency, and a justification for the rejection of Western values. Nonetheless, the universal nature of these European problems, and their implicit relevance to the Africa situation is reflected in the transposition of some European themes into the Africa environment. For instance, Sophocles' King Oedipus is transposed as The Gods are not to Be Blamed by Ola Rotimi, Antigone is transposed as The Island by Athol Fugard, Kani, and Ntshona, while Euripides' The Bacchae is transposed as

The Bacchae of Euripides by Wole Soyinka. Such a critical approach to foreign values indicates that the acceptance of those Western values some of
which have become the center of protest was partly as a result of a conscious
selection and free choice by the colonized. Again, it is in this context that Senghor could elaborate his literary dicta such as "Assimilate, don't be Assimi-
lated," and "Cultural Cross-breeding." When all is said and done it will be
realized that the introduction to Africa of new ways of doing things is essentially an offer of an opportunity to choose between different options, at least
the old and the new, the Western and the indigenous.

The hybrid nature of literary expression of African resistance to the colonial experience and its consequences as mirrored in the pioneering written literary works validates this position. For instance, in his assessment of the
nature and origin of the Negritude Movement, Hymans notes that: "There are
many *negritudes*: the aggressive *Negritude* clamouring for recognition of
African values; the conciliatory *Negritude* advocating cultural miscegenation
or cross-breeding; and an inventive *Negritude* tending toward a new humanism. These three major currents have been present from 1931 onwards; but
according to the period and the 'militant', one of these aspects has taken prece-
dence over the other" (Hymans 1977, 23). These three "Negritudes" contain
elements that can be considered legitimate reactions to the type of negation to
which colonialists subjected their territories. It is not surprising that in clamoring for recognition Negritude counted on the method of confrontation and
demystification. Sartre notes concerning the negritude writer that: "pour con-
struire sa Vérité, il faut qu'il ruine celle des autres" (Sartre 1948, xxiii). The
aggressiveness of Negritude is thus explicable in the logic of vengeance that is
essentially an imitation in so far as it is one's reaction to another's action. When
we avenge or retaliate we simply imitate. The adversary who argues that: "My
(exaggerated) action is a reaction to the enemy's action" is only indicating that
he has followed the precedent of the aggressor. The imitation embodied in the
retaliation or vituperative vengeance of the negritude writer was not wantonly
destructive. It was not meant to question the humanity and intelligence of any
race. It was constructive in that it sought the restoration of the truth of racial
equality. One of the means of doing this was to imitate the culture of the written word to complement that of the oral. That same language and method
used to denigrate him becomes his instrument of revalorization and pride, and
restitution. The inferiority attributed to him by imposition is thus rejected by
imitation. This imitation then seems imposed in a way since he is obliged by

circumstances to address the colonizer in a language and logic that the colonizer can understand, hence the use of European languages and literary forms as instruments of post-colonial literary expression.

The distinction between imitation and imposition in the evolution of modern African literary discourse is pertinent to the question of responsibility for the contemporary crisis of post-colonial Africa—a continent that is believed to have taken its destiny into its own hands. This is because imitation presupposes choice, and choice implies responsibility for the consequences thereof. Two opinions have been expressed on this issue. The first tends to presume the virtuous innocence of pre-colonial African culture and society. This makes, by implication, the African the lethargic entity in a world of so-called foreign evils. Ademola in the following poem expresses this position thus: "Here we stand / infants overblown / poised between two civilizations / finding the balancing irksome,/ itching for something to happen, / to tip us one way or the other, / groping in the dark for a helping hand / and finding none . . ." (Ademola 1962, 65).

The imagery of the African as an "infant overblown" who is finding it difficult to balance the effects of two civilizations is essentially a facile one. The impression is further created that the persona (the African) lacks initiative and is simply "itching for something to happen," Such notions have been propagated by the erroneous idea that it is unacceptable for an African to imitate practices and values which were originally European even when such imitation is realistic and pragmatic. The rejection of such imitation is flawed on at least two grounds: First, the African of today cannot in any significant or participatory sense claim membership of the erstwhile pre-colonial culture to which the personas of some poets are so idyllically attached. This is because the contemporary African has been born into a cultural setting which is a blend of the pre-colonial traditional past and the introduction of "foreign" notions. Second, the pre-colonial past can only be claimed but never reconstituted. The failure to distinguish between what can be recovered in its purity and what is irremediably lost to hybridization can lead to a literal misinterpretation of the ideas expressed in the works such as this poem of Guy Tirolien entitled: "Je ne veux plus aller à leur école" in which the persona advocates the rejection of European values and education in favor of the traditional African way of life: "Je veux suivre mon père dans les ravines fraîches / Quand la nuit flotte encore dans le mystère des bois / Où glissent les esprits que l'aube vient chasser./ Je veux aller pieds nus par les rouges sentiers / Que cuisent les flammes de midi . . ." (Tirolien 1981, 137–38). The essence of the standard and models of these societies, like those of other pre-industrial ones elsewhere (Greek, Roman, Chinese) is a construct that is not static. Such pre-colonial nostalgia among African writers can be appreciated only when they evoke history as guide for the future.

Another issue of imitation and hybridization in pos-colonial African literature is that of language. Frantz Fanon had already indicated that "The use of language as a tool of assimilation and subsequent rebellion against linguistic integration and alienation have become familiar aspects of colonial life" (qtd. in Gendzier 1973, 47). It was clear that some advocates of African authenticity have been swift to brand foreign languages as instruments of colonial domination whose public practices must be discontinued at least in postcolonial African literature. Basing their arguments on the debatable premise that the imitation or introduction of a foreign language presupposes the inferiority of the imitator, Ngugi, for instance, has argued that: "The bullet was the means of the physical subjugation. Language was the means of the spiritual subjugation" (Ngugi 1972, 282) and "Language carries culture, and culture carries, particularly through orature and literature, the entire body of values by which we come to perceive ourselves and our place in the world" (Ngugi 1972, 290). This idea falls in with the disputable opinion according to which the possession of a particular language indicates that the possessor shares or even approves of the ideological and cultural worldview of the society in which the language is born and practiced. Frantz Fanon puts this as follows: "Tout peuple colonisé c'est-à-dire tout peuple au sein duquel a pris naissance un complexe d'infériorité du fait de la mise au tombeau de l'originalité culturelle locale se situe vis-à-vis du langage de la nation civilisatrice c'est-à-dire de la culture métropolitaine" (Fanon 1963, 209).

The very premises of such contentions begin to falter upon little deliberation and interrogation. When we understand that political decolonization was achieved through a combination of the very same instruments of colonial oppression—the intelligentsia, the armed forces, and a colonial middle-class, among others. Will it be awkward to expect that the freedom from "the spiritual subjugation" about which Ngugi speaks can be achieved through the subversive influence of this same foreign language? In fact this is what happened. The legitimacy or appropriateness of this question resides in the fact that these same foreign languages have been the cementing factor for communication and the spread of ideas among countless African societies, which were hitherto separated and linguistically inconsonant entities lacking any form of inter-comprehensibility. Again, different section of African communities differ as to what constitutes spiritual "subjugation" in the final analysis. While some advocate a return to pre-colonial values others have not hesitated to indicate that: "we do not intend to revive the past as it was. . . . We want to integrate into modern life only what seems valuable from the past. Our goal is neither the traditional African nor the Black European, but the modern African" ("Ntu Editorial" 1964, 79).

It follows from these opposing perspectives that while some may see a reconstitution of pre-colonial culture as redemptive others may not only see it as impossible but also undesirable. To the latter the post-colonial reality is not a physical mixture but a chemical compound that cannot be separated into its initial constituents. Imitation of language, like that of cultural value, then becomes not only positive but also a means of inevitable hybridization. Paul Ansah has observed concerning pioneering African poets that: "But the virtually total rejection of western civilization never constituted a major theme in the writing of the pioneer poets of Anglophone West Africa, and this is sharp contrast to the violence with which western culture is rejected, even if only symbolically or as a mere poetic attitude, by the francophone black poets of Negritude persuasion both West Indian and African" (Ansah 1974, 48). The position of Fanon and Ngugi can be summed up in the contention that foreign languages in Africa are imposition which must be rejected on the grounds that they are vehicles of a foreign culture whose continuing imitation or acceptance in the literature of post-colonial society is indicative of persisting subjugation. Ngugi notes in "Towards a National Culture" that: "by acquiring the thought-process and values of his adopted tongue . . . becomes alienated from the values of his mother tongue, or from the language of the masses" (Ngugi 1972, 16). It must, however, be pointed out that any language is capable of carrying any culture just as any culture can carry any language: Witness the transformation of diverse ancient cultures and societies when they fell under Greek and Roman sway). Languages and cultures have demonstrated a capacity to adapt to "foreign" cultures and novelties in science, philosophy and art by the introduction of new words and borrowing from other languages to express the new notions. Such borrowing underscores the phenomenon of linguistic exchange that is essentially a process of imitation and hybridization. A careful study of the etymology of words like "bank," "police," and "association" and their introduction into various European languages indicates how language, rather than being static, is a medium of imitating new realities. Language can be deemed capable of supporting the mutable and dangling weight of such a dynamic a thing as culture. The adoption of foreign words like "taboo" and "kwashiorkor" into the English language, for instance, as well as the existence of structurally ethnographic sentences in novel written by Anglophone and Francophone African writers is equally indicative of the rich exchange which already exists and can be developed to foster understanding.

The real problem arises when we classify literature into realms of linguistic expression rather than into representations of cultural experience; when we consider the works of Joseph Conrad as English literature, those of Ionesco and Beckett as French literature rather than a classification that will emphasis content rather than medium. It will therefore be more realistic to refer to a classification such as "Commonwealth Literature" to be more realistic than say "Francophone Literature" or "Lusophone Literature." The reference here is made to a common (cultural) colonial/imperial experience that unites Great Britain and its former colonies; and these experiences can be expressed in African languages as well. Such a definition of Commonwealth goes beyond mere linguistic expression. As it is, the rejection of foreign languages as mediums of African literature will logically devour every idea of African Literature. There will rather be ethnic literatures of all types. In this degeneration, language rather than a common experience will be the determinant of literary classification.

African literature will dissolve and polarize into a situation akin to what Achebe seemed to be hinting at when he said: "I'm an Igbo writer, because this is my basic culture; Nigerian, African and writer . . . no, black first, then a writer. Each of these identities does call for a certain commitment on my part" (qtd. in Appiah et al. 1991, 19). Here culture and experience rather than language becomes the essence of literature. Ngugi's claim to linguistic rejection on the grounds that the linguistic indigenization of African literature will rid Africans of so-called corrupt foreign "thought-processes and values of [their] adopted tongue" is equally enfeebled by the fact that there are countless instances in history where people of one and the same language and culture have been divided over everyday issues of central importance, and have even gone to war over them. The legitimate question then arises: If ideology is a derivative of linguistic structure (the adoption of which, it is believed, will corrupt African minds) how do Fanon and Ngugi explain such fratricidal wars? More important, their contention dangerously undermines the very effort at peaceful multiethnic nation-building in Africa since the linguistic diversity of the various states would imply—following the logic of Ngugi and Fanon and those who share their opinion—the existence of opposing ideologies, conflicting and irreconcilable values, and world views. In fact, to purport that a given language possesses any measure of intrinsic oppressive, imperial domineering tendencies and must therefore be rejected as a medium of the emancipatory account of post-coloniality is not only objectionable but also patently idealistic and superstitious, especially when the cultures of such languages are the cradles of *The Magna Charta* and *The Rights of Man.* Contrary to the claims of the proponents of the rejection of foreign languages as a medium of African literature, the stylistic legacy bequeathed to post-colonial writers found meaningful expression in the works of Negritude writers. Sartre, for instance notes that: "le surréalisme, mouvement poétique européen, est dérobé aux Européens par un Noir qui le tourne contre eux et lui assigne une fonction rigoureusement définie" (Sartre 1948, xxviii). This assertion made in connection with the work of Aimé Césaire attests to the efficacy of imitation in matters of artistic expression (see, for example, *Présence Africaine*).

Another area in which post-colonial literature imitates colonial discourse is myth making. This mythical dimension consists of opposing myth with myth. To the idea of African inferiority the post-colonial writer opposed that of African intrinsic goodness and incorruptibility. The rejection of a supposedly foreign tainted present by Negritude naturally led to the desire to reclaim and imitate the past. This was attractive for several reasons among which is the natural psychological desire to be part not only of a distinct and exclusive and glorious past but also to acquire a sense of an appurtenance which links one to an indissoluble group that stretches across eternity. It is, therefore, clear that far from constituting an expression of freedom, the rejection of European values as advocated by post-colonial African critics and writer has meant the imposition of prohibitions and inhibitions which tend to coerce individuals into sticking to limited choices in matters of cultural values and language. It therefore has implications for marriage, profession, migration, food, and dress. It might close the door to profitable hybridization and universalism. Again, Mphalele, for instance, has indicated the inevitability of imitation and hybridization in these terms: "I personally cannot think of the future of my people in South Africa as something in which the white man does not feature. Whether he likes it or not, our destinies are inseparable. I have seen too much that is good in western culture—for example, its music, literature and theater—to want to repudiate it" (Mphalele 1962, 40).

In concluding this brief discussion I would like to reiterate that the ubiquity (or even dominance) of "imperial" culture and language may provoke reactions of nationalism but it does not constitute subjugation *per se*. The modern concept and role of African literature must be founded on the solid rock of universal patrimony so that we can begin to see its linguistic medium and themes as part of a global heritage. This will belong to a humanism which eschews the Manichean perception that whatever language or culture is introduced into Africa by the "oppressive institution of colonialism" must be opposed and rejected in favor of pre-colonial ones. Such advocacy is patently misleading because it divides the partners of cultural exchange in Africa into makers and imitators rather than parties engaged in an exchange in which all are both makers and imitators, drawing vision and change from a common source that belongs to humanity as a whole. The choice to imitate foreign languages and cultures in African literature will continue to provide a unifying center for the myriad of African languages and cultures for which the political and legal implications of a return to pre-colonial multilingualism and culture diversity are neither desirable nor possible.

WORKS CITED

Ademola, Francis. *Reflection: Nigerian Prose and Verse*. Lagos: Africa UP, 1962.

Ansah, Paul A.V. "Black Awareness in African Poetry in English." *Legon: Journal of Humanities*. Accra: Ghana Publishing Corporation, 1974. 35–53.

Appiah, Athony Kwame, et al. "Interview with Chinua Achebe." *Reading Chinua Achebe: Language and Ideology in Fiction*. Ed. Simon Gikandi. Nairobi: Heinemann, 1991. 30–36.

Chevrier, Jacques. *Littérature nègre*. Paris: Armand Colin, 1984.

"Ntu Editorials." *Which Way Africa? The Search for a New Society*. Ed. Basil Davidson. London: Penguin Books, 1964. 74–80.

Dei-Anang, Michael. *Africa Speaks*. Accra: Guinea P, 1959.

Gendzier, Irene L. *Fanon: A Critical Study*. London: Wildwood House, 1973.

Fanon, Frantz. *Les Damnés de la terre*. Paris: Présence Africaine, 1963.

Mpalele, Ezekiel. *The African Image*. London: Faber & Faber, 1962.

Hymans, Jacques Louis. *Leopold Sedar Senghor: An Intellectual Biography*. Edinburgh: Edinburgh UP, 1977.

Ngugi wa Thiong'o. *Decolonizing the Mind: The Politics of Language in African Literature*. London: J. Currey, 1986.

Ngugi wa Thiong'o. *Homecoming: Towards a National Culture*. London: HEB, 1972.

Ngugi wa Thiong'o. "The Language of African Literature." *The Post-Colonial Studies Reader*. Ed. Bill Ashcroft, Gareth Griffiths, and Helen Tiffin. London: Routledge, 1995. 285–90.

Présence Africaine: Revue culturelle du monde noir / Cultural Review of the Negro World. Special Issue *Hommage à Aimé Césaire* 151–152 (1995): 3–253.

Sartre, Jean-Paul. "Orphée noir." *Anthologie de la nouvelle poésie négre et Malgache*. Ed. L.S. Senghor. Paris: PU de France 1948. ix–xliv.

Tirolien, Guy. "Je ne veux plus aller à leur école." *Anthologie Négro-Africaine. Littérature de 1918 à 1981*. Ed. Lylian Kesteloot. Verviers: Marabout, 1981. 135–38.

Wauthier, Claude. *The Literature and Thought of Modern Africa: A Survey*. London: Pall Mall P, 1966.

The Goethean Concept of World Literature and Comparative Literature

Hendrik Birus

There is currently little agreement about the systematic localization or methodology of comparative literature. What is far less controversial is the description of the field of comparative literature as world literature. But what is world literature? The answer seems trivial: The literature of the entire world. Yet this entails certain problems, since today noone will be able to simply say, as Goethe could over 160 years ago: "European, i.e., world literature" ("europäische, d.h., Weltliteratur"; as reads the heading of a late outline of Goethe's [Werke. Sophien-Ausgabe; further on referred to as WA [I, 42.2, 500]). This is why Etiemble's lecture at the IVth Congress of the 1964 ICLA/AILC: International Association of Comparative Literature in Fribourg posed the pro-·grammatic question: "Fautil réviser la notion de *Weltliteratur*?" (Etiemble 1975). Etiemble's demand for a "littérature universelle" (Etiemble 1982)—or a "littérature (vraiment) générale" (Etiemble 1966, 1975)—offered the tempting prospect of a "comparatisme planétaire" (Etiemble 1988). At the same time, however, it also suggested a concept of "world literature" too vast to be grasped by anyone, regardless of linguistic and literary education. After all, even the "decaglottism" proposed a century ago by the comparatist Hugó Meltzl von Lomnitz—Meltzl had suggested focusing on German, English, French, Icelandic, Italian, Dutch, Portuguese, Swedish, Spanish, and Hungarian (see Berczik)—would remain, in its Eurocentrism, a far cry from the well-founded principles established by Etiemble (1975, 19–20). Should we then, for the sake of feasibility, view as "world literature" only the best examples of all literatures from different epochs and regions? It was in this sense that Horst Rüdiger, the post-IInd World War founder of the German section of the

ICLA/AILC, stood up for the "right and duty of literary evaluation according to supra-national standards" ("das Recht und die Pflicht zur literarischen Wertung nach übernationalen Maßstäben"), arguing that "the qualitative canonical concept of 'world literature' is an aesthetically necessary correlate to the quantitative, geographical concept of 'literatures of the world'" ("Dem quantitativen, dem extensiv-geographischen Begriff der 'Literaturen der Welt' stellt sich der qualitative, der kanonische Begriff der 'Weltliteratur' als ästhetisch notwendiges Korrelat zur Seite") (1972, 51, 1973; Marino 204–05). But, as noted contemptuously by Werner Krauss, the doyen of Romance Languages and Literatures in the German Democratic Republic, world literature "accordingly rises above all literatures as a superliterature, with its masterpieces towering above every normal horizon. World literature thus turns into a great pandemonium in which Cervantes and Rabelais, Dante and Voltaire nod to each other" ("Sie erhebt sich dann als eine Spitzenliteratur mit ihren unsterblichen, den Normalhorizont überragenden Meisterwerken über alle Literaturen. Weltliteratur ist dann zu einem Pandämonium geworden, in dem sich Cervantes und Rabelais, Dante und Voltaire zunicken") (347–48).

This was in no way Goethe's concept of "world literature," which he coined in the last decade of his life as a reaction to Romantic—even pre-Romantic—literary criticism's breaking through of the traditional limits of Occidental literature by revaluating popular poetry and the literatures of the Middle Ages and of the Orient. Indeed, in the present use of the term, the quantitative aspect of world literature—its extensional universality considering all particular literatures—is often paralleled by the qualitative aspect of the exemplary value of those texts that belong to it. But contrary to this interpretation of world literature as a comprehensive and hierarchically structured thesaurus, Goethe had pointed out that it was presently, that is, contemporaneous to him, emerging. After all, from 1827 on Goethe asserts in the most varied ways that "such a world literature will soon come into being, as is inevitable given the ever-increasing rapidity of human interaction" ("eine solche Weltliteratur, wie bey der sich immer vermehrenden Schnelligkeit des Verkehrs unausbleiblich ist, sich nächstens bildet") (WA I, 42.2, 502]; similarly in a letter to Adolph Friedrich Carl Streckfuß, 27 January 1827 [WA IV, 42, 28] and in *Maximen und Reflexionen* [WA I, 42.2, 202]), he even compares his situation to that of the sorcerer's apprentice, with the advancing world literature "streaming towards him as if to engulf him" ("daß die von mir angerufene Weltliteratur auf mich, wie auf den Zauberlehrling, zum Ersaufen zuströmt") (Goethe to Carl Friedrich

Zelter, 21 May 1828 [WA IV, 44, 101]). And Goethe himself, like the later authors of the *Communist Manifesto*, related the resulting "universal world literature" ("allgemeine Weltliteratur") not only in a general way to the "contemporary, highly turbulent epoch" ("gegenwärtige, höchst bewegte Epoche") and its "vastly facilitated communications" ("durchaus erleichterte Communication") (WA I, 41.2, 299), but also quite concretely to the "constantly spreading activities of trade and commerce" ("immer mehr umgreifende Gewerks- und Handelsthätigkeit") (WA I, 42.2, 505) in which he saw the "human spirit gradually attaining the desire to participate in the more or less untrammeled intellectual trade" ("kam der Geist nach und nach zu dem Verlangen, auch in den mehr oder weniger freien geistigen Handelsverkehr mit aufgenommen zu werden") (WA I, 42.1, 187).

Yet, for Goethe the significance of the concept of world literature is not merely limited to such current or future relevance. Marx and Engels' *Communist Manifesto* had responded to the new quality of class antagonism by representing not only the present, but also the "history of all previous societies" ("die Geschichte aller bisherigen Gesellschaft") as "the history of class-struggle" ("die Geschichte von Klassenkämpfen") (Marx and Engels 1974, 462; note Engels' clearly restricting annotation to the English edition of 1888). Goethe similarly lends his new concept of "world literature" further retrospective significance when he insists: "If we have dared to proclaim a European literature, indeed a universal world literature, then we have hardly done so simply to point out that different nations acknowledge each other and their respective creations, for in this sense it has existed for a long time and continues more or less to flourish" (1975, 295) ("Wenn wir eine europäische, ja eine allgemeine Weltliteratur zu verkündigen gewagt haben, so heißt dieses nicht daß die verschiedenen Nationen von einander und ihren Erzeugnissen Kenntnis nehmen, denn in diesem Sinne existiert sie schon lange, setzt sich fort und erneuert sich mehr oder weniger" [1970, 295]). What both applications of the term have in common, however, is Goethe's conviction that "like all things of supreme value, [art] belongs to the whole world and can only be promoted by a free and general interaction among contemporaries" ("[Kunst] gehöre wie alles Gute der ganzen Welt an und könne nur durch allgemeine freie Wechselwirkung aller zugleich Lebenden, in steter Rücksicht auf das, was uns vom Vergangenen übrig und bekannt ist, gefördert werden") (WA I, 48, 23). Naturally, a discourse of this kind must "always remain attentive to what has been inherited from the past," as we read in the famous stanza from the West-Eastern Divan: "He who cannot be farsighted / Nor three thousand years assay, / Inexperienced stays benighted /Let him live from day to day" ("Wer nicht von dreytausend Jahren / Sich weiß Rechenschaft zu geben, / Bleib im Dunkeln unerfahren, / Mag von Tag zu Tage leben (Und wer franzet oder brittet)" (1994, 59).

Although this historical field of reference cannot be excluded from the concept of "world literature," it by no means constitutes its core as a kind of treasury of humanity, but rather has its function solely with regard to the experience and interaction of contemporaries. Contrary to Gadamer's assertion of the "normative significance" ("normativer Sinn") of "world literature" (167), then, Goethe represents just the opposite of a normative concept of world literature. Rather, in the famous conversation with Eckermann on 31 January 1827, he introduces his proclamation of the "epoch of world literature" with the following observation:

> "I see increasingly that poetry is a common property of mankind and that it emerges in all places and at all times from many hundreds of people. Some are a little better at it than others and stay on top a little longer, that is all there is to it . . . everyone must realize that the gift of poetry is not so rare a thing, and that nobody has reason to let it go to his head if he produces a good poem" (Ich sehe immer mehr, daß die Poesie ein Gemeingut der Menschheit ist und daß sie überall und zu allen Zeiten in Hunderten und aber Hunderten von Menschen hervortritt. Einer macht es ein wenig besser als der andere und schwimmt ein wenig länger oben als der andere, das ist alles. . . . jeder muß sich eben sagen, daß es mit der poetischen Gabe keine so seltene Sache sei und daß niemand eben besondere Ursache habe, sich viel darauf einzubilden, wenn er ein gutes Gedicht macht). (Eckermann 198).

Eckermann's diligent question whether the novel of manners of the Ming Era (*Yü-chiao-li* [*Red Jade and Dream Pear*]; Goethe read this novel in French translation [see Era]) with which Goethe was so preoccupied was not "perhaps one of the era's finest" ("vielleicht einer ihrer vorzüglichsten"), is accorded the casual answer: "Not at all. The Chinese have thousands of such novels, and had them while our ancestors were still living in the forests" ("Keineswegs, die Chinesen haben deren zu Tausenden und hatten ihrer schon, als unsere Vorfahren noch in den Wäldern lebten") (Eckermann 198). Of course, whenever the "need for something exemplary" ("Bedürfnis von etwas Musterhaftem")—

a true model—arose, Goethe resolutely drew on the "ancient Greeks": "We must view every-thing else historically and, as far as possible, learn from the good in it" ("Alles übrige müssen wir nur historisch betrachten und das Gute, so weit es gehen will, uns daraus aneignen") (Eckermann 198). If classical antiquity loses its exceptional status, the question of whether or not a hierarchical factor is indispensable to the concept of "world literature" takes on a significance quite different from that which it still had for Goethe. Just such a hierarchical factor underlies not only Etiemble's counter-proposals to the Eurocentric reading-lists he criticizes, but also and particularly the following description of the situation: "qu'au lieu de gaspiller son temps à lire mille mauvais livres dont tout le monde parle, on saura choisir parmi les dizaines de milliers de grandes oeuvres qui n'attendent que notre bonne volonté" (1975, 30). But not only is it difficult to derive a canonical notion of "world literature" from Goethe's comments. Goethe asserts, on the contrary, that popular literature plays a role—indeed a central role—in the process of "world literature's" formation: "If such a world literature will soon come into being, as is inevitable given the ever increasing rapidity of human interaction, then we may not expect anything more or different from [this literature] than what it can and does achieve . . . whatever pleases the masses will expand without limit and, as we are already witnessing, find approval in all areas and regions" (Wenn nun . . . eine solche Weltliteratur, wie bey der sich immer vermehrenden Schnelligkeit des Verkehrs unausbleiblich ist, sich nächstens bildet, so dürfen wir nur nicht mehr und nichts anders von ihr erwarten als was sie leisten kann und leistet. . . . was der Menge zusagt, wird sich gränzenlos ausbreiten und, wie wir jetzt schon sehen, sich in allen Zonen und Gegenden empfehlen) (WA I, 42.2, 502f).

　　And his sole consolation in the face of the "English spring tide" ("englische Springflut") (Goethe to Streckfuß, 27 January 1827 [WA IV, 42, 28]) is that "some individuals will be blessed" by the "advancing world literature . . . even if the general cause suffers" ("Dies sind aber schon die Folgen der anmarschirenden Weltliteratur, und man kann sich hier ganz allein dadurch trösten, daß, wenn auch das Allgemeine dabey übel fährt, gewiß Einzelne davon Heil und Segen gewinnen werden") (Goethe to Zelter, 4 March 1829 [WA IV, 45, 187]; see also Auerbach 303–04]) for "those who have devoted themselves to higher things, to what is fruitful on a higher level, will get to know each other all the more quickly and closely" ("diejenigen aber die sich dem Höheren und dem höher Fruchtbaren gewidmet haben, werden sich geschwinder und näher kennen lernen") to "resist the everyday deluge" ("der breiten Tagesfluth sich entgegen zu setzen") and work together toward a world literature that would promote the "true progress of mankind" ("den wahren Fortschritt der Menschheit") (WA I, 42.2, 503). Even the recently debated thematic criterion for the applicability of the notion of "world literature"—namely that it reflects "the problems, experiences, expectations and fears of the western industrial world" (Steinmetz 1988b, 132, 1988a, 136–41)—even this criterion originates with Goethe, who had related the formation of a "world literature" to the "advancement of the human race" ("Vorschreiten des Menschengeschlechts"), to "long-term human and global prospects" ("weite Aussichten der Welt- und Menschenverhältnisse") (Goethe to Streckfuß, 27 January 1827 [WA IV, 42, 28]) and to the interest of nations in "gaining knowledge of the mutual relations of all to all" ("die Verhältnisse aller gegen alle kennen lernen") (WA I, 42.2, 505). Goethe considered that German Romantic and Biedermeier works, given their inadequate roots in the contemporary world, were hardly worthy of the name "world literature" in comparison with contemporary French literature. Goethe writes: "German poetry . . . really provides nothing but the expressions, sighs and interjections of well-meaning individuals. Each person makes his appearance in accordance with his nature and education. Hardly anything attains to a universal, lofty level. Least of all does one find situations common to the domestic, urban or rural sphere. As far as Church and State are concerned, nothing is to be seen" (Die deutsche Poesie bringt . . . eigentlich nur Ausdrücke, Seufzer und Interjectionen wohldenkender Individuen. Jeder Einzelne tritt auf nach seinem Naturell und seiner Bildung; kaum irgend etwas geht in's Allgemeine, Höhere; am wenigsten merkt man einen häuslichen, städtischen, kaum einen ländlichen Zustand; von dem, was Staat und Kirche betrifft, ist gar nichts zu merken) (Goethe to Hitzig, 11 November 1829, WA IV, 46, 144–45).

On the other hand, it does indeed amount to a quantitatively comprehensive concept of world literature when, in the Eckermann conversation of 31 January 1827, Goethe echoes Herder in stressing that poetry is the common property of mankind, and that it emerges in all places and at all times. . . . this is why I study foreign nations and advise everybody else to do the same. National literature does not mean much at present, it is time for an era of world literature, and everybody must endeavor to accelerate this epoch (198) ("daß die Poesie ein Gemeingut der Menschheit ist und daß sie überall und zu allen Zeiten . . . hervor-tritt. . . . Ich sehe mich daher gern bei fremden Nationen um und rate jedem, es auch seinerseits zu tun. Nationalliteratur will jetzt

nicht viel sagen, die Epoche der Weltliteratur ist an der Zeit, und jeder muß
jetzt dazu wirken, diese Epoche zu beschleunigen") (Eckermann 198). As a test,
Goethe refers to the contrast between the highly-talented Béranger's "indecent,
dissolute" ("unsittliche, liederliche") songs and the aforementioned "thoroughly decent" ("durchaus sittlich")—if also thoroughly mediocre—Chinese
novel. Moreover, he underlines the novel's contrasts with and similarities to
both his own "bourgeois idyll" *Herrmann and Dorothea* and to Richardson's
epistolary novels (Eckermann 197–98). But an understanding of world literature as extensive as that documented in Goethe's works cannot be realized without a substantial revaluation of literary translation that places it above the
category of a makeshift solution and Árpád Berczik even forwarded—with critical intention—the exaggerated thesis that "World literature, following Goethe's
concept, is nourished foremost by transla-tions; more, it is almost identical to
the art of translation ("Die Weltliteratur nach Goethes Konzeption wird vor-
wiegend durch Übersetzungen gespeist, ja, sie ist mit der Übersetzungskunst
nahezu identisch") (288; see also Tgahrt). It is true that Goethe held the strong
conviction that one should, as far as possible, "seek out, get to know and cher-
ish each poet in his own language and within the specific area of his time and
customs" ("daß man jeden Dichter in seiner Sprache und im eigenthümlichen
Bezirk seiner Zeit und Sitten aufsuchen, kennen und schätzen müsse") (1994,
270)—why else would he, for the sake of Hafiz, have begun to learn Persian
at the age of 65? Yet in a review of Carlyle's *German Romance* he states with
equal conviction: "Whatever one may say about the shortcomings of translation, it nonetheless remains one of the most important and most worthy activities in the business of this world. *The Koran* says: 'God has given each people
a prophet in its own tongue.' Every translator is thus a prophet in the midst
of his own people" ("was man auch von der Unzulänglichkeit des Übersetzens
sagen mag, so ist und bleibt es doch eines der wichtigsten und würdigsten
Geschäfte in dem allgemeinen Weltverkehr. *Der Koran* sagt: 'Gott hat jedem
Volke einen Propheten gegeben in seiner eigenen Sprache.' So ist jeder Über-
setzer ein Prophet in seinem Volke") (WA I, 41.2, 307).

   To this extent, Goethe regards the process of development of world literature as profoundly bound up with the medium of literary translation, over
and above our striving for the widest possible direct knowledge of the various
literatures, and over and above the lively interaction among Literatoren (that
is poets, critics, university teachers, etc.). Goethe had seen the "great value that
world literature yields and that will increasingly manifest itself" above all else

in the fact "that we are now, with close contact between the French, the English and the Germans, beginning to correct each other" ("Es ist aber sehr artig, daß wir jetzt, bei dem engen Verkehr zwischen Franzosen, Engländern und Deutschen in den Fall kommen, uns einander zu korrigieren. Das ist der große Nutzen, der bei einer Weltliteratur herauskommt und der sich immer mehr zeigen wird") (Eckermann 227–28) and, moreover, in the fact that "the disagreements that prevail within one nation are smoothed out by the views and judgment of the others" ("die Differenzen, die innerhalb der einen Nation obwalten, durch Ansicht und Urtheil der übrigen ausgeglichen werden") (Goethe to Sulpiz Boisserée, 12 October 1827 [WA IV, 43, 106]). Goethe had no high-flown illusions about this and expressly emphasized that "it is not a matter of nations being obliged to think in unison; rather, they should become aware of and understand each other, and, if love proves impossible, they should at least learn to tolerate one another" (WA I, 41.2, 348). He concedes that "it cannot be hoped that this will produce a general peace, but it can be hoped that the inevitable conflicts will gradually become less important, that war will become less cruel and victory less arrogant" ("German Romance," WA I, 41.2, 306). Of course, our present century's history has ensured that even these moderate hopes would come to nothing. And, as Auerbach notes, the process of cultural "conciliation" ("Ausgleichsprozeß") that Goethe regards with some optimism is increasingly eroding every distinctive tradition, with the result that ultimately, "in a uniformly organized world, only one single literary culture—indeed, in a relatively short time, only a few literary languages, soon perhaps only one—will remain alive. And with this, the idea of world literature would be at once realized and destroyed" ("auf einer einheitlich organisierten Erde nur eine einzige literarische Kultur, ja selbst in vergleichsweise kurzer Zeit nur wenige literarische Sprachen, bald vielleicht nur eine, als lebend übrigbleiben. Und damit wäre der Gedanke der Weltliteratur zugleich verwirklicht und zerstört") (301).

And in a similar sense T.S. Eliot proposes "that a world culture which was simply a uniform culture would be no culture at all. We should have a humanity de-humanised. It would be a night-mare. But on the other hand, we cannot resign the idea of world-culture altogether" (62) while Lévi-Strauss suggests that "c'est la différence des cultures qui rend leur rencontre féconde. Or ce jeu en commun entraîne leur uniformisa-tion progressive: les bénéfices que les cultures retirent de ces contacts proviennent largement de leurs écarts qualitatifs; mais, au cours de ces échanges, ces écarts diminuent jusqu'à s'abolir"—with

the result, "que, dans leur évolution, les cultures tendent vers une entropie crois-
sante qui résulte de leur mélange" (206). These views overlap with Etiemble's
view—arrived at differently, of course—that "qu'au moment précis où la
Weltliteratur devient enfin possible, elle devient du même coup quasiment
impossible" (1975, 33–34).

In contrast, one of Goethe's last essays, entitled "Epochs of Social Education" ("Epochen geselliger Bildung"), leads one to the conclusion that Goethe
directed all of his hopes towards exactly this progression away from the seclu-
sion and intimacy of life in what he called the "idyllic epoch," to its gradual
convergence and fusion, and finally to the point where it is wholly united with
the "universal epoch." And four stages of literary education ("Bildung") are
assigned to this progression: in the first, one sings only of the beloved and
"prefers to head toward one's mother tongue" ("halten . . . mit Vorliebe auf
die Muttersprache"); in the second and third, "one does not resist the influence of foreign languages" ("den fremden Sprachen verweigert man die Ein-
wirkung nicht"); and in the fourth, one is "convinced of the necessity of
informing oneself about the present course of world events, in their real as
well as ideal sense. All foreign literatures, together with our native literature,
become part of the same phenomenon, and we are not left behind by world
events" ("die Überzeugung, wie nothwendig es sei, sich von den Zuständen
des augenblicklichen Weltlaufs im realen und idealen Sinne zu unterrichten.
Alle fremde Literaturen setzen sich mit der einheimischen ins Gleiche, und wir
bleiben im Weltumlaufe nicht zurück") (WA I 41.2, 361–62). This latter state
can indeed be called "world literature."

Yet, this linear scheme of progression is somewhat deceiving. For just as
all four historical stages must be experienced anew by each individual, and just
as "world piety" ("Weltfrömmigkeit"), which seeks to embrace the whole of
humanity, requires "home piety" ("Hausfrömmigkeit") as its basis (WA I, 24,
378), so even the most advanced world literature remains dependent on "naïve
poetry" (Goethe 1994, 140) or "nature poetry" ("Naturdichtung"; see "Ein
Wort für junge Dichter" [in a letter to Melchior Meyr, 22 January 1832 (WA
I, 42.2, 106–08, esp. 106–07); see also WA I, 42.2, 120)—as its origin and its
source of regeneration. Thus, if Goethe praises the dawning epoch of world literature for the fact that "the efforts of the best poets and aesthetic writers of
all nations have, for some time now, been directed toward humanity in general," so that "in every particular of nationality and personality the general significance can be seen to shine through" ("Offenbar ist das Bestreben der besten

Dichter und ästhetischen Schriftsteller aller Nationen schon seit geraumer Zeit auf das allgemein Menschliche gerichtet. In jedem Besondern . . . wird man durch Nationalität und Persönlichkeit hin jenes Allgemeine immer mehr durchleuchten und durchscheinen sehen") ("German Romance," WA I, 41.2, 305), and if even he, to Eckermann's astonishment, stresses not the exotic features of this Chinese novel, but rather the fact that in it "the people think, act and feel almost exactly as we do" ("die Menschen denken, handeln und empfinden fast ebenso wie wir") (Eckermann 196) then this does not amount to a submergence of the particular in the general—even in "humanity in general" ("das allgemein Menschliche")—but rather (in a language that is quite Hegelian) to "mediation and mutual recognition" ("Vermittelung und wechselseitige Anerkennung"): "One must get to know the peculiarities of each nation to then see past them and establish a relationship with the nation; for the characteristics of a nation are like its language and its coins — they facilitate dealings with it, in fact they make such dealings possible in the first place" ("Die Besonderheiten einer jeden muß man kennen lernen, um sie ihr zu lassen, um gerade dadurch mit ihr zu verkehren: denn die Eigenheiten einer Nation sind wie ihre Sprache und ihre Münzsorten, sie erleichtern den Verkehr, ja sie machen ihn erst vollkommen möglich") ("German Romance," WA I, 41.2, 306).

And Erich Auerbach has the same idea in mind when he writes: "'World literature' refers not simply to what is common and human as such, but rather to this as the mutual fertilisation of the manifold. It presupposes the felix culpa of mankind's division into a whole host of cultures" ("Weltliteratur . . . bezieht sich nicht einfach auf das Gemeinsame und Menschliche überhaupt, sondern auf dieses als wechselseitige Befruchtung des Mannigfaltigen. Die felix culpa des Auseinanderfallens der Menschheit in eine Fülle von Kulturen ist ihre Voraussetzung") (301). Goethe, however, has the advantage over Auerbach's assessment of the situation not only in his astounding anticipation of Marx and Saussure on the comparative levels of culture, language, and economy, but also in the fact that, rather than identify the diversity of cultures as the precondition of the formation of a common world literature, he focuses instead with greater historical specificity on the modern antagonism among different nations. It was thus no unreflected Eurocentrism when he described the developing world literature as being, for the present, limited to European literatures, above all those of France, England, Scotland, Italy, and Germany (see especially Goethe's diverse outlines on "world literature" [WA I, 42.2, 491–501])—even if the non-European literatures were increasingly becoming the focus of attention, as vividly demonstrated by Goethe's *West-Eastern Divan* (*West-östlicher Divan*, 1819 and 1827) and his Chinese-German *Seasons and Hours of the Day* (*Chinesisch-deutsche Jahres- und Tageszeiten*, 1829).

Goethe's famous dictum: "National literature does not mean much at present, it is time for the era of world literature and everybody must endeavour to accelerate this epoch" ("Nationalliteratur will jetzt nicht viel sagen, die Epoche der Weltliteratur ist an der Zeit, und jeder muß jetzt dazu wirken, diese Epoche zu beschleunigen") (Eckermann 198, 31 January 1827) is not to be taken at face value. For, what we meanwhile observe is not the replacement of national literatures by world literature, but the rapid blossoming of a multitude of European and non-European literatures and the simultaneous emergence of a world literature (mostly in English translations) as two aspects of one and the same process. The understanding of this dialectic—should not this be one of the main targets of comparative literature today?

WORKS CITED

Auerbach, Erich. "Philologie der Weltliteratur." *Gesammelte Aufsätze zur romanischen Philologie*. Bern: Francke, 1967. 301–10.

Berczik, Árpád. "Eine ungarische Konzeption der Weltliteratur. (Hugo v. Meltzls vergleichende Literaturtheorie)." *La Littérature comparée en Europe orientale*. Ed. István Sőtér, et al. Budapest: Akadémiai, 1963. 287–94.

Eckermann, Johann Peter. *Gespräche mit Goethe in den letzten Jahren seines Lebens*. Ed. Regine Otto and Peter Wersig. Berlin: Aufbau, 1987.

Eliot, T.S. *Notes towards the Definition of Culture*. London: Faber & Faber, 1949.

Etiemble, René. "Faut-il réviser la notion de Weltliteratur?" 1966. *Essais de littérature (vraiment) générale*. By René Etiemble. Paris: Gallimard, 1975. 15–36.

Etiemble, René. *Ouverture(s) sur un comparatisme planétaire*. Paris: Christian Bourgois, 1988.

Etiemble, René. *Quelques essais de littérature universelle*. Paris: Gallimard, 1982.

Gadamer, Hans-Georg. *Gesammelte Werke*. Vol. 1. *Hermeneutik I: Wahrheit und Methode. Grundzüge einer philosophischen Hermeneutik*. Tübingen: Mohr, 1986.

Goethe, Johann Wolfgang von. *Die Schriften zur Naturwissenschaft*. [Leopoldina-Ausgabe]. Vol. 11. *Aufsätze, Fragmente, Studien zur Naturwissenschaft im allgemeinen*. Ed. Dorothea Kuhn and Wolf von Engelhardt. Weimar: Böhlau, 1970.

Goethe, Johann Wolfgang von. *West-östlicher Divan* (Frankfurter Ausgabe). Ed. Hendrik Birus. Frankfurt: Der Deutsche Klassiker Verlag, 1994.

Goethe, Johann Wolfgang von. *Werke.* [Sophien-Ausgabe]. Weimar: Böhlau, 1887–1919. 133 vols. Rpt. München: deutscher taschenbuch verlag, 1987.

Iu-kiao-li ou Les Deux cousines. Trans. J.P. Abel-Rémusat. Paris, 1826.

Krauss, Werner. "Probleme der vergleichenden Literaturgeschichte." *Zur Dichtungsgeschichte der romanischen Völker.* Leipzig: Reclam, 1965. 100–113, 345–48.

Lévi-Strauss, Claude, and Didier Eribon. *De près et de loin.* Paris: Jacob, 1988.

Marino, Adriano. "Wo ist der Ort der 'Weltliteratur'?" *Vergleichende Literaturforschung in den sozialistischen Ländern 1963–1979.* Ed. Gerhard R. Kaiser. Stuttgart: Metzler, 1980. 189–208.

Marx, Karl, and Friedrich Engels. "Manifest der Kommunistischen Partei." *Werke.* Berlin: Dietz, 1974. Vol. 4, 459–93.

Marx, Karl, and Friedrich Englels. "Manifesto of the Communist Party." Trans. Samuel Moore. *Great Books of the Western World.* Ed. Mortimer J. Adler. Chicago: Encyclopaedia Britannica, 1994. 413–34.

Rüdiger, Horst. "Klassik und Kanonbildung. Zur Frage der Wertung in der Komparatistik." *Komparatistik. Aufgaben und Methoden.* Ed. Horst Rüdiger. Stuttgart: Kohlhammer, 1973. 127–44.

Rüdiger, Horst. "'Literatur' und 'Weltliteratur' in der modernen Komparatistik." *Weltliteratur und Volksliteratur.* Ed. Albert Schaefer. München: Beck, 1972. 36–54.

Steinmetz, Horst. "Weltliteratur. Umriß eines literaturgeschichtlichen Konzepts." *Literatur und Geschichte. 4 Versuche.* München: iudicium, 1988. 103–26, 136–41.

Steinmetz, Horst. "Response to Claus Clüver's 'The Difference of Eight Decades: World Literature and the Demise of National Literatures'." *Yearbook of Comparative and General Literature* 37 (1988): 131–33.

Tgahrt, Reinhart, et al., eds. *Weltliteratur. Die Lust am Übersetzen im Jahrhundert Goethes. Eine Ausstellung des Deutschen Literaturarchivs im Schiller-Nationalmuseum Marbach am Neckar.* München: Koesel, 1982.

Comparative Literature in India

Amiya Dev

In this paper, I discuss an apriori location of comparative literature with regard to aspects of diversity and unity in India, a country of immense linguistic diversity and, thus, a country of many literatures. Based on history, ideology, and often on politics, scholars of literature argue either for a unity of Indian literature or for a diversity and distinctness of the literatures of India. Instead of this binary approach, my proposal involves a particular view of the discipline of comparative literature, because I argue that in the case of India the study of literature should involve the notion of the interliterary process and a dialectical view of literary interaction. Let me begin with a brief account of linguistic diversity: previous censuses in 1961 and 1971 recorded a total of 1,652 languages while in the last census of 1981 some 221 spoken languages were recorded excluding languages of speakers totalling less than 10,000. Many of the 221 language groups are small, of course, and it is only the eighteen listed in the Indian Constitution as major languages that comprise the bulk of the population's speakers. In addition to the eighteen languages listed in the Constitution, four more are recognized by the Sahitya Akademi (National Academy of Letters) for reasons of their significance in literature (Assamese, Bengali, Dogri, Indian English, Gujarati, Hindi, Kannada, Kankani, Kashmiri, Maithili, Malayalam, Manipuri, Marathi, Nepali, Oriya, Panjabi, Rajasthani, Sanskrit, Sindhi, Tamil, Telugu and Urdu). However, this total of twenty-two major languages and literatures is deceiving because secondary school and university curricula include further languages spoken in the area of the particular educational institution. This diversity in languages and literatures, however, is not reflected in either the general social discourse or in literary scholarship.

In general, the perspective of India as a hegemonious language and literature area is ubiquitous.

We are all aware that the so-called major Indian literatures are ancient—two of them (Sansjrit and Tamil) ancient in the sense of Antiquity while the rest of an average age of eight to nine hundred years—except one recent arrival in the nineteenth century as an outcome of the colonial Western impact (Indian English). We also know that although some of these literatures are more substantial than others and contain greater complexities, no further gradation into major and minor major ones is usually made. A writer in any one is counted as much Indian by the Sahitya Akademi as a writer in any other and no distinction is made between one literature prize and another. Thus, while we have a plurality of so-called major literatures in India, we are confronted by a particular problematic: Is Indian literature, in the singular, a valid category, or are we rather to speak of Indian literatures in the plural? Eighteenth- and nineteenth-century Western Indologists were not interested in this question, for Indian literature to them was mainly Sanskrit, extended at most to Pâli and Prakrit. For example, with all his admiration for *Sakuntala,* William Jones was oblivious of literatures in modern Indian languages. Non-Indian Indianists today, too, are more often than not uninterested in the question. Although they do not consider Sanskrit-Pâli-Prakrit as "the" only literature of India, these scholars are still single literature specialists. Similarly, literary histories written in India by Indian scholars also focussed and still focus on a single literature.

This single-focus perspective is a result of both a colonial and a post-colonial perspective, the latter found in the motto of the Sahitya Akademi: "Indian literature is one though written in many languages" (Radhakrishnan). However, this perspective was opposed by scholars who argued that a country where so many languages coexist should be understood as a country with literatures (in the plural). The argument was formal and without any serious political overtones, only insisting that instead of Indian literature, singular, we should speak of Indian literatures, plural. Presently, a different kind of resistance has emerged to the unity thesis in the form of what may be called "hegemonic apprehensions." This perspective includes the argumentation that the designation "Indian literature" will eventually be equated with one of the major literatures of India, perhaps or likely with the largest single spoken language and literature. What speaks against this argument is that, for example, the literature of one of the smallest spoken languages—of a non-Indian origin too—is sometimes claimed to be the only truly Indian literature because of its freedom from regional ties.

In brief, arguments of unity in diversity are in my opinion suspect, for they encroach upon the individualities of the diverse literatures. In other words, a cultural relativist analogy is implied here, difference is underlined and corroborated by the fact that both writers and readers of particular and individual literatures are overwhelmingly concerned with their own literature and own literature only. It is from this perspective that to the Akademi's motto "Indian literature is one though written in many languages," the retort is "Indian literature is one because it is written in many languages."

The above briefly outlined problem of unity in diversity and its perspectives are the bases of Comparative Literature as a discipline in India. Let me first mention Gurbhagat Singh who has been discussing the notion of "differential multilogue" (see Singh). He does not accept the idea of Indian literature as such but opts for the designation of literatures produced in India. Further, he rejects the notion of Indian literature because the notion as such includes and promotes a nationalist identity. As a relativist, Singh accords literatures not only linguistic but also cultural singularities. With regard to the history of comparative literature as a discipline, he rejects the French and the American schools as well as the idea of Goethe's *Weltliteratur*. Instead, he argues for a celebration of difference and has anticipated Charles Bernheimer's much discussed *Comparative Literature in the Age of Multiculturalism*. For Singh, comparative literature is thus an exercise in differential multilogue. His insistence on the plurality of logoi is particularly interesting because it takes us beyond the notion of dialogue, a notion that comparative literature is still confined to. Singh's proposal of differential multilogue as a program will perhaps enable us to understand Indian diversity without sacrificing the individualities of the particulars. Singh's notion of differential multilogue reflects a poststructuralist trend in Indian discourse today, a trend that manifests itself among others by a suspicion of the designation of Indian literatures as one. One of the reasons for this suspicion is that the key to the notion is held centrally, whether by an institution or a synod of experts leading to an accumulation of power. If we agree that power is the most ubiquitous social evil then the more decentralization the better. Decentralization minimizes the aggression from above as well as impels grass-roots movements from below. In such a situation, the matter of difference is thus thoroughly contextualized. In literature, difference does not deny the possibility of interliterary spaces but, on the contrary, welcomes them provided they do not come as a program of action organized from above. The notion of difference and interliterary processes has, in fact, recently engaged Indian scholars with regard to the problematic of inter-Indian translation particularly in the day-to-day interaction of different languages (for a full-fledged theoretical framework of the interliterary process, see Durišin; Gálik in this volume).

If difference is understood and enacted as self-containment and concomitant self-complacency, then there is a problem with regard to the concept of mutuality. However, poststructuralism understands difference as a notion of inclusion, that is, mutuality. Thus, it cannot accept the single-focus category "Indian" without deconstructing its accompanying politics. In other words, if the deconstruction of politics involves the weeding out of things excessively local or peripheral, it is appropriate because all value loading is suspect. If, on the other hand, "Indian" is a mere description, a general signifier, then there is no need for the act of deconstruction. Poststructuralism is by no means purist; what matters more than anything else is the historical perspective that upholds difference. In turn, if we deconstruct this predilection for difference, we will see that our predilection is not so much a matter of *Weltanschauung* but rather a reaction to the possibility of power accumulation in the name of "Indian literature." If Indian literature had not been so heavily publicized and hammered down, as it were, into our national psyche, if our individual literatures had been left alone and not asked to pay their dues to "Indian literature," there would be no resistance to the notion of unity in diversity. And it cannot be denied that in the pursuit of "Indian literature" some of us have shown negative discrimination towards texts produced in "less important" and "different" literatures. The poststructuralist stance is particularly wary of rhetoric in the name of integration and a call to emotion in the name of nation runs against its basic principles. Nationalism and fundamentalism of any type are built on regimentation and exclusion.

Yet, there are some problems with poststructuralism in Indian scholarly discourse and that is the prominence of theory to the detriment or non-existence of application. Instead of fitting theory to the experience of literature, the latter is fit to theory, thus resulting in an over abundance of meta-theory. Ironically, Indian poststructuralism inflicts upon itself a sameness with difference-speakers elsewhere and does not seem to recognize that difference speaking in India may be different from difference-speaking elsewhere. At the same time, this poststructuralism does not seem to recognize that given all the differences pertaining to the Indian experience, underlying it and tying together the different entities, there may be a commonality, a *sensus commu-*

nis of a broadly cultural kind. Jaidev, criticising the fad of existentialist aes-theticism in some contemporary Indian fiction, develops an argument for this cultural differential approach. However, and importantly, Jaidev's notion of an Indian *sensus communis* is not that routine Indianness which we often encounter from our cultural ambassadors or in the West, that is, those instances of "national" and racial image formations which suggest homogeneity and result in cultural stereotyping. The concept of an Indian *sensus communis* in the context of Singh's differential multilogue or Jaidev's differential approach brings me to the question of situs and theory. That is, the "site" or "location" of theory and of the theorist are important factors here. I am convinced that situs is as important as theorization, particularly in a country where the decol-onization process is still incomplete and where a neo-colonial situation is in the making. A wrong theory is bad, but a right theory from a wrong situs is equally bad. It is situs that Tagore spoke of in many of his prose texts and it is situs that Gandhi so consistently practised. And in Indian Marxism, too, the question of situs has again and again appeared as a particular problematic. Now, if situs means cultural and linguistic rootedness then the notion of com-monality is applicable, although we cannot ignore the danger of commonal-ity turning itself into self-referentiality or even nationalism or racism. At this point of potential danger, the enactment of a dialectic may be the solution. Let the Indian theorist have his/her situs right by heeding to commonality, but let him/her also stand guard against commonality turning self-referential. In other words, the theorist must make sure that commonality will not be turned into an ideological and political commodity. But under no circum-stances should the theorist deny commonality because of expediency or fear and neither should he/she take refuge in suggesting a superior and detached intellect. That way lays alienation, and alienation is a further aspect that the Indian theorist must resolutely resist.

Commonality and the oneness I am suggesting here as a primary situs of the Indian theorist and theory is not exactly the cultural commonality Jaidev had in mind in his critique of cultural pastiche, however. Jaidev's concept of oneness provides an ambience for particular concerns with regard to cultural and artistic expression such as the case of language overlaps, the bi- and mul-tilinguality of authors and their readership, openness to different genres, the sharing of themes based in similar social and historical experiences, emphasis on the oral and performing modes of cultural and artistic transmission, and the ease of inter-translatability. On the other hand, these characteristics of

Indian cultural commonalities Jaidev suggests in turn are rooted in a situs of the premodern age of Indian literatures (that is, in periods prior to the advent of print). Where Jaidev's structure is applicable, instead, are our contemporary literatures in India because it is here that the danger of an oneness construction—the process of nation-state construction—looms.

Another example where nation-state orientation and nation-state cultural and literary identity construction is discussed in detail is Aijaz Ahmad's *In Theory: Classes, Nations, Literatures.* Ahmad describes the construct of a "syndicated" Indian literature that suggests an aggregate and unsatisfactory categorization of Indian literature (see 243–85). Ahmad also rules out the often argued analogy of Indian literature with that of European literature by arguing that the notion of "European literature" is at best an umbrella designation and at worst a pedagogical imposition while Indian literature is classifiable and categorizable. Further, he argues that while European and African literatures have some historical signifiers in addition to their geographical designation, these are recent concepts whereas Indian homogeneity has the weight of tradition behind it. In Ahmad's argumentation, the problem is that in the "Indian" archive of literature, Indianness ultimately proves limited when compared with the differential literature comprised in each of the twenty-two literatures recognized by the Sahitya Akademi. While it is evident that in each of these languages and literatures there is material taken from the others or another, their totality does not constitute one archive. Rather, they constitute twenty-two different archives. An "Indian" archive of literature as represented by an "English" archive—while non-hegemonious on the one hand by removal from a differential archive but hegemonizing by a latent colonial attitude on the other—also reflects the official language policy of the government: English, while not included in the Indian Constitution, is still recognized as a lingua franca of government, education, etc. For example, until recently the government sponsored the National Book Trust, an entity entrusted with the task of inter-Indian translation by a process of a first translation into English followed by translation from that into the other languages.

The notion of an "English" archive of Indian literature came about two decades ago by the suggestion of V.K. Gokak and Sujit Mukherjee who were speaking of an Indo-English corpus of literature that was created out of English translations of major texts from major Indian languages (see Mukherjee). Thus, the idea of Indian literature was authenticated and not only that, a history too was proposed for it with forms and techniques varying from age to

age. Further, Gokak and Mukherjee suggested the canonization of their proposal by inserting the Indo-English corpus into university curricula. It was along
these lines of ideology and political economy that a decade ago recommendations were made by a government committee to institute a Master's program
in Indian literature following an undergraduate degree in any single Indian literature ("University Grants Commission Circular Letter"). Ahmad's concern
is with the hegemony of English, although he does not suggest its abolition in
a way that would be close to Ngugi's arguments. On the other hand, Gokak,
Mukherjee, and Motilal Jotwani—who was a committee member for drafting
the above circular—suggested to implement English as a function, owing to
the ever-growing corpus of translations from the various Indian literatures into
English, thus making this new corpus of Indo-English literature available to
all. In turn, this new corpus would suggest an Indian communality resulting
in a more or less homogeneous Indian literature. In addition to the argument
against this construction of a national literature advanced by Ahmad, there
are other problems with the notion and its implementation. It is true that the
ideal of one language in India has been made real by now by ideological and
political mechanisms. The official national language is Hindi and if literary texts
from the other languages could be in toto translated into Hindi, we could possibly arrive at a national Indian literature. However, in this case we would again
arrive at a hegemonizing situation. On the other hand, it is clear that in the
realm of education, English is the largest single language program in our col-
leges and universities.

It is for the above reasons that I propose, instead, the notion mentioned
previously: Indian literature is not an entity but an interliterary condition in
the widest possible sense of the concept which is related to Goethe's original
idea of *Weltliteratur* and its use by Marx and Engels in *The Communist Manifesto*. The interliterary condition of India, we should remember, reaches back
much farther than its manuscript or print culture. For instance, bhakti—a popular religious movement as both theme and social issue (stretching from the
eighth to the eighteenth century)—had a variety of textual manifestations in
various Indian languages. There are many other similar literary and cultural
textualities in India whose nature, while manifest in different other systems of
a similar nature are based primarily on themes or genres, forms and structures
observable in historiography. It is possible, in other words, to think of a series
of such sub-systems in which the individual literatures of India have been inter-
related with one another over the ages. For example, Swapan Majumdar takes

this systemic approach in his 1985 book, *Comparative Literature: Indian Dimensions,* where Indian literature is neither a simple unity as hegemonists of the nation-state persuasion would like it to be, nor a simple diversity as relativists or poststructuralists would like it to be. That is, Majumdar suggests that Indian literature is neither "one" nor "many" but rather a systemic whole where many sub-systems interact towards one in a continuous and never-ending dialectic. Such a systemic view of Indian literature predicates that we take all Indian literatures together, age by age, and view them comparatively. And this is the route of literary history Sisir Kumar Das has taken with his planned ten-volume project, *A History of Indian Literature,* whose first volume, *1800–1910: Western Impact / Indian Response,* appeared in 1991.

The approach Das has taken is methodologically pragmatic: He has a team of scholars working with him (at least one scholar for each language) who collect the initial data which he then processes through a number of checks resulting in a chronological history of literature. In it we have simultaneous listings of similar events from all the twenty-two recognized literatures: Authors' births and deaths, dates of text composition and publication, classification in genres, text dissemination, reception, literary reviews and their impact, literary society formations and debates, translations from both inside and outside, and so on. These constitute, on the one hand, literary data; but on the other hand they are also data of relevant social events. The mode of assortment will naturally vary from volume to volume depending on the nature of the data. The work Das proposed is not only a comparative chronology but it will include a narrative based on it. Of course, the narrative is his own reading of the chronology, and other readings are possible. One of the interesting conclusions he arrived at with the first volume in question and based on his reading of the established chronology, is a structure of pro-phanes and meta-phanes. Certain features of these phanes may be generic, thematic, stylistic, or found to have appeared in one literature early, in another late. It is an engaging discovery and may also be true of the other ages. However, the underlying and most important finding is a pattern of commonality in nineteenth-century Indian literatures. Das's work on the literatures of the nineteenth century in India does not designate this Indian literature a category by itself. Rather, the work suggests a rationale for the proposed research, the objective being to establish whether a pattern can be found through the ages. One age's pattern may not be the same as another age's and this obviously pre-empts any given unity of Indian literature. Thus, Das's method and results to date show that Indian literature is neither a unity nor is it a total differential.

Interestingly, although Das does not call himself a comparatist and does not locate the project in that discipline, his work is comparatist. In many ways, Das's work is similar to K.M. George's two-volume *Comparative Indian Literature* of 1984–85 that was researched and published under the auspices of Kerala Sahitya Akademi. George's work was not as comprehensive as Das's: it only dealt with fifteen literatures and that too in a limited way. It had a generic bias, that is, it approached the literatures in terms of a few given genres. George's genealogy too is by and large given and not arrived at from the literatures themselves. In my view, George's work also demonstrates Western hegemony. Poetry, for instance, was discussed in terms of "traditional" and "modern" but as if traditional was exclusively Indian and modern the result of a Western impact. Another problem of George's two volumes was that although they were titled Comparative Indian Literature, there was no comparison built into the findings and the fifteen individual literatures were placed simply side by side. Thus, comparison was only suggested, that is, the reader was required to make whatever comparison was necessary or appropriate.

With regard to the inherently and implicitly advantageous discipline of comparative literature it is interesting that the Gujarati poet Umashankar Joshi—a supporter of the unity approach—was the first president of the Indian National Comparative Literature Association, while the Kannada writer U.R. Anantha Murthy is the current president of the Comparative Literature Association of India in addition to being the president of Sahitya Akademi. The discipline of comparative literature, that is, its institutional manifestation as in the national association of comparatists reflects the binary approach to the question of Indian literature as I explained above. However, the Association also reflects a move toward a dialectic. This is manifest in the fact that Murthy's approach concerns a subtle move away from the routine unity approach and towards aspects of inter-Indian reading. In other words, the method of Comparative Literature allows for a view of Indian literature in the context of unity and diversity in a dialectical interliterary process and situation. There was a time when I spoke in terms of an extra consciousness on the part of individual language writers: for Bengali literature, for instance, I saw a Bengali+, for Hindi literature a Hindi+, for Tamil literature a Tamil+, etc. My understanding of Indian literature consisted of the author's extra consciousness and not of an archival entity as such but rather a state of mind in order to justify the unity of Indian literature. However, today, with a focus on reception and the theoretical premises offered by the notion of the interliterary process, I understand Indian literature as ever in the making.

Apart from reception studies, there are of course other aspects that support my understanding of Indian literature in an interliterary process: we are located in our own languages—whether with an active or passive binguality—where we have access to one or two other languages. Through inter-Indian translation we have also access to texts from a fourth and more languages. Now, as readers, consciously or subconsciously we place the texts in additional languages beside our original and first text. Or, one may say that alternatively these other language texts impel us to do so. Here is an example of this process: recently, while reading an early twentieth-century Oriya novel, I was reminded of an acclaimed pioneer of Bengali fiction. Thus, the case of Bengali influence on Oriya may be argued here, although evidence to the contrary may also be the case. Sisir Kumar Das's concept of pro- and meta-phanes may explain this, but my point here is whether or not we can use this active juxtaposition towards a possible commonality in genre history. Suppose my reading of a Marathi classic of the late nineteenth century induces a similar juxtaposition with a Malaylam novel of about the same time or a Hindi or Urdu or Gujarati novel. Juxtapositions do not mean that we have already made up our mind about the so-called Indian novel of the first phase and reduce these texts to their common denominator. On the other hand, the texts are very much themselves, the Oriya absolutely Oriya, the Marathi absolutely Marathi, and so on. This is far from setting up initial postulates for the Indian novel of the first phase and testing the texts against them. Thus, inter-Indian reception presupposes that our situs is in our first text, that is, first language literature. This is crucial for there is no no-man's land or neutral territory between Indian literatures.

Finally, let me assure you that, obviously, the problematic of unity and diversity are not unique to India. However, in keeping with my proposal that the situs of both theorist and theory is an important issue, I demonstrate here the application of the proposal. If I had discussed, for instance, Canadian diversity, it would have been from the outside, that is, from an Indian situs. I am not suggesting extreme relativism, but Comparative Literature has taught us not to take comparison literally and it also taught us that theory formation in literary history is not universally tenable. I am suggesting that we should first look at ourselves and try to understand our own situations as thoroughly as possible. Let us first give full shape to our own comparative literatures and then we will formulate a comparative literature of diversity in general.

WORKS CITED

Ahmad, Aijaz. "'Indian Literature': Notes towards the Definition of a Category." *In Theory: Classes, Nations, Literatures.* By *Aijaz Ahmad.* London: Verso, 1992. 243–85.

Bernheimer, Charles, ed. *Comparative Literature in the Age of Multiculturalism.* Baltimore: The Johns Hopkins UP, 1995.

Das, Sisir Kumar. *A History of Indian Literature.* Vol 1: *1800–1910: Western Impact / Indian Response.* New Delhi: Sahitya Akademi, 1991.

Ďurišin, Dionýz. *Theory of Interliterary Process.* Bratislava: VEDA/Slovak Academy of Sciences, 1989.

Gálik, Marián. "Interliterariness as a Concept in Comparative Literature." *Comparative Literature and Comparative Cultural Studies.* Ed. Steven Tötösy de Zepetnek. West Lafayette: Purdue UP, 2002. 34–44.

George, K.M., ed. *Comparative Indian Literature.* Madras and Trichur: Macmillan and Kerala Sahitya Akademi, 1984–85. 2 vols.

Jaidev. *The Culture of Pastiche: Existential Aestheticism in the Contemporary Hindi Novel.* Simla: Indian Institute of Advanced Study, 1993.

Majumdar, Swapan. *Comparative Literature: Indian Dimensions.* Calcutta: Papyrus, 1985.

Mukherjee, Sujit. *Translation as Discovery.* New Delhi: Allied Publishers, 1981. 15–73.

Ngugi, wa Thiong'o. "On the Abolition of the English Department." *Homecoming: Essays on African and Caribbean Literature, Culture and Politics.* By Ngugi wa Thiong'o. London: Heinemann, 1972. 145–50.

Singh, Gurbhagat. "Differential Multilogue: Comparative Literature and National Literatures." *Differential Multilogue: Comparative Literature and National Literatures.* Ed. Gurbhagat Singh. Delhi: Ajanta Publications, 1991. 11–19.

"University Grants Commission Circular Letter." No. F5-5-85 (HR-1) New Delhi (25 March 1986).

Interliterariness as a Concept in Comparative Literature

Marián Gálik

The concept of interliterariness has a very short history and is used mainly in Central European literary scholarship. Proponents of the notion are indebted to Russian Formalists and Czech Structuralists; "literariness" as a fore-runner of interliterariness has been coined in the *Werkstätte* of Roman Jakobson in 1921: "The object of literary scholarship is not literature but literariness, i.e. which makes a given work a literary one. Up to now literary scholars were more similar to policemen who, aiming to arrest some person, will round up everybody and everything to be found in the flat, even the people passing by chance on the street. Prey to the literary historian was human existence, psychology, politics, philosophy" (11; my translation; see also Gálik 1996). A similar concept of literariness has been briefly stated by René Wellek in his well-known study on the "crisis of comparative literature" in 1959: "literary scholarship will not make any progress methodologically, unless it determines to study literature as subject distinct from other activities and procedures of man. Hence we must face the problem of 'literariness,' the central issue of aesthetics, the nature of art and literature" (293). Here "aesthetics," of course, does not mean aesthetics as a philosophy of beauty and art, or the laws governing its manifestations, but an embodiment of aesthetic value, and other values, in the works of literature.

Ďionýz Durišin, in his *Theory of Interliterary Process* (1989), characterizes literariness even in a more succinct way, as the "basic and essential quality" (21) of all literature embodying all relations within the literature, their intensity, amount, and manner of their conditionality within the framework of various individual literatures. If this intensity, variability, mutual relations, or affinities transcend the boundaries of individual literatures, then "literari-ness" transforms itself automatically into "interliterariness." Thus, interliter-ariness is the basic and essential quality of literature in an international and inter-ethnic context and ontological determination. This determination and its framework comprise all possible relations and affinities, individual literatures, supra-ethnic, and supra-national entities of various kinds, and the highest embodiment of interliterariness, world literature. In his *Les Communautés interlittéraires spécifiques* Ďurišin writes: "Interlittérarité exprime la base ontologique du processus interlittéraire supranational, c'est-à-dire du déroule-ment et de l'evolution littéraire, de la vie littéraire" (1993, 14). For Ďurišin, the concept of interliterariness forms the main notion for a theory of interlit-erary process as comparative literature and as such it deserves more attention by theoreticians of comparative literature as well as theoreticians of literature and culture in general. And this attention does occur although in my opinion not in a sufficiently critical mass. For example, according to the editors of the 1989 *Comparative Literature: Theory and Practice* (Amiya Dev and Sisir Kumar Das, eds.), there is a need for a new epistemology in comparative lit-erature, and also for the "redefining [of] its areas in terms nearer to . . . inter-literariness . . . as yet the *prime rationale* of the discipline" (my emphasis; inside back cover).

Ontologically speaking, interliterariness is secondary to literariness. Because of their "division of labor," they are distinct entities: Although interliterariness always comprises literariness, the reverse is not always the case. From an epis-temological point of view, the question of interliterariness—its scope, contents, and characteristics of its various manifestations in comparative literature, that is, in the interliterary process—is not as deeply studied as questions concerned with literariness. One of the most important features of interliterariness is its implied or implicit processual character, a system(at)ic series of related liter-ary facts within the ethnic or national framework presupposing the temporal and spatial changes in the course of their literary development. Particular lit-eratures, from the oldest Sumerian and Egyptian to the most recent emerging ones, have always been in the state of permanent flux, in a tension that might be defined as a "coming to be," i.e., a flux of construction (Piaget 140).

If we look at the facts of process over a period of one hundred years of one of the first great works of literature, *The Epic of Gilgamesh*, starting with its first version by G. Smith in 1872 and the numerous translations and ver-sion including the Czech translation by L. Matouš in 1975, we may see the process of interliterary metamorphosis of Sumerian, Accadian, Assyrian, and Hittite bases. Here, at the dawn of literary civilization, we find a systemo-cultural filter or sorter of interliterariness. The different copies (no one complete) reflect differentiated literary development and show the structure of individual literatures and their overall sociopolitical and ideological frameworks. Different attitudes to gods among Sumerians and probably more sophisticated Semitic Akkadians have found their various representation of *sujet* and their literary processing (see Berdnikov 99, 102–11). The Hittite version was shorter than others owing probably to once again to a different receiving structure. These were first links of an extremely long chain, or knots in the immense fabric of literature of all ages and broad territories of *orbe universo*. The impact of this work and many of its components we may find in Moses' *Genesis* or Homer's *Odyssey*. The genetic relations are plausible in both cases. The existence of a Euro-Afro-Asian intercultural community is beyond doubt in the pre-Antique age; it comprises Egypt, Mesopotamia, Crete, and the Aegean civilization with its Mycenian stratum (Berdnikov 53).

If we add up old Indian epics and the literary products of the pre-Antique intercultural community, then we find not only genetic relations but also clear structural-typological affinities between the literatures of a Euro-Asian world. Its interliterary unity and variety, for instance, is reflected in the similar use of epithets and similes, and in resembling themes, such as the abduction of a woman (Helen and Briseis in the *Iliad* and Sita in the *Ramayana*), or her seduction (Draupadi in the *Mahabharata* and Penelope in the *Odyssey*), or the hero's dream affecting the epic action, or a heavenly messenger announcing something to other celestial or to terrestrials (Hermes in the *Odyssey* or Impaluri in the Hittite *Song on Ullikumi*). Also similar is the use of narrative within narrative, as so abundantly seen in the *Mahabharata*, the *Gilgamesh*, and the *Iliad*, although to a lesser extent in the latter two (see Dev and Das 118).

Interliterariness is concerned with that part of the process at first regional or zonal and in the last centuries global which leaves aside the purely ethnic or national aspects of literatures (or the aspects that define their individualities or individual qualities) and focuses on the trans-ethnic, trans-national, and lately on the geoliterary development as a whole. It involves all possibilities of literary impact and response. To put it more specifically, a literary fact or a literary phenomenon as the most basic element of literature and of its study and research may be the outcome of stimuli that have an extra-ethnical or extra-national character in their vertical or horizontal continuity, surpassing the confines of ethnic, national, or single literatures. Thus, a literary fact or phenomenon changes into the interliterary and becomes in the process a basic element of interliterariness. An interliterary impact and response to it is, as a rule, a prerequisite for a literary production in every literature—with the exception of the possible existence of only one literature in the world at the beginning of human civilization or a scattered existence of a few at great distance from each other—if it satisfies the overall structural requirements of the receiving literatures which in themselves are the representations of ethnic, national, or individual characteristics. Geoliterary development seems to be a new term in interliterary studies and represents the most recent state in the interliterary process. More recent concepts emerged based on the theoretical developments starting at the end of the nineteenth century, when the countries of Asia and North Africa began to respond to the literary and cultural impact of the West. Recent developments came with the advent of the post-colonial era and are connected with wholesale cultural globalization, where the broadest East-West synthesis is an aim to be achieved in interliterary process and its concrete realization, as well as its geoliterary and geocultural globalization.

Interliterariness is most conspicuous in the field of genetic-contact relations (or within the framework of influence and response) comprising all the phenomena in the interliterary process where contacts between literatures are a *conditio sine qua non* of their development. External contacts, i.e., those which did not leave any deeper traces in the structure of the receiving literatures, and internal contacts, where the impact could be reasonably proved, establish the different qualities of interliterariness. The first qualities are shallower while the second ones are deeper. This process of interliterariness becomes most common in times of great cataclysms in literary evolution, where the whole systemo-structural entities of individual literatures change their overall habitus owing to the metamorphoses in ideology, aesthetics, literary kinds, genres or forms. This is the case, for instance, with many new literatures in Asia and Africa of the second half of the nineteenth and during the twentieth centuries and following the enormous impact of the Euro-American world (see Král et al). The genetic-contact relations in the pre-Antique time were certainly different from those of later ages. If there were any traces of the external contacts, they were certainly not preserved for later generations. But without internal contacts existing between the Egyptian, Accadian, Cannanite, and even Sumerian poetry, we are not able to properly analyze the interliterary process leading to the Hebrew poetry of the *Bible*, and especially to the *Song of Songs*, probably the most beautiful love song of the world literature (Leick 69, 72, 238; Albright 131, 221). It was, among other reasons, also owing to the high level of interliterariness that the *Bible* became the "book of books" in Western literature especially after the translation of the *Old Testament* into Greek as *Septuagint* and whose style had an influence on the *New Testament* and on the Christian world as a whole. The interliterariness connected with the genetic-contact relations does not appear to be always effective when two well-developed literatures meet. On the other hand, if the contact occurred in a relatively new environment, and provided there were enough possibilities of free development, as in Chinese Turkestan (now Xinjiang in Mainland China) between the second century B.C. and the eighth century A.D. These literatures developed into the first world culture in history: the Silk Roads connected Chang'an (now Xi'an) with the Tarim Basin through the passes of Pamir, the towns of Samarkand, Bukhara or Balkh, Merv, Palmyra, Tyrus, Antioch, Alexandria and ended in Rome, or later in Byzantium. Here, four most advanced cultural areas met: European Greco-Roman and Oriental, i.e., West, South, and East Asian, in a fruitful clash and harmony. Here, interliterary development, combined with interartistic and intercultural processes, formed the first specimen of the highest embodiment of the world's intercultural process. Gandharan (Greco-Roman and Indian) interartistic symbiosis, religious (Buddhist, Manichean, and Nestorian) *oecumene*, polylinguism reminiscent of the mythic Tower of Babel (with Sanskrit as the most important among them), cultural pluralism, intensive translating, and artistic activities made it possible to enrich the local environment and to make their impact on the regions eastward of China and the whole Far East. The world culture of the Oasean cities between the Himalayas and Tianshan remained for more than one millennium a paradigm of liberal spirit, intercultural, and interliterary tolerance and understanding (see Gálik 1993).

In the realm of structural-typological affinities, that is, literary parallels, we may find another kind of interliterariness. Here it is not the concrete, material evidence that is important, but its value in the history and development of individual literatures. Affinities (parallels) in the structural-typological field are equivalent to relations in the genetic-contact field; their study could be even more valuable than that of the real substance of the literary facts concerned, since it could supply us with new knowledge and lead to a deeper understanding in various areas of literature, its history, theory, and criticism. Influence and reception studies helped literary scholars to illuminate the problems of the genesis of works in their continuity within the dialectical tension between the tradition (coming mostly from ethnic or national literatures) and innovation (coming very often from the interliterary field). The structural-typological realm, exploring analogies in the interliterary process of different literatures of the same period, or of different epochs, and sometimes spatially very remote from each other, meant or at least could mean a deeper penetration into the study of the interliterary process, and its results could lead to the discovery of the higher forms of interliterariness. While the field of genetic-contact relations reveals the mechanism of continuity that exposes the course of the interliterary process in its most visible way, the field of structural-typological affinities is securing the same effect in a more sophisticated and not so immediate form. For this reason, it compels the researcher to study not only various forms of social consciousness, political situations or contexts in which the works were written or to which they corresponded in a creative manner, but also literary traditions and conventions, literary genres, and trends. Especially new knowledge within the framework of literatures outside the Euro-American cultural area is needed now.

In the list of terms distributed to the participants of the XIIIth ICLA/AILC Congress in Tokyo (1991) and connected with the *International Dictionary of Literary Terms*, we find only six terms related to old and modern Chinese literature among about six hundred devoted to the rest of the literatures of the world, mostly to the Euro-American West. If we look into James J.Y. Liu's *Chinese Theories of Literature* (1975), we find there at least thirty important terms concerning old Chinese poetry alone, not including fiction and drama (183–97). Interliterary poetics, as one of the objectives of comparative literary theory, is still in its embryonic stage, and will not achieve any even relatively serious results without taking into account comparative study of the literary genres, traditions, and conventions at least of Sanskrit and post-Sanskrit Indian literatures, Arabian literatures, and the literatures of the Far East. With attention to such a wider scope of areas, I believe it possible to find a common metalanguage in the field of comparative literary scholarship. It is within human cognitive abilities to come to the core of terms very different from those we use in Europe, to define their adequate meanings, to detach ourselves from their pure sign forms, presented very often with the veil of ineffability to the indigenous and foreign experts, to focus on their content and range, particularly in concrete cases, and endeavour to give it approximately precise delimitation within the framework of comparative literature, concretely within the proposed comparative, that is, interliterary, poetics.

Earl Miner's *Comparative Poetics: An Intercultural Essay on Theories Literature* (1990), taking into account mostly Sino-Japanese and European literary and theoretical legacy, is probably the best book of its kind in the last years. A thorough investigation of the literary areas mentioned above will not be enough in order to study the most basic aspects of the structural-typological affinities. According to Earl Miner, other literatures, including the literatures of Africa and Latin America, and lesser known literatures of Europe and Asia deserve the attention of scholars: "the consideration of the other three quarters or four-fifths of the race must enter into any literary study denominating itself comparative" (11). Interliterariness as a quality of literature surpassing the confines of national, ethnic or individual literatures, according to Durišin, finds its broadest implementation in the field of interliterary communities (or commonwealths), i.e., supranational and supraethnic conglomerates of literatures coming into existence, changing and disappearing in historical developments conditioned spatially and temporally by ethnic, linguistic, national, and even ideological factors. Interliterary communities are literary "families" similar to each other owing to factors just mentioned. We may speak about many interliterary communities of different kinds (their typology has not been scholarly elaborated as yet), e.g., the community of English and American literatures, the different communities of Slavic literatures, the specific community of Swiss literatures, the interliterary community of the Far East up to the end of the nineteenth and the beginning of the twentieth centuries, Balkan interliterary communities during the last two millennia, contemporary interliterary communities in Sub-Saharan Africa, etc. These communities that exist in the "commonwealth of world literature," are fulfilling certain functions which help them to realize their special nature in order to exist as interliterary communities, whether in a positive or a negative direction (see Durišin 1987–93).

In interliterary communities, the literatures in contact—and all literatures forming interliterary communities are in contact—are fulfilling some functions that are not visible in the field of ordinary genetic-contact relations. Owing to the great extent of mutual impact and response, individual literatures and their various strata behave mostly in two different, opposing ways: either taking the foreign impulses and integrating them into their own receiving structure (an integrational function), or trying to filter or sort out stimuli in order to select the most convenient one, and to repudiate inconvenient elements of the giving systemo-structural entity (a differential function). These two functions can be fulfilled only if certain factors of interliterary community are at work:

e.g., the existence of a common language as in the case of German speaking countries—the community of German and Austrian literatures together with a part of Swiss literature, Jewish Prague literature up to 1939, and even Jiddish literature; or in the case of different communities within the framework of Anglophone, Francophone, Lusophone, or Hispanic literatures, as well as contemporary Chinese literature on the Mainland, in Taiwan, Hong Kong, Singapore, Malaysia, and elsewhere (as ethnic minority literature, for instance). The last one mentioned, i.e., literature written in Chinese in different parts of the world, may serve as a paradigm of interliterary flux through the centuries and millennia. Its history is more than three thousand years old and its great era was connected with the interliterary community of the Far East comprising the Chinese, Korean, Japanese and in the second millennium B.C. for some periods also a part of Vietnamese, Manchu, and Mongolian literatures. This interliterary community began to develop in the last decades B.C. or in the first decades A.D. in harmony with the Chinese concept of *Zhongguo* (The Middle Kingdom), or *Zhonghua* (The Middle Civilization) and in its relation to the peripheral "barbarian" territories. An essential difference between the Chinese and the "barbarians" was to reside in *wen* that may be roughly translated as the "spiritual culture." From China, which was highly endowed with it, this *wen* radiated like rays of the sun into the surrounding world, surpassing the integrational function working in most other interliterary communities, and spread Chinese literature into neighbouring countries. During the rise and development of non-Chinese literature of this interliterary community, Chinese literature fulfilled its "culturalist" function and served for many centuries as a substitute for the indigenous literatures of the area. Only after centuries, or even after a millennium, did this function decline until it disappeared altogether. Literary works of Japan, Korea, or Vietnam, especially of the last two, if they were written in their own languages, for many centuries had only a complementary function. This traditional interliterary community disappeared in the last decades of the nineteenth and in the first two decades of the twentieth century (see Gálik 1995). A new interliterary community of the Far East did not come into being owing to political, ideological, cultural, and literary reasons.

Bilingualism or biliterarity, such as in the interliterary communities of the Balkans, India, Central Asia, or Africa, or polylinguism and polyliterarity of certain groups, e.g., in Switzerland or in Malaysia, is another example of interliterariness. These phenomena are usually accompanied with another kind of interliterariness, even more important than that just mentioned: That of *dioicousness* and *polyoicousness*. These terms, borrowed and applied from the Greek *oikia* (a house or dwelling), mean in the first instance an ability to be at home in two different literatures, usually but not always in two different literary languages and cultures. *Dioicousness* and *polyoicousness* prove to be important in times of great social and political mobility. For example, P.J. Šafárik was writing in Czech and German and *dioicous* in Czech and Slovak literature, Ivo Andric was present at first in Croatian and later in Serbian literature, and Alisher Navoi (1441–1501), who wrote in three languages, has been "at home" in Old Uzbek, Persian, as well as Arab literatures.

Theoretically, the highest quality of interliterariness may be found in the concept of world literature, which in its literary-historical and evolutionary apprehension within the interliterary process is its highest hypostasis. World literature is a *summa litterarum universarum* not in their overall quantity but in their mutual relationships and affinities within the complicated systemo-structural reality of the interliterary process. This interliterariness is uniting all other kinds mentioned above, but on the highest possible level, owing to its deeper, broader, and mutual contextuality. This does not mean that all inter-literariness in the dimensions of world literature is the most worthy from an axiological point of view. It means only that specific literary facts went through all the interliterary filters mentioned above. This interliterariness depends on the measure of the knowledge of inter-literary facts and processes and therefore it is much more variable within the flux of time and space than those in subordinated spheres of the interliterary process. There is a great difference between the interliterariness during the time of Homer's *Odyssey* and Joyce's *Ulysses* (1922) or Giono's *La Naissance de l'Odyssée*.

If we consider the first known literatures of history: Sumerian, Egyptian, and Akkadian and the "last" known accumulation of literatures based on a numerical account of languages (about six thousand languages), we may imagine the differences in the degree of variety, complexity, and intricacy existing in this kind of interliterariness. As far as the theory of inter-literary process is concerned, I argue against the concept of world literature as a *summa* of all literary works produced in individual literatures in the course of their evolution, as I argue against *Weltliteratur* as *Wertliteratur*, i.e., a *summa* of all literary masterpieces. Neither do I agree with theoreticians of literature—such as Horst Steinmetz—who connect world literature with the literatures, mostly of the Euro-American cultural area, produced in the nineteenth and twentieth centuries (see Steinmetz 1988). More than five millennia of the existence of literature in world history and about some hundred of single literatures existing today provide the researchers with unimaginable numbers of different relationships and affinities within the interliterary process, including so far unknown and never studied concrete relations between individual literatures of the world. These were not researched yet, and when proposed, as in Durišin's case, then in relation to the lower level components of the interliterary process, these possible relationships and processes can be regarded as a pure hypothesis to be researched and extrapolated (see Durišin 1992, 7–56, 174–95). In sum, while in literary study the application of the theory of interliterariness as the basic and essential quality of literature in its international or interethnic realm awaits realization, it is, most importantly, an evolutionary concept that changes in time and space. Thus, new theoretical and methodological frameworks and applications are necessary for its deeper and broader understanding.

WORKS CITED

Albright, William Foxwell. *Yahweh and the Gods of Canaan: A Historical Analysis of Two Contrasting Faiths*. London: Athlone, 1968.

Berdnikov, G.P., ed. *Istoria vsemirnoi literatury* (*A History of World Literature*). Moscow: Nauka, 1983–.

Dev, Amiya, and Sisir Kumar Das, eds. *Comparative Literature: Theory and Practice*. New Delhi: Associated Press, 1989.

Ďurišin, Dionýz. *Theory of Interliterary Process*. Bratislava: Veda, 1989.

Ďurišin , Dionýz. *O je svetová literatúra?* (*What is World Literature?*). Bratislava: Obzor, 1992.

Ďurišin , Dionýz, et al., eds. *Les Communautés interlittéraires spécifiques*. Bratislava: Veda, 1987–93. 6 Vols.

Epos o Gilgamešovi (*Epic of Gilgamesh*). Trans. L. Matouš. Bratislava: Tatran, 1975.

Gálik, Marián. "Some Remarks on the Process of Emancipation in Modern Asian and African Literatures." *Asian and African Studies* 23 (1988): 9–29.

Gálik, Marián. "Viae sericae or Silk Roads as the Intermediaries between Asia and Europe." *Human Affairs* 3.2 (1993): 118–30.

Gálik, Marián. "Some Theoretical Problems of the Interliterary Community of the Far East." *The Force of Vision: Inter-Asian Comparative Literature*. Ed. K. Kawamoto, H. Yuan, and Y. Ohsawa. Tokyo: Tokyo UP, 1995. 222–28.

Gálik, Marián. "Comparative Literature in Slovakia." *Comparative Literature: History and Contemporaneity*. Ed. Milan V. Dimić and Steven Tötösy de

Zepetnek. Thematic Cluster, *Canadian Review of Comparative Literature / Revue Canadienne de Littérature Comparée* 23.1 (1996): 101–11.

Jakobson, Roman. *Noveishaia russkaia poezia (Recent Russian Poetry)*. Prague, 1921.

Král, Oldrich, et al., eds. *Contributions to the Study of the Rise and Development of Modern Literatures in Asia*. Prague: Academia, 1965–70. 3 Vols.

Leick, Gwendolyn. *Sex and Eroticism in Mesopotamian Literature*. London: Routledge, 1994.

Liu, James J.Y. *Chinese Theories of Literature*. Chicago: U of Chicago P, 1975.

Miner, Earl. *Comparative Poetics: An Intercultural Essay on Theories of Literature*. Princeton: Princeton UP, 1990.

Piaget, Jean. *Structuralism*. New York: Harper & Row, 1968.

Steinmetz, Horst. *Literatur und Gesellschaft. 4 Versuche*. München: iudicium, 1988.

Steinmetz, Horst. "Response to Claus Clüver's 'The Difference of Eight Decades. World Literature and the Demise of National Literatures'." *Yearbook of Comparative and General Literature* 37 (1988): 131–33.

Wellek, René. "The Crisis of Comparative Literature." *Concepts of Criticism*. Ed. Stephen G. Nichols Jr. New Haven: Yale UP, 1963. 282–95.

The Impact of Globalization and the New Media on the Notion of World Literature

Ernst Grabovszki

The notion of world literature is never static, as Yves Chevrel states: "la notion de *Weltliteratur* est sans cesse à réviser" (27). In this context, I would like to suggest that the contemporary situation of world literature should be discussed with regard to the phenomenon of globalization in a perspective of its social processes and the impact of new media from a systemic and empirical point of view. However, first I would like to elaborate briefly on "globalization" in the context of comparative literary studies, especially for the reason that many disciplines in the human sciences have already developed their own notion of the said term while there has been little written about it in comparative literature. Jan Nederveen Pieterse suggests that in general terms, globalization means boundlessness and/or the internationalization of social, political, and economic processes and he argues that globalization should also be understood as a process of modernism as well as postmodernism (87). He also argues that internationalization may not necessarily be a result of globalization; rather, it was a basis for the process of globalization itself. This explanation of modernism and globalization characterizes globalization as a Eurocentric phenomenon insofar as it is spreading from Europe and results in the Occidentation of the cultures of neighboring countries as well as the global community.

Anthony Giddens offers a more neutral definition of globalization: "Globalization is definable by an intensification of global social interrelations by which distant localities are connected to one another in such a manner that events taking place at one locality effect those that happen many kilometers away, and vice versa" (qtd. in Nederveen Pieterse 92; my translation; on Giddens, see Tucker). Between the two definitions—that of Nederveen Pieterse and

Giddens—there is agreement that globalization means no unification, the flattening or the levelling of culture. Rather, contrary to the perceived dangers of globalization, regionalism, postmodern fragmentation, localism, the questions about and the formations of identity and community, and the contrasts or delimitations of these notions and acts have remained social, political, economic, etc., factors. Nevertheless, the process of globalization is considered troublesome by some and a positive development by others. Ralf Dahrendorf, for instance, foresees a new class society as a result of a reduction of employees due to the efforts of trans- or international enterprises to keep their labor costs to a minimum. On the other hand high incomes keep increasing and the rich are getting richer (47; see also, for example, Buell; Bird et al.; Dev; Featherstone; Friedman; Jameson and Miyoshi; Menzel; Moses; Wilson and Dissenayake).

For my discussion, I would like to take my point of departure with Giddens' notion of globalization being "an intensification of global social interrelations" and in an extension of his suggestion, I argue that that globalization also means the intensification of literary relations and of communication including that of artistic, i.e., literary communication and production. In the context of an empirical approach to the situation of globalization and world literature I propose the following preliminary aspects for discussion:

1) Copyright: The sale of copyright is an important pre-requisite for the global distribution of literature. In the German book trade, for instance, the sale of subsidiary rights has gained as of yet incalculable importance for publishers as a source of income in order to equalize the ever increasing costs of production, marketing, and inventory. The tendency towards selling copy rights—to book clubs, paperback and special editions, anthologies, as well as film, TV, radio, video, foreign rights and merchandising, etc. (see Owen; Wittmann 427)— results in an ever increasing international traffic of cultural production, including literature. In this respect it is also important to consider the role of literary agents (especially in English-speaking countries) and translators not only as mediators between literary institutions but also between cultures.

2) The role and function of literary institutions: The regional densities of literary institutions such as publishers, libraries, bookstores, distributors, etc. means that the circulation and knowledge of literature depend on the existence and function of the said institutions. In consequence, we must pay attention of the how of these institutions in their appropriate context. For instance, when considering African literature one would be misguided to assume that literary production and the business of literature in Africa is similar to the production

and consumption of literature in European countries or North America. Obviously—and this is not a value judgement, simply a reference to the realities of production, distribution, and consumption—because of the high quota of illiteracy in certain parts of Africa, printed texts are less used than media which do not require reading abilities such as radio, TV, theater, or video. Our Eurocentric notion where literature is more often than not equated with the written and/or printed text will not serve us well here. Literature, clearly, is not only the printed text and there are parts in the world where oral literature has a much broader tradition as well as social and cultural importance. And here again we may want to pay attention to the paradigmatic function of the method of comparison. Historians Heinz-Gerhard Haupt and Jürgen Kocka state that "in the light of alternatives observed one's own development loses its former matter of course. Comparison allows the view of other constellations, it expands the awareness of potentialities . . . and identifies the case being observed as one alternative among others" (14; my translation).

3) The question of global economics and the reading of literature: Again, using the example of Africa, there might be people who are able to read but are they in turn able to afford books? In many African countries, the price of a book ranges up to 25 percent of the monthly average income! (see Loimeier 8). As to European conditions (see also point 6) the recently adjourned resolution on the abolition of the "common book price-fixing" within the European Union is expected to affect the book trade seriously. Owing to their relatively stable financial background, large chain bookstores are able to sell books and other media products at low prices which will lead to the drastic reduction of book stores and, consequently, of publishers because of their inability to compete. This, of course, effects also the range of literature offered to the reader.

4) The problematics of the development of electronic media and the cultures of information with regard to their technical and content development in their global and regional settings: This point is again suited for making us realize that literature is not only bound up with the book as its traditional medium but that it is also perceived and functions as an oral form. Thus we have to draw our attention to such media which are dominant in a certain region such as certain parts of Africa and Asia. In the technologically advanced countries of the world, the role of the internet as a medium of communication between distributors and customers is still insignificant, at least for the German book trade, for example. In 1998 the German internet book trade

could register sales of 30 million German Marks, which is no more than 0,00176 percent of the trade's total turnover! (see "Seifenblase Internet?" 60). Further, an analysis of the content of the media taken into consideration has to cover the ways and manners literature is dealt with in its different manifestations. The following questions can be posed: How is literature discussed? What rank does literature hold within the program of a radio or TV station or within literature-related sites on the world wide web? Which literature is discussed (high-brow, trivial literature, etc.)? Is there also foreign literature that receives attention or only literature in the national language(s) and if yes, is it dealt with in its original language or in translation? Especially radio or audio media allow to present literature in an authentic way. Audio books, for instance, may intensify the authenticity of literature by presenting a text read by its author in the original language. In addition, this kind of authenticity proceeds from the assumption that, according to the old model of literary communication a piece of literature is always linked with the name of a person.

5) The problematics of control and censorship: The control and censorship of literature occurs in both democratic and non-democratic countries and with regard to all kinds of media. However, censorship exists in Western democracies in subtle and at times more intangible ways (see, for example, <http://www.clairescorner.com/censorship/banned.htm>; <http://www.luc.edu/libraries/banned/ecen.html>) . In the last decade, the discussion about censorhip and the internet has developed on a large scale. Governments of all ideological orientations are earnestly discussing to what degree freedom of speech should be granted to the internet and its users. In whatever manner this discussion will develop, there is evidence that censorship of the digital space is hardly comparable with censorship of the book. From the censor's, the consumer's, and the producer's point of view, one aspect is of particular importance, namely that it is virtually impossible to monitor the traffic of information and material on the internet. Craig Atkinson puts it as follows:

> For example, China is attempting to restrict political expression, in the name of security and social stability. It requires users of the Internet and electronic mail (e-mail) to register, so that it may monitor their activities. In the United Kingdom, state secrets and personal attacks are off limits on the Internet. Laws are strict and the government is extremely interested in regulating the Internet with respect to these issues. . . . In France, a country where the press generally

have a large amount of freedom, the Internet has recently been in the spotlight. A banned book on the health history of former French president Francois Mitterrand was republished electronically on the World Wide Web (WWW). Apparently, the electronic reproduction of *Le Grand secret* by a third party wasn't banned by a court that ruled that the printed version of the book unlawfully violated Mitterrand's privacy" and finally sums up that "the internet cannot be regulated in the way of other mediums [sic] simply because it is not the same as anything else that we have. It is a totally new and unique form of communication and deserves to be given a chance to prove itself. Laws of one country can not hold jurisdiction in another country and holds true on the Internet because it has no borders (see <http://www.freqwerks.com/censor>; for restrictions imposed on the internet in Asia and Africa see also <http://www.ccpj.ca/publications/internet/ch1.htm>).

6) The monopoly of media giants and its implications: The concentration of media businesses, enterprises, and publishers suggests increasing tendency towards the globalization of their operations. In turn, this may lead to a monopoly of conglomerates which means undue control of what gets produced and what does not, including the type of literature and the contents of the types of literature. With regard to specifics of the economics of the European Union, for example, this concentration poses the question whether the implementation of market prices based on competition of literary products in the European Union would help the preservation of the diversity of literary forms or destroy it.

7) In addition to the above points of consideration I am suggesting for a study of globalization and world literature, there is of course the broader implications of the event, processes, and consequences of cyberspace, or, in the words of Homi Bhabha, "third space". Personally, I prefer the term "digital space" instead of cyberspace because of the latter's inflationary use in connection with computer games, music, or techno-culture. Digital space in my opinion is a neutral enough term to circumscribe the technical as well as the contents-related aspects of new media and fulfills the idea of a global net which facilitates communication, information retrieval, and, of course, artistic representation freed from national, linguistic, or cultural assignments and value judgments. As to the global impact of the internet and the world wide web, the English language is indeed prevailing on account of the dominant influence of the United

States and other English-speaking countries but serves, in this case, rather as a lingua franca than as an expression of imperialism (see Tötösy 17).

The term cyberspace was coined, interestingly, by an author of literature, William Gibson, who depicts it as an imaginary world "behind the screen" in his 1984 novel, *Neuromancer* (see Bollmann 163). "In his novel, Gibson describes cyberspace as a computer generated landscape into which his figures shift, sometimes by connecting electrodes directly to implants in their brains. What they see when they arrive there is a 'graphical reproduction of information from the banks of all computers in the system of mankind', in large department stores and skyscrapers of data. In a key scene of *Neuromancer* Gibson describes the cyberspace as follows: 'A consensual hallucination, witnessed daily by billions of people entitled to in all countries, by children to illustrate mathematical terms . . . Incredible complexity. Light lines packed in the non-space of the mind, data packages arranged in groups'" (Bollmann 163; my translation). Stefan Bollmann expands on Gibson's ideas and suggests that cyberspace may be defined as "the new manner of interactivity and intersubjectivity which develops when the computer is connected to the telephone line" (165). In other words, the said interactivity does not just cover further means of communication but offers the opportunity to work on texts in a "third space."

Here I would like to expand on my last point of area I suggest for further discussion on the problematics of globalization and world literature today. New media, especially the internet and the world wide web, I argue, impact on the model of literary communication. As we know, this structuralist model consists of the author (the primary producer of the text), the distributors (the producers, distributors, and marketers of the product), and the readers (the consumers of the text who also include critics and scholars) (see, for example, Darnton). In view of contemporary literary scholarship, comparative or other, it is astonishing that the presence and impact of new media has seldom been considered to be of importance for the notion of world literature in any of its aspects and perspectives despite the fact that such intellectuals as Walter Benjamin already noted in 1936 that world literature—or any kind of literature—should be discussed with regard to its medium (23, 32). In recent times, although there has been much discussion about the demise of reading or the book and the various relationships of this to the event of new media and the electronic revolution (see, e.g., Birkerts; Donatelli and Winthrop-Young; Kernan; Kerckhove), the discussion has been scarce with regard to scholarship specifically (for a recent example, see Tötösy 249–59;

Jochum and Wagner <http://www.klostermann.de/verlegen/jochu_02.htm>). In the following, I will present selected points I believe are worthy of attention with regard to the impact of new media in the context of globalization on world literature and the study of literature (for the impact of new media on scholarly publishing see, for example, Jäger <http://www.klostermann.de/verlegen/jaege_10.htm>):

1) The author is no more an author of "texts" in the traditional sense but has the possibility to add audio-visual and/or pictorial elements ("clips") to his/her "text" on account of the world wide web's technical spectrum. Such an author potentially creates a *Gesamtkunstwerk* in the romantic sense, provided that he/she is skilled enough to cope with the mentioned technical spectrum available. Since the web represents an open medium unlike the book (i.e., the text of a book cannot be altered whereas the "text" on the web can continuously be modified and "updated"), the author in certain cases may lose the clear and unequivocal ownership of his/her "text" (I am not referring to copy right here but to the author as the creator of the product.) The web offers the possibility and, indeed, opportunity to change, complete, modify, vary etc., a text, thus the participants in the process become its (co-)authors.

2) In many instances, in literary production collective authorship replaces the single author associated with his/her proper name and work (see Foucault). This alteration of authorship has an impact on both the form and the content of creative texts. For example, there is now on the web the new literary genre called "fan fiction": "Fan fiction's roots trace back to the underground fanzine culture of the '60s and '70s. Fans further imagined adventures for the characters of their favorite TV shows, wrote them down, xeroxed them and distributed them by hand. But in the current decade, the Internet has spawned hundreds of fiction sites" (Dolan). For a central directory of fan fiction web sites, ranging from Jane Austen to MacGyver, see <http://members.aol.com:80/ksnicholas/fanfic/index.html>.

3) The web text itself is subject to a formal—and content-related—reshaping. With the use of hypertext (a text of whose elements refer to elements of other texts linked electronically; thus becoming a dense network of texts), it mirrors its medium: the texts stored in the internet also represent a network. Thus, their formerly clearly defined visual and tactile form (the book) and content-related (plot, line of reasoning, etc.) elements become permeable to changes in meaning or to deviations from linearity by other texts or other elements fraught with meaning.

4) Traditional distributors of literary and scholarly products such as publishers become increasingly redundant. This will become evident particularly in the area of scholarship but also in the distribution of primary literature. The impact on the economics of production and distribution here is such that it results in the lowering of costs but in turn this resulting in redundancy.

5) The internet and the world wide web as well as other digital media require new abilities and skills from the reader and this also has an impact on the process of reading. In addition to the knowledge of how to navigate in digital spheres in order to track down information or "text" wanted, the medial variety of a text calls for a higher level of activity by the reader because of the medium's demand not only on the visual faculty but on other sensory organs. This higher activity is a result of reading in the internet on the one hand but on the other hand—and more likely—it is also a consequence of the increasing flood of information through other media which in turn requires selection. Readers of digital texts have, therefore, more responsibility both toward themselves and their information because they have to decide *on the screen* which information is relevant to them. It is their decision that requires a different level and type of mental activity and responsibility than previously.

6) Paul Gilster characterizes the ability to use digital media for information recovery in a purposeful manner as "digital literacy is the ability to understand and use information in multiple formats from a wide range of sources when it is presented via computers" (1); market science distinguishes between the so-called high-involvement and the low-involvement customer: both categories can be differentiated above all by their specific way of information processing. High involvement means active search for information whereas low involvement rather means passive irrigation. Whoever searches the web for data displays a different degree of involvement and interest than someone who uses the new media for entertainment. Today, using the web and the internet in the high-involvement mode probably means membership in a relatively small— and not necessarily concentrated in technologically advanced societies although it is true that the density of such is at present higher in western societies— information-oriented elite (scholarship) and/or business and sales. From studies of the book market we know that the ratio of this information-oriented elite constitutes no more than 20 percent of the world population ("Seifenblase Internet?" 64).

7) In addition to the above mentioned skills, reading hypertexts requires a different way of reading than reading books in the traditional tactile mode.

We can distinguish between linear reading (books and printed texts) and structural reading ("texts" electronically linked to other "texts"). On account of the network structure of hypertexts, the reader is forced to examine this structure, their construction, and references and to recognize these structures in their entirety.

With regard to my central question as to how the above areas of new media in their entirety would have an impact on the notion of world literature, I suggest the following. Because of new media, literature obtains an additional public as well as individual dimension by means of the digital sphere. A consequence of this impact is a democratization of literary production in a range of its processes extended to not only the economics of production but also to the creative process of the production of the primary text and further extends to its scholarship and criticism. On the other hand—and this is a consequence of this democratization—there is much text in the internet and on the web which most likely would have never been published in the traditional printed form precisely because of the change in the processes of production and adjudication. Therefore, the democratization of literary production and distribution means an increase of the quantity—although not necessarily the quality—of literature.

In principle, the notion of world literature today finds its most relevant expression in infinite digital space. Goethe argued that national literatures depict different forms of human existence and that these fictional representations should be adopted for mutual returns resulting in an interplay that in turn would determine a new world (Albrow 428). In our age of new media and digital space this notion of world literature changes to a situation where: "In the global society globality shapes the frame for all social relations. Globality is indeed not simply the outcome of the interaction between social groups, be they nationally or internationally oriented. This is the big difference to the situation, Goethe had in mind" (Albrow 432). Further, the notion of the digital space gives rise to the democratization and a decentralization of the literary system (the primary text as well as its economics and business). However, this decentralization can also be understood in the postcolonial paradigm, although with an important distinction: a constituent aspect of postcolonial discourse is the tension between center and periphery. I will use the example of Salman Rushdie and the fate(s) of his novels to exemplify my point. His example shows that on the one hand we have the implicit and explicit differentiation between a "home" culture and a culture of the "Other." On the other hand, Rushdie's novels have made us realize a certain loosening of the said tension between "home" and

"Other" on an institutional level, namely via the appreciation of a (mitigated) Third World writer in the West's literary system. In new media and its digital space, there are no reasons for such tensions (on the surface?) except maybe between the digital and the "real" or non-virtual space in the sense of a systems theoretical understanding of social interaction. In other words, within digital space there is no location of a centre or centres of a cultural or social kind. Consequently, world literature loses its determinable locations.

It is not only that the business of literature undergoes a process of decentralization, it is also that the text and the producer of the text become decentralized entities and hybrids precisely because of their infinite travel in digital space, therefore not belonging to any "nation" or even an imagined community (Anderson) because this travel is directed by data and information. Note that digital space is characterized as a duplicate of real space by the use of the term *netizen*, a "person" traveling in digital space but equipped with the same consciousness and the same rights as a *citizen* (see Rötzer 39, 48). A *netizen* of digital space is able to be anywhere and the text itself—also literature, for example—is not located anywhere specifically either (although this is not as clear cut as that: the exact location of the web site where a text is "housed" and therefore controlled from may be an analogue of the library of tactile books). Importantly, this is a kind of literature that does not seem to stem from any national or cultural setting but comprises the world as a net, and thus becomes a world literature in a new sense of the notion. At the same time, I hasten to add, this type of "new" world literature is still written by authors with different cultural origins while digital space allows the same authors to produce a literature that contains a conglomerate of different cultural symbols traveling without discernable centers and locations.

In closing, I would like to discuss briefly Vilém Flusser's *Die Schrift. Hat Schreiben Zukunft?*, for the reason that he discusses literature from a traditional as well as progressive points of view. Flusser conflates elements of the old and the new models of literary communication. For my discussion, he raises the following relevant issue: today, we are leaving the age of writing (inscribing) for a new age of programming (prescribing), that is, we are abandoning alphabetical writing by progressing to a way of *indirect* communication by computer. This is because writing in the electronic age means communication *via* as well as *with* the computer in that one does not write alphabetically but in binary codes in order to prescribe the computer what to do. Flusser argues that alphabetical writing served a "historical" purpose: writing on paper with a pen or other writing utensils makes us aware of history and of our responsibility for history and it is this responsibility we are going to lose in the electronic age: "Every way of action becomes profane, scientific, functional, non-political, and people are free to give a sense of this way of action. . . . A new, post-historical mentality comes to the fore, giving sense to the absurd. Whether this optimism really satisfies all persons concerned, remains to be seen" (62; my translation). Here, Flusser makes an important observation: Programming—that is, the use of computers for writing and communication—has to be differentiated from poetic writing. This leads him to the conclusion that literature is not only composed of commands, rules, and instructions: "And these other threads in the tissue of literature are by no means programmable. Therefore we will go on with writing. And the historical, political and valuing mentality may be preserved by this resumption of writing" (62; my translation). Thus, for in my understanding of Flusser's thought as related to new media is that digital space is an addition to communication, creativity, and social interaction rather than a replacement. In creative writing whether with a pen or a computer, we maintain intrinsically the factor of the poetical while we add to it and the process of writing further dimensions and possibilities not available previously.

WORKS CITED

Albrow, Martin. "Auf dem Weg zu einer globalen Gesellschaft?" *Perspektiven der Weltgesellschaft*. Ed. Ulrich Beck. Frankfurt: Suhrkamp, 1998. 411–34.

Anderson, Benedict. *Die Erfindung der Nation. Zur Karriere eines folgenreichen Konzepts*. Trans. Christoph Münz and Benedikt Burkard. Frankfurt: Campus, 1996.

Appadurai, Arjun. *Modernity at Large: Cultural Dimensions of Globalization*. Minneapolis: U of Minnesota P, 1996.

Atkinson, Craig. "Censorship and the Internet" (1999–): <http://www.freqwerks. com/censor> .

Bachmann-Medick, Doris. "Multikultur oder kulturelle Differenzen? Neue Konzepte von Weltliteratur und Übersetzung in postkolonialer Perspektive." *Kultur als Text. Die anthropologische Wende in der Literaturwissenschaft*. Ed. Doris Bachmann-Medick. Frankfurt: Fischer, 1996. 262–90.

Beck, Ulrich. *Was ist Globalisierung?* Frankfurt: Suhrkamp, 1998.

Beck, Ulrich, ed. *Perspektiven der Weltgesellschaft*. Frankfurt: Suhrkamp, 1998.

Benjamin, Walter. "Das Kunstwerk im Zeitalter seiner technischen Reproduzierbarkeit." *Das Kunstwerk im Zeitalter seiner technischen Reproduzierbarkeit.
Drei Studien zur Kunstsoziologie.* Frankfurt: Suhrkamp, 1963. 7–44.

Bhabha, Homi. *The Location of Culture.* London: Routledge, 1994.

Bird, Jon, Barry Curtis, Tim Putnam, George Robertson, and Lisa Tickner, eds.
Mapping the Future: Local Cultures, Global Change. London: Routledge,
1993.

Birkerts, Sven. *The Gutenberg Elegies: The Fate of Reading in an Electronic Age.*
New York: Fawcett Columbine, 1994.

Bollmann, Stefan. "Einführung in den Cyberspace." *Kursbuch Neue Medien.
Trends in Wirtschaft und Politik, Wissenschaft und Kultur.* Ed. Stefan Bollmann. Mannheim: Bollmann, 1996. 163–65.

Buell, Frederick. *National Culture and the New Global System.* Baltimore: The
Johns Hopkins UP, 1994.

Chevrel, Yves. *La littérature comparée.* Paris: PU de France, 1989.

Dahrendorf, Ralf. "Anmerkungen zur Globalisierung." *Perspektiven der Weltgesellschaft.* Ed. Ulrich Beck. Frankfurt: Suhrkamp, 1998. 41–54.

Darnton, Robert. "Was ist die Geschichte des Buches?" *Der Kuss des Lamourette.
Kulturgeschichtliche Betrachtungen.* Trans. Jörg Trobitius. München: Hanser,
1998. 66–97.

Dev, Amiya. "Globalization and Literary Value." *The Search for a New Alphabet:
Literary Studies in a Changing World.* Ed. Harald Hendrix, Joost Kloek,
Sophie Levie, and Will Van Peer. Amsterdam: John Benjamins, 1996. 62–72.

Dolan, Deirdre. "When Spock Beamed Down to the Lesbian Space Colony." *The
Globe and Mail* (23 July 1999): B5.

Donatelli, Joseph, and Geoffrey Winthrop-Young, eds. *Media Matters: Technolo-
gies of Literary Production.* Special Issue of *Mosaic: A Journal for the Interdisciplinary Study of Literature* 28.4 (1995): 1–186.

Featherstone, Mike. *Undoing Culture: Globalization, Postmodernism and Identity.* London: Sage, 1995.

Flusser, Vilém. *Die Schrift. Hat Schreiben Zukunft?* Göttingen: European Photography, 1992.

Foucault, Michel. "Was ist ein Autor?" *Schriften zur Literatur.* Trans. Karin von
Hofer. Frankfurt: Fischer, 1993. 7–31.

Friedman, J. *Cultural Identity and Global Process.* London: Sage, 1993.

Gilster, Paul. *Digital Literacy.* New York: John Wiley & Sons, 1997.

Haupt, Heinz-Gerhard, and Jürgen Kocka. "Historischer Vergleich. Methoden, Auf-
gaben, Probleme. Eine Einleitung." *Geschichte und Vergleich. Ansätze und
Ergebnisse international vergleichender Geschichtsschreibung.* Ed. Heinz-
Gerhard Haupt, Jürgen Kocka. Frankfurt: Campus, 1996. 9–45.

Jäger, Georg. "Vom Text der Wissenschaft. Überlegungen zum Wandel des Textbe-
griffs im Rahmen vernetzter EDV-Kommunikation." (27 July 1999): <http://
www.klostermann.de/verlegen/jaege_10.htm> .

Jameson, Fredric, and Masao Miyoshi, eds. *The Cultures of Globalization*. Durham: Duke UP, 1998.

Jochum, Uwe, and Gerhard Wagner. "Cyberscience oder vom Nutzen und Nachteil der neuen Informationstechnologie für die Wissenschaft." (27 July 1999): <http://www.klostermann.de/verlegen/jochu_02.htm>.

Kerckhove, Derrick de. *The Skin of Culture: Investigating the New Electronic Reality*. Ed. Christopher Dewdney. Toronto: Somerville, 1995.

Kernan, Alvin. *The Death of Literature*. New Haven: Yale UP, 1990.

Lietsch, Jutta. *Zum Beispiel Internet*. Göttingen: Lamuv, 1997.

Loimeier, Manfred. *Zum Beispiel afrikanische Literatur*. Göttingen: Lamuv, 1997.

Menzel, Ulrich. *Globalisierung versus Fragmentierung*. Frankfurt: Suhrkamp, 1998.

Moses, Michael Valdez. *The Novel and the Globalization of Culture*. New York: Oxford UP, 1995.

Nederveen Pieterse, Jan. "Der Melange-Effekt. Globalisierung im Plural." *Perspektiven der Weltgesellschaft*. Ed. Ulrich Beck. Frankfurt: Suhrkamp, 1998. 87–124.

Owen, Lynette. *Selling Rights. Rechte vermarkten*. Trans. Marianne Sparr. Friedrichsdorf: Hardt & Wörner, 1997.

"Seifenblase Internet?" *BuchMarkt* 33.9 (1998): 60–69.

Rötzer, Florian. *Digitale Weltentwürfe. Streifzüge durch die Netzkultur*. München: Hanser, 1998.

Tötösy de Zepetnek, Steven. *Comparative Literature: Theory, Method, Application*. Amsterdam-Atlanta, GA: Rodopi, 1998.

Wilson, Robert, and Wimal Dissanayake, eds. *Global/Local: Cultural Production in the Transnational Imaginary*. Durham: Duke UP, 1996.

The Culture of the Context: Comparative Literature Past and Future

Jan Walsh Hokenson

On the brink of the new millennium, as we look back over literary history and the recent past of comparative literature as an academic discipline, it seems timely to ask: What have we learned, in Mario Valdés's words, about "literature in the context of the culture it represents"? How will those lessons shape literary histories in the next millennium?

Having recently, often nervously moved along the Great Divide between theory and text, most comparatists have struggled to keep the discipline's traditional emphasis on literary history at least visible on the horizon. Meanwhile, it often seemed that the figure of Theory loomed so large as to blot out mere text, and literary history—not to mention aesthetics—seemed lost to literature; then Culture shouldered Theory aside and emerged as equally immense, ahistorical, and aesthetically numb. Between text as Foucauldian, authorless discursive construct and text as Geertzian, authorless cultural artefact, literary history *as* a history seemed to splinter into discrete freeze-frames, sliced for theoretical consumption.

Some of the most brilliant work of recent years (by such diverse figures as Hayden White, Stephen Greenblatt, Richard Terdiman, Stephen Kern, Lydia Liu) seems like preparatory spadework, providing the tools *for* re-envisioning literary history rather than the thing itself. Just as early Structuralism had such difficulty getting beyond the paragraph, so perhaps we are in an early stage of historico-cultural work that cannot yet get beyond the delimited period or even generation, in order to attain the perspective of the overview of "literary history" that was once basic to comparative critical training and study.

Now, as we scan the horizon, adjusting our many, many lenses for viewing local historicities, shall we be forever in the trenches? Can we, and indeed should we ever hope to regain the panoptic view?

We do know that literary history is a dynamic and fluid sequence, spilling over centuries and over national borders and languages, presenting each young writer with a blueprint of the genre and the formal tradition in which he or she then invents.

By way of approaching the burdens and challenges of literary history in the next millennium, I should like to focus for a moment on one particular kind of critical problem—cross-cultural intertextuality—that has always characterized comparative study and that suggests the sorts of problems and new directions that comparatists will face in the coming epoch of global life and art.

I. CULTURAL INTERTEXTS

Many writers who have in part shaped Western literary history (Cervantes, Goethe, Balzac, for example, or Joyce, Proust, Mann) wrote texts intensely conscious of the full sweep of European literary history which they critiqued, synthesized, and redefined. Balzac drew upon the long history of French prose fiction since Rabelais but also relied heavily on Dante and Shakespeare—Italian and English *summas* of their respective national literary traditions—to reconfigure French literary history, and reflexively critique French culture of 1830–50; accordingly, Proust so used Balzac, plus Tolstoy and Dostoevsky, even as Joyce was invoking Homer to write the modernist national epic of Ireland and Mann was using the Bible to construe the German tradition since romanticism. At one time, to study such issues was to undertake "comparative authors" or "sources and influences," terms that became anathema in the postmodern, authorless decades.

Now, still on our brink, how do we describe the literary-historical context of this cultural wedge—Dante-in-Balzac, say, or Japanese Noh in Yeats or *négritude* in Modernism: Is there a critical category of analysis which, now moving beyond outworn forms of author-based studies, can embrace all that we have learned about discursive moments in time and cultural fields in social space? It is already clear that this sort of cross-cultural borrowing, which Earl Miner and others are beginning to theorize as comparative poetics, will become more frequent and more global in the coming era of globalization. Concerning these few examples I have mentioned, how do we historically and culturally contextualize them? As a "history" of intertextualities? Surely not. They are intersections that, on our brink, we cannot yet insert in "culture" or any satisfactory locus of comparative cultural "context."

When Wellek and Warren unfurled the banner of intrinsic criticism in the 1940s, such textual intersections of literary histories and cultures (nationalist internationalism, author-focused) was the core of comparatists' work. Such work was construed not as cross-cultural study (culture was considered the purview of anthropologists), and definitely not as literary history (rather a pseudo- or at best a smuggled history). History itself was largely still considered to be public events orchestrated by great white men. Now, in the wake of the epistemological revolutions in the Humanities disciplines, not least in historical and cultural studies, do we know what literary history is or should be?

As we conjecture a future for literary history, we must draw upon recent lessons from theoretical and cultural studies to reconfigure old, still recurrent questions.

It is clear that literary history in the next millennium must contextualize literature in the culture it represents. My question is: Are we sure we know which culture the text seeks to represent?

Certainly, we know that Balzac represented a certain view of French national culture. But the Dante-in-Balzac problem indicates some of the difficulties of situating *La Comédie humaine* in a literary history which embraces both aesthetic innovation and historico-literary tradition. Exactly this type of critical comparative problem will become crucial in the next millennium.

Wellek's students studied the state of 1830 French translations of Dante, in a return to original or primary texts. But now we recognize that in Balzac's literary-historical cultural context, comparatists are also well advised to study the history of reader-reception of Dante in France, the pan-European *idea* of the inferno, and the European cultural contexts of Realism (in painting, political theory, journalism, photography, etc.), all as mediated in Balzac's texts.

II. MILLENNIAL CONTEXTS

Culture, having moved from margin to center of literary study, is in several respects the new vessel for the old wine of "comparative authors" and "sources and influences." Now recognizing that no culture is singular, that even within Europe national cultures implicate and replicate aspects of one another endlessly, and that African, Middle Eastern, and Asian cultures long ago threaded their way into the foundations of Europe, comparative study must come to grips with the need to pluralize its own methods of analyzing "culture" and "context," in order to construct literary histories.

Three problems ensue. First, the next millennium will surely see an increasing globalization of culture. Already, the new European Union is taking steps toward the kind of pan-continental cultural continuities not seen since Latin Christendom. In the United States, programs in comparative literature are offering courses in the literatures of the Americas, the Latina writer, Caribbean poetics, East-West aesthetics—blurrings of national boundaries in favor of regional constants or parameters. It is clear that, slowly but surely, national cultures will no longer obtain. Cultural contexts for modern texts—and, I suggest, retrospective accounts of erstwhile national conceptions of traditions and regional poetics—will change, and with them the categories of analysis for "culture" and historico-literary "context."

Second, the electronic imperialism of the English language will surely vitiate foreign-language study—and critical training in Greek and Latin, Hebrew and Sanskrit—in favor of translation studies. Even in comparative studies, the notion of primary text, and primary linguistic and cultural context, will change as we evolve lateral, relative modes of considering past single-language traditions and new artistic innovations. What does "in context" mean, in an increasingly univocal mode of writing and reading across global time-space?

Third, the linchpin of the last millennium of literary study, indeed the very coherence of the term "literary," will also crumble, as "mimesis" loses coherence in an increasingly open and, I trust, fruitful exchange between the arts and literatures of the Eastern hemisphere with those of the Western part of the world. Already we speak easily of Postmodernism's radical critique of the foundations of Western literature and thought, but we rarely stop to consider the meaning of "Western" in that project. (In fact, in most European languages "occidental" means "ce qui remonte à la Grèce," whereas in English, as Christopher Coker has shown in *Twilight of the West,* "Western" is a recent Anglo-American conception denoting the liberal, market-driven democracies as distinct from Russia and China.) It is not for long that, absent any real comparative context, we will use the term "Western" so blithely, without an East in sight, utterly unaware of which East is being used to demarcate this West.

Occident and Orient will perhaps recover contrastive value, as we explore the major Indian, Japanese, Chinese, and other alternatives to the long Western tradition of mimesis, with all its (still) unstated assumptions.

Already the once stable metropolitan centers of national cultural traditions are diffusing, through mass migrations, outward from the old cultural capitals of Paris, Berlin, Tokyo, Rio de Janeiro, into regional, continental, and even hemispheric radials. Tracing literary histories along those lines will entail new challenges.

III. THE TECTONIC PLATES OF LITERARY HISTORY

The question of the role of literary history itself, then, must be contextualized in global, millennial terms. A significant, even operative literary history will necessarily be comparative and the components will be hemispheric and then surely global.

Already, comparatists are producing scholarly studies of Euro-Asian comparative poetics, United States literature in Spanish, "Overseas Chinese" literature, Japanese literature in Brazilian Portuguese. Such cultural intersections entail but greatly magnify our stodgy example of Dante-in-Balzac: already we read South America-in-the-United-States or, conversely, Aristotelian mimesis in Caribbean poetics. These are small steps toward a new literary history of transcultural, global intertextuality, on the order of Dante-in-Balzac writ large.

Writ global. As we begin to realize, here on our brink, how adopted languages, adopted cultures, adopted genres change radically under the pressures of modern migrations and at the hands of bi-cultural writers, we will begin to see continuities that we failed to notice in the hey-day of national literatures. In the creeping erasure of national, canonical, disciplinary, and other borders, we must re-vision the literary past of the *last* millenium in order to locate sites of cultural transfer in medieval, renaissance, augustan, romantic, modernist intertextuality, and thereby develop the analytical, comparative tools to accommodate literary history in the new millennium.

Recent trends in translations studies suggest the dimensions of the task. Twenty years ago (at an MLA meeting in Chicago), Glyn Norton called for recognition of "the vital contribution of French Renaissance translators" to the development of Renaissance literary consciousness; he stressed translation as "an area frequently overlooked yet inseparable from" periodization and literary history (190). At that time, the primacy of translation was often acknowledged but rarely studied as one of the bases of literary history. Since then André Lefevere, Lawrence Venuti, Susan Bassnett, Anthony Pym, Douglas Robinson have evolved categories of analysis for translation as cultural transfer between languages and culturo-poetic systems. Still, English poet Charles Tomlinson argues that the history of English poetry has never been taught (not even at Cambridge!) because the standard view still excludes the major poets' crucial apprenticeships as translators of French, Italian, Latin, Greek; so he calls for intercultural readings of Chaucer, Wyatt, Surrey, Marlowe, Pope, Dryden, Shelley, Arnold, Pound. For centuries, theories of nation and genius erased the intercultural origins of English poetic innovation.

In another call to reinvigorate "source studies" within English literature, in 1985 Stephen Greenblatt made the scholarly turn back to "source study," which, he noted, had become "the elephants' graveyard of literary history" (97). Deconstructionist theory had provided essential tools for new work, he said, even though we now recognize that the autonomous text is itself a theoretical construct, and that actual literary practice entails localized strategies in particular historical encounters. He positioned his own study of Shakespeare in the critical method that he called "cultural poetics" (situating the text in the cultural contexts of late sixteenth-century English struggles to redefine the central values of society [e.g., the sacred], and requiring "a rethinking of the conceptual categories by which the ruling elites constructed their world" [100]). Thence Shakespeare's sources *as* English cultural contexts.

Whether one uses the Victorian notion of culture as the manners and morals of a nation, or the Postmodern notion of culture as a society's system for the organization of meaning and the production of ideology, it is clear that the "culture" of the context occupies a larger time-space than does individual "author." Cultural intertexts across languages occupy even larger spaces, indeed global reaches. It is from this global vantage that comparative study of the culture of the context will *de facto* require an increasingly panoptic view across national and canonical frontiers, both past and present ones. The critical gaze over this sweep of terrain, which can be characterized as "intercultural poetics," to use Miner's terms (231), will entail new comparative methods and new categories of analysis. Perhaps, indeed, as we struggle to regain a panoptic view, it is "nation studies" (English, French, Japanese, American) that have become the millennial elephants' graveyard. For it is a new and quite different mode of source studies, exploring transcultural intertexts, that is opening a way toward future, global types of panoptic literary history.

At the moment our rhetorical consciousness is limited to two or three languages in comparative literature and to a few continental, at best hemispheric traditions. To *think* globally, around and across languages and contrastive poetics—and then global cybersites of cultural transfer—is very difficult (much more difficult than the recent challenge to become truly interdisciplinary). Truly global intercultural conceptions of literary history, diachronic and synchronic, still elude us.

The millennial challenge requires at a minimum (a) reconceptualizing the transcultural contexts of intertextuality and (b) ultimately reconceiving the literary in terms of global amalgamations, i.e., in the global context of an emerging world poetics.

In the kinds of planetary tectonic shifts in poetics that are bound to occur, the nature of comparative literature will change in ways we, on our brink, cannot imagine.

IV. MAGMA OF METHOD

The future of comparative literature as academic discipline was just as unimaginable to the founders—to Goethe and Germaine de Staël, of course, but equally to the academicians Abel François Villemain or Philarète Chasles in the 1830s, amid the drumbeats of modern nationalisms. From the beginning, as Claudio Guillén has shown, critical focus on the transmissive connections between national literatures almost always occurred within a vague but distinctly supra-national conception of "the Republic of Letters," a loose and baggy notion of literary universals. In the universities, during the academic institutionalization of literature in the late nineteenth and early twentieth centuries, the multinational blazon of Goethe's *Weltliteratur* was broken down into three components. Paul Van Tieghem, for instance, stipulated that an understanding of Rousseau's *La Nouvelle Héloïse* required appreciating three contexts or "domaines": the French novel of the eighteenth century, "comparative" literature or Richardson's influence on Rousseau, and "general" literature or the sentimental novel in Europe (175).

This early notion of literary contexts seems today like a sequence of abstract categories of analysis arranged as concentric circles, ever widening out from Rousseau's text across national borders. In contrast to contemporary cultural studies, as rooted in the sociology of creativity and knowledge, the three contexts look like critical conceits, circling far above mere "culture." Like many pioneering comparative formulations of the critical enterprise, moreover, when pushed to extremes the project seemed to become tautological: in this case, it resulted in characterizing Rousseau's text by the "context" of the very genre that the text helped define.

René Wellek and other (often immigrant European) Americans, rejecting this distinction between "comparative" and "general" literature as specious and untenable, conflated them. One result in 1940–60 was the new binary of world literature, in translation for sophomores, and comparative literature, for scholars in multiple languages. Reading only in the original languages, comparatists studied the interrelations of multiple literatures, charting their relationships along the intellectual axis of the history of criticism, meaning the foundational poetics of Aristotle and subsequent developments in critical principles and criteria, period and genre characteristics, and European intellectual and literary history. If context broadened to include critical history, it deepened only by demarcating "extrinsic" elements (the facts of editions and manuscripts, biography and psychology, economic and social conditions of authorship) from the primary "intrinsic" or textual elements. Wellek and Warren's magisterial *Theory of Literature,* in several major editions after 1949, never used the word "context," as far as a quick re-reading reveals, and preferred instead "scheme of relationships between methods" of textual analysis (269), as buttressed by historico-critical research.

Wellek's concept of comparative literature, which shaped American graduate curricula for two generations, was itself Euro-American, stressing close multilingual textual study within national frames of the history of criticism. Thus through 1975 the ideal graduate course was a seminar on Conrad-Nietzsche-Gide or Flaubert-Dostoevsky-Eliot, within a Eurocentric optic trained on the great novels as constitutive elements of literary and intellectual history. Gide's homosexuality, Nietzsche's dementia, Dostoevsky's epilepsy, not to mention the writers' gender, social class, and often aberrant politics entered the course, if at all, chiefly as a lecturer's footnotes on gossip irrelevant to the aesthetics of the text and its place in critical history.

One of the unstated premises of nation-focused comparative study and, I think, these post-war decades of comparative literature in the United States in particular, was the primacy of originality. The ways in which local and even "folk" traditions wove their way into a text mattered chiefly as local color, as indicators of how the artist characteristically transubstantiated such raw material. The European, basically romantic notion of artistic originality has long been a mainstay of comparatists' conception of their work. In their *Qu'est-ce que la littérature comparée?* What Is Comparative Literature? (1983), the French team of Pierre Brunel, Claude Pichois, André-Michel Rousseau have noted that in the beginning comparative literature was a scholarly means of appreciating the originality of each literature; it should have been called Comparative National Literatures, they said (16), since so many comparatists were in effect tracking the distinctive contributions of each national literature to Literature, or Goethe's hallowed notion of *Weltliteratur,* an amalgam of originalities in a play of contrasts. Inspirited with the liberal winds of anti-isolationism among Voltaire and the Encyclopedists, followed by the romantics and later nineteenth-century comparatists in philology and religion, the new literary discipline measured borrowings against national traditions and local originalities: German into French, medieval into modern, graphic into verbal, always general into particular. However widely the net was cast, its center long remained the individual author's unique idiolect, within the national language in the text as local transformative production. At one point, Wellek and Warren justified their entire project as a defense of originality: Just as the principles of criticism are essential to the literary historian, so

> literary history is also highly important for literary criticism as soon
> as the latter goes beyond the most subjective pronouncement of likes
> and dislikes. A critic who is content to be ignorant of all historical
> relationships would constantly go astray in his judgements. He could
> not know which work is original and which derivative; and, through
> his ignorance of historical conditions, he would constantly blunder
> in his understanding of specific works of art. . . . The common divorce
> between literary criticism and literary history has been detrimental
> to both. (44)

In one respect, this is to state the obvious for young comparatists: the critic who does not know Aristotle and Shakespeare will misapprehend Brecht and, worse, will esteem Brecht's mere imitators. In another respect, however, one more crucial to the past and especially the future of the discipline, this is to restate the cardinal tenet of originality as the centerpiece of all critical evaluation.

Aside from the fact that "derivative" is pejorative only in the West, such pronouncements indicate how intricately the question of "influence" has bedeviled Eurocentric literary study and comparative literature in particular. If through the 1970s "influence" was worthy but "derivative" base, the conceptual entanglement was never sorted out. The reasons for consigning the issue to the graveyard included the fact that influence was notoriously difficult to prove, even by author-focused scholars, and the fact that postmodern writers were repositioning quotation and intertextuality as higher values than outworn ones of genius and originality.

Similarly, the hierarchy of values in curricula changed, even reversed position in the American decades of "relevance," when "greats" tumbled, the pedestals of canon seemed for a while to be disintegrating, and recent French critical theory furnished analytical tools for exposing the ideological and authoritarian assumptions of the text, and the unwitting author.

In comparative literature, as Clayton Koelb and Susan Noakes suggested, erstwhile assumptions about nation dispersed into scattered and often conflicting models of intertextuality (such as Freudian, feminist, deconstructionist). They also pointed out that "We have learned all too well that Wellek was correct in his caution and that literary studies in North America, as well as in most European universities, will continue to be conducted for the most part in departments organized according to the model generated by nineteenth-century German philology" (9). Comparative literature as a discipline, and most comparatists as scholars, continued to be based within national frames. Always the bridge, never the bride, comparative literature served national academic departments as an avenue to critical theory, and, said Koelb and Noakes, thereby became less a set of critical practices, such as comparing texts in different languages or media, than "a shared perspective that sees literary activity as involved in a complex web of cultural relations" (11).

Wellek and Warren's "scheme of relationships" (a critical function of "methods") and "historical conditions" (a textual function of the history of the genre) had evolved by the end of the century into a complex "web" (nonspecific but pointedly non-hierarchical) of "cultural relations."

By 1990 indeed the text's cultural relations had become the *sine qua non* of literary study, the context that defined the text, by situating it in the sociology of its ideolect. The new discipline of cultural studies, in England and the United States, positioned comparative literature itself as a group of ancients being overtaken by media-savvy moderns more in tune with popular culture and thereby the roots of all creativity, literary included. It is at this point, in the fractious tensions of the 1990s between comparative literature and cultural studies, that the traditional aims and methods of comparative literature themselves seemed to splinter, crumbling under the weight of accusations that, as Susan Bassnett put it, "Today, comparative literature is in one sense is dead" (47), because even modern foreign-language study is too onerous, and because mass globalization of culture requires using translations, notably as a subset of cultural studies. In the British political and intellectual lineage of Raymond Williams, Bassnett dismissed comparatists' scholarly traditions as a Eurocentric body of knowledge and as an elitist enterprise.

Bassnett's position is extreme, coming from the far end of the spectrum of critical discussion today while at the other end is Steven Tötösy's proposal of a "comparative cultural studies," a merger of comparative literature and cultural studies (see in this volume). Yet it is a useful challenge. It spotlights the need to re-vision the past of comparative literature as a discipline in order to clarify its future. If comparative literature *as* literary study is to surmount such challenges, it must restore its cultural credentials.

Which brings us back to Dante-in-Balzac, to nation, cultural context, translation, and originality.

V. MAPPING

Some of the finest work comparatists have ever done identifies the meanings of different terms in different cultures, such as "sentimentalische" in comparison with "sentimentale." What might seem today like critical conceits circling over culture is really a function of contemporary definitions of the term "culture" itself. Comparatists have always been deeply engaged in cross-cultural study; it is clearly impossible to read such analyses as Auerbach's *Mimesis*, Curtius's *European Literature and the Latin Middle Ages*, Abrams's *The Mirror and the Lamp*, Steiner's *After Babel* without understanding how, in the contemporary lexicon, local historicities and cultural fields served them as the very basis for their inquiry. In their day, national frontiers were organizing principles of cultural alterity. Within and across them, however, before Foucault,

Auerbach examined *The History of the Franks* by Gregory of Tours in the context of Greek and Latin historiographers' and clerics' use of indirect discourse and intellectual paradigms, Curtius glossed texts as a function of the branches of learning and medieval sociologies of knowledge, Abrams constructed derivations of one nation's poetry from another's philosophy. In turn, we must now look back at their own use of a periodized scholarly lexicon, explain how it worked in the analysis of the cultures of the text, and champion their work as the historical bases of cultural studies.

Similarly, concerning method, no comparatist to my knowledge has ever staked out a disciplinary claim to a delimited body of knowledge. On the contrary, infinity or the global reach has been (to appropriate T.S. Eliot's terms for India) both the horror and the glory of comparative literature. In my view, pace Bassnett, comparative literature has since Goethe always been a mode of inquiry, never a body of knowledge. Two centuries of comparatists have professionally championed cross-cultural study while always lamenting, on a personal note somewhere in the text, their own linguistic and cultural limitations, or foreshortened horizons, thus overtly recognizing that comparative literature should be global but can only be a function of individual comparatists' linguistic reach. At some point, almost all current textbook introductions to the field nod, at least, toward East-West studies as a significant aspect, often even the optimal goal of comparative work.

The "culture" of the context has always been, in various critical vocabularies and periods, a complex concept, whether it was subsumed under "history," "nation," "people," or "language." Perhaps, following Wellek's lead, we ought to be disentangling the history of this concept, as he did the history of criticism, from its multiple instantiations over the past two hundred years of comparative work—in critical studies published in Asia and Latin America no less than in Euro-America. By specifying and defining the cultural bases of the discipline, one can see quite precisely how well it is suited to become the primary mode of critical inquiry in the global millennium. By contrast, to dismiss , like a rather offhanded Darwinian, all previous comparative scholarship because it failed to differentiate between elite and popular culture, is to mistake the premises of the discipline and, I think, to misread European literary history.

It was, after all, Raymond Williams who furnished an important model for historical studies when he pointed out that, at any given time and place, the monad "culture" comprises three types of components: residual, dominant, and emergent (121–7). As elements always in dynamic interplay in society and in varying emphases in the text, these rubrics are a useful way to relativize originality, and to examine influence more specifically as cultural intertexts—in Shakespeare as in haiku. As the author of *Mythologies,* Barthes would be the first to point out that popular culture cannot be dissociated from elite culture, since a society's culture is their amalgam, and their shared (national) language produces a shared text, co-extensive with ideolect. Since Lukács and Bakhtin, if not Taine and Philarète Chasles, comparatists have long been examining such relationships between (national) social milieux and discourses. The discipline needs to clarify this plank of its own history.

Looking back from this brink over the past two centuries, one can see deeper patterns of continuity beneath the shifting surfaces and styles of comparative scholarship apropos of the text in its cultural relations. Even a cursory review of the discipline's history reveals the social axis of comparatists' work. The object of study remains continuous, i.e., the text as intersection of the foreign and the domestic, while the requisite critical faculty evolves from imaginative empathy to theorizing analysis. Thus in his founding documents Philarète Chasles in 1835 spoke of "this great work of sympathies" (qtd. in Brunel et al. 19; my trans.), which Wellek and Warren were still explicating in 1949 when they insisted that "this conception of [comparative] 'literary history' requires an effort of imagination, of 'empathy,' of deep congeniality with a past age or a vanished taste" (41). Critical readings are inseparable from historical reconstruction of "the general outlook on life, the attitudes, conceptions, prejudices, and underlying assumptions of many civilizations" (41), together illuminating the cultures of the context.

In the age of waning romanticism, Chasles called for "sympathy" in the construction of a tableau of French and foreign literary interrelations, just as in the waning psychologies of modernism Wellek and Warren were still appealing to 'empathy' in the construction of literary histories in order, in both cases, to appreciate what their successors call "intercultural" texts (see Pichois and Rousseau 197). For comparatists, varying conceptions of social context have always been the Ariadne's thread through literary interrelations, of different types and extent.

Already sharpening the focus on social analysis in 1886, in the age of Taine's "man, milieu, and moment," Hutcheson Posnett in New Zealand adopted "the gradual expansion of social life, from clan to city, from city to nation, from both of these to cosmopolitan humanity, as the proper order of our studies in comparative literature" (qtd. in Clements 4).

Concerning the ([inter] national) culture of the context, I doubt that any one of these scholars would have disagreed with Bakhtin's point that criticism errs when it locks stylistic phenomena "into the monologic context of a given self-sufficient and hermeneutic utterance, imprisoning it, as it were, in the dungeon of a single context" (669). Writing in the 1930s but postmodern *avant la lettre,* Bakhtin restates in a new lexicon the age-old relations of culture and context in European comparative literature: "[The text is] determined by its dialogic orientation, first, amid others' utterances inside a *single* language (the primordial dialogism of discourse), amid other "social languages" within a single *national* language and finally amid different national languages within the same *culture,* that is, the same socio-ideological conceptual horizon" (669). This (still emergent) model of "dialogized heteroglossia" (668) serves cross-cultural study both within as well as across the political frontiers of nation, region, and hemisphere, depending upon where one puts down the claim-stake of conceptual horizon.

VI. RADIALS

If the concept of national character seems to be foundering on modern multi-cultures and cybersites, the new field of translation studies is coming to grips with the opposite dilemma. It appears to Venuti and Pym, for instance, that (national) culture is that which cannot be translated. Venuti thus calls for "foreignizing" translations that highlight cultural alterity, through alienation techniques which make the text appear strange, foreign, other. More historically oriented, Pym calls for scholarly histories of the "points of resistance" between source texts and translations, by way of cultural differentiation. Translation studies is *de facto* becoming comparative cultural study (see also Tötösy 2001).

In the kind of East-West work that seems to me the comparative terrain of the next millennium, Lydia Liu examines the advent into China of the Western notion of national character and culture, in *Translingual Practice: Literature, National Culture, and Translated Modernity—China, 1900-1937.* She is interested in how Asian languages and literatures must create new spaces of meaning when receiving Western concepts. Her first step is to drop the inappropriate lexicon of source and target languages, and re-equilibrate them as "host language" and "guest language" in order to "stress the agency of the host language (modern Chinese in this case) in the meaning-making process of translation so that the guest language need not carry a signature of authenticity in order to make sense in the new context" (29). She finds that "serious methodological problems arise when a cross-cultural comparative theory is built upon the basis of an essentialist category, such as 'self' or 'individual,' whose linguistic identity transcends the history of translation and imposes its own discursive priority on a different culture" (8). In a millennial caution, she warns that Western comparatists must beware of conceptual horizons: "The knowledge obtained in this way cannot but be tautological" (9). More useful is the study of language reception, or how writers' translingual practice opens new conceptual fields in the language and the text:

> The Chinese compound *guomin xing* . . . is a Meiji neologism (*kokuminsei*), or one of several neologisms, that the Japanese used to translate the modern European notion of national character. . . . [it] was first used by late Qing intellectuals to develop their own theory of the modern nation-state . . . identifying the cause of the evils responsible for the deplorable state of the Chinese *guomin* (citizen). . . . The fact that Liang Qichao and Sun Yat-sen were the foremost critics of Western imperialism of their time and yet still had to subscribe to a discourse that European nations first used to stake their claims to racial superiority points to the central predicament of the Chinese intellectual. This predicament . . . characterizes all subsequent attempts either to claim or to reject Chinese national identity. (48–49)

Given the tumultuous decades of conflicting definitions of Chinese (national) identity, as a constructed amalgam of elite and popular culture, such West-to-East work is crucial in reading Chinese literature of the past century. At least for another century or so, clearly it is only bilingual comparative study that can elucidate the text's place in the East-West web of cross-cultural relations.

In my own work on a history of *japonisme* in French literature, as well as in another project on literary self-translation, I find that it is precisely this kind of new conceptual space that characterizes, say, Proust's use of Japanese art to critique European aesthetics, or the bilingual canons of Ungaretti and Beckett: neither purely Irish nor purely French, Beckett's texts exist as "an interculture" in Pym's term, or a "translingual" space in Liu's. Whatever the vocabulary comparatists develop, these are the sorts of conceptual configurations that will become increasingly necessary in future comparative study, spanning languages and hemispheres with common methods of inquiry.

CIRCUMFERENCES

Hemispheres is of course a term already being outdated by the world wide web. Indeed all four of the terms originally introducing this essay have become matters of controversy in recent decades: literature, context, culture, representation. Their geographies will similarly need re-mapping in the electronic millennium. Meanwhile the old maps, lessons from the discipline's past since 1800, suggest that comparatists have traditionally engaged the cultures of the context at rather more basic levels than they are usually credited for doing. As the next millennium proceeds, in the short term we shall have to continue setting the conceptual horizon ever further outward from our local intellectual fields and regional intercultures toward global ones. Logically, the most appropriate methods of literary study will be increasingly—or rather perhaps remain continuously—comparative, in the sense of addressing texts in the widening contexts of a global intercultural poetics. To Euro-American, South American, Asian, and African comparatists, knowledge of at least two Western and Eastern languages will be essential, no longer merely desirable. The state of languages in the longer term, particularly as enmeshed in machine translations, remains conjectural.

On a more somber note, it may be that we in the United States are witnessing, for the first time in human history, the mass evaporation of culture. Certainly when a word is as intensely contested as the term "culture" is today, the concept is in crisis. Even as the historically palimpsestic structures of culture are disaggregating around the world into discrete language groups and ethnic assertions, including post-colonial canon formation, the electronic means of overarching all these cultural groups are being perfected. If it is in a metalanguage of the world wide web that the next millennium eventually writes its literary histories, then the local vanishes into the global, culture becomes a digital context, and ideolect warps into cybertext. Even so, only the comparatist will really know what happened.

WORKS CITED

Abrams, Morris. *The Mirror and the Lamp.* Oxford: Oxford UP, 1953.
Auerbach, Eric. *Mimesis: The Representation of Reality in Western Literature.* Trans. Willard Trask. New York: Doubleday, 1957.

Bakhtin, Mikhail. "Discourse in the Novel." Trans. Caryl Emerson and Michael Holquist. *Critical Theory Since Plato.* Ed. Hazard Adams. New York: Harcourt Brace, 1971. 665–78.

Bassnett, Susan. *Comparative Literature: A Critical Introduction.* Oxford: Blackwell, 1993.

Bassnett, Susan, and André Lefevere, eds. *Translation, History and Culture.* London: Pinter, 1990.

Brunel, Pierre, Claude Pichois, and André Michel Rousseau. *Qu'est-ce que la littérature comparée?* Paris: Colin, 1983.

Clements, Robert J. *Comparative Literature as Academic Discipline.* New York: Modern Language Association of America, 1978.

Clifford, James. *The Predicament of Culture.* Cambridge: Harvard UP, 1988.

Coker, Christopher. *The Twilight of the West.* Oxford: Westview, 1998.

Curtius, Ernst Robert. *European Literature and the Latin Middle Ages.* Trans. Willard Trask. New York: Harper & Rowe, 1953.

Foucault, Michel. *Les Mots et les choses.* Paris: Gallimard, 1966.

Geertz, Clifford. *The Interpretation of Culture.* New York: Basic Books, 1973.

Greenblatt, Stephen. "Shakespeare and the Exorcists." 1985. *Shakespeare's King Lear.* Ed. Harold Bloom. New York: Chelsea, 1987. 97–119.

Guillén, Claudio. *The Challenge of Comparative Literature.* Trans. Cola Franzen. Cambridge: Harvard UP, 1993.

Kern, Stephen. *The Culture of Time and Space: 1880–1918.* Cambridge: Harvard UP, 1983.

Koelb, Clayton, and Susan Noakes, eds. "Introduction: Comparative Perspectives." *The Comparative Perspective: Approaches to Theory and Practice.* Ithaca: Cornell UP, 1988. 3–17.

Liu, Lydia H. *Translingual Practice: Literature, National Culture, and Translated Modernity—China, 1900–1937.* Stanford: Stanford UP, 1995.

Miner, Earl. *Comparative Poetics: An Intercultural Essay on Theories of Literature.* Princeton: Princeton UP, 1990.

Norton, Glyn P. "French Renaissance Translators and the Dialectic of Myth and History." *Renaissance and Reformation* 17.4 (1981): 189–202.

Pichois, Claude, and André-Michel Rousseau. *La Littérature comparée.* Paris: Colin, 1967.

Pym, Anthony. *Method in Translation History.* Manchester: St. Jerome, 1988.

Robinson, Douglas. *What Is Translation? Centrifugal Theories, Critical Interventions.* Kent: Kent State UP, 1997.

Steiner, George. *After Babel: Aspects of Language and Translation.* 2nd ed. New York: Oxford UP, 1992.

Taylor, E. B. *Primitive Culture: Researches into the Development of Mythology, Philosophy, Religion, Art, and Custom.* 1871. 2nd ed. London: John Murray, 1913.

Terdiman, Richard. *Discourse/Counter Discourse: The Theory and Practice of Symbolic Resistance in Nineteenth Century France*. Ithaca: Cornell UP, 1985.

Tomlinson, Charles. "The Presence of Translation: A View of English Poetry." *The Art of Translation: Voices From the Field*. Ed. Rosanna Warren. Boston: Northeastern UP, 1989. 258–76.

Tötösy de Zepetnek, Steven. "From Comparative Literature Today Toward Comparative Cultural Studies." *Comparative Literature and Comparative Cultural Studies*. West Lafayette: Purdue UP, 2002. 235–67.

Tötösy de Zepetnek, Steven. "Comparative Cultural Studies and the Study of Translation: Concepts and Terminology." *CLCWeb: Comparative Literature and Culture: A WWWeb Journal (Library)* (2001–): <http://clcwebjournal.lib.purdue.edu/library/translationstudy.html>.

Valdés, Mario. "Opening Remarks." Panels on "Literary History in the Next Millennium." Chicago: MLA: Modern Language Association of America Convention, 1999.

Van Tieghem, Paul. *La Littérature comparée*. 1931. Paris: Colin, 1951.

Venuti, Lawrence. *The Translator's Invisibility: A History of Translation*. New York: Routledge, 1995.

Wellek, René, and Austin Warren. *Theory of Literature*. 1949. 3rd ed. New York: Harcourt, Brace, 1956.

White, Hayden. *The Content of the Form: Narrative Discourse and Historical Representation*. Baltimore: Johns Hopkins UP, 1987.

Williams, Raymond. *Marxism and Literature*. Oxford: Oxford UP, 1977.

On Literariness: From Post-Structuralism to Systems Theory

Marko Juvan

In his paper, "The Literary in Theory," Jonathan Culler claims that although the problem of literariness is central to literary theory from Russian formalism to French structuralism, it appears that "the attempt to theorize . . . the distinctiveness of literature . . . hasn't been the focus of theoretical activity for some time" and that questions which have become central to theory are far less about aesthetics than issues of race, gender, and class (Culler 2000, 274–75 and passim). In my opinion, the impression that the question of literariness has become surpassed or irrelevant emanates from a specific cultural location and space: the asking about the essence or distinctive features of literature has to do with the history of the discipline, in this case Euro-American literary theory. When a literary theorist—in this case someone guided by Jakobson's phenomenological imperative that the object of literary scholarship must be literariness (Jakobson 1921, 11)—discusses what the essence of literature may be, what discriminates texts deemed literary from other forms of communication, or, rather, what exactly changes their status into works of art, he/she not only asks questions about the object of inquiry. By asking this question the theoretical observer is also seeking an excuse for limiting the territory in which it is possible to utilize legitimately his/her explanatory concepts, tools, and plans. Or, as Culler puts it: "To ask 'what is literature?' is in effect a way of arguing about how literature should be studied" (Culler 2000, 276). In Pierre Bourdieu's understanding, "it is clear that theoretical writings . . . are also (and more especially) contributions to the *social construction of the very reality* of this object" (1996, 294, Bourdieu's emphasis; for constructivism, see Riegler). Thus, posing the question about literariness is indirectly and implicitly aimed also towards the observer as a representative of the discursive field that has well defined and institutionally inherited cultural functions as well as a meta-language with a specific history.

In his paper, "Why did Modern Literary Theory Originate in East-Central Europe?," Galin Tihanov argues that modern literary theory was actually born in the decades between World War I and II in East Central Europe owing to the disintegration of philosophical discourses (Marxism, phenomenology), to dissatisfaction with positivist and historicist legacies, and to changes in litera-ture itself (i.e., its self-reflective and responsible uses of form). In his opinion, the emerging discipline of literary theory adopted ideas of Romantic aesthetics and philosophy of language and established its specific discourse in the uniquely multilingual and multicultural academic environment of Russia, Czechoslova-kia, Poland, and Hungary (see Tihanov 2001). Further, the field of the theory of literature has become institutionalized as late as in the mid-twentieth cen-tury with such seminal texts as Wellek and Warren's *Theory of Literature* (1942) while the discipline now as a standard part of literary studies was draw-ing exhaustively on the tradition of ancient poetics and rhetoric (see, e.g., Glaser 15–23; Groden and Kreiswirth; Ocvirk 6–12). However, since Aristotle, poet-ics and rhetoric used to reflect, describe, classify, and normalize the domain of communication that was either narrower or larger than what has been for approximately two hundred years considered *belles lettres* and written and read for aesthetic purposes: poetics dealt mostly with poetry, which, for instance, did not include prose genres, while rhetoric cultivated and studied the skill (in the sense of *ars*) of any kind of public speaking, not just that inspired by artistic muses (see, e.g., Lausberg). From poetics and rhetoric, literary theory adopted a series of issues and notions such as the principles of representation/mimesis, *topoi*, disposition, literary kinds and genres, diction, figures of speech, meter, etc. In literary theory such notions have become independent from practical-normative aspects and have become anchored in a new *epistemè* and practi-tioners of the discipline presupposed the awareness of art as an autonomous system of social communication, i.e., a system governed by its own principles. From the Enlightenment on, these ideas were built on aesthetics such as Bat-teux's channeling of all *beaux arts* into a single, imitative principle, Schiller's idea that art creates rules for itself, or Kant's notion of beauty and aesthetic experience as contemplative enjoyment, devoid of practical interests (see, e.g., Tatarkiewicz 23–30). Aesthetics reflected and with its infiltration into ideology also encouraged one of the two great restructurings of traditional Europe: the

transformation of the estate system into functional differentiation of modern-
ized bourgeois societies, in which the *beaux arts* as a special and increasingly
autonomous social field assumed the role of the only remaining guardians of
the crumbling wholeness of an individual's existential experience. In light of other
major process such as the formation of national identities, the arts confirmed
the individuality and creative ability of the collective individual emanating from
a "national spirit" (Schmidt 1989, 25, 282–83). Finally, the "literary field" has
become fully developed in the period of post-romanticism to modernism: it
included texts, practices, life-style, notions, presuppositions, institutions, groups
and activities, etc., which were (or seemed to be) regularly emancipated from
constraints and direct pressures of economic or political power and within that
field the specific *nomos* (auto-nomy) was instituted "both in the objective structures of a socially governed universe and in the mental structures of those who
inhabit it" (Bourdieu 61, 289–92).

The *object* and the methods of literary scholarship are constructed and
maintain each other's existence, autonomy, and functions: questions about the
nature and essence of literature can be articulated with real consistency only in
the framework of a specialized field, i.e., literary theory, and only if freed from
explicit normativity and close entanglements with matters of poetic production.
In other words, only after literary genres—at least in their most representative
cases—had been autonomized under the new and uniform understanding of literature as artistic production. The *differentia specifica* of literature is found primarily in its social function: it became *literature* pertaining to the social domain
of arts and standing in opposition to "literatures" of other fields of social activity, e.g., religion, politics, science, or education (see Rusch 97–98). Viewed from
within literary scholarship, the meaning of literary theory can thus be explained,
namely that it helps us understand what we, as "ordinary" readers experience
when reading a work of art (this can also be explicated in the spirit of the Emil
Staiger's lucid *paronomasia*, namely, "dass wir begreifen, was uns ergreift" (qtd.
in Rusterholz 344). However, from the critical perspective of a higher-order
observer, literary theory might lose its apparent distance from the object of study
as an analytical and descriptive undertaking. Seen from the outside, literary theory turns out to be a discursive practice intertwined with literature, science, and
education (incl. Pedagogy). In these domains of social and cultural interaction,
literary theory helps to establish interpretative languages and practices among
writers, scholars, critics, readers, teachers, and students. Such interpretive structures with sets of concepts and mental operations refine the sense that litera-

ture as art is a special class of phenomena as well as of extraordinary cultural value (see Eagleton 200–03). By inquiring what gives texts a literary character, literary theory as a discipline participates in the identity construction of its object and with it, theory secures its own existence as well as the relevance of its conceptions and methods.

In the development of literary theory in the twentieth century, two opposing lines of thinking followed one another: modernism in the arts and theory—with its phenomenological reductionism, elitism, "formalism," "theologico-aesthetics," and "the animus against the everyday, the ordinary, the popular, the wordly, the techno-scientific, and the public" (Leitch 41)—elevated the idea of the aesthetic autonomy of (verbal) art. A part of Russian formalism, the Chicago School, New Criticism, and *Werkimmanente Interpretation* strove, in a parallel manner with modern artistic currents (e.g., abstract painting), to elaborate the particular ontology, specific structure, and/or singular meaning of the literary work of art by concepts such as de-familiarization, iconicity, or ambiguity. On the other hand, for the last thirty years the category "literature" shared the same fate with other totalities: it was exposed to postmodern deconstruction and de-hierarchization. As a symptom of that move, there has been growing doubts about the possibility to claim what the essence of all literature would be and to recognize and display general literary-artistic structures in every item of this class of objects. Ever since French structuralism and its mutations in post-structuralism in the late 1960s, literature was more and more often studied as a discourse, as one among other discursive practices in society. It became basically equal to, say, myth or soap operas on television. Literary texts were observed as "communal documents" (Leitch ix), their literariness was moving out of focus. Among libertarian or left-wing academics, critical of unreflected elitism hidden behind preceding notions of literariness, literature is no more axiologically privileged over science, religion, politics, popular culture, and new media, including productions in new media such as hypertext (see Sanchez-Mesa <http://www.dipoli.hut.fi/org/TechNet/org/humanities/lite/summary.html>), nor it is treated as a totality, ontologically different from other genres of communication. As Vincent Leitch puts it, "literature turns into a modulated functionalist notion of 'literatures'"(60), which implies that "there is no ontology of literature; there are only literature functions—functions in relation to specific languages, intertexts, institutions, regimes of reason" (Leitch 59). Literature as a heteroglot discourse intertextually affiliated to societal and historical *heteroglossia* is the notion that has supplanted the once homogeneous category of *belles lettres.* Gebhard Rusch's conviction, that modes of literary reception are not uniform, since they differ for different social groups, textual genres as well as "different types and concepts of literature" is (98–99), although based on empirical evidence, no exception within the general trend of pluralizing and opening of the literary canon(s).

Arguments against the notion of literature as an aesthetic and homogeneous expression as well as the questioning the boundaries between art and non-art come from various viewpoints (see García-Berrio 25–27, 39–44). On the one hand, theorists of socio-historical or reader-response orientations point out that literariness is only one of the social conventions or psychic expectations which form the background for the understanding of texts, but it is by no means neither their internal essence nor their objective feature, be it structural, stylistic, or semantic. Texts which could have not been written and in their time understood as pure verbal art are nowadays treated as literature. For example, the old Attic comedy, which was a kind of "poetry," but inseparably connected with Dionysian festivities, could therefore not be reduced to the function that today understood as aesthetic. Marxist, psychoanalyst, feminist, and postcolonial scholars and critics are well skilled in reading "against the grain"; they are eager to disclose traces of economic, bodily, social, ideological, political, and other non-aesthetic investments even in the subtlest poetic literature. On the other hand, precisely linguistics—which, according to Jakobson, should be understood as a kind of semiotic meta-theory ensuring objective identification of literariness (i.e., the poetic function) in the texts themselves (1981, 18–21, 766)—turns increasingly to pragmatics. Practitioners of the pragmatic turn agree to the thesis that all linguo-stylistic features which should objectively distinguish the literary text from a non-literary one and it is argued that this is wide spread in non-artistic communication, too, so that the deciding factor in literariness is the circumstance or the context of a given speech act. No need to mention that post-structuralist "rhetoric," as well, makes out literary features, such as tropes, fiction, and story-telling, in other domains, e.g., in philosophy (Derrida, de Man), law, and history (White). More, to the dismay of some more traditionalist scholars, instead of observing literature, their colleagues follow the example of Barthes and, rejecting the dichotomy between language and meta-language, create an essayist mixture of literature, philosophy, hermeneutics, and semiotic ludism. In Culler's observation, "the literary in theory . . . has migrated from being the object of theory to being the quality of theory itself" (2000, 286).

The above-mentioned practitioners of theoretical "anti-essentialist" work in the study of literature agree that "literature" "refers to a heterogeneous group of objects between which there is no more than a family resemblance" (Olsen 73–74). Culler comments on the logic of anti-essentialist and conventionalist approaches and, quoting John M. Ellis, compares the concept of "literature" to the position of the concept "weeds": weeds are plants that do not have some common botanical denominator, structure or essence; rather, the semantic range of this concept depends on the (noxious) *function* of these plants in a particular society or its (agri-)culture, namely, on the convention governing people's handling of plants or their view of plants (1989, 32). Similarly, Stein Haugom Olsen speaks in favor of the term "literary work of art" as the name of a class of functions, where the identity of the objects which are members of such a class could be only "defined through the function they serve in a community of practitioners using the objects" (74). But if for Olsen defining the literary work in the context of a practice involving it seems to cause no crucial problems, Culler came to the fatal conclusion that, based on the notion that literariness is only a convention, literary theory would be redundant, since the common features of literature would be better explained by sociology, anthropology, or history (1989, 32). Beside Olsen and his *The End of Literary Theory* there are in fact some literary theorists who sign their names to the obituary for the attribute "literary." Their reasoning is as follows (particularly provocative is, for instance, Eagleton's): if there are no ontological boundaries between literature and other discourses, if literature is only some kind of ideological fiction, an umbrella term for heterogeneous genres and linguistic registers, historically created constructs with a set date of expiration, then there is no need for theory to fancy or burden itself with the attribute "literary," since all texts—from a sonnet to a court document of indictment—are justified to be explained with the same conceptual tools (Eagleton 194–217). Literary theory is said to be "passé" (Tihanov 3), or, more optimistically, to be transformed into "post-theory," i.e., into "the theoretical discussions animated by the questions of the death of theory" (Culler 2000, 277). After a period of scrutinizing its own premises and the object of analysis, literary theory is self-obliterating (see Smirnov 6–10) or, rather, flows into the sea of Theory: sociology, semiotics, discourse analysis, cognitive science, cultural or media studies, etc.

It is therefore evident to me that the problem of literariness is related to the question of the existence or dissolution of literary theory as a discipline. It is a symptom of a permanent crisis, which is, according to de Man, immanent to all modern literary scholarship: The succession of various scientific schools since positivism has proved the elusiveness of its object, methods, concepts, and results. The question whether literariness is an "internal" trait of the text or just an "external" convention (Culler 1989, 39–40) is exciting, since it brings to the fore far-reaching epistemological dilemmas between realism, nominalism, constructivism, and/or between hermeneutic and psycho-sociological approaches to literature. It can even have considerable implications for policies and the situation concerning the present study of literature, especially as characterized dramatically by Steven Tötösy as a process of a marginalization of the study of literature (20–23). In sum, the question is, within what institutional framework should literary theory be advanced and taught, if at all.

LITERARINESS AS AN "OBJECTIVE" CHARACTER OF THE TEXT

Culler summarizes current, post-Jakobsonian definitions of literariness as a set of traits, objectively present in the text itself, into two basic groups of criteria: typical of literary texts are a special use or, rather, arrangements of language on the one hand, and a particular attitude towards reality on the other (1989, 34, 41). Considering the growing, differing, and heteroglot production of literature, the conception according to which literary/poetic language exists as one of social dialects or, rather, as a separate functional style (see Mukařovský 45, 80), different from the other varieties of standard language owing to the domination of the aesthetic function can presently hardly hold true. Jan Mukařovský, who was the first to introduce this kind of theory into modern discussions, was already well aware that the boundaries of poetic language were fuzzy. He found that poetic language is characterized only by a thin layer of "poeticisms" while sharing the rest of linguistic elements with other styles and also benefiting from them (82–83). But despite the semiological view that art as well as poetic language are social facts, dependent on norms, conventions, and values, Mukařovský nevertheless reified poetic language—he discussed it as a relatively autonomous sub-code, even if it is impossible to prove its autonomy with immanently linguistic criteria and with no reference to statistical data. The thesis of the stylistic peculiarity of literary language could perhaps hold true only for discursive dictionaries and grammars, developed—by imitation of patterns, recurrence, and variance of clichés—in the traditions of literary genres and kinds in particular periods or currents such as the language of the romantic sonnet or the poetic languages of the nineteenth century, of decadence, or expressionism.

To me, much more convincing than the conceptions of the literary language as a linguistic sub-code seems to be the thesis that in a text that is written with artistic intentions, the author uses and arranges linguistic material differently and with other goals than in standard communication. Hence, the actualization of linguistic levels in the text written for aesthetic purposes differs from conventions of practical, scientific, or any kind of non-artistic communication: Its reader can therefore discover not only deviations from "normal" sociolects and styles, i.e., various kinds of figurativeness, additional or superordinate organization of sound, lexico-syntactic, and semantic material, but most of all their greater density and structural coherence (García-Berrio 39–79; Markiewicz 45–55). This means a higher frequency of uncommon language features in artistic texts as well as a richer network of intra- and intertextual relationships between these elements and their patterns. From such views the "objectivistic" theory of literariness extrapolated two basic tendencies of literary usage of language: the inclination towards the polysemy of words, phrases, and larger units of discourse (this is the opposite of the ideal of the monosemy in non-literary languages) and the tendency towards textual self-reference, i.e., towards the fact that the reader is paying more attention to structural homologies, to playing with recurrent forms and ambivalent meanings, and to spatialized patterns of parallelisms and oppositions, so that his/her reading is not limited only to the linear quest for referential information (see Eco 145–67; García-Berrio 52, 61–70).

In a literary text an important peculiarity of every writing is stressed; unlike speech, written word is devoid of the "physical" presence of the author and the original communicative context. Once being recorded, a literary text detaches itself from its contingent circumstances. Its meaning has to be tied more to what is stored in the cultural memory through writing. In a literary text the context of uttering cryptically vanishes. Because of such "depragmatization" of the literary text (Culler 1989, 34) extratextual referentiality and the performativity of literary signs are reduced or, rather, mutated. The author, educated in this kind of tradition of writing, makes sure that the depragmatization is counter-balanced by an outburst of semiotic inter-connectivity: This way the ties between linguistic signs in the text strengthen, intertwine, and increase in number, while the meanings also come into being with intertextual reference to the literary tradition and by hypothetical (re)constructions of the author's original socio-cultural milieu through symptomatic textual representations. The literary text, separated from its author and context, must itself receive special attention by its receiver (in reading as well as analysis). Because of the material character of the recording or, rather, the fetishism of the Book as a standard medium of presentation of a literary work of art, many readers are still inclined to experience the text as an organic, complete unit, in which nothing is coincidental and everything is meaningful and/or functional. Hence, its stylistic patterns and even its substance and forms of expression (e.g., the quality and distribution of vowels) can make up parallelisms, isomorphisms, ambiguity, semantic density, and iconic connotation (see Culler 1989, 34, 37–38; Eco 147–49; García-Berrio 64). But, in fact, many of these traits would hardly be noticed by the same reader in the context of "ordinary language," i.e., if the text were not already treated as a literary work by a prior reading decision and expectation (see Olsen 80).

The depragmatization of utterance in literature means the transition between literariness viewed through a peculiar use of language and literariness as a particular textual relationship towards reality. To Aristotle, already, the stylistic and formal criteria alone were not sufficient for defining poetry. For that reason he introduced criteria of significance concerning content (*mimesis* as the relationship between a poetic work and reality), pragmatics and reception (catharsis as the impact of dramatic act on the reader's psyche). According to Aristotle, unlike the historian's attitude towards reality, the "poet's responsibility is not to tell what in fact happened, but rather what could have happened, i.e., what could have happened according to the laws of probability and necessity" (*Poetics*, Chapter 9); this thought fed not only the notions of aesthetic *vraisemblance*, but also the determinants of literariness concerning the relationship between the textual and extra-textual worlds.

While in the classicist tradition the evidence of poetic art was mostly formal artistry, since pre-Romanticism and Romanticism the criteria of content, such as imagination, fantasy, and in newer theories particularly fictionality, have been more important (Meletinski 13–29). In the literary text, the world represented, the subject expressing this world (narrator's, poet's voice), and the author's speech acts (quasi-judgments, quasi-referential presentation) are all fictional (Culler 1989, 41–43; Markiewicz 99–122). As Lubomír Doležel has stressed, Aristotle's comparison between historiography and poetry was used as a base for a redefinition of the relationship between textual world and reality as early as the eighteenth century when after a period of absolute domination of mimetic-imitative poetics a tendency for aesthetic justification of individual creative imagination emerged. This thought wrests itself from the vulgarized norm of imitating the outside world, since it puts the nature and the author or, rather, the actual and poetic reality into an equal position—in that of a parallel co-existence. J.J. Bodmer, A.G. Baumgarten, and J.J. Breitinger, Swiss aesthetists, relied on logic and ontology by Leibniz and Wolff, and to legitimize the poetic world-building used their notion that fictional stories are "possible worlds," which exist as alternatives to actual reality, having their own logic, chronology, and cosmology. The theory of possible worlds was then forgotten until recently (see Doležel 1990, 67, 39–52, 1998, 231).

The fact that the literary text can be detached from its original context and actualized in different ways, marks its relationship towards reality yet in another way, not just the one discussed in theories of fiction. This relationship implies its referential indeterminacy and polyvalence (García-Berrio 49–52, 66–70). Since the authorial intention no longer controls the signs in the text, and they are not determined by the context of utterance, they can more freely relate to loosely limited and overlapping cognitive domains and thematic fields. Especially through the history of reading, signs evoke heterogeneous and sometimes even incompatible contexts, while their meanings are grafted intertextually into experientially or socially distinct discursive fields, texts, thematic networks, and contingent horizons of expectations (see Culler 1982, 122–25, 134–35; De Berg 24–27). Such polyvalence and semantic indeterminacy of the artistic text results in the dynamics and condensation of its meaning; it gives the represented textual world a touch of "the concrete universal" (Culler 2000, 281), which means that literary fictions are applicable to historically, culturally, and socially particular levels of understanding where they function as a kind of example or as an implicit model of how the identity is being formed (Culler 2000, 282). Discussing Steven Knapp's *Literary Interest*, Culler—in a Bakhtinian vein—maintains that the specific interest in literature originates precisely in the ability of literary writing's "staging agency" and its "engagement with otherness": literary representation, which according to Knapp particularizes the emotive and other values of its referents by foregrounding their dependency on complex, even contradictory, lingual framings, helps to defamiliarize stereotyped knowledge and "makes us self-conscious agents"; literature gives us "an unusually pure experience of what agency . . . is like" (Culler 2000, 280–81).

After the above compressed summary of the main components of theories of literariness, I present here an example of a post-structuralist interpretation of a text, one that is considered, arguably, literary, Edvard Kocbek's poem
"The Tree": "I hear the tree and I catch sight of it, / I lay down under its shade
/ or I touch it and tear it down, / I cut it up and put it in the stove / or I build
a log-house from it, / whatever I do with it, / it will always remain a tree, /
indivisible, indestructible / rustling of the wind day and night, / in the stove,
on the bed, in the shade, / between the lines in a newspaper, / and in the smoke
between the sky and earth, / the tree as shade and respite / the tree as cradle
and coffin, / the tree as center of the paradise, / the tree as noise and hush, /
the tree as tree, / and the tree as word" (Kocbek 86, trans. M. Pirnat-Greenberg). The word "tree" in this poem avoids any specific extra-textual reference, it even eludes the reference derived from the experience (typical of lyrics),
which opens the textual space in the beginning ("I *hear* the tree and I *catch
sight* of it, / I lay down under its shade"); "tree" does not indicate the characteristics, story or condition of a concrete, individual tree nor it represents a
particular concept "tree" within one of the discursive fields, e.g., botany, fruit-
growing, forestry, paper-making, etc. In non-literary communication a word
is only as relevant as it can be used for informative regulation of the practice
with which one comprehends the living environment or acts within it, e.g.,
"Look, a tree! There will be some shade" or "A tree is torn down, cut up, and
used as a fire-wood." Kocbek's poetic voice argues against the reduction of
the sign, against its stable, definite, and operative reference. By listing alternative possibilities, various ontological modalities of the tree, the poem suggests that the meaning of a poetic sign ("tree") cannot be exhausted by
automated views of it, which were shaped by repeating contextual connections
of the word in various genres of every-day communication. Kocbek's tree
evokes some kind of elusive "tree-ness" which escapes stabilized categorical
or pragmatic schemes. This unique, merely poetically contrived meaning
emerges only in this literary text, i. e., with the play of alternative possible
worlds of the tree (it is shade, a cradle, a coffin, paper, a tree of Eden, a word,
a noise, silence), by juxtaposing heterogeneous and even contradictory areas
of imagination, and by crossbreeding of the evaluative perspectives that the
word had gone through in its cultural context during the course of its historical life. Poetic writing revives the recorded cultural memory instead of rely-
ing on the outside reality. Kocbek's "The Tree" evokes the connotations that
this word has gained through culture and the poet's personal experience. The

poem lists contexts that can be entirely practical (the tree as an object of perception, a place of respite, raw material for a carpenter and a paper maker, etc.) or the contexts which acquired symbolic, archetypal dimensions——existential, religious, poetic (tree of Eden, smoke, sky, earth, cradle, coffin, word). Hence, the literary text takes part in imaginary-symbolic anthropological universals, with which members of a particular culture orient their lives (García-Berrio 86–93); the poem with its unique linguistic-structural fabric gives a special semantic design and evaluative accent to this supra-historical imagery.

The textual world can refer primarily to itself, since it only exists in this text and because of it. Self-referentiality is disclosed on the final margin of the text in a kind of *mise en abyme*; the ending gives a new sense to the previous whole. The point in question is the tautology "the tree as tree," which with the sentence of identity replaces previous predications ("the tree as a/b/c"), and metafictional loop "the tree as word." In fact, the tree constantly appears in Kocbek's text as a word, a signifier, even if its word-only character is disguised by the iconic fictions of the referents. However, precisely as a poetic, literary word the tree is capable of the evasive excess of meaning. Kocbek's poem interpreted in this way, satisfies all the major criteria that provide a text with literary features: The poem is linguistically designed in a special way, semantically dense, highly structured (this way it draws attention and provides the possibility of picturesque image), the poet's fictional substitute (lyrical subject) expresses an imaginary world, amalgamated from possible, alternative stories. Also, the meaning of the poem—symbolized by "the tree as word"—is polyvalent and undetermined. All these characteristics seem to be objective properties of the text. Therefore, with respect to Kocbek's poem one could claim that literariness is structural essence, which is realized in every (single) artistic text and is accessible for objective theoretical description.

LITERARINESS AS CONVENTION

Opponents of essentialist conceptions of literariness, e.g., Eagleton (1–16), on the contrary, claim that all the aforementioned features are also characteristic of genres that are by no means considered literature. Fictional are, for instance, word math problems ("On the market Johnny bought 3 red apples and 2 pears. How many pieces of fruit did he bring home?"). Usually, they do not forget to add that Mukařovský and Jakobson—as the main proponents of a linguistic circumscription of literariness—have already detected the poetic function of language in non-literary texts such as political advertisements (e.g., the notorious "I like Ike") as well. Moreover, for Vincent Leitch it is precisely by Jakobson's notion of the poetic function that "the structuralist concept of literariness . . . helps us think past literary aestheticism and strict formalism, opening the whole field of social communication to semiotic analysis attentive to matters beyond, but inclusive of, 'poeticity'" (42).

If on the one hand literariness is by no means limited to the works which are deemed literary, on the other hand one can see how a hermeneutic-evaluative presupposition that one is dealing with a literary text changes his/her reading and understanding of a simple newspaper note (see, e.g., Genette 150): "His Cry": "As he stepped / to the machine / to fix its / sensor, / the machine automatically turned on. / He did jump back, but too late, / since / the moving part / of the machine squeezed / him against the static part." A piece of news from a police and fire report about a work-related accident which I simply rewrote in verse could be read differently as in its original shape. Verse is a standard signal that triggers a reading according to poetic conventions. Therefore, the newspaper news about a work-related accident loses realistic attributes and concrete temporal-spatial determinants. Instead of referring to actual reality in a particular factory, the intra-textual ties between linguistic elements strengthen, and so does the intertextual harmony of the "poem" with codes and works recalled from the literary tradition. For that reason the transformed journalistic text could even be interpreted—forgive my ludistic exaggeration—as a minimalist, tragicomic ballad about a fatal conflict between a person and technology. The message about a particular event would be universalized to a degree of exemplariness and deeper, eternal meanings, detached from a concrete situation, would be searched for. A skilled interpreter would not have greater troubles to corroborate this kind of reading by "objective" data found in the text (e.g., the contrast between the moving and static parts of the machine, between the broken sensor and destructive functioning). Here is yet another and different example:

the newcomer in the second national league belišće / is no doubt a pleasant surprise for / the western group since this team let / everybody and particularly the favorites know that / it is not planning to be satisfied just with average / achievements this is best indicated by the results / and the placement in the ranks since this / team prides itself among other things with / the fact that it is the only undefeated league member among / all national teams there-

fore it is no surprise / that the belišće players because of this initial / success
are confident and that / before the game with aluminum their predictions / are
optimistic with the game so far that / we have shown at the championship
matches / there is no reason to hide hope / for a complete success in ljudski
vrt as well / said one of the best players / who proved himself this past sun-
day / jozić (Šalamun 45, trans. M. Pirnat-Greenberg) .

If someone reads the above text to us, we would say without much hesi-
tation that it belongs to the journalistic genre. It would be regarded as sports
commentary. The language seems natural, prosaic, the message is non-ambigu-
ous, and it might have helped the readers with entirely practical interests (e.g.,
with filling out sports forecasts); the textual world refers to well-known realities from soccer life in Slovenia. But if we know that we have in fact listened
to a poem by Tomas Šalamun, all these "objective" properties are seen in a
completely different light and their function is changed. Unlike Kocbek's "The
Tree," in this case the context of the utterance, its medium and presentation,
as well as the reading conventions applied are really crucial for establishing
literariness. Already the author's name as a paratextual information evokes
expectations of genre, style, perspective, etc. Following Foucault it can be said
that the author functions not only as the owner of the text/the copyright, and
the guardian of its proper understanding, but also as a special socio-cultural
role, through which people classify, evaluate, and stratify the universe of discourse (see Pease). For reasonably educated Slovene readers the name of Šalamun functions as a repository of "symbolic/cultural capital" (Bourdieu),
containing of literary-cultural associations, either originating in reading the
author's better known texts or derived from journalistic, scholarly, or school
metaliterature and from the image created by the public media. The medium
or the place of publication of the poem "Belišće" also reset its character: By
moving it from the newspaper column to the context of the collection of poems
(*Namen pelerine*, 1968) the text becomes fictional, depragmatized, since to a
reader it is not important whether the facts in the poem are true or not, once
he/she decides to process it according to conventions of poetry. Naturally, the
poem "Belišće" is in apparent discrepancy with the majority of these conventions. Against the background of the canonized poetic texts and traditional
codes it loses any meaning. Its artistic significance can only be legitimized by
the reader's reliance on avant-garde aesthetic conventions, on principles of the
so-called ready-made. Philosophizing about similar artistic practices of
Duchamp and Warhol, Arthur C. Danto maintains, that artistic statement of

the kind "By this gesture I make this simple object an artwork" is only possible on the background of the tradition, when the history of art has been internalized in the conceptual frameworks of both the artist and observer/critic (51). As a member of the neo-avantgarde group OHO, Šalamun took a ready-made newspaper fragment and with some minor changes moved it to the aesthetic context: His collection of poems is a parallel to the gallery where Marcel Duchamp once exhibited a urinal under the title "A Fountain" (see Danto 93–94).

Under these circumstances readers perceive a sports commentary in its aesthetic function. One observes, as Bakhtin would say, the "image of language" shown from a distance. Šalamun's manipulation encourages the reader that she/he, as well, looks at the iconized sociolect from a reflexive, and ironic distance. Šalamun's "ready-made" verse undermines traditional ideas about poetry. The text is artistically relevant precisely as a means of critical laying bare of such expectations—by revealing them as conventions, which are institutionalized and socially consecrated. With the provoking absence of the expected, "Belišće" talks about the hidden nature of literariness, yet with relaxing, parodic laughter.

It should be noticed that it is this kind of avant-garde act that prompted the theoretical notion that literariness cannot be an objective property of texts, but rather something "external," what is *assigned* to texts: in a particular circumstance, the context of the text's reception is based on conventions of literarines. After reader-response theory and post-structuralism had tried to convince us that the essentialist explication of literariness was unjustified, it is nevertheless necessary to pose some seemingly trivial questions: would one be willing, for instance, to satisfy her/his needs for literature (if one has them, of course) by consuming journalistic texts printed as collections of poems, grinding philosophic treatise between the covers of a novel or by watching TV round-tables staged as absurd grotesques? And on the other hand, would one even try to derive anything useful and every-day pragmatic from, for instance, Kocbek's "The Tree" if she/he found it with a signature "E.K." in the column "For Home and Family" in some magazine? If literariness is only a convention, how did it come to be, what is the basis for the consensus that, for instance, *The Divine Comedy, Don Quixote*, or Prešeren's romantic verse tale *The Baptism at the Waterfall* are undoubtedly literary works, pieces of verbal art? I postulate that all these questions are not merely rhetorical. They imply that texts, in order to be read as literature, have to serve a certain social (existential) function that is irreducible to other discourses. From a similar standpoint, Olsen argues that "the term 'literary work of art' is the name of a function-class constituted by an institution of concepts and rules defining a practice" (75). In my view this is not far from a sound answer to the question about literariness, but seeing the literary of the literary text only through the function the text serves in the practices of a given cultural context still fails to explain *how* texts do it and *why*, on what basis such function is at all expected from them.

LITERARINESS AS AN EFFECT BASED ON A CANON

Kocbek's poem—as all "objective" symptoms of literariness were found in it—belongs to the opus of a poet who is considered a classic of modern Slovene poetry and is therefore respected among scholarly and lay readers alike and who are favorably disposed towards poetry. With their reading, metatexts, enthusiastic or critical reviews, conflicting interpretations, etc.—critics, essay writers, literary historians, philosophers, and teachers gradually recognized Kocbek's literature as particularly valuable, culturally representative, exciting, stimulating discussions and proliferation of further literary works. Thus, the author and his work were installed in the core of the Slovene literary canon. Literary canon is a repertoire of works, authors, and norms, principles, conventions, and explanations related to them, which—owing to the success among readers, recognition among the elites, abundant and diverse metatextual responses by writers and scholars as well as educational or political "applicability"—in a particular culture become selected as representations of general notions and "supra-historical" values: canonized texts function as paradigms not only of beautiful, correct and eloquent writing, of rules of literary genres, of ethical, cognitive and other values, but also of the concept of "literature" (see Juvan 277–89).

Most agree that literature in the sense of verbal art has not been around forever and that as a conception it is historical (Kos 5–12), not without ideological investments, and that, in Europe, it represents an outcome of large restructurings of society, within which a relatively autonomous domain of communication—the system of art or the "literary field"—gradually developed. However, there might be too little attention paid to the fact that the notion of literature was established on the basis of concrete, highly valued texts, namely, by their recording, conserving, reproducing, reading, celebrating, and commenting through individuals, groups, and institutions, such as salons, eminent journals, academies or university departments of literary study. These complex practices lead to establishing a set of descriptive and evaluative terms for commenting on art, sometimes adopted from other fields (religion, politics). Such terms, together with normative generalizations and practices of classification (e.g., genres or high vs. popular literature, etc.) engendered a discourse about works of art, which, according to Bourdieu, is "not a simple side-effect, designed to encourage its [i.e., the work's] apprehension and appreciation, but a moment which [was] part of the production of the work, of its meaning and its value" (170); this discourse turned attitude towards objects, classified and perceived as artworks, into a kind of "literary *doxa*" or quasi-religious "belief" in their transcendent meanings and in demiurgic authority of their authors (172). This means that literariness as a convention with great ideological charge evolved along the canon of representative texts—along the so-called world literature and classics of national literatures. Those texts function among professional and amateur readers alike not only as exemplary realizations of ethical, stylistic, or gnoseological ideas, but also of what an artwork should be like and which approaches to literariness are considered legitimate. For these reasons it is not surprising that in Kocbek's poem one can recognize all the characteristics of literariness; the concept of "literature" was created precisely by a process of normalizing canonical works, i.e., the texts that have or used to have the socio-cultural status equal to, for example, "The Tree" in Slovene literature. Literariness can thus be defined as the culturally specific effect and functioning of a particular and specific text, perceived on a formal, semantic, and value-ideological levels –and so within the aesthetic discourse of the last two centuries not only on the landscapes of literatures in Europe or the Americas (in the so-called West) but globally.

A text can have this kind of effect because of several interdependent factors: if it was conceived and written with the purpose of being perceived as literature, if it was thematically and linguistically organized according to some of the conventional clues to literariness, if it was published in media that establish and recall literary milieu, and—last, but not least—if the readership (including critics, essay writers, scholars, and other authors of meta-literature) in the course of reception, based on at least one of the aforementioned factors, activated the appropriate expectations, frameworks, and conventions. The effect of literariness originates in a complex (systemic) interaction of mental processes, metatexts, actions, and activities related to the texts: Hence, besides the physiognomy of the text itself, there are other factors determining literariness, namely, who published the text and where, with what intentions, who reads it, with what kind of knowledge and expectations, and how it is subsequently or simultaneously commented on, explained, and classified (see, in particular, Schmidt). I rephrase this definition by a quotation from Rusch: "Literariness appears to be a time-, culture-, and milieu-sensitive variable within the interactional network of authors, texts, publishers, printers, readers, etc. Rather than an immanent feature of texts or the psychological characteristics of an author or the decisions of readers, literariness turns out to be a matter of 'arrangement' and mutual adjustment" (97).

From the overview I present here we can come to the following conclusions. First, literariness is a flexible, historically, socially and culturally differentiated convention, derived from the immanent characteristics of some literary works (canonized, classic, paradigmatic; see Schmidt 1997, 144). Second, along with Bourdieu's sociology of the literary field, it is the contextual and systemic approach to literature (see, for example, Miall and Kuiken <http://www.ualberta.ca/~dmiall/reading/igel98.htm>; Schmidt 1980, 1989, 1997; Tötösy 1998) that provides us the most convincing answers to the complexities of literariness. Systems theory as a contextual approach in and for the study of literature, such as proposed in Schmidt's *Empirische Literaturwissenschaft* (*Empirical Study of Literature*) or Steven Tötösy's proposal of a "comparative cultural studies (see in this volume) neither reduces literariness to a textual property nor it denies the fact, that a text as a material "scheme" and basis for processing has something to do with its own (and other text's) cultural and social effects. Instead, systems theory elaborates on a series of interdisciplinary conceptual tools which allow for the description of the subtlest socio-historical, psychic, linguo-pragmatic, and actional (behavioral) ramifications, in which literariness can be intended, planned, textualized, and grasped, i.e, contexts of the construction and functioning of literariness. Third, those who are concerned with explaining the problem of literariness cannot be considered pure observers of literature; instead, they should be aware of their identity as participants who—at least indirectly, via systems of culture including science and education—collaborate in the construction of the notion and conventions of literature as well as the study of literature and culture.

WORKS CITED

Aristotle. *Poetika*. Trans. Kajetan Gantar. Ljubljana: Cankarjeva založba, 1982.

Bakhtin, Mikhail M. *The Dialogic Imagination: Four Essays by M.M. Bakhtin.* Ed. Michael Holquist. Trans. Caryl Emerson. Austin: U of Texas P, 1981.

Bakhtin, Mikhail M. *Teorija romana (On the Theory of the Novel)*. Ed. Aleksander Skaza. Trans. Drago Bajt. Ljubljana: Cankarjeva založba, 1982.

Bourdieu, Pierre. *The Rules of Art: Genesis and Structure of the Literary Field.* Trans. Susan Emanuel. Stanford: Stanford UP, 1996.

Culler, Jonathan. *On Deconstruction: Theory and Criticism after Structuralism.* London: Routledge, 1982.

Culler, Jonathan. "La littérarité." *Théorie littéraire. Problèmes et perspectives.* Ed. Marc Angenot, Jean Bessière, Douwe Fokkema, and Eva Kushner. Paris: PU de France, 1989. 31–43.

Culler, Jonathan. "The Literary in Theory." *What's Left of Theory? New Work on the Politics of the Literary Theory.* Ed. Judith Butler, John Guillory, Kendall Thomas. New York: Routledge, 2000. 273–92.

Danto, Arthur. *The Transfiguration of the Commonplace: A Philosophy of Art.* Cambridge,: Harvard UP, 1981.

De Berg, Henk. "Reception Theory or Perception Theory?" *The Systemic and Empirical Approach to Literature and Culture as Theory and Application.* Ed. Steven Tötösy de Zepetnek and Irene Sywenky. Edmonton: Research Institute for Comparative Literature, U of Alberta and Siegen: Institute for Empirical Literature and Media Research, Siegen U, 1997. 23–30.

De Man, Paul. *Blindness and Insight: Essays in Rhetoric of Contemporary Criticism.* 2nd ed. Minneapolis: U of Minnesota P, 1983.

Doležel, Lubomír. *Occidental Poetics: Tradition and Progress.* Lincoln: U of Nebraska P, 1990.

Doležel, Lubomír. *Heterocosmica: Fiction and Possible Worlds.* Baltimore: The Johns Hopkins UP, 1998.

Eagleton, Terry. *Literary Theory: An Introduction.* Oxford: Blackwell, 1983.

Eco, Umberto. "Die ästhetische Botschaft." *Einführung in die Semiotik.* By Umberto Eco. Trans. J. Trabant. München: Fink, 1988. 145–67.

García-Berrio, Antonio. *A Theory of the Literary Text.* New York: de Gruyter, 1992.

Genette, Gérard. "Langage poétique, poétique du langage." *Figures II.* By Gérard Genette. Paris: Seuil, 1969. 123–53.

Glaser, Horst Albert. "Literaturwissenschaft und Textwissenschaft." *Grundzüge der Literatur- und Sprachwissenschaft. Band 1: Literaturwissenschaft.* Ed. Heinz Ludwig Arnold and Volker Sinemus. München: DTV, 1990. 15–23.

Groden, Michael, and Martin Kreiswirth, eds. *The Johns Hopkins Guide to Literary Theory and Criticism.* Baltimore: The Johns Hopkins UP, 1994.

Jakobson, Roman. *Noveishaia russkaia poeziia* (*Modern Russian Poetry*). 1921. *Selected Writings 5*. The Hague: Mouton, 1985. 299–344.

Jakobson, Roman. *Selected Writings 3*. The Hague: Mouton, 1981.

Juvan, Marko. "Slovenski Parnasi in Eliziji: Literarni kanon in njegove uprizoritve" ("Slovenian Parnassus and Elysium: Literary Canon and Its Representations"). *Individualni in generacijski ustvarjalni ritmi v slovenskem jeziku, književnosti in kulturi* (*Individual and Generational Creative Rhythms in Slovenian Language, Literature, and Culture.*). Ed. Marko Juvan and Tomaž Sajovic. Ljubljana: Znanstveni inštitut Filozofske fakultete, 1994. 277–315.

Kocbek, Edvard. *Zbrane pesmi* (*Collected Poems*) 2. Ljubljana: Cankarjeva založba, 1977.

Kos, Janko. *Literatura*. Ljubljana: DZS, 1978.

Lausberg, Heinrich. *Handbuch der Literarischen Rhetorik. Eine Grundlegung der Literaturwissenschaft*. München: Max Hueber, 1960. 2 vols.

Leitch, Vincent B. *Cultural Criticism, Literary Theory, Poststructuralism*. New York: Columbia UP, 1992.

Markiewicz, Henryk. *Glavni problemi literarne vede* (*The Main Problems of the Literary Scholarship*). Trans. N. Jež. Ljubljana: DZS, 1977.

Meletinski, Eleazar. "Sociétés, cultures et fait littéraire." *Théorie littéraire. Problèmes et perspectives*. Ed. Marc Angenot, Jean Bessière, Douwe Fokkema, and Eva Kushner. Paris: PU de France, 1989. 13–29.

Miall, David, and Don Kuiken. The Reader Response Research Group (1998–): <http://www.ualberta.ca/~dmiall/reading/igel98.htm>

Mukařovský, Jan. *Kapitoly z české poetiky I.* (*Chapters in Czech Poetics I.*) Prague: Svoboda, 1948. 41–77, 78–128.

Ocvirk, Anton. *Literarna teorija* (*The Theory of Literature*). Ljubljana: DZS, 1978.

Olsen, Stein Haugom. "Defining a Literary Work." *The End of Literary Theory*. By S. H. Olsen. Cambridge: Cambridge UP, 1987. 73–87.

Pease, Donald E. "Author." *Critical Terms for Literary Study*. Ed. Frank Lentricchia and Thomas McLaughlin. Chicago: U of Chicago P, 1990. 105–17.

Riegler, Alexander. Radical Constructivism (1998–):<http://www.univie.ac.at/constructivism/>

Rusch, Gebhard. "Literature, Media, and Society: Toward a Media Description Standard." *The Systemic and Empirical Approach to Literature and Culture as Theory and Application*. Ed. Steven Tötösy de Zepetnek and Irene Sywenky. Edmonton: Research Institute for Comparative Literature, U of Alberta and Siegen: Institute for Empirical Literature and Media Research, Siegen U, 1997. 91–105.

Rusterholz, Peter. "Verfahrensweisen der Werkinterpretation." *Grundzüge der Literatur- und Sprachwissenschaft. Band 1: Literaturwissenschaft*. Ed. Heinz Ludwig Arnold and Volker Sinemus. München: DTV, 1990. 341–57.

Sanchez-Mesa Martinez, Domingo. "Literatures in Multimedia Context." *Humanities* (2000): <http://www.dipoli.hut.fi/org/TechNet/org/humanities/lite/summary.html>

Schmidt, Siegfried J. *Grundriss der Empirischen Literaturwissenschaft.* Wiesbaden: Vieweg, 1980. Vol. 1.

Schmidt, Siegfried J. *Die Selbstorganisation des Sozialsystems Literatur im 18. Jahrhundert.* Frankfurt: Suhrkamp, 1989.

Schmidt, Siegfried J. "Empirical Study of Literature: Why and Why Not?" *The Systemic and Empirical Approach to Literature and Culture as Theory and Application.* Ed. Steven Tötösy de Zepetnek and Irene Sywenky. Edmonton: Research Institute for Comparative Literature, U of Alberta and Siegen: Institute for Empirical Literature and Media Research, Siegen U, 1997. 137–53.

Smirnov, Igor P. *Po puti k teorii literatury (On the Way to the Theory of Literature.).* Amsterdam-Atlanta, GA: Rodopi, 1987.

Šalamun, Tomaž. *Namen pelerine (The Purpose of a Raincoat).* Ljubljana: Published by the author, 1968.

Tatarkiewicz, Wladyslaw. *Istorija šest pojmova: Umetnost, lepo, forma, stvaralaštvo, podražavanje, estetski doživljaj (The History of Six Notions: Art, Beauty, Form, Creation, Imitation, Aesthetic Experience.).* Trans. P. Vujičić. Belgrade: Nolit, [1985].

Tihanov, Galin. "Zakaj moderna literarna teorija izvira iz Srednje in Vzhodne Evrope?" ("Why did Modern Literary Theory Originate in East-Central Europe?"). Trans. Marko Juvan. *Primerjalna književnost* 24.1 (2001). 1–15.

Tötösy de Zepetnek, Steven. *Comparative Literature: Theory, Method, Application.* Amsterdam-Atlanta, GA: Rodopi, 1998.

Tötösy de Zepetnek, Steven. "From Comparative Literature Today Toward Comparative Cultural Studies." *Comparative Literature and Comparative Cultural Studies.* Ed. Steven Tötösy de Zepetnek. West Lafayette: Purdue UP, 2002. 235–67.

Comparative Literature and the Ideology of Metaphor, East and West

Karl S.Y. Kao

Traditional confidence in the ability of conceptual thinking to control the working of rhetorical figures started to receive serious challenges in the nineteenth century. Nietzsche pointed out that thinking is always and inseparably tied to the rhetorical devices that are part and parcel of language itself. Not only does the philosophical discourse lack epistemological superiority over other kinds of discourse, it is self-deluding for us to think that any kind of discourse could be exempted from rhetorical penetration and contamination. Set forth mainly in the well-known essay that describes "truth" as a used-up, worn-out metaphor, Nietzsche's criticism of the truth-claim of philosophical discourse as illusory has to do with his mistrust of metaphysics. Reality and truth are not accessible without mediation, while interpretations and "anthropomorphisms" have their roots not in some transcendental source but the drive to appropriate and conquer, the "will to power" (42–47).

Deconstructive criticism follows up on this by inquiring into the problematics of rhetoric and figural discourse, making inquiries in this respect a fundamental aspect of its project. Both Derrida and de Man have examined the question in detail and exposed how thinking is bound to rhetorical devices, how figures are connected with metaphysics and ideology. To briefly recapitulate, in Derrida's view, the Western tradition since the time of Plato has been confused by the thinking that there are fixed truths and non-linguistic facts "out there," that through the tools of reason, argumentation, and evidence, philosophy and science could capture or uncover these truths. This thinking follows from a belief in the "metaphysics of presence" which, however, could never be reached or realized through language. All discourses, philosophical or scientific, are in reality but varieties of "writing," systems of signs, which are characterized by différance and the free play of signs. The logocentric purpose, the pursuit of "transcendental signified," arrests this play by suppressing the difference in the sign and freezing the differing process. This is also the moment when, in Derrida's words within *Of Grammatology* (1976), "a metaphoric mediation has insinuated itself into the relationship [between the signifier and the signified] and has simulated immediacy" (15). What is called "literal truth" is but a willful interruption of the free play of language and the restriction of the sense of the sign as determinate. As David Novitz puts it in his 1985 article "Metaphor, Derrida, and Davidson," "When once we freeze this play, when once we speak determinately, we are . . . speaking metaphorically" (105). In a logocentric system, where language is used in such a "determinate" way, speaking will appear to have definite meanings.

Philosophers have dreamt for language to be purified of its contamination by figures and rectified of the aberration, but it is only through a "double effacement" of the metaphor that this illusion is sustained. Exploring the question of "metaphor in the text of philosophy," Derrida shows in "White Mythology" that philosophy is a "process of metaphorization which gets carried away in and of itself" (211); it is not so much that metaphor is in the text of philosophy but theses texts are in metaphor. In reading a text, says Derrida in *Of Grammatology* that "it is not . . . a matter of inverting the literal meaning and the figurative meaning but of determining the 'literal' meaning of writing as metaphoricity itself" (15).

The choice of a metaphor inevitably entails the positing of a perspective or frame, a positioning of the discourse in its "will to power." In this view, dominant values and ideologies of a given time are supported by the ruling metaphors, as Foucault's conception of discursive formation would also argue. Philosophy, then, is a kind of writing that cannot help being contaminated by metaphoricity; concepts only become such by a process of metaphorization of language. But this process is often hidden from epistemological scrutiny, as metaphoricity has also often been rendered transparent and invisible. Deconstructive reading of philosophical texts exposes how privileged terms in Western culture, in their striving for a metaphysics of presence, are held in place by the force of dominant metaphors rather than undisputable logic. Exposure of the hidden metaphor and the metaphoricity of the text in general also disrupts the logic of rational argument, resulting in the instability and undecidability of the meaning of a text. As Derrida urges in *Dissemination*, "Metaphoricity is the logic of contamination and the contamination of logic" (149). Richard Rorty remarks, in his "Philosophy as a Kind of Writing," that the function of deconstruction of metaphoricity in the text is to show "that there is an alternative to the metaphysics of presence and the logocentrism which it encourages" (98).

Like Derrida, de Man sees rhetoricity and its subversive force as the most tenacious and inescapable characteristics of Western literary and philosophical discourses. To him figurality is ingrained in the act of cognition itself; no conceptualization and abstract thinking can escape it. In the words of his "The Epistemology of Metaphor," as "soon as one is willing to be made aware of their epistemological implications, concepts are tropes and tropes concepts" (21).

Rhetoricity therefore is tied to the questions of knowledge and representation. At another level, de Man deals with the issue of specific tropes and their literary functioning, relating them ultimately to the question of the ideology of aesthetic (see Norris 1988). In the Western tradition, rhetoric from the very beginning has been opposed to logic as an alternative faculty. The addition of grammar to the classical opposition between logic and rhetoric to form the trivium of an integral liberal arts education in Medieval times could be seen as a measure introduced to diffuse the tension between oratory and scientific discourse. Grammar is expected to work together with logic to ensure the accuracy of language's mediation of conceptual reasoning so that language may better represent the phenomenal reality, and through this representation we may gain better control of the world. At the same time, the devious operation of rhetoric "making the worse appear as the better cause" may be contained by its "grammatization," subjugated by the rules to serve the enhancement of the expressive power of language. De Man questions such an assumption of collaborative functions. Rhetoricity is not something added to the rules of language, but something inherent in it. Contrary to serving language's purpose of conveying or accurately describing reality, rhetoric cannot but disrupt this function. As de Man sees it in *Allegories of Reading*, "Rhetoric radically suspends logic and opens up vertiginous possibilities of referential aberration" (10). Since concepts are metaphors and language itself is structured by conflicting systems of signification, under rigorous reading the text will deconstruct itself. Hence de Man's dictum: "The paradigm for all texts consists of a figure (or a system of figures) and its deconstruction" (205).

De Man also examines and reads specific figures and their cultural and ideological valorizations. Traditionally, metaphor is considered as the foremost trope, more powerful or fundamental than metonymy, or for that matter, any other tropes and figures. This privileging of metaphor over metonymy has much to do with the fact that the former, through its ability to induce the perception of sameness in difference, is thought to have the power of capturing the essence of things, even providing a hope to reach the metaphysical; whereas, metonymy, based on association by contiguity, establishes relations that are accidental, non-essential. With Aristotle, artists themselves also believe in the power of metaphor. In Proust's texts, besides being a trope of necessity as opposed to that of arbitrariness, metaphor is considered superior to other figures also because it has a "totalizing" ability it is superior even to reality which can be experienced only in fragments. For example, reading a passage from *Du Coté de chez Swann,* where the young Marcel defends his preference of reading indoors to playing outside, de Man notices that through the use of metaphors, "Marcel's imagination finds access to 'the total spectacle of summer,' including the attractions of direct physical action, and that he possesses it much more effectively than if he had been actually present in an outside world that he then could only have known by bits and pieces" (60). But in a close analysis, the impression of such a total experience turns out to be created by the use of metonymy, rather than metaphor as such, and the latter's alleged ability to capture essences relies in fact on the accidental contiguity effects of the former. There is an inversion of our normal valorization of these two tropes in de Man's reading of Proust.

De Man's deconstructive reading of metaphor corroborates his revaluation of symbol and allegory carried out in relation to a study of Romantic poets. Again, questioning the traditional view held since the late eighteenth century which assumes the superiority of symbol over allegory as a poetic mode or device, he contests, in "The Rhetoric of Temporality," the notion that symbol could effect the reconciliation of man and nature. The promotion of symbol at the expense of allegory may be related to an aesthetics that attempts to bridge the gap between experience and the representation of that experience. De Man describes this aesthetics by paraphrasing Gadamer in his "The Rhetoric of Temporality" thus: "The subjectivity of experience is preserved when it is translated into language; the world is then no longer seen as a configuration of entities that designates a plurality of distinct and isolate meanings, but as a configuration of symbols ultimately leading to a total, single, and universal meaning" (188). For de Man, this is a delusion. Symbol allures by its promise of organic unity and oneness with the transcendental, which is but a mystification. On the other hand, allegory and irony, with their operations based on the explicit discrepancy between signifier and signified, are considered a more authentic understanding of language, just as temporality would serve as a better model for the relation between figuration and interpretation. His "allegorical reading," with an "ironization," exposes the discontinuity and non-identity in symbolism that the aesthetic ideology of the "organic world" poetics which has implications for political totalitarianism has prevented us from seeing. Thus, Derrida and de Man both see figurality as inherent in philosophical and literary discourses: its motivation and function is to arrest the free play of signification by imposing a "centric" perspective for the reading of the "proper" meaning. Derrida sees this "logocentric" impulse come from the drive for "the transcendental signified," the supposed originary point of meanings. His reading exposes the figural source of the value hierarchy and points to the instability of the text under close scrutiny. De Man further looks to the referential implications of figures and their disruption of the signification process. In *Resistance to Theory* (1986) de Man sees ideology as "the confusion of linguistic with natural reality, of reference with phenomenalism" (11), his reading thereby uncovers the ideological aberrations caused by figural interference.

Deconstruction is a project designed for the critique of Western metaphysics; it aims to debunk the belief that some truths external to language exist "out there." The basic assumption about language here is its truth-claim. Parallel to this, the referential aberration exposed by the deconstructive reading of the literary and philosophical texts is based on a mimetic-representational theory of language. Early Chinese theories of language, however, do not seem to share such an orientation or assumption. Chad Hansen argues, for instance, in the 1985 article "Chinese Language, Chinese Philosophy, and Truth" that early Chinese theory of language has had a pragmatic orientation (also see Hansen's 1983 book *Language and Logic in Ancient China*). And neither the tension sustained opposition between logic and rhetoric, nor anything like the trivium of the Medieval curriculum, has been established to exert an influence in the formation of discursive systems in this tradition. As a consequence, a different set of problematics may have evolved in relation to the question of rhetoric and rhetoricity in Chinese. This will become clear from the theories that underlie the use of metaphors or metaphor-like figures to be discussed below. But first it might be pointed out that not all languages have the same figures and that the same, or equivalent, figures may not operate in exactly the same way in different languages. Figures are language-specific. There is a figure (trope) frequently used in early Chinese poetry that shows operations similar to metaphor. But closely associated with it in the same context is another figure that has been interpreted to operate like a metaphor, and yet at the same time functions quite differently. An examination of these tropes in the settings of their usages, and the controversies surrounding particularly the latter in its readings, could throw light on the specific ideological questions of Chinese metaphor.

Of the three basic "modes of composition" recognized in the *Shijing* (*Book of Songs*) exegeses, *bi* and *xing* have been considered to operate like metaphors. *Bi,* meaning basically "comparison (by contiguity)," is in fact generally taken to be an equivalent of metaphor (including simile), while *xing* "evocation, stirring" often invites a metaphoric reading of the image involved. A most important and fundamental device in early Chinese poetry, *xing* continued, in a transformed guise, to dominate the theory of poetic composition and reading for much of the imperial period after the Han dynasty (206 BCE to 220 CE), when the interpretation of *Shijing* began to be codified. *Xing's* literary operations, however, are ambiguous. They have "stirred" up much controversy in the Chinese exegetic tradition and different attempts have been made trying to explain how xing works or simply define what it is is it a mode, a generic style, a kind of imagery, a rhetorical device, or a trope? In *The Reading of Imagery in the Chinese Poetic Tradition* (1987), Pauline Yu translates *xing* as "stimulus" and spends ten dense pages of her book on the imagery in the Chinese tradition to explain its history and the various theories about it (57–67; for other essential studies of the question of *xing*, see also Chou 1980; Cai 1986; Saussy 1993). For a succinct summary of different interpretations of this term throughout Chinese history, see the entry "fu, bi, xing" in Yue 153–56). Stephen Owen in his *Readings in Chinese Literary Thought* (1992) renders the term as "affective image" and cuts the Gordian knot of its interpretive history with a concise explanation of the concept: "*Hsing* [*xing*] is an image whose primary function is not signification but, rather, the stirring of a particular affection or mood: *hsing* does not "refer to" that mood; it generates it. Hsing is therefore not a rhetorical figure in the proper sense of the term. Furthermore, the privilege of *hsing* over *fu* and *pi* [*bi*] in part explains why traditional China did not develop a complex classification system of rhetorical figures, such as we find in the West. Instead there develop classifications of moods, with categories of scene and circumstance appropriate to each. This vocabulary of moods follows from the conception of language as the manifestation of some integral state of mind, just as the Western rhetoric of schemes and tropes follows from a conception of language as sign and referent" (46).

One of the most illuminating statements ever made about the nature of Chinese poetry, this passage accords well with the affective-expressive orientation of Chinese literature (as opposed to the mimetic-representational one of the West). For all its perceptiveness and explanatory efficacy, the passage's definition of *xing* as "an image" however is most baffling. The term *xing* is usually taken to designate not an object or entity but an activity: an "evocation," "rousing," or "stirring" and "generation," just as *fu* is "exposition" and *bi* "comparison." I would like to add that Yu's translation of the term as "stimulus" is ambiguous if not misleading as well. But from her discussion, it is clear that the term refers not so much to the object that stimulates as to the activity or process of stimulation (57) and Yu's translation of the term as "stimulus" may be motivated by the topic of her book as about the "reading of imagery" in the Chinese tradition (this is true of Owen too). However, *xing* is known for its ambiguity and this unusual translation should evoke no surprise. Like *fu* and *bi, xing* may be used also to refer to a mode of composition that implies a particular kind of relationship between the image and the mood or meaning of the poem (the thematic reading of *xing* imagery is not uncommon; see below). It involves the question of how the image is to be understood in relation to the rest of the poem and in what way the reader may be affected in his/her reading. The main controversy of *xing* is not over its designation of a process of stimulation or "stirring" (that leads to the generation of a mood and the affecting of the reader by the poem). It is concerned with two other issues: 1) Exactly how the image that serves as the stimulus is related to the event of the poem and its mood is it like a bi comparison? is the relationship "allegorical"? or something else? and 2) What is the provenance of the stimulating, affecting image is it something external that the poet becomes aware of on the spot, or something arising internally in his/her mind at the moment of composition? or is it a stock image used in a formulaic composition and typically associated with some set theme or mood the poem wants to present or evoke? Only the first question (the relationship between the image and the rest of the poem) is of immediate interest to us here.

An image posed (or read) in the *xing* mode stirs up feelings or generates a mood. But as the interpretive history from Zheng Xuan (127–200) to Zhu Xi (1130–1200) has testified, there has always been an urge to assign a thematic or cognitive meaning to the image in the context of the poem as a whole by an allegorical reading. The different conceptions of the image as mood-generating and as thematic seem to suggest that a xing image operates in several

ways, and we need to see in it a more complex structure than has been recognized. In his analysis of metaphor "The Metaphorical Process as Cognition,
Imagination, and Feeling," Paul Ricoeur sees three kinds of activities as intrinsic to an interactive metaphorical process. With an intentionality of their own,
feelings are "integrated thoughts" that "abolish the distance between knower
and the known without cancelling the cognitive structure of thought and the
intentional distance which it implies" (154). Ricoeur alludes to Aristotle's
analysis of catharsis as well as Northrop Frye's definition of "mood" as "the
way in which a poem affects us as an icon" and as something that gives unity
to a poem (155; for an analysis of *xing* imagery in terms of Ricoeur's concept
of "predicative assimilation," see Weiqun Dai's 1991 "Xing Again: A Formal
Re-investigation"). There is a structural analogy between the cognitive, the
imaginative, and the emotional components of the complete metaphorical act,
and that "the metaphorical process draws its concreteness and its complete-
ness from this structural analogy and this complementary functioning" (157).
A *xing* image may be seen to have an interactive structure like a metaphor,
with three similar components or dimensions relating to three respective
processes. The semantic dimension provides the ground on which the cognitive operation is based; it requires a thematic reading of the image. The emotional dimension evokes feelings and leads to the development of the poetics
of moods in Chinese tradition. With a proper metaphor, the cognitive (semantic) dimension of the image will be dominant, while in the case of a *xing* image,
it is its emotional (affective) dimension that is preeminent. Such a theory
would more easily account for the various kinds of readings in the history of
Shijing interpretations.

Ricoeur is vague in his analysis of the imaginative dimension, but this component may be compared to another way of traditional reading of the *xing*
imagery. A *xing* image is sometimes thought to function in such a way that it
connects the events of the poem to a larger, "cosmic" order. It can do this
because the image is said to belong to or to be correlative of a "category" with
a cosmic significance. Unlike the bi comparison which derives its meaning from
some recognizable common semantic grounds between the two things juxtaposed, the relationship here is based on a "categorical correspondence" predicated on an organic view of the universe. This relationship between a particular
object and the "category" (or class: *lei*) it belongs to is described as "organic,"
as that between genus and species, but from a linguistic point of view the
"semantic features" presumably shared by the two entities are only assumed,

not identified. Ultimately the "category" itself is a metaphor; it can only be conceived and represented metaphorically in terms, for instance, of yin and yang which "literally" mean the sunny and shady side (respectively) or those of the Five Elements defined as the correlatives of the Five Directions, the Five Internal Organs, etc. This reading may be understood as a kind of schematization that transcends both the dimensions of senses and feelings.

Initially, a free sign that evokes a certain mood or poetic ambience, a *xing* image theoretically need not incur the problem of "referential aberration" nor succumb to the seduction and mystification of the metaphysics of presence. However, as in the Western discourse, the desire for a determinate reading stops the free play of meanings and the indefinite affective associations. Ricoeur's analysis of the cognitive component of metaphor identifies, in place of Derridian différance and aporia, a split between "the literal incongruence and metaphorical congruence" at the semantic level, and analogically there is at once "a suspension and commitment" at the other levels as well. In the Chinese context, this split, or tension, is put in terms of "ambiguity" or "obscurity" of signification. In *Wenxin diaolong* (*The Literary Mind Carves Dragons*), Liu Xie (465–520) sees the commentaries given by the interpretive authorities as a shedding of light on the originally dim configuration of meanings, a revealing of the "correct" relationships and their significance: "It is getting brighter but not yet full sunlight: Thus they can be visible only after commentary has been given" (Owen 258). Since the significance of the image exists, presumably, a priori the authoritative interpreter's job is point out this significance, not create one there can be no split of reference, only "potent" meaning awaiting discovery and revelation. In a thematic reading, the cognitive dimension of a xing image is often given political or didactical interpretations. Thus "the song of ospreys" (birds that "makes a distinctions between the sexes") is said to suggest "the virtue of the Queen Consort"). The emotive content, on the other hand, seems more likely to escape the ideological co-option. This aspect of the image has in fact led to the later mainstream theory that sees poetry as a combination of *jing* and *qing*, or a fusion of verbalized external "scenes/situations" with that of subjective "feelings/affections." Such a content is more or less purely aesthetical, but it is not entirely immune to contamination. By Ricoeur's analysis, feeling involves an internalization of the world as well as assimilation by it. "To feel, in the emotional sense of the word, is to make ours what has been put at a distance by thought in its objectifying phase" (154). From an opposite perspective, this assimilation in relation to what we "feel" is also a self-assimilation vis-à-vis the world, just as we are "made similar" in relation to what we "see." The poetic mood of the "happy air of a good era," or the "licentious song of a degenerate time," can be understood then as an ideological assimilation of the feeling: it is an "interpellation" in the emotional sense. As for the dimension of the image's "categorical correspondence," it also yields easily to the co-option by the state or its contending powers. Poetic images believed to be correlative of the "alternation of Cosmic Phases" had been enlisted, for instance, to legitimize the overthrow of a dynasty, for the change-over in power was said to correspond to a due course of the "natural" process that was already reflected in the poem and that no one should try to reverse.

As the account above indicates, the *xing* imagery contains in it various dimensions that make it more complex in structure than *bi*. *Bi* does not occupy a predominant position in Chinese poetry as metaphor does in Western discourse, although the pieces in *Chuci* (*Songs of the South*) (3rd century BCE to 2nd century CE) composed after the *Book of Songs* rely on a system of imagery that is heavily emblematic (see Yu 84–117). Liu Xie considers *xing* a "superior" operation to bi because the former is "covert" and the latter "overt" (Owen 256–58). This judgment is based on different political functions of these literary devices, on the suitability of their linguistic mechanism for social comment. The covert *xing* is more appropriate for the important task of making political and social comments which must be done through "indirection" or circumspection. On the other hand, the overt quality of *bi* makes it a more suitable tool for philosophical argument and explanation. In this respect, there is an inherent tendency in this trope that is ideological in nature. While theoretically *bi* could emphasize contrast, distance, and dissimilarity characteristic of Western metaphor, its metaphoric operation is based on comparison, rather than substitution. As Michelle Yeh observes in her 1997 article "Metaphor and Bi: Western and Chinese Poetics" uses of *bi* often stress similarity (237–54), unwittingly privileging unity over diversity and valuing continuity above break with tradition and the status quo.

Although not essential in poetry, the analogical mechanism of *bi* was employed frequently in early philosophical prose essays in the figural forms of *piyu* and *yuyan*. Functioning mainly as an explanatory device in the contexts of both the Confucian and Taoist discourses, *yuyan* refers to a parable-like story or anecdote which sometimes also looks like an allegory (*piyu* usually designates a short explanation by analogy). *Yuyan* serves best in a discourse where an abstract point is in need of concrete explanation. As such it is an

important tool frequently employed by the pre-Qin writers in their philosophical debates and by persuaders in state policy deliberations (the retention
of many of these *yuyan* in the condensed form of four-syllabic idioms in
today's vocabulary also attests to their continuing currency and vitality).

The pervasive use of *yuyan* in place of a syllogistic logic for argumentation constitutes both the strength and weakness of the philosophical discourse
in early China. Using analogy to illustrate a point, *yuyan* is a valid device of
explanation, but generally speaking it lacks the force of logical inference. Such
a metaphorical or analogical illustration does not constitute a premise for a
valid deduction, even though occasionally an illustration may form the ground
for a sound inference. Usually the analogues are not homologous. But the effec-
tiveness and vividness of analogical *yuyan* give it the ability to insinuate homo-
logicality between the two things compared. Like metaphor, *yuyan* is creative
for its bringing together two disparate, incompatible things, and this creative-
ness may have enhanced the misconception of it as a figure of proof. The way
yuyan develops in the Confucian and Taoist discourse shows a marked difference which seems to betray the divergent ideological appropriation of the
form by the two schools of philosophy. By the Han dynasty, it was clear that
the use of *yuyan* had greatly diminished in frequency in Confucian texts, its
place taken by a related figure called *yongshi*, i.e., historical allusion. A hall-
mark of the classical literary discourse after the Han, yongshi is ostensibly a
figure also of comparison, but it has a modeling (framing) function as well.
The speaker's own situation or the current affair is related to, compared with,
the historical (or supposedly historical) situation alluded to. This general intertextual device of using the past as a frame of reference for the present is appropriated by Confucianism and made a primary device of the school to transmit,
disseminate, and perpetuate its values. The subject or the personage alluded
to often attains the quality of an archetypal symbol or cultural icon through
frequent invocations. Like the appeal to authority as an argumentative device
where the authorities are usually the "past sages," "ancient worthies," or Con-
fucius himself historical allusions look to the past to define one's own situation, and thereby the present also carries on the traditional values. *Yongshi*
allusions are similar to *yuyan* in that both provide a frame or standard for
measuring the situation at hand, but *yuyan* is usually constituted by fictitious
stories whereas *yongshi* involves history, reflecting a pragmatic Confucian
mentality that values wisdom derived from past experiences rather than pure
inventiveness. This particular kind of metaphoric operation promotes to the

full the tendency of bi to emphasize similarity in comparison, and in so doing it also makes itself lose much of metaphor's "world making" creative power.

In contrast to this development in Confucian discourse, the *yuyan* told in the Taoist texts tend to be, not only imaginary, but fantastic in nature Zhuangzi's *zhongyan* parables also feature "historical personages," but mostly only their names are historical not the events associated with them. Zhuangzi's *yuyan* are made of imagery such as the transformation of the tiny kun-fish into a *peng*, a giant bird with wings spanning hundreds of miles, soaring like a whirlwind for a journey to the mythic "Southern Deep," and the picture of the Lord of the Yellow River traveling downstream with autumn floods in the survey of the vast expanses of the sea, there to carry on a lofty conversation with the Spirit of the Ocean, which in turn contains many fantastic *yuyan* anecdotes. But more importantly, most such Taoist *yuyan* have images that work like metonymy and synecdoche, rather than metaphor; there is often an ontological common ground between the illustration and the illustrated. For the explanation of the concept of *xuanjie*, "Freedom from the Bonds," we are given in the Zhuangzi the image of a wizened but wise old man whose left arm gets transformed into a rooster to keep morning watch, the right arm into a crossbow to shoot pellets, and so on. Or to illustrate the concept of *wuhua*, the "Transformation of Things," we have the intriguingly ambiguous concomitant possibilities of a Zhuangzi himself dreaming that he is a butterfly and/or a butterfly dreaming that it is Zhuangzi dreaming of itself dreaming of Zhuangzi. Besides the mise-en-abime quality of the imagery, the intended message of "transformation" is illustrated by a not entirely metaphorical change of a person into a different being or an object the change is consubstantial (see Kenneth Burke's use of the term "consubstantial." The term is used here in a different, but related, sense).

Transformation or transmutability of things is in fact not merely a transferring of sense, as with a metaphor, but a central theme of Zhuangzi's philosophy. The Taoist imagination displays a belief in physical transformation, akin to the philosophy of *tianren heyi* ("Union between Man and Heaven") and the later metaphysics of "immanent transcendence" characteristic of Neo-Confucian thought based on the Doctrine of Mind. Seemingly harmless in the context of "spiritual cultivation," this belief in the transmutability of things and consubstantialism could have consequences similar to de Man's warning against the mystification of the aesthetics of ideology. Zhuangzi and Liezi use the image of the True Man (*zhenren*) or the Ultimate Man (*zhiren*), a being endowed with the supernatural qualities of cosmic power and impervious to fire and water, to describe the state of attainment to Tao and the spiritual unity with the Universe. When later converts took literally such figurative descriptions, attempting to give a "proper" reading of the metaphoricity of the language, the belief led not only to the phenomenon of the immortality cult in the tradition of internal alchemy. It also led to such disastrous histories as the Boxer Uprising, which took place, not during the Han or the Six Dynasties, but at a time not so remote from our own.

WORKS CITED

Cai, Yingjun. *Bi, xing, wuse, yü qingjing jiaoron (Comparison, Evocation, Colours of Things, and the Fusion of Feeling and Scene)*. Taipei: Da'an, 1986.

Chou, Ying-hsiung. "The Linguistic and Mythical Structure of Hsing as a Combinational Model." *Chinese and Western Comparative Literature: Theory and Strategy*. Ed. John J. Deeney. Hong Kong: Chinese UP, 1980. 51–78.

Dai, Wei-qun. "Xing Again: A Formal Re-investigation." *Chinese Literature: Essays, Articles, Reviews* 13 (1991): 1–14.

De Man, Paul. *Allegories of Reading: Figural Language in Rousseau, Nietzsche, Rilke, Proust*. New Haven: Yale UP, 1979.

De Man, Paul. "The Epistemology of Metaphor." *On Metaphor*. Ed. Sheldon Sacks. Chicago: U of Chicago P, 1979. 11–28.

De Man, Paul. *The Resistance to Theory*. Minneapolis: U of Minnesota P, 1986.

De Man, Paul. "The Rhetoric of Temporality." *Blindness and Insight: Essays in the Rhetoric of Contemporary Criticism*. By Paul de Man. Minneapolis: U of Minnesota P, 1983. 187–228.

Derrida, Jacques. *Dissemination*. Trans. Barbara Johnson. Chicago: U of Chicago P, 1981.

Derrida, Jacques. *Of Grammatology*. Trans. Gayatri Chakravorty Spivak. Baltimore: Johns Hopkins UP, 1976.

Derrida, Jacques. "White Mythology." *Margins of Philosophy*. Trans. Alan Bass. Chicago: U of Chicago P, 1982. 209–71.

Hansen, Chad. *Language and Logic in Ancient China*. Ann Arbor: U of Michigan P, 1983.

Hansen, Chad. "Chinese Language, Chinese Philosophy, and Truth." *Journal of Asian Studies* 44.3 (1985): 491–518.

Nietzsche, Friedrich. "On Truth and Lie in an Extra-Moral Sense." *The Portable Nietzsche*. Ed. Walter Kaufmann. New York: Viking, 1954. 42–47.

Norris, Christopher. *Paul de Man: Deconstruction and the Critique of Aesthetic Ideology*. London: Routledge, 1988.

Novitz, David. "Metaphor, Derrida, and Davidson." *The Journal of Aesthetics and Art Criticism* 105 (1985): 34–52.

Owen, Stephen. *Readings in Chinese Literary Thought.* Cambridge: Harvard UP, 1992.

Ricoeur, Paul. "The Metaphorical Process as Cognition, Imagination, and Feeling." *On Metaphor.* Ed. Sheldon Sacks. Chicago: U of Chicago P, 1979. 141–58.

Rorty, Richard. "Philosophy as a Kind of Writing." *Consequences of Pragmatism.* By Richard Rorty. Minneapolis: U of Minnesota P, 1982. 90–109.

Saussy, Haun. *The Problem of a Chinese Aesthetic.* Stanford: Stanford UP, 1993.

Yeh, Michelle. "Metaphor and Bi: Western and Chinese Poetics." *Comparative Literature* 39.3 (1987): 237–54.

Yu, Pauline. *The Reading of Imagery in the Chinese Poetic Tradition.* Princeton: Princeton UP, 1987.

Yue, Daiyun, et al., eds. *Shijie shixue da cidian (An Inclusive Dictionary of World Poetics).* Beijing: Shenyang Chunfeng wenyi, 1993.

Comparative Literature in Slovenia

Krištof Jacek Kozak

The first and foremost problem of any (scholarly) endeavor in Slovenia is the size of the country. It is inhabited by only two million people whose lives pass by almost unnoticed by other larger nations. This fact per force limits the scope and horizon of its professional endeavors when compared with other European countries. Consequently, any scholarly activity undertaken by such a small nation is left to oscillate or arbitrate between potentially mutually exclusive poles. On the one hand, between a comfortable and self satisfied inwardness and self reliance. On the other hand, between an uncomfortable, aggressive and, quite frankly, uncharacteristic openness to the "outside" world. Irrespective of the size of a country, however, any scholarly venture must constantly reassert its distinctiveness, uniqueness and the essential differences of its own particular field. A nation with a small population finds itself asking questions concerning the adequacy or relevance of its own research, especially how (if at all) it can or should relate to the rest of the world. Thus, any area of research in Slovenia has to establish and prove itself within these rather narrow national boundaries and simultaneously define itself as equal to that of any other nation. Consequently, comparative literature in Slovenia is no exception when it comes to answering these questions. It, too, strives to define its distinctive features, to catch up, and to be in accord with the latest scholarly currents in the world, but at the same time to develop the characteristics through which it appears distinctive and unique; it wants to partake in international debates while drawing upon its own distinguishing Slovenian roots. Its drawback in comparison with other disciplines is that it first had to establish itself, that is, to become comfortable in "its own skin," which appears to be the problem of comparative literature in general and, second, it had to define itself as a very modern and non-problematic area of research in today's humanities. Yet, not everything appears to be so bleak.

Janko Kos provides us with the most comprehensive account of the development of comparative literature in Slovenia thus far. This doyen of the field is a long-standing professor who long occupied the position of the Chair of the Department of Comparative Literature and Literary Theory at the University of Ljubljana. He is the author of (amongst others) "Teorija in praksa slovenske primerjalne književnosti" (1978), "Primerjalna zgodovina slovenske literature" (1987), "Oddelek za primerjalno književnost in literarno teorijo" (1989), "Literarna veda kot znanost, ki se mora odpirati tudi filozofiji" (1991), "Theory and Practice of Comparative Literature" (1994), and *Duhovna zgodovina Slovencev* (1996) (for English translations of the Slovenian titles, see the Works Cited). Within these texts, Kos simultaneously documents and maps out the journey of Slovenian comparative literature via historical sources and contemporary liaisons. The primary movement and recurrent contention is that Slovenian comparative literature (such a label does not mean a particular kind of comparative literary scholarship but rather comparative literature as it is practiced in Slovenia) developed predominantly on the basis of the French comparative literary school, although on more than one occasion it reached beyond this limited view and attempts to embrace a more inclusive perspective of the field.

The French approach in early comparative literature, as defined and developed by Baldensperger, Brunetière, Hazard, van Tieghem, Carr, etc., concentrates on relations (*rapports*) studied in a rather strict historical-positivist manner. In this approach to comparative literature, the utmost significance is attributed to facts, factual evidences, and documents. The only relevant relations are therefore *rapports de fait,* for example, scholarly elements requiring empirical proof. Another essential element used by "orthodox" French comparativists is the actual act and hence, the method of "comparing." In its strictest sense this approach amounts to limiting comparative literary scholarship to the study of binary relations in their "factual" form. It comes as no surprise that the main subject of comparative literature thus becomes the "sources of literary works, reactions and mediators, the fate of the works and the success of the authors, their influence" (Kos 1978, 31; some North American universities have also chosen this model for teaching comparative literature. Hence the prospective student has to choose his/her first [major] and second [minor] language and literature so that the comparative attitude is a priori secured). This kind of positivist scholarship, despite being less of a scholarship than of a literary history, which works its way towards a thorough description of one's own national literature and its influences, exerted a significant influence on comparative literature as such. Yet, when this approach came under critique, two kinds of criticism of French comparative literary scholarship developed. The first was more ideological claiming that it was too nationally oriented and consequently, did not treat "other" literatures equally, whereas the second was methodological stating that comparing per se was already the foundation of the discipline hence there was no need for stressing the comparison. The bottom line of this criticism of the French school was that because of its concentration on factual comparisons it turned into empirical, positivist literary history. Such criticism provoked a strong reaction from the French ranks compelling Marius François Guyard among others to refute those accusations and to proclaim that "comparative literature is not comparing" (1994, 5).

While Slovenian comparative literature has certain traditional ties with the French school, the more modern approach appears to be all-inclusive, in theoretical and in methodological as well as in subject matters. In this vein, modern Slovenian comparative literature reaches out towards the American school. Nevertheless, due to notable French influences, the Slovenian comparative literary discipline remains very European with respect to its general view of the area of research. While North American scholarship today tends more towards issues in cultural studies, the European tradition—very generally viewed in German-, French-, Italian-, Spanish-, Portuguese-language, etc., scholarship including Central and East Europe—appears to hold a philosophical and essentialist point of view in and for the discipline (with regard to this observation, see Peter V. Zima's *Komparatistik*). The division between the two can be said to run along these lines: It is clear that the first and foremost problem for Slovenian comparative literature, as with other national comparative literary disciplines, is to establish its own independent position between the "general" (*littérature générale, Weltliteratur*) and the "national" literature. Here there are two different sides: If one is too inclusive, the other is too exclusive. Where, then, is the place for comparative literature per se?

As a general guideline, Slovenian scholars, most notably Anton Ocvirk, Dušan Pirjevec, and Janko Kos suggested precisely the space between the two, a zone that in effect creates a platform where both "parties" can meet. According to Kos in the 1978 article "Teorija in praksa slovenske primerjalne književnosti," the Slovenian interest in comparative literature has its roots within Romanticism (9). This common source is also cited as the origin of the development of comparative literature within Germany and France (9; citing the Schlegel brothers and Villemain, respectively). Kos attributes the determinate role of Romanticism within Russia's own development of comparative literature, and Drago Bajt in his 1989 article "Primerjalna književnost v vzhodnoevropskih socialističnih deželah" similarly cites (via Mickiewicz) Romanticism as origin of Poland's development of a comparative literature (45). Matija Čop (1797–1835), an enlightened scholar whose main interest lay in European literature and in transferring its models to his native soil is considered as one of the founders of modern Slovenian comparative scholarship. According to Kos, Čop's publications strove to bridge the gap between European and domestic literary production and then, very much in the vein of today's cultural studies' approach, suggested discussing the relationship between literature and the social basis of language (Kos 1978, 9). Recognizing the connections among literary genres as well as the importance of the initial paradigm, he broadened this area of interest to include a European perspective. Čop's life may be perceived as an epitome of the existence of the Slovenian nation in the Austrian monarchy. A librarian and teacher overlooked by many, he worked in Rijeka, Lvov, and Ljubljana as a philologist, historian, theoretician of literature, and literary critic. Very much in the spirit of the time, Čop's interest lay in taking a holistic look at the cultural and literary endeavors of his day. Whilst Kos observes that Čop did not differentiate between comparative and general literature, this does not diminish his value as an early proponent of a comparative concept. Through his analyses Čop became aware of the importance of contemporary forms of poetry, which resulted in the introduction of those to the greatest Slovenian poet, Romantic bard, France Prešern. Čop's broad interest, building a bridge between European literatures and his own, thereby considering the wide in order to understand the "narrow" element, set a paradigm pregnant with consequences for a comparativist stance in Slovenia.

After the demise of Romantic period that had brought about this type of research, it was of no great surprise that this "open" comparative characteristic waned. Realism took the place of Romanticism and consequently introduced a different awareness of the previously mentioned questions. The attention of literary scholars turned inward again into the national realm itself and there was little interest in following events elsewhere. The interest in literary scholarship was revived in 1850 for a short time when Ivan Macun published a treatise on literary theory, the first one written in Slovenian. After this, the first analyses of European influences on Slovenian literature were written by, among others, Fran Levstik and Fran Levec towards the end of the nineteenth century. A very important shift happened around 1900 with a younger generation of literary scholars such as Matija Murko (1861–1952), Ivan Prijatelj (1875–1937), France Kidrič (1880–1950) and Ivan Grafenauer (1880–1964). Coming without exception from the positivist scholarship and working predominantly on Prešern, they volens nolens became more interested again in the larger, in fact, European picture. Because of their position this meant that it was not enough to explain literary works only through the close reading, but rather they had to be situated within a broader perspective. Suddenly, connections with European literatures appeared in the forefront of scholarly investigations and, with them, one could see the influence of foreign authors on Slovenian ones. In response to this foreign influence a riposte was initiated in the formation of artistic and literary periods, directions, and currents. Yet, it is hard to say that conscious efforts of Slovenian scholars were connected to this strategy, even though their scholarship pointed out many comparative questions and problems. Theirs was an approach within the scope of the general (world) literary scholarship more in the vein of literary history. This is particularly true for Ivan Prijatelj and France Kidrič who were particularly interested in Slavonic literatures, specifically their interrelations and mutual horizons. According to Kos, the efforts of these two men could have been in the literary field regarded as the beginning of a particular branch of comparative literature, namely "Slavonic comparative literature" (1994, 11), but this labeling tends to limit the field of scholarly investigation only to Slavonic literatures and their mutual influences. Arguably, it would delineate a correct approach only in the case where there were other specific fields of comparative literature, such as "Germanic" or "Romance." Insofar as comparative literature as a discipline would be limited to particular fields, this would also in all likelihood be its form. However, the essence of comparative literature is precisely to put up no borders, no limitations, hence to allow no confinements. Its proposed or avowed frame of reference is literature as whole with its very disparate contacts and connections. For some, even this might appear to be too bold a statement. At the 14th ICLA congress in Edmonton, Wang Ning (Peking U) had to admit in the discussion ensuing from his presentation that e.g., Chinese postmodern literature does not have too many similarities with European, North- and Latin-American. (see Virk 1994, 71). Since this conclusion may be also valid for other literary examples, one has to exert great caution with effusive generalization and broad inclusiveness.

Therefore, it is clear that the above mentioned fields are all constituent parts of one comparative literary discipline which consequently cannot be split into smaller "groups of interest." Suffice to state that these scholars came only very close to starting the study of comparative literature. The position of comparative literature in Slovenia is branded by this particular predicament. Although there were scholars who wrote and published in this field it was hard to confirm its existence without any academic or scholarly supporting evidence. Its systematic development can be traced back to the development of the Department of Comparative Literature at the University of Ljubljana. Prijatelj and Kidrič instituted the teaching and research of more modern Slovenian literature in the Institute for Slavonic Philology at the newly opened Faculty of Arts at the University of Ljubljana. Kos records that in 1926 Kidrič initiated lectures on the "European frame" (1989, 223) of Slovenian literature, and was thus able to lecture in a distinctive Seminar for Comparative Literature (Comparative Literary History, as it was called then) which has existed as a separate entity from the Institute of Slavonic Philology since 1930. Prijatelj lectured there until 1935 and in 1937 he was replaced by Ocvirk. (Note: The University of Ljubljana in its present form was inaugurated on 31 August 1919 by the king of the then Kingdom of Serbs, Croats, and Slovenians who appointed the first eighteen professors to their positions. On 12 November 1919, the first president of the university, mathematician Josip Plemelj, and the deans were elected. The first lecture took place on 3 December 1919; see Melik).

The true founding of comparative literature as a discipline in Slovenia is attributed to Anton Ocvirk (1907–1980). Today the publication of his book *Theory of Comparative Literary History* in 1936 is considered to mark the birth of the Slovenian comparative literature. In the early 1930s Ocvirk began consolidating the inherited views within the Slovenian literary scholarship with those which he deemed the most influential in the field. In his lectures and publications from as early as 1938, Ocvirk reached beyond previously established European limits and started discussions on the latest issues in literary theory and methodology together with selected chapters from literary history. From the outset Ocvirk did not reject the possibility of such a synthesis; his was the perspective of a maximalist, a synthesist who is satisfied only when the horizon in question appears to be and is also seen as unlimited. In his case this limitlessness meant both, expanding his interests first to Europe then to the entire world as the frame of reference on the other. As far as the methodology was concerned, the most emphasis was placed on "comparing" as such, on (f)actual influences, those which could be empirically proven and positively asserted (see also van Tieghem's *La Littérature comparée,* 1931). Consequently, the foundations of a viable Slovenian comparative literature which he laid, were based on conclusions of the French school. Stemming namely from Hazard's circle—Hazard happened to be Ocvirk's teacher and mentor; he completed his Ph.D. under the supervision of Hazard in 1933—Ocvirk used Hazard's scholarly approach as his own starting point which he eventually left behind in search for a more encompassing standpoint because he felt that such a perspective could not be fully satisfactory. Nonetheless, Ocvirk also added other components to the essential elements considered by the French school in order to equilibrate the emphasis of the nascent discipline in Slovenia. He broadened the questions of influences, responses, and intermediaries with more "classical" themes usually considered in German scholarship where Goethe's *Weltliteratur* collected plaudits. Ocvirk recognized the need for a less literal approach while dealing with literary styles and genres on one hand as well as literary periods and movements on the other. It was obvious to him that broader issues should go hand in hand with strictly literary concepts. The historical positivism and empiricism represented by Ocvirk's point of departure became a determinate factor within the scholarly and speculative procedures of comparative literature. Its importance may be attributed to the question of redress or emphasis. Specifically, Ocvirk was the first scholar in Slovenia to seriously consider the issues of literary theory as the beacon of literary studies. His significance lies in the fact that he successfully combined the theoretical literary issues with literary history and through his work he manifested the interconnection of both thereby laying firm foundations for the *geistesgeschichtliche* approach later assumed by Kos, and today still practiced at the Department. By bringing these very diverse elements together and by putting "timeless" theory and historical interpretation on the same level, he opened a path, a bivium, from where the future development of comparative literature in Slovenia could not escape. In fact, this path proved to be the rewarding and fertile middle ground between the two extremes. On one hand the traditionalists, such as Ocvirk himself, rejected the theory as too philosophical for independent consideration since their main issues usually revolved around the essence of a work of art, cf. the phenomenological approach. On the other hand, "les modernes" wanted to reach out towards the known substance with new tools which included particular elements borrowed from the philosophical methodology.

Through this Ocvirk remained attached to both the meta—or theoretical—level as well as on the basic, factual, historical one. It should be pointed out that Ocvirk never discarded the framework or outlook of the French School, even though he thus attempted to broaden the horizon of contemporary literary studies. While remaining in fundamental accord with the latter, he saw himself only as a scholar who expanded the scope of investigation. As another of Ocvirk's invaluable contributions to Slovenian comparative literature Kos also lists the investigation of "literary-aesthetic, formal-stylistic or psychological-personal facts" (1994, 12). In this light it is evident that he was pitted against any excessive application of theoretical construction or, for that matter, against any philosophically based scientific method. Thus, the crossing of this barrier and the introduction of philosophical methods into Slovenian comparative literature were left for generations to come. Only with the appearance of younger scholars tempted by the ontological as well as the epistemological, cognitive, and ethical issues of literature did the field predominantly develop in the new direction. But it was not until 1945, after the end of World War II, that the Department of Comparative Literature and Literary Theory was finally established at the University of Ljubljana. As already stated, it was not only instrumental but also essential in constituting the base for comparative literary studies in Slovenia, and still is the most vibrant and intense forum where up-to-date issues in comparative literature are discussed.

Another important step towards establishing comparative literature in Slovenia was taken in 1948. Under the auspices of the Slovenian Academy of Sciences and Arts, the Institute for Slovenian Literature and Literary Science was founded to boost the work on literary theory as well as in comparative literature. In a reorganized form the Institute has survived to the present day. It was also in 1948 when Kidrič retired from lecturing at the University. This prompted Ocvirk to switch entirely to the Department of Comparative Literature which in 1950 changed its name to the Department of World Literature and Literary Theory. For more than a decade Ocvirk was the sole professor in the department until 1963 when another important figure of Slovenian comparative literature appeared at the University. However, the man who, at least for a period of time, fundamentally changed the theoretical paradigm by opening new horizons was Dušan Pirjevec (1921–1977), one of the three professors who began teaching in the Department after World War II. Pirjevec, a very spirited lecturer, at first followed Ocvirk's positivistic scholarly paradigm but in the early 1960s opted for a shift in both the methodology and the substance of comparative literature. His major sources can be traced down to the following philosophical platforms. Having been initially influenced by the French, he converted to existentialist philosophy, particularly the strand of Jean-Paul Sartre. Another paramount authority for Pirjevec manifested the philosophical tradition of phenomenology: The theoretical stances of Edmund Husserl and Roman Ingarden, yet, his most viable theoretical source was Martin Heidegger. Pirjevec was mostly interested in pursuing the questions of the ontology and phenomenology of literary work into which he successfully introduced Heidegger's notion of the "ontological difference," which grew to be his starting point in basing and directing his research. Pirjevec was also the first scholar to introduce the concept of hermeneutics and its methodology into literary studies in Slovenia.

Owing to his primarily philosophical orientation, Pirjevec naturally saw literary problems from a different perspective from that of Ocvirk. For him literary works of art functioned as "external" phenomena, epitomes of what could be described as "essence." They were intentional objects, embodiments of exoterically inaccessible ontological components, and in this respect he stood in fundamental accord with Ingarden whose phenomenological theory he supported wholeheartedly. For Pirjevec literary works of art have an independent existence beyond factual reality. Stemming from this line of thought, it seemed most natural that Heidegger's "ontological difference" between the "being" [Sein] and "entity" [Seiende] would also prove to be of the utmost usefulness for Pirjevec's theoretical scheme. He searched for truth which was necessarily hidden and unattainable, particularly attributing such truth to poetry, although even the novel was not a total stranger to it either. Here another influential thinker must be mentioned. In the case of the novel it is György Lukács who established great authority with his *Theory of the Novel* (1916) and this genre became one of the Pirjevec's preferred genres and he published some incisive studies on the subject of the European novel.

In transferring the philosophical and aesthetic discourse into literary scholarship Pirjevec automatically transposed some of its problems. While today's literary science exercises the highest caution when seeking the "truth" of a work of art, Pirjevec's contemporaries were less reluctant to look for absolute and universal terms and concepts. For him there was the ultimate truth of an artwork that we know about but cannot reach and is linked to the "being" [Sein] of the work and in turn asserts its existence. Pirjevec was the only comparativist who concentrated predominantly on the philosophical aspects of literary problems. By resolutely transferring the weight of research towards philosophy and the aesthetic, Pirjevec stirred the moderate comparative literary scholarship. According to Kos, Pirjevec's ideas were too one-sided and therefore too remote from the realm of proper scholarship. Kos went so far as to insist that Pirjevec "disturbed its unity" (1994:14). Pirjevec had taught with Ocvirk for almost a decade when a third colleague Janko Kos joined them in 1970. Soon afterwards, in 1971, the Department changed its name again and became the Department of Comparative Literature and Literary Theory which it still retains today. In the mid-1970s the Department reached its apogee in relation to the quota of its teaching staff: Three professors and two assistants, and remained at this level for many years—in fact, until 1999.

We have observed that Ocvirk started on the premises of French comparative literary scholarship and departed from orthodoxy by adopting a more reconciliatory stance. Pirjevec, on the other hand, moved in a different direction by emphasizing and underlining the philosophical aspects of literary works of art. Kos—born in 1931—sought to mediate the differences between distinct emphases and approaches by moving towards a synthesis within Slovenian comparative literary scholarship. Literature, usually the main object of research, came under the influence of philosophical, aesthetic, cognitive issues which, in the hermeneutic process, relegated it to the periphery. It is safe to say that, in Kos's opinion, opening comparative literature so much to philosophical questions and to methods of examination would remove the balance necessary for a thorough and non-biased scrutiny. Nevertheless, this toned down stance was not formed from the outset. Kos records in 1991 that in the early 1970s he favored the opinion that literary scholarship had to become as scientific as possible, which actually meant that the scholarship had to get rid of the multitude of "foreign influences" and, conversely, to focus strictly on literary methods. This changed around 1980 when, under his guidance, Slovenian comparative literature was set on a course of reconciliation. Kos wanted to remain faithful to Ocvirk's heritage yet he did not want to keep philosophical elements too far at bay. After he became the senior comparativist in Slovenia, Kos realized that pure literary scholarship enabled scholars to achieve only partial results, thus "on the one hand literary scholarship was focused on pure science and on the other had to open itself towards philosophy" (1994, 14). Kos's rather cautious scholarly demeanor nonetheless showed his determination to bridge the previous gap with a moderate and consolidating stance and subsequently to bring a certain degree of unity and synthesis to former extremes as well as to enrich purely scientific literary scholarship. The best examples are provided by his publications where Kos exerts extreme caution in approaching an endless array of issues. Moreover, he scrupulously and in a truly original "poly-historian's" way avoids radical and one-sided and thus also less purely "scientific" conclusions. In his opinion, this development went in the direction of appeasement, where both extremes were brought closer to a mutual understanding and where togetherness of traditional and modern approach to Slovenian comparative literature could be achieved. As a true comparativist, Kos took pains to bring Slovenian comparative literature onto the same level as it occupied in the world. His efforts can be particularly well seen in his seminal book *A Comparative History of Slovenian Literature* (1987). Despite being similar in title to Philippe van Tieghem's *Les Influences étrangères sur la littérature française 1550–1880* (1961), Koren urges in a 1988 article that Kos actually follows an entirely different path (52). Contrary to the Frenchman's "external" (foreign sensu stricto) influences, Kos embraced a perspective unraveling the said influences on Slovenian works of art. Via this distinct vantage point, Kos gives Slovenian literature a more commendable epistemological advantage.

Although remaining on the firm ground of the European tradition in methodology, Kos—as the Chair of the Department of Comparative Literature and Literary Theory at the University of Ljubljana—strove to broaden the horizons of scholarship. He opened the door for new currents such as "reception aesthetics, poststructuralism, deconstruction, theoretical psychoanalysis, new historicism, feminism, etc." (1994, 15). Although these currents in comparative literature were not unknown in Slovenia, their acceptance and usage was somewhat more reluctant than, for example, in North America. This reveals the unease of the comparative literature in Slovenia today which is, in Kos's own words, "still being determined primarily by the bases created . . . in the first decades after World War I" (1994, 15). Ocvirk's model of historical empiricism was subjected to modern philosophical, psychoanalytical, hermeneutic, and other theoretic approaches. In more than one instance, the limits between two extremes (historical-empirical and philosophical-theoretical) become blurred and shifted. Despite this blurring and shifting, Ocvirk remains a highly regarded and frequently cited theorist. Kos, in his professorial role, paid great attention not to favor any of the above-mentioned approaches; according to him, the balance and moderation in views ultimately reflected the true scientist. This attitude helped in specifying the method which intrigued Kos for a good number

of years; moreover, it seems to have become his primary one. Instead of Pirjevec's Heideggerian *seinsgeschichtliche* problems he favored much more classical, *geistesgeschichtliche* questions. In Kos's words it was: "exactly this which
enables scientific methodology in Slovenian comparative literature not to be
placed in exclusive opposition to non-empirical or even explicitly philosophical approaches " (1994, 16). Equal emphasis is put on every aspect of scholarship, be it theory or empirical research, be it "pure" theorizing or factual
analysis, be it in discussions about literary genres or in particular study cases.
Kos's personal scholarly attitude had a tendency towards synthesis, towards
inclusion of both previously separated issues under discussion. For him Ocvirk's
position was not yet good enough and Pirjevec's attitude, because of its purely
philosophical bend, was unacceptable and no longer viable. By virtue of his dissatisfaction with those rather metaphysical problems Kos supported "more rational and also differentiated geistesgeschichtlich studies" (1994, 16). In Kos's
opinion, any particular theoretical position due to its unilateral approach, either
in dealing with history or with theory, cannot be completely useful. The most
appropriate illustration of these statements is Kos's recently published book,
Duhovna zgodovina Slovencev (*An Intellectual History of Slovenians*) (1996),
a tour-de-force of his intellect that crowns his endeavors. Over the years, Kos's
students have applied his approach as can bee seen, for example, in Tomo Virk's
Duhovna zgodovina (*Intellectual History and Literary Scholarship*) (1989).

Under his auspices two main research topics have emerged in Slovenian
comparative literary studies. The first is the methodology of comparative literature which, having shaken off Pirjevec's predominantly Heideggerian direction,
became open to the multiplicity of different approaches and towards "methodological pluralism" (16). The second topic is represented by the increased presence of Slovenian literary themes in comparative literary studies. Slovenian
literature, in addition to the less cosmopolitan approach necessarily embraced
by the Department of Slavics at the University of Ljubljana, is being considered
within a bigger picture encompassing Europe and the world. In light of recent
trends in comparative literary scholarship, new movements and directions
within the discipline are being developed. In the above-mentioned interview Kos
described Slovenian comparative literature today by claiming it stands on a
world level. Having developed methodological pluralism, he did not at the same
time allow it to deviate into empty eclecticism or pure methodological volun-
tarism, although it approached other fields that would not fit into pure science,
like literary criticism or essay writing. By retreating from pure science and by

offering its hand to philosophical and semi-literary methods, comparative literature became "very versatile, open and flexible" (Kos 1991). Still, not all the formal bodies needed for the normal functioning of a discipline were in place by this time. The piece that was missing was a formal organization, which would open up the secluded academic and scholarly circles to an interested public. It was not until 1973, however, that the Slovenian Association for Comparative Literature was founded. This association, gathering both scholars and nonprofessionals around comparative literature, started with quite an ambitious program. Its main task was to spread the notion of comparative literature in addition to providing the scholarly community with a platform for discussions outside the institutional framework. At the same time the Association became an enlivened place for extra-curricular lectures and talks by scholars and authors as well as the successful organizer of symposia. In 1993 the Slovenian Comparative Literature Association took the first steps towards institutional internationalization by becoming a paying member of the International Comparative Literature Association.

Since an association without its own "voice" was not fully operational, a scholarly journal devoted only to comparative literature was established in 1978. It remains in publication to this day. From the outset, though, there was a sense—if not an outright question—concerning the need for such a journal in a nation so small. And yet it was this sensibility—and the corresponding questions—which continue to give the bi-annual *Primerjalna književnost* (*Comparative Literature*) its contemporary resonances. Indeed, it contributed to solidifying the position of comparative literature, its field of study, its methodologies, and its meaning in the Slovenian literary space and society in general. Comparativists are not the only scholars encouraged to contribute to the general discourse—scholars from other fields are more than welcome to publish there, with only one restriction: The topic has to be discussed from a comparative point of view. Currently, the journal effortlessly secures its position among plethora of other scholarly journals in Slovenia and boasts remarkably high ratings throughout its issuance.

Among the important achievements of Slovenian comparative literature one should mention at least two. The first is a series of monographs entitled *Literarni leksikon* (*Encyclopedia of Literature*) and published by the Institute for Slovenian Literature and Literary Science at the Slovenian Academy of Sciences and Arts in Ljubljana. The series began in 1978 and its first volume Ocvirk's *Literary Theory*. With this book he set the tone for the entire series in that its focus is on literary theory. According to Ocvirk's introductory words the edition does not favor any particular aspect but is fully open to any and all methodological approaches and theoretical and philosophical views. Its aim is to construct a totality (which, nota bene, can never be achieved) out of which the comparative literary discipline will appear as a whole. In this vein the scholarly format was set for all ensuing publications. Every author has to cover the concept under discussion ab ovo, elaborate on its basic meaning, and link it to its presence in Slovenian literary realm. Among the published books there are volumes on diverse topics such as positivism in the study of literature (D. Dolinar), cybernetics, communication and information studies (D. Pirjevec), the sociology of literature (D. Rupel), popular literature (M. Hladnik), drama and theatre (A. Inkret; L. Kralj), the essay (D. Poniž), gothicism (K. Bogataj-Gradišnik), and romanticism, postmodernism (both J. Kos). From these topics it is obvious that the emphasis by and large lies in concepts accepted and discussed by the international scholarly community. Slovenian authors and scholars have taken this into account, have successfully elaborated on them, and have linked them to the Slovenian cultural, social, and literary realm. It is worth noting that the on-going work on the series of the *Literarni leksikon* entails throughout the elucidation of the relationship between international and global and "local" (Slovenian) literature and literary theory. The edition has grown considerably and now numbers forty-five volumes, the most recent of which features M. Juvan's monograph on intertextuality.

A great editorial effort of a different kind was to publish the one hundred most important novels figuring in the world's heritage. Each one is accompanied by a lengthy and very studious introduction written by one of the comparativists. Through this editorial achievement Slovenian comparative scholarship established itself as the mediator between the achievements of world literature together with its theory and the readers' (professional or amateur) community. Not only does the development and success of Slovenian scholarship speak for itself, but of related importance are those people who have been associated with the Department. If one browses through the list of those who graduated or at least studied there, it reads almost as a "Who's Who" in Slovenia. An amazingly large number of people who remained active in public life had an "affair" with comparative literature. Among them and this is only a very arbitrary list one can find writers (A. Blatnik, J. Javoršek, M. Pevec, J. Virk), poets (A. Debeljak, M. Dekleva, N. Grafenauer, M. Jesih, J. Menart, B. A. Novak, J. Snoj), playwrights (E. Flisar, I. Svetina), politicians (J. Pučnik,

D. Rupel), literary scholars (M. Dolgan, D. Dolinar, H. Glušič, M. Hladnik, M. Juvan, J. Koruza, D. Moravec, M. Stanovnik, J. Škulj), publicists, editors, translators (A. Berger, M. Bogataj, K. Bogataj-Gradišnik, M. Crnkovič, T. Štoka). This colorful roster of names shows only a very limited number of the professions followed by former students of comparative literature. The department always had a reputation of being the one among those in Arts which provided its students with broad and firm foundations. It has kept this good, not to say elite, standing since.

When considering the situation of Slovenian comparative literature at home and abroad, one comes to the conclusion that there are few things working to the detriment of the scholarship. The most notable of which is the size of Slovenia, modest in both its population and its size. Here the everyday sophism about the relation between quantity and quality cannot even come into effect because "the happy few" partaking in Slovenian comparative literature are simply too few to permit themselves not to be dedicated scholars. Nevertheless, comparative literature in Slovenia boasts a paramount significance for the nation's cultural realm. It is one of the few disciplines connecting characteristically Slovenian enterprise, that is literature and literary events, with mundane happenings. In this respect its role is a commendable one: the only question is its reach. Succinctly put, Slovenian comparative literature lacks the "critical mass" to break out and establish itself internationally. This is not for a lack of thorough and weighty scholarship, but simply because of its collective presentation that always remains precarious. Even if scholars are now and then personally successful, it is still Slovenian comparative literary scholarship in general that lacks holistic validation and acknowledgement by the international community. In this respect the Slovenian comparative literature resembles a "Sleeping Beauty."

Be that as it may, a great portion of the responsibility for such a condition lies with the Slovenian scholars themselves. They have so far neglected the ultimate importance, even the essential necessity, of international contacts and their own presence abroad. For Kos, Slovenian comparative literature has both a special nature and a particular position, incomparable to that of the Slavics department which has its counterparts in most other countries. Slovenian comparative literature, again in Kos's opinion, is not just a "simple imitation of international events," on the contrary, in many instances it is "original" (1996, 70) because of its foundation in Slovenian *Geistesgeschichte*. Kos prefers to shift the focus to the reluctance of the international community to open up its interests in the direction of less populated nations. Nonetheless, not all Slovenian scholars supported such a standpoint and attitude of "hibernation." It is possible to say that Kos modeled his stance after Ocvirk who was rather reluctant to partake in different scholarly activities abroad. Such a self-sufficient attitude can be understood only from the point that for Ocvirk the development of Slovenian comparative literary scholarship was represented by examples taken only from Slovenian literary heritage.

Soon afterwards this task ceased to be so pressing since comparativists successfully established comparative literature as an independent and meaningful discipline within Slovenia. Pirjevec was, in Kos's words, more interested in contacts with philosophers than comparativists, whereas Kos himself "does not believe overly in international scholarly contacts on personal level, or that of exchanges or symposia etc. A true contact . . . is always spiritual—and from a distance" (1996, 70). In his opinion, the establishment and maintenance of those kinds of contacts invite the danger of "watering down" the discipline itself. Another danger to intellectual scholarship contributes "international scholarly tourism" (1996, 70). Since Kos, as Chair of the Department, was the most prolific and consequently, the most prominent comparativist, his influence was such that, with few noteworthy exceptions, many scholars followed his example thus giving the tone and shape to the general attitude of the entire field. Nonetheless, even though all those years with the prevailing inhibited attitude towards the international scholarly community are gone, nothing was irretrievably lost. The period of the last twenty or so years was precisely the time when many efforts should have gone to promoting Slovenian comparative literature, to opening it to the world, and to positioning it on the international map. Today, after the many political and ideological changes in Central, East, and Southern Europe, the institutional internationalization of Slovenian comparative literature is increasingly taking place. One example of this is a recently undertaken move has been the reestablishment of affiliation with the neighboring Department of Comparative Literature at the University of Klagenfurt, Austria, in the summer of 2000. For Slovenia trying to establish itself as a Central European country these contacts now seem to be of particular importance. Comparative literature as a discipline and its parameters with regard to the relative potential in crossing linguistic as well as political borders should in this case only help in establishing its position. By emphasizing the development and maintenance of links between different spaces and locations—culturally and geographically—comparative literary scholarship represents a relevant force in society. Today, the Department of Comparative Literature at Ljubljana boasts the largest number of teaching staff and students since its inception after World War II. There are now five professors (Lado Kralj, Chair, Janez Vrečko, Boris A. Novak, Tomo Virk, and Vid Snoj), three assistants (Matevž Kos, Vanesa Matajc, and Tone Smolej), and a full-time librarian (Vera Troha), all of whom contribute to the strengthening of the discipline not only in Slovenia but in Europe and the world.

WORKS CITED

Bajt, Drago. "Primerjalna književnost v vzhodnoevropskih socialističnih deželah" ("Comparative Literature in Eastern European Socialist Countries") *Primerjalna književnost (Comparative Literature)* 12.2 (1989): 41–51.

Bogataj-Gradišnik, Katarina. *Grozljivi roman (The Tale of Terror) Literarni leksikon* 38 (1991).

Clemenz, Majda. "Znanstveni in strokovni spisi Antona Ocvirka" ("Anton Ocvirk's Scientific and Professional Texts") *Primerjalna književnost (Comparative Literature)* 1.1-2 (1978): 62–68.

Dolinar, Darko. *Pozitivizem v literarni vedi (Positivism in the Study of Literature) Literarni leksikon* 5 (1978).

Dolinar, Darko. "A Chronological Outline: Institutions, Scholars and Selected Publications." *Primerjalna književnost (Comparative Literature)* 17.1 (1994): 19–24.

Hladnik, Miran. *Trivialna literatura (Popular Literature) Literarni leksikon* 21 (1983).

Inkret, Andrej. *Drama in gledališče (Dramatic Literature and Theatre) Literarni leksikon* 29 (1986).

Juvan, Marko. *Intertekstualnost (Intertextuality) Literarni leksikon* 45 (2000).

Koren, Evald. "Primerjalna književnost na Slovenskem. Ob Kosovi Primerjalni zgodovini slovenske literature" ("Comparative Literature in Slovenia: Kos's *Comparative History of Slovenian Literature*") *Primerjalna književnost (Comparative Literature)* 11.2 (1988): 51–54.

Kos, Janko. "Teorija in praksa slovenske primerjalne književnosti" ("The Theory and Practice of Slovenian Comparative Literature") *Primerjalna književnost (Comparative Literature)* 1.1-2 (1978): 30–44.

Kos, Janko. *Romantika (Romanticism) Literarni leksikon* 6 (1980).

Kos, Janko. *Primerjalna zgodovina slovenske literature (A Comparative History of Slovenian Literature)*. Ljubljana: ZIFF Partizanska knjiga, 1987.

Kos, Janko. "Oddelek za primerjalno književnost in literarno teorijo" ("The Department of Comparative Literature and Literary Theory"). *Zbornik Filo-*

zofske fakultete v Ljubljani 1919–1989 (*Collection/Miscellany of The Faculty of Arts, University of Ljubljana 1919–1989*). Ljubljana: Filozofska fakulteta, U of Ljubljana, 1989. 223–25.

Kos, Janko. "Literarna veda kot znanost, ki se mora odpirati tudi filozofiji" ("Literary Scholarship as a Discipline that Must be Open to Philosophy") *Delo* 13 (1991).

Kos, Janko. "Theory and Practice of Comparative Literature." *Primerjalna književnost* (*Comparative Literature*) 17.1 (1994): 3–16.

Kos, Janko. *Postmodernizem* (*Postmodernism*). *Literarni leksikon* 43 (1995).

Kos, Janko. "Nikoli ne bi odšel na samotni otok." ("I Would Never Leave for a Deserted Island"). *Literatura* 55 (1996a): 66–82.

Kos, Janko. *Duhovna zgodovina Slovencev* (*An Intellectual History of Slovenians*). Ljubljana: Slovenska matica, 1996b.

Melik, Vasilij. "Predhodniki in začetki ljubljanske Filozofske fakultete" ("The Forefathers and the Beginnings of the Faculty of Arts at Ljubljana"). *Zbornik Filozofske fakultete v Ljubljani 1919–1989* (*Collection/Miscellany of The Faculty of Arts, University of Ljubljana 1919–1989*). Ljubljana: Filozofska fakulteta, U of Ljubljana, 1989. 9–15.

Ocvirk, Anton. *Teorija primerjalne literarne zgodovine* (*The Theory of Comparative Literary History*). Ljubljana: Znanstveno društvo, 1936.

Ocvirk, Anton. "Pesniška umetnina in literarna teorija" ("A Literary Work of Art and Literary Theory"). *Primerjalna književnost* (*Comparative Literature*) 1.1-2 (1978): 4–21.

Pirjevec, Dušan. "Filozofija in umetnost" ("Philosophy and Art"). *Primerjalna književnost* (*Comparative Literature*) 1.1-2 (1978): 21–30.

Pirjevec, Dušan. *Strukturalna poetika. Kibernetika, Komunikacija, informacija* (*Structural Poetics: Cybernetics, Communication, and Information*). *Literarni leksikon* 12 (1981).

Poniž, Denis. *Esej* (*The Essay*). *Literarni leksikon* 33 (1989).

Strutz, Janez [Johann]. "Casarsa, Mat(t)erada, Vogrče/Rinkenberg ali medregionalnost in literatura: koncept regionalnega težišča celovške komparativistike" ("Casarsa, Mat(t)erada, Vogrče/Rinkenberg or Inter-regionality and Literature: The Concept of Regional Gravitation of Comparative Literature in Klagenfurt"). *Primerjalna književnost* (*Comparative Literature*) 13.1 (1990): 1–14.

Van Tieghem, Paul. *La littérature comparée*. Paris: Armand Colin, 1931.

Virk, Tomo. *Duhovna zgodovina* (*Intellectual History and Literary Scholarship*). *Literarni leksikon* 35 (1989).

Virk, Tomo. "14. kongres ICLA." ("The 14th ICLA Congress"). *Primerjalna književnost* (*Comparative Literature*) 17.2 (1994): 69–73.

Zabel, Igor. "Problem razumevanja literarnih del pri Antonu Ocvirku" ("Problems in the Understanding of Literary Artworks by Anton Ocvirk"). *Primerjalna književnost* (*Comparative Literature*) 13.2 (1987): 1–18.

Zabel, Igor. "Literarna interpretacija v slovenistiki šestdesetih let" ("Literary Interpretation in Slovenian Studies in the Sixties"). *Primerjalna književnost (Comparative Literature)* 13.2 (1990): 25–43.

Zima, Peter V. *The Philosophy of Modern Literary Theory.* London: Athlone, 1999.

Zima, Peter V., and Johann Strutz. *Komparatistik. Eine Einführung in die Vergleichende Literaturwissenschaft.* Tübingen: Franke, 1992.

Comparative Literature in
the United States

Manuela Mourão

In this paper, I present an updated version of my observations with regard to the history and current situation of the discipline of comparative literature in the United States I published in the collected volume, *Comparative Literature Now: Theories and Practice / La Littérature comparée à l'heure actuelle. Théories et réalisations* (see Mourão). The 1993 "Bernheimer Report" of the ACLA: American Comparative Literature Association made very clear that the discipline had evolved to such an extent that an expanded definition of the field has become essential. The report stressed that "the different ways of contextualizing literature in the expanded fields of discourse, culture, ideology, race, and gender are so different from the old models of literary study according to authors, nations, periods, and genres, that the term literature may no longer adequately describe our object of study" (Bernheimer 42). The debate sparked by this and related statements is not quite over yet. Inevitably, there are those who perceive such an evolution as a threat to the fundamental nature of the discipline and who therefore reject the on-going broadening of the scope of literary studies. But the evidence of the work of comparatists in the last few years proves that the broadening of the field has happened irreversibly; moreover, and even if there is still talk of crisis, it has energized the discipline in very significant ways.

If we put the present situation in perspective and look back more or less a half a century, we realize that from the very beginning comparative literature has been in some crisis or other, contending with, among other things, problems of definition and method. As early as 1958, addressing those at the IInd Congress of the International Comparative Literature Association, René

Wellek stresses that "the most serious sign of the precarious state of our study [was] the fact that it [had] not been able to establish a distinct subject matter and a specific methodology" (282). Literariness, aesthetics, and art, Wellek maintains, should be the focus of the discipline. By 1961, Henry Remak's "Comparative Literature: Its Definition and Function" lamented the trouble, controversy, and confusion in the field (18). In 1963, Etienne Etiemble's famous "comparaison n'est pas raison" claimed that the crisis in the discipline had been going on for at least two decades (9) and cited differences in the methodologies of the so-called French and American schools as part of the problem.

Comparatists' frustration with the endless discussions about the problems with the discipline became rather noticeable and by the end of the 1960s and A. Owen Aldridge and Harry Levin, among others, were pleading for the methodological polemics to stop (see Aldridge 110–16; Levin 5–16). But the discussions of the proper object of comparative literature and of its methodological problems showed no signs of abating. In fact, the shift in emphasis in literary studies brought about by the widening of critical debate—particularly noticeable in American scholarship from the 1970s on—actually increased them. In 1981, Henry Remak acknowledged the tendency of the discipline towards interdisciplinarity and urged caution: "It is therefore necessary to work into our volumes new approaches and areas: . . . structuralism, semiotics, reception and communications theory, the sociology of literature (including *Trivialliteratur*), linguistics, rhetoric and the interdisciplinary study of literature . . . while making sure they are used primarily to make the literary phenomenon more understandable, more significant, more authentic" (1981, 221). Four years later, however, he had come to believe that such a tendency was proving to be one of the causes of the problem with comparative literature and writes that "As the interdisciplinary ambitions of supposedly 'literary' scholars have mushroomed (linguistics, structuralism, history of ideas, philosophy, political and economic ideology, communication theory, semiotics), their literary sense and their knowledge of foreign languages and cultures have declined. Comparative literature is not well served in and through such a subservient arrangement" (1985, 10).

As Remak expressed them, the perceived dangers to the discipline had become quite different from those of twenty years before. Standards remained an issue, but the crux of the matter, it was rapidly becoming apparent, was no less than survival itself. Decades of polemics and insecurity had translated, by the 1980s, into open questioning of the future of comparatism at the institutional level. The symptoms of this were unmistakable then and became consistently more substantial. For example, as I started graduate work at the University of Illinois in Urbana in 1986, there were attempts at merging the Comparative Literature Program with different language departments. Then, students and faculty succeeded in preventing what would have amounted to a dissolution of the program; still, by the summer of 1994 the program was scheduled to be terminated. Fortunately, a change in deanship saved it, but the prospect of dissolution still looms on the horizon of this and other American programs and there are many examples of similar situations with a less fortunate outcome at American universities. Thus, mere survival has been very much on the mind of American comparatists. For some of the scholars of earlier generations this survival continues to be equated with the enforcement of standards, a clear object, and a set of methodologies. Etiemble, his anti-chauvinistic understanding of comparative literature notwithstanding, still discussed methodology in his 1988 book on the future of the discipline:

> Une fois fix, le sens des mots de la tribu comparatiste, il importerait d'étudier systématiquement les diverses méthodes dont il est loisible au comparatiste, au généraliste, de s'armer pour exercer correctement son dificil métier" (178). Like the new generation of comparatists, he sees comparative literature perishing unless it refuses to be Eurocentrist—but unlike them, he sees it perishing unless it upholds its traditional methods: "Nul avenir . . . pour la littérature générale et comparée, si elle ne s'applique pas . . . toutes les littératures qui ont vécu ou qui survive sur la planète; nul avenir non plus si, acceptant toutes ces littératures, écrites et orales, elle refuse de les scruter selon les méthodes que je viens de suggérer. (182).

Arguing for the keeping to traditional approaches continues to be the advice of more than one prominent scholar of the discipline. For example, Michael Riffaterre, at the 1993 convention of the Modern Language Association of America voices his concern with, among other things, what he perceives as the multiculturalist comparatists' downplaying of literature and its literariness (as he sees it, the true object of comparative literature) in favor of non-literary texts. And he is very skeptical of the efforts to expand the field by teaching literature in translation in undergraduate classes, despite the obvious limitations this imposes (see Riffaterre). Thus, at the closing of 1993, there was, as always, a sense of crisis in comparative literature. Unlike previous ones, however, this crisis is no longer just a disagreement about methodologies or schools. The gradual disappearance of comparative literature programs owing to diminishing institutional support but also to a scarcity of students, and the lack of positions available to comparatists—this is considerably more dramatic than in English or other foreign languages—makes the debates more poignant and relevant.

The question of what had to be done in order to stop this downhill trend was largely addressed via commentary on the 1993 ACLA report by Charles Bernheimer. Attacked as it was for having remained prescriptive (although in my opinion it really was far less so than its predecessors) and for a lingering stress on "standards," the report was also praised for offering significant insights. It recognized, on the one hand, that its function should be to describe the current critical practices in the field, rather than to continue the polemics about what these ought to be; on the other hand, it pointed out that those practices did show the broadening of the scope of literary studies: More and more scholars were approaching literature as one discursive practice among many others and did not necessarily view aesthetic value as the primary criteria for their interest in a text. If, as we saw, several comparatists have repeatedly worried about the boundaries of the field, the fact of the matter was that by 1993 comparative literature as a discipline had already been significantly transformed by a broadening of its scope. The general sense of the coming to an end of a practice of comparatism exclusively modeled on the traditional approaches was poignantly obvious in *Building a Profession: Autobiographical Perspectives on the History of Comparative Literature in the United States* (Ed. Gossman and Spariosu). Published in 1994, shortly after the "Bernheimer Report," *Building a Profession* offered a retrospective of the early days of comparative literature in the United States. Through autobiographical sketches by some of its most influential comparatists, it mapps the beginning and the development of the discipline in the United States. As they describe well over a half a century of American comparatism, these senior comparatists also reflect on their vision of the future of the discipline. Some show strong concern about the changes; others acknowledge the need to follow the new directions being carved out for literary studies. All, however, and regardless of their position on this matter, unequivocally express a sense that a moment in the history of the discipline had come to a close.

Marjorie Perloff, in her essay "On Wanting to be a Comparatist," discusses the changes comparative literature started undergoing in the mid-1980s and notes that "in the abstract, the demand for the 'opening of the field' made perfect sense" (133) but that what "seemed at first like a simple and much needed opening of the canon . . . effectively spelled the end of Comparative Literature as René Wellek and his colleagues had conceived it [although that] was not immediately clear to those who taught the subject" (134). Thomas G. Rosenmeyer's essay "Am I a Comparatist?," reveals his distance from the practices of today's younger comparatists whose tendency "to philosophize about and generalize from texts, or to use the texts to vindicate pre-established theories, has made the loose and exhaustive study of the primary texts unfashionable" (62). But he acknowledges—even if he is not pleased—that comparative literature had become a "laboratory for exploration at the margins" (62). This is also acknowledged, and much more positively, by Thomas M. Greene. In his "Versions of a Discipline" he states that "the growth of cultural studies, the growth of political methodologies, the hegemony of theory, are disturbing developments only if they betoken an indifference to the marvel of the text" (48). Greene's sense of the future of comparative literature might well have proved accurate. According to him, the discipline crosses linguistic and cultural boundaries; it presupposes the mutual reinforcement of theory and interpretation; it transgresses disciplinary barriers without sacrificing the autonomy of the poetic text; it gestures toward the still inchoate field of historical semiotics (48). Two other scholars, Anna Balakian and Gerald Gillespie, offered the most openly critical views of the process of change comparative literature was then already undertaking. Gillespie was particularly upset at the attacks made by multiculturalists who claim that comparative literature is Eurocentric and elitist: "The consequences of the altered cultural climate have been devastating for CL," he writes. Furthermore, he is angry at practitioners who, in his words, "learned to tolerate the most banal assaults on one of the most complex civilizations imaginable (Europe and its extensions)" (171). He calls our attention to the wide acceptance of what he considers another potentially Eurocentric practice: The application of Western critical theories to the analysis of non-Western literatures and cultures and claims that the redefinition of the discipline was, in some institutions, taking place "without the agreement of the experts involved" (172). Anna Balakian's reservations are, for example: "We have arrived on dangerous ground. We are threatened . . . with a host of scholars crossing over without union cards to participate through our discipline in the newer concepts of interpretation of literature and the study of socio-cultural texts within the context of comparative relationships. . . . Innovations are what keeps a discipline vigorous and dynamic but each generation cannot reinvent Comparative Literature from scratch" (84). In particular, she worries that comparative literature might be "headed towards a struggle with political correctness" (87), and she fears that the current rejection of Eurocentrism might damage comparative literature's study of relations between literatures if one of them is a literature of a "so-called developing country" (85).

By contrast, other senior comparatists such as Mary Louise Pratt believe that the survival of the field entails openness and the tearing apart of boundaries. When she addresses this issue at the 1993 MLA meeting, she urges comparatists to end "fencing" and "vigilance." Unafraid of mixtures, unafraid even of the inevitable disorder that, she admits, must temporarily ensue, her belief that "literature does not lose its power and expressive force because of other things being brought into the picture" was most encouraging for those of us who believed, and continue to believe, that the best possible course for comparative literature is to refrain from censoring the on-going redefinition of its goals and methods in light of current multiculturalist, interdisciplinary practices. The concerns these scholars voice, and others like them share, continued to be echoed in a number of articles and books published since the "Bernheimer Report." The essays in *Comparative Literature in the Age of Multiculturalism* (Ed. Bernheimer), for example, offer an ideal overview of the immediate shape of the debate. In his essay "Must We Apologize?" Peter Brooks criticizes the report for what he saw as a passive acceptance of the devaluation: "Far from believing with the ACLA report that 'the term "literature" may no longer adequately describe our object of study,' I would hence urge that literature must very much remain our focus, while by no means restricting its dialogic interaction with other discourses and its various contexts" (104). In turn, Jonathan Culler, in "Comparative Literature at Last" points out that treating literature as a discourse among others seems an effective and commendable strategy . . . [but] the turn from literature to other cultural productions will not help to differentiate or define comparative literature. . . . If it resists the rush into cultural studies, comparative literature will find itself with a new identity, as the site of literary study in its broadest dimensions" (117–19). In "Between Elitism and Populism: Whither Comparative Literature," Elizabeth Fox-Genovese addresses the charge of elitism carefully against traditional comparative literature studies and concludes that "Comparative Literature is and should remain an intellectually elitist enterprise, on the proud conviction that intellectual elitism may not be taken as a proxy for social elitism" (142). Marjorie Perloff, in "Literature in the Expanded Field" asks "what is the role of a discipline that trains people for a jobless future?" and emphasizes that "if you don't yet have a position, you won't get one by entering the so-called expanded field of the discipline" (178).

In all, these and other essays in *Comparative Literature in the Age of Multiculturalism* reflect a general understanding of the fact that literature is at the center of our field. The disagreement—and the anxiety—is not so much about that; rather, it is about whether the expansion of the field of comparative literature would eventually lead to a marginalization of literature, and about how to achieve this "pluralized and expanded contextualization of literary study" (Bernheimer 11). But if there is something comparatists are used to doing, it is precisely to scrutinize their discipline. A steady stream of publications has continued to engage in this dialogue. Gathered in the 1996 volume *Multicomparative Theory, Definitions, Realities* (Ed. Nemoianu), Gerald Gillespie's "The Internationalization of Comparative Literature in the Second Half of the Twentieth Century," Virgil Nemoianu's "Globalism, Multiculturalism, and Comparative Literature," and Anne Paolucci's "National Literatures in a Comparative Spectrum: Theory Practice and the Marketplace," among others, continued to explore possible although more conservative paths for the discipline. Also published in 1996, *The Search for a New Alphabet: Literary Studies in a Changing World* (Ed. Hendrix et al.) features short essays from comparatists the world over. Among them, Hans Bertens's "From Over-Confidence to Clear and Present Danger," Yves Chevrel's "On the Need for New Comparative Literature Handbooks," Amiya Dev's "Globalization and Literary Value," Earl Miner's "Canons and Comparatists," Mihály Szegedy-Maszák's "Universalism and Cultural Relativism," and Wang Ning's "Cultural Relativism and the Future of Comparative Literature: An Oriental Perspective," offer a more international view of the issues under discussion. Their positions are representative of the range of the debate: Bertens, for example, warns that "where comparatism assumes an underlying common identity for all human beings, multiculturalism assumes irreconcilable differences, an assumption that puts an awkward spoke in the comparatist wheel" (10). In turn, Dev stresses the distinction between internationalism and globalization: "Cultures," he maintains, "are resilient," and "rather than cultures going global, only their surfaces will do so—the result will be a limited sameness everywhere" (66). He urges comparatists to subvert the hegemony of globalization and to remain committed to "holding up cultural identities" (66). Wang Ning focuses more centrally on the literature versus cultural studies issue and concludes that "it is unnecessary to be afraid of the strong impact of cultural studies" (294).

This overview, while far from exhaustive, clearly indicates that sustained attention to the shaping of comparative literature remains at the heart of comparatists' endeavors (about this, see also, e.g., Foley; Franci; Lorant and Bessière; Tötösy). But alongside work debating what the discipline should be, comparative work has steadily continued. Much of it shows not only a willingness to accept the expanded definition of the field announced in the Bernheimer report, but also that such changes have neither entailed a lowering of standards nor a marginalization of literature. *Borderwork: Feminist Engagements with Comparative Literature* (Ed. Higonnet), published in 1994, and *Cultural Interactions in the Romantic Age: Critical Essays in Comparative Literature* (Ed. Maertz), published in 1998, are wonderful examples of the renewed energy of comparative work that represents the ideological and multicultural concerns of the present intellectual climate. These volumes demonstrate unequivocally that comparative literature can, more easily than national literatures, commit itself to the kind of broad understanding of literary studies entailed by contemporary critical thinking. In their cross-cultural, interdisciplinary approaches, the essays in these works show that branching out into cultural studies does offer relevant points of departure for the comparative analysis of literature and culture without posing a threat to more traditional, exclusively textual studies.

While institutionally the fate of comparative literature remains uncertain, the practice of comparatism, the evidence suggests, has been systematically revitalized since the Bernheimer report. Moreover, scholars specifically concerned with the institutional future of comparative literature have begun to offer practical strategies to address the problem. Steven Tötösy's *Comparative Literature: Theory, Method, Application*, for example, proposes an approach to the discipline with a view to make its relevance apparent to those outside the academy and, consequently, to facilitate a strengthening of its institutional standing. Tötösy's answer to "the question of the social relevance and legitimization of the study of literature and culture" (262) is a contextual approach which borrows from the social sciences, and that, as his analyses of problems and texts seek to demonstrate, can contribute in no small measure to a revitalization of the study of literature and to an ease of the "current marginalization of the humanities" (19; see also Tötösy's proposal for a "comparative cultural studies" in this volume). Another new model of comparative literature is advanced by Ed Ahearn and Arnold Weinstein in "The Function of Criticism at the Present Time: The Promise of Comparative Literature." This "engaged" model, in place at the authors' home institution, Brown University, has resulted in a thriving department with strong undergraduate and graduate programs (see 80–81). As the authors describe it, the program is at once culture specific and cross-cultural (80), interdisciplinary and engaged with cultural studies (81–82). "Most strikingly," they explain, the program has "developed and pursued an interest in secondary education which is unique for comparative literature programs in the country but which demonstrates the particular pertinence of the comparatist stance for today's educational needs" (82). While the first model (Tötösy) calls for a more radical re-thinking of the practice of comparative literature and the second for a wider dissemination of "the comparative principles that undergird the discipline" (Ahearn and Weinstein 85), both require an imaginative and flexible understanding of the nature of, and the place for, comparatist work that leaves no room for intellectual rigidity. Indeed, the institutional future of the discipline may well depend on our willingness to overcome such rigidity. It may also, as Tobin Siebers suggests, depend on our efforts to overcome skepticism (203). But while there are still very few positions available for comparatists, and while there are still problems with the discipline at the institutional level, the vitality of the current scholarship in the field is undeniable, as is the commitment of comparatists to doing.

WORKS CITED

Ahearn, Ed, and Arnold Weinstein. "The Function of Criticism at the Present Time: The Promise of Comparative Literature." *Comparative Literature in the Age of Multiculturalism*. Ed. Charles Bernheimer. Baltimore: The Johns Hopkins UP, 1995. 77–85.

Aldridge, A. Owen. "The Comparative Literature Syndrome." *Modern Language Journal* 53 (1969): 110–16.

Balakian, Anna. "How and Why I Became a Comparatist." *Building a Profession: Autobiographical Perspectives on the History of Comparative Literature in the United States*. Ed. Lionel Gossmann and Mihai I. Spariosu. New York: State U of New York P, 1994. 75–87.

Bernheimer, Charles. "The Bernheimer Report, 1993: Comparative Literature at the Turn of the Century." *Comparative Literature in the Age of Multiculturalism*. Ed. Charles Bernheimer. Baltimore: The Johns Hopkins UP, 1995. 39–48.

Bernheimer, Charles, ed. *Comparative Literature in the Age of Multiculturalism*. Baltimore: The Johns Hopkins UP, 1995.

Bertens, Hans. "From Over Confidence to Clear and Present Danger." *The Search For a New Alphabet: Literay Studies in a Changing World*. Ed. Harald Hendrix, Joost Kloek, Sophie Levie, and Will van Peer. Amsterdam: John Benjamins, 1996. 7–12.

Brooks, Peter. "Must We Apologize?" *Comparative Literature in the Age of Multiculturalism.* Ed. Charles Bernheimer. Baltimore: The Johns Hopkins UP, 1995. 97–106.

Chevrel, Yves. "On the Need for New Comparative Literature Handbooks." *The Search For a New Alphabet: Literary Studies in a Changing World.* Ed. Harald Hendrix, Joost Kloek, Sophie Levie, and Will van Peer. Amsterdam: John Benjamins, 1996. 53–56.

Culler, Jonathan. "Comparative Literature at Last." *Comparative Literature in the Age of Multiculturalism.* Ed. Charles Bernheimer. Baltimore: The Johns Hopkins UP, 1995. 117–21.

Dev, Amiya. "Globalization and Literary Value." *The Search For a New Alphabet: Literay Studies in a Changing World.* Ed. Harald Hendrix, Joost Kloek, Sophie Levie, and Will van Peer. Amsterdam: John Benjamins, 1996. 62–66.

Etiemble, René. *Ouverture(s) sur un comparatisme planétaire.* Paris: Christian Bourgois, 1988.

Franci, Giovanna, ed. *Remapping the Boundaries: A New Perspective in Comparative Studies.* Bologna: CLUEB, 1997.

Foley, John Miles, ed. *Teaching Oral Traditions.* New York: Modern Language Association of America, 1998.

Fox-Genovese, Elizabeth. "Between Elitism and Populism: Whither Comparative Literature." *Comparative Literature in the Age of Multiculturalism.* Ed. Charles Bernheimer. Baltimore: The Johns Hopkins UP, 1995. 134–42.

Gillespie, Gerald. "Home Truths and Institutional Falsehoods." *Building a Profession: Autobiographical Perspectives on the History of Comparative Literature in the United States.* Ed. Lionel Gossmann and Mihai I. Spariosu. New York: State U of New York P, 1994. 159–75.

Gillespie, Gerald. "The Internationalization of Comparative Literature in the Second Half of the Twentieth Century." *Multicomparative Theory, Definitions, Realities.* Ed. Virgil Nemoianu. Whitestone: Council of National Literatures World Report, 1996. 13–42.

Gossman, Lionel, and Mihai I. Spariosu, eds. *Building a Profession: Autobiographical Perspectives on the History of Comparative Literature in the United States.* New York: State U of New York P, 1994.

Greene, Thomas M. "Versions of a Discipline." *Building a Profession: Autobiographical Perspectives on the History of Comparative Literature in the United States.* Ed. Lionel Gossmann and Mihai I. Spariosu. New York: State U of New York P, 1994. 37–48.

Hendrix, Harald, Joost Kloek, Sophie Levie, and Will van Peer, eds. *The Search For a New Alphabet: Literay Studies in a Changing World.* Amsterdam: John Benjamins, 1996.

Higonnet, Margaret R., ed. *Borderwork: Feminist Engagements with Comparative Literature*. Ithaca: Cornell UP, 1994.

Levin, Harry. "Comparing the Literature." *Yearbook of Comparative and General Literature* 17 (1968): 5–16.

Lorant, André, and Jean Bessière, eds. *Littérature comparée. Théorie et pratique*. Paris: Honoré Champion, 1999.

Maertz, Gregory, ed. *Cultural Interactions in the Romantic Age: Critical Essays in Comparative Literature*. New York: State U of New York P, 1998.

Miner, Earl. "Canons and Comparatists." *The Search For a New Alphabet: Literary Studies in a Changing World*. Ed. Harald Hendrix, Joost Kloek, Sophie Levie, and Will van Peer. Amsterdam: John Benjamins, 1996. 151–55.

Mourão, Manuela. "Comparative Literature Past and Present." *Comparative Literature Now: Theories and Practice / La Littérature comparée à l'heure actuelle. Théories et réalisations*. Ed. Steven Tötösy de Zepetnek, Milan V. Dimić, and Irene Sywenky. Paris: Honoré Champion, 1999. 165–72.

Nemoianu, Virgil. "Globalism, Multiculturalism, and Comparative Literature." *Multicomparative Theory, Definitions, Realities*. Ed. Virgil Nemoianu. Whitestone: Council of National Literatures World Report, 1996. 43–73.

Nemoianu, Virgil, ed. *Multicomparative Theory, Definitions, Realities*. Whitestone: Council of National Literatures World Report, 1996.

Paolucci, Anne. "National Literatures in a Comparative Spectrum: Theory, Practice, and the Marketplace." *Multicomparative Theory, Definitions, Realities*. Ed. Virgil Nemoianu. Whitestone: Council of National Literatures World Report, 1996. 83–102.

Perloff, Marjorie. "On Wanting to be a Comparatist." *Building a Profession: Autobiographical Perspectives on the History of Comparative Literature in the United States*. Ed. Lionel Gossmann and Mihai I. Spariosu. New York: State U of New York P, 1994. 125–40.

Perloff, Marjorie. "Literature in the Expanded Field." *Comparative Literature in the Age of Multiculturalism*. Ed. Charles Bernheimer. Baltimore: The Johns Hopkins UP, 1995. 175–86.

Pratt, Mary Louise. "Comparative Literature and Global Citizenship." *Comparative Literature in the Age of Multiculturalism*. Ed. Charles Bernheimer. Baltimore: The Johns Hopkins UP, 1995. 58–65.

Remak, Henry H.H. "Comparative Literature: Its Definition and Function." *Comparative Literature: Method and Perspective*. Ed. Newton P. Stallknecht and Horst Frenz. Edwardsville: Southern Illinois UP, 1961.1–57.

Remak, Henry H.H. "Comparative History of Literatures in European Languages: The Bellagio Report." *Neohelicon: Acta Comparationis Litterarum Universarum* 8 (1981): 119–228.

Remak, Henry H.H. "The Situation of Comparative literature in the Universities." *Colloquium Helveticum* 1 (1985): 7–14.

Riffaterre, Michael. "On the Complementarity of Comparative Literature and Cultural Studies." *Comparative Literature in the Age of Multiculturalism*. Ed. Charles Bernheimer. Baltimore: The Johns Hopkins UP, 1995. 66–73.

Rosenmeyer, Thomas. "Am I a Comparatist?" *Building a Profession: Autobiographical Perspectives on the History of Comparative Literature in the United States*. Ed. Lionel Gossmann and Mihai I. Spariosu. New York: State U of New York P, 1994. 49–62.

Siebers, Tobin. "Sincerely Yours." *Comparative Literature in the Age of Multiculturalism*. Ed. Charles Bernheimer. Baltimore: The Johns Hopkins UP, 1995. 195–203.

Szegedy-Maszák, Mihály. "Universalism and Cultural Relativism." *The Search For a New Alphabet: Literay Studies in a Changing World*. Ed. Harald Hendrix, Joost Kloek, Sophie Levie, and Will van Peer. Amsterdam: John Benjamins, 1996. 239–44.

Tötösy de Zepetnek, Steven. *Comparative Literature: Theory, Method, Application*. Amsterdam-Atlanta, GA: Rodopi, 1998.

Tötösy de Zepetnek, Steven. "From Comparative Literature Today Toward Comparative Cultural Studies." *Comparative Literature and Comparative Cultural Studies*. Ed. Steven Tötösy de Zepetnek. West Lafayette: Purdue UP, 2002. 235–67.

Wang Ning. "Cultural Relativism and the Future of Comparative Literature: an Oriental Perspective." *The Search For a New Alphabet: Literary Studies in a Changing World*. Ed. Harald Hendrix, Joost Kloek, Sophie Levie, and Will van Peer. Amsterdam: John Benjamins, 1996. 290–95.

Wellek, René. "The Crisis in Comparative Literature." *Concepts of Criticism*. Ed. Stephen G. Nichols, Jr. New Haven: Yale UP, 1963. 282–95.

Comparative Literature and Cultural Identity

Jola Škulj

The problem of cultural identity involves the question of the self and of culture. In other words, this means reflecting on the essence of culture itself and the implication that there is a reasonable motive of self-questioning. In turn, we may also ask whether the self-questioning is motivated in the problematic, uncertain, or insufficiently reflected idea of our selves or in a desire to analytically reaffirm the fragility of culture. From the viewpoint of literary studies, the question of cultural identity is primarily with reference to literary identity in the community we are living in. Here, Bakhtin's argumentation that "Literature is an inseparable part of the totality of culture and cannot be studied outside the total cultural context. It cannot be severed from the rest of culture and related directly (by-passing culture) to socio-economic or other factors. These factors influence culture as a whole and only through it and in conjunction with it do they affect literature. The literary process is a part of the cultural process and cannot be torn away from it" (Bakhtin 1986, 140) is most relevant for my discussion. However, if the very existence of literature can be defined in terms of structuralism (and, in another context, by Heidegger) as a re-examination of the possibilities of language itself (and through it refracted historical consciousness), then the problem of literary identity would logically be reduced to the natural environment of native language, that is, to one's national culture. Such a view cannot, of course, be a relevant interpretation of literary identity at the end of our century because it reveals a concept of identity implying characteristics unacceptably finite and self-referential. The identification of literary identity with national culture is regression to the idea of identity conceived in the nineteenth century. The literature of Romanticism and Post-Romanticism was acceptable as a factor confirming national entities and as a genuine representation of the cultural self. This understanding of identity was a result of the romantic interpretation of the self as the inner reality of a given subject. It revealed in itself the concept of the subject as an absolute and autonomous being and denied any decisive or obligatory references outside itself. It denied transcendence outside oneself and identified itself only with its immanent reality or with its own immanent validity. The subject of Romanticism defined itself by its own subjectivity, interpreted as being self-aware, self-sufficient, and self-referential. In Romanticism, being was recognised to be authentic while comprehensible only as interior consciousness.

The insufficiency of such a reductionist view on culture and literature, for example, the "soul of nation" (Herder) was, in fact, already conceptualised by Goethe when he constructed the concept of world literature. But any gesture of openness in the *geistesgeschichtliche* frame of Romanticism was only understood as self-affirmation of the romantic absolute and autonomous subject. Any notion of an understanding of openness as a feature of transgressing or of the self-revaluation of the romantic self can be found only in the phenomenon of romantic irony. Thus, the problematic of cultural identity undoubtedly refers us to a question of cross-cultural interactions. Considered this way, it is pre-eminently a concept belonging to the field of comparative literature. Literary works, genres, trends, and periods of artistic orientation in a given nation, as manifested through history, cannot exist as isolated events of the closed national existence of cultural history and cannot be understood without contacts with literary phenomena of other national cultures. No cultural identity can be identified or analysed only on its national ground. Any national culture was given form on the borders of other influential cultures. For example, *The Freising Manuscript* (a Slovenian text from the end of the eighth or the beginning of the ninth century) bears evidence, among others, of Latin and Old High German traces. Clearly, literature cannot be but an intercultural historical phenomenon of mutual artistic and other influences from several cultures, of mutual interactions of artistic expression produced in different cultural circumstances, and thus of mutual reception of Otherness. "Otherness" is, irrevocably, cultural reality. The Other does not necessarily endanger its selfness or its principles of identity: "The reality principle coincides with the principle of otherness" (de Man 103). According to this notion, the validity of cultural identity cannot be an equivalent to the measure of originality of an inherent national subjectivity in it.

Formations of cultural identity pass through their own "deconstruction" and permanent multiplication of cultural relations. Consequently, the interweaving of cultural and literary influences does not result in loss of identity. Rather, it constructs a multiple plane where yet inactivated possibilities interact and merge. In Europe, the convergence of different cultures has been a permanent factor of their existence. On the other hand, the role of marginal phenomena and traces of contacts with minor cultures were not insignificant in European cultural and literary history. Concepts of identity cannot mean simply "to be something" or to be "identical with oneself," or, in other words, identity should not be seen as "the first way of being" (Descombes 35, 37). Rather, the principle of identity coincides with the principle of otherness or— to use Bakhtin's terminology with the principle of dialogism: "The self is the gift of the other" (qtd. in Kershner x). As a historical concept, cultural identity implies an introduction of difference into itself, i.e., an element of reciprocity into its own being (Descombes 38). Cultural identity—as an element of the historical process cannot remain of the same nature and is never a perpetuation of itself; it cannot be preserved in a fixed, unchanged form; it inherits the "divine privilege" to introduce its authentic construct of alterity and innovative nature into itself through its continuous contact with the Other and Otherness. According to this, cultural identity as expressed in literature is reestablished through constant dialogue with other cultures and literatures. This dialogic nature pre-determines that the study of cultural identity and/in literature is best performed in and with the tools of the discipline of comparative literature.

Within comparative literature, I propose that a most appropriate methodology for the study of cultural identity be provided by the work of Bakhtin. More precisely, I mean Bakhtin where he goes beyond the metaphysical orientation of the earlier formalists and where he developed his ideas under the specific circumstances of prescribed ideological monism and totalitarianism. Both contexts, the formalist and the totalitarian, evoked specific philosophical and theoretical responses by Bakhtin and his followers and served the unmasking of fundamental flaws in the organization of Western rationality. Bakhtin's views of dialogism, in fact, extricate European rationality from its predicaments in that they mediate toward an ideology of otherness. The event of Bakhtinian ideology of otherness as overcoming ideological monologism was due to the historical changes in the self-consciousness of European thought after the initial manifestations of Modernism.

A critical reading of Bakhtin's work on the background of contemporary poststructuralist premises may prove influential in literary theory. But even more important are Bakhtin's specific terminological solutions that have brought to light some ethical and ideological dimensions of art. In the eighties, after a decade of extremely good acceptance of Bakhtin's issues in theoretical debates, Paul de Man intervened with scepticism: "why the notion [could] be so enthusiastically received by theoreticians of very diverse persuasion and made to appear as a valid way out of many of the quandaries that have plagued us for so long" (1983, 100). However, de Man misread in Bakhtin the inherent quality of dialogism, namely conflict and contradiction, i.e., the quality implying the inscribed space for Otherness as something different and opposing. In his *Marxism and Philosophy of Language*—published in 1929 under the name of Voloshinov—Bakhtin presented an ontological frame to his ideas and dialogism is disclosed as a notion indicating awareness of competing views on the same thing. It implies the presence of relativized, de-privileged truth of something or, in other words, it implies the de(con)struction of the authoritative or absolute word about it. This concept, established in the philosophy of concreteness, poses anew the problem of truth and its certainty. It presupposes a non-finite character of truth, a multiplicity of focuses on it, a notion of its inexhaustiveness, i.e., an immense, boundless "wealth of its being."

If a dialogic word is an antonym to authoritative discourse (*avtoritetnoe slovo*), and dialogism means decentralizing or a centrifugal force in the conception of the subject or of truth (as evident in marginal comic genres), then these two Bakhtinian concepts have similar value as Heideggerian philosophy in that it has brought elaborated concepts for the de(con)struction of the history of ontology. This Heideggerian call for de-(con)struction—the German *Destruktion* and not *Zerstörung*—which later echoed in American poststructuralist deconstructive hermeneutics, means that the "task of destroying is an effort at a creative preserving of history" (Leitch 66). Further, there are corresponding implications in the notion of dialogue and in the Heideggerian thought on "defamiliarization and unconcealment of truth" (Leitch 1983, 70). Also, "a word, discourse, language or culture undergoes dialogization"' (Holquist 1981, 427). This is argued in comments on Bakhtin by Michael Holquist, who gave a most accurate translation to the North American reading public as well as an extensive survey on the problems of Bakhtin's dialogism (1990).

Some other notions from Bakhtin's taxonomy are important for the discussion of cultural identity: "Alien" or "other"—as in someone else's word (*cuzoj, cuzoje slovo*), "otherness" (*cuzdost*) "re-accentuation," a quality of incompleteness or absence of capability of definitive finalisation (*nezaversennost'*) or in the appropriate English translation (as used by Holquist) "inconclusiveness" or "openendedness." There are also some seminal attributes like "re-accentuated," "dialogized," "refracted," all of them assuring the presence of at least two different words or views on the given object. This implies Bakhtin's fundamental assertion that "truth cannot triumph or conquer" (Bakhtin 1986, 141). In his view, the basis for the one and only truth concerning cultural identity is "thwarted," if not eliminated, while the problem of cultural identity is to be viewed through the principle of Otherness. The identity of culture is multiform in its being and its actual individuality functions as cultural dialogism. Thus, through dialogism the heterological nature of literary or cultural phenomena in the tradition of a given national history can be explored with fairly consequent argumentation. Cultural identity is complexly structured and it represents a non-finite wholeness. The identity of any national literature is undoubtedly multiform through its historical stages.

In Bakhtinian thought, motivated by the search for a concrete philosophy, the quest for the real self shows a reverted Cartesian position. In his *Problems of Dostoevsky's Poetics,* Bakhtin argues that the self is a stream of statements and that so long as man lives, he is "never coincident with himself" (Bakhtin 1973, 48). The self cannot serve as the subjectum to all existing things any longer, or in other words, it has lost its own Cartesian substantiality: "I realise myself initially through others," Bakhtin argues, continuing, "From them I receive words, forms, and tonalities for the formation of my initial idea of myself" (1986, 138). Actually, he points to the insufficiency of the Cartesian subject being defined in cogito. Bakhtin finds it as a "false tendency toward reducing everything to a single consciousness, toward dissolving in it the other's consciousness" (1986, 141) and he argues that "quests for my own word are in fact quests for a word that is not my own, a word that is more than myself; this is a striving to depart from one's own words, with which nothing essential can be said" (1986, 149). *Cogito, ergo sum* or, as it goes in a later dictum, *ego cogito, ergo sum, sive existo,* is for him an inadequate answer about the self. Instead, truth is not defined as adequatio any longer or, in the sense of identity, as being the same. The real face of truth is agonistic, defined as a field of contradictions. Truth could be defined as undecidability: the realm of the Cartesian certitude is annihilated. Truth is acknowledged not to be univocal and the concept of identity is to be redefined. The truth of the real self of culture is defined as not remaining the same; it is defined in an inscribed will to difference (Descombes 1980, 35). Modern philosophy, as well as Bakhtin in his philosophical anthropology, introduces difference into the very definition of identity.

Cultural identity as revealed through history of literature and other forms of art is an entity, which is very concrete in its being. Culture should not be understood as a sum of phenomena, but as a concrete totality, where the notion of totality should be understood pragmatically (not metaphysically), i.e., as something open, non-finite, as something inconclusive in its character. Bakhtin explains the study of literature and cultural identity as follows:

There exists a very strong, but one-sided and thus untrustworthy, idea that in order better to understand a foreign culture, one must enter into it, forgetting one's own, and view the world through the eyes of this foreign culture. . . . In the realm of culture, outsideness is a most powerful factor in understanding. It is only in the eyes of another culture that foreign culture reveals itself fully and profoundly. . . . A meaning only reveals its depth once it has encountered and come into contact with another, foreign meaning: they engage in a kind of dialogue, which surmounts the closedness and one-sidedness of these particular meanings, these cultures. We raise new questions for a foreign culture, ones that it did not raise itself . . . Such a dialogic encounter of two cultures does not result in merging or mixing. Each retains its own unity and open totality, but they are mutually enriched. (1986, 6–7).

One should not forget that even "consciousness" is a real fact for Bakhtin. In *Marxism and Philosophy of Language* he asserts that consciousness is materialised in the material of signs. The sign or, to follow strictly his views on language, the word (Russian *slovo*, Greek *logos*) or utterance (as the smallest unit of language), refracts the social and historical entities in itself. He also reminds us of the constant interplay between the sign and its related historical being. At this point, again, Bakhtin's views are very close to Heidegger's: When Heidegger elaborates his ideas of the existential meaning and the role of art and explains why man is "located in the world and situated historically" only "through poetry" (qtd. in Leitch 65), he also points out that the historical being itself is emerging into the unconcealedness only through the language of poetry: "Thus art is: the creative preserving of truth in the work of art. Art then is the becoming and happening of truth. . . . All art, as the letting happen of the advent of the truth of what it is, is, as such, essentially poetry. The nature of art . . . is the setting-itself into-work of truth" (Heidegger 1986, 274). The domain of poetic composition in the wider sense, i.e., of the arts and of culture, has a privileged position in that it is "a mode of the lighting projection of truth" (Heidegger 1986, 275). Thus, according to both Bakhtin and Heidegger, language and thinking imply the presence (facticity) of the historical consciousness or of the historical being.

The identity of a culture is established through a complex reality of historical processes. The question of cultural identity should then legitimately be posed on a very concrete level. Bakhtin's gnoseological point of departure is based in his philosophy of concreteness. My methodological expectation that the implications of Bakhtin's notion of dialogue epitomises in itself the complexity of reality should then prove relevant in the discussion of cultural identity as well. When posing the question of cultural identity methodologically on the ground of the reality principle, a move into the field of comparative literature is inevitable. However, not only the reception of one culture by another is meant here by comparative literature. Much more than in cultural influences through direct or indirect contacts, comparative literature is interested today in a re-examination of the historicality of being entrapped in the languages of different literatures and arts. The question of analyses of literary texts (or other works of art) refers us to the historical being concealed in them, and how it participates in the truth of a global self-understanding of man/woman and, consequently, in the truth of historical subjectivity of different cultures. On the other hand, the question of mutual relations between world literatures only on the basis of empirically realised contacts and influences is insufficient in modern comparative literature. Today literatures cannot be studied ignoring the questions of history itself; neither can they evade matters of their national being—both of which provide answers concerning the situation of individual literatures in a given historical segment of global thought. The study of cultural identity also gives answers connected to the very "facticity" of the historical being which defines the situation of a literature. The problem of English or of Slovenian cultural identity, for instance, has to be compared through analyses with other literatures.

Cultural identity of a given national history is its "primordial founding" (Leitch 69) and it brings forth its existence while its mode of existing is in a multitude of its own faces through history. It is a complex image of the many-sided interests of its own self. The identity of culture, if we follow Bakhtin and his notion of dialogue, is not univocal and it is neither a sum of different qualities nor of characteristics that clearly set the given culture apart from others. As any individuality, cultural identity is a meeting point of several cross-cultural influences. It is of a complex plurivocal character, open to its own changes in order to preserve its own being in a new context of interests. Our cultural identity is our intertext. The immense and boundless world of Otherness constitutes a primary fact of existence of our cultural identity. In his later notes Bakhtin states the following: "The study of culture (or some area of it) at the level of system and at the higher level of organic unity [implies the following notions]: open, becoming, unresolved and indterminate, capable of death and renewal, transcending itself, that is, exceeding its own boundaries" (1986, 135). The presence of interests in Bakhtin's definition of cultural identity reveals that the question of politics is indispensably inherent in the event of culture through history.

Forming itself and existing through cross-cultural interactions, cultural identity exposes its inevitable intertextual character. This intertextual character of cultural identity suggests infinite diversity of its being: "The world of culture and literature is essentially as boundless as the universe," argues Bakhtin (1986, 140). Openness and indeterminateness are the most evident characteristics of culture and its identity. The formation of the self of a given culture through encountering with Otherness cannot, as Bakhtin reminds us, change the existence of it, but only the sense of its existence. Here, Bakhtin puts in another crucial remark that sounds very much in accord with Post-structuralism: "Authenticity and truth inhere not in existence itself, but only in the existence that is acknowledged and uttered" (1986, 138). The interacting of cultural identities, as follows, results in a change of the sense of their existence. As a reflection of the self in the empirical, the Other should always lead to the self-affirmation of one's existence. Thus, self-confidence of a culture—or self-consciousness, can only be activated and creatively flourish through the principle of Otherness. Cultural dialogism does not mean obliteration of individual cultural identities. Rather, as history witnesses, it reassures the pertaining of a gap between existing cultural identities and their evolutionary possibilities.

Although being constantly re-established through Otherness, cultural identity cannot be deprived of its own evolution and of its own evolutionary interests. Through creative contacts it participates in its own change of sense. Cultural consciousness today, in an awareness of the infinite diversity of cross-cultural influences on its own being, is not endangered of being dissolved in another cultural identity. Uniqueness of identity of a culture lies in its very features of differences and its Otherness throughout history. Identity features of a given national literature cannot be exhausted. This inexhaustiveness, inscribed in cultural identity through its dialogism, is a guarantee, which enables its persistent existence. In my opinion, the professed fear of European cultures—especially now with the on-going plans of an extension of the European Union—that they will lose their distinct cultural identities is groundless. Two thousand years after the beginnings of literary genres and literary "languages," literary history bears witness to the differentiation of distinct European literatures and cultures. In their mutual interactions of cultural identities and literatures, the existing differences of individual national literatures were even increased at the period of Romanticism and since. However, the condition of a permanent flux of contacts and influences, the cultural identity of a national literature is continuously undergoing the impacts of new qualities and peculiarities. Linked to features of another cultural identity, one cultural identity re-accentuates its own inexhaustible characteristics. It can be changed radically or be enriched, but its transformation cannot discredit its very existence (Bakhtin 1986, 137).

And as to the practicality and application of my arguments, the future of European integration processes, as is evident in the perspective of the proposed reflection on the identity principle as dialogism, is not likely to endanger the existence of several cultures and their individual identities in Europe. Based on Bakhtin's dialogism, one might only say that a cultural identity awakens in another's consciousness and lives on its own unrepeatable existence. In conclusion, cultural identity represents non-finite wholeness. Openness and indeterminateness are its most evident characteristics. Through its complexity of influences, cultural identity defies predictability. Its own creativity, when being enacted in a dialogue with other cultures, changes itself only to a new sense of its existence. Comparatively speaking, the creativity of individual cultures exists through permanent re-interpretations of their own image of identity. While taking into account the processes of cross-cultural interactions and the permanency of re-interpretations in the formation of individual cultural identities, the role of the marginal and peripheral and their validity has evolved into a new context. In a dialogism that results in overcoming monological or hegemonistic views and statuses, demarcations between majority cultures and marginal cultures is becoming a real possibility. Enacted dialogism is democratic in its origin and in its essence. In history, the marginal and the peripheral has proved influential through its will to power. The role of the marginal, following Bakhtin's philosophy of Otherness, has ultimately changed the historical transformations of thought in the twentieth century.

WORKS CITED

Bakhtin, M.M. *Problems of Dostoevsky's Poetics.* Trans. R.W. Rotsel. Ann Arbor: Ardis, 1973.

Bakhtin, M.M. *Speech Genres and Other Late Essays.* Ed. and trans. Caryl Emerson and Michael Holquist. Austin: U of Texas P, 1986.

De Man, Paul. "Dialogue and Dialogism." *Poetics Today* 4.1 (1983): 99–107.

Descombes, Vincent. *Modern French Philosophy.* Cambridge: Cambridge UP, 1980.

Heidegger, Martin. *Being and Time.* Trans. John Macquarrie and Edward Robinson. Oxford: Blackwell, 1973.

Heidegger, Martin. "The Origin of the Work of Art." *Deconstruction in Context: Literature and Philosophy.* Ed. Mark C. Taylor. Chicago: U of Chicago P, 1986. 256–79.

Holquist, Michael. *Dialogism: Bakhtin and His World.* London: New Accents, 1990.

Holquist, Michael, ed. *The Dialogic Imagination: Four Essays by M.M. Bakhtin.* Austin: U of Texas P, 1981.

Kershner, R.B. *Joyce, Bakhtin, and Popular Literature.* Chapel Hill: U of North Carolina P, 1989.

Leitch, Vincent B. *Deconstructive Criticism.* New York: Columbia UP, 1983.

Voloshinov, V.N. [M.M. Bakhtin]. *Marxism and the Philosophy of Language.* Trans. Ladislav Matejka and I.R. Titunik. New York: Seminar P, 1973.

Theory, Period Styles, and Comparative Literature as Discipline

Slobodan Sucur

INTRODUCTION

It is sometimes said that the origins of comparative literature are tied to debates concerning the renewal of the notion of literature, tied together because such theoretical debates on literariness, text, aesthetics, etc., and theoretical debates in general which still affect us, appear to originate with the Jena-Berlin school of Romanticism (the first phase), the approximate period from which the origins of comparative literature emanate as well. The question which looms large here is the following: Can a rapprochement be brought about between various, often antagonistic, literary-theoretical views and the concept of comparative literature itself, which requires accord, consensus, agreement, etc., for it to function as a concrete body and discipline? I will deal with the question by splitting this paper into three parts. In the first part, I will expose the antagonistic nature of theory by looking at some formalist, deconstructionist, and humanist views, views which seem to feed on each other for survival, and which pose a threat to the notion of smoothly operating disciplines such as Comparative Literature, Art History, etc.; the antagonism, inconsistency, and confusion which is present in and arises because of the polemic nature of these views will be traced back to early Romanticism. In the second part of the paper, I will use Ali Behdad's concept of "belatedness," juxtaposed onto Virgil Nemoianu's argument for a Biedermeier style, to explain why comparative literature as a discipline seems to be a product of the same Romanticism that gave birth to high theorizing but simultaneously seems to be divided and at odds with this "other," theoretical product; I will attempt to account for this supposed paradox. In the third and final part of the paper, I will attempt to reconcile theory and discipline (i.e., comparative literature) by bringing in the notion of literary history as a medium through which antagonisms can be subsumed, and perhaps even cancelled out, by larger narrative accounts of literary and theoretical development, by meta-endeavors, as it were; I will also speak of other concepts in this final section.

THEORY, DISCORD, AND EARLY ROMANTICISM

It may be odd that I am beginning a discussion on theory, discord, and Romanticism by citing examples from Russian Formalism, because the latter school of thought is often said to be anti-Romantic, especially in its reaction against Symbolist poetics, as Selden says in his *A Reader's Guide to Contemporary Literary Theory*: The Futurists, who provided the initial impetus for Formalism, directed their artistic efforts "against 'decadent' bourgeois culture and especially against the anguished soul-searching of the Symbolist movement in poetry and the visual arts . . . [and against] the mystical posturing of poets" (30). Nonetheless, certain Formalist assumptions were later attacked by poststructuralism, leading to conceptual opposition and discord, and besides, while Selden believes that Formalism was anti-Romantic owing to its avoidance of Symbolist assumptions, we may also argue that Symbolism was itself anti-Romantic owing to its elaboration on earlier, romantic tendencies, and so on.

As I have said, certain Formalist assumptions were later attacked, and this is why I mention such assumptions. One of the clearest examples of Formalism is found in Victor Shklovsky's article, "Art as Technique," where one of the major points is that the very phrase, "works of art," designates those "works created by special techniques designed to make the works as obviously artistic as possible" (17). What Shklovsky is working towards with such a comment is the idea of art, in this case poetry, as an autonomous construct, a self-sufficient entity that is set up through conscious craftsmanship: He cements the essence of his argument later by saying that what is required is a proper distinction "between the laws of practical language and the laws of poetic language" (19). Further on, Shklovsky offers a sentence that has been quoted and criticized often: "*Art is a way of experiencing the artfulness of an object; the object is not important*" (20; italics in the original). Near the end of the article, he once again reaffirms his views be saying "a strong tendency

. . . to create a new and properly poetic language has emerged. In the light of
these developments we can define poetry as *attenuated, tortuous* speech. Poetic
speech is *formed speech*. Prose is ordinary speech—economical, easy, proper,
the goddess of prose [*dea prosae*] is a goddess of the accurate, facile type, of
the 'direct' expression of a child" (28). In his article, "Linguistics and Poetics," Roman Jakobson continues with this thrust towards an autonomous definition of literature, a thrust which is representative of the earlier phase of
Formalism. He speaks of how "the terminological confusion of 'literary studies' with 'criticism' tempts the student of literature to replace the description
of the intrinsic values of a literary work by a subjective, censorious verdict.
The label 'literary critic' applied to an investigator of literature is as erroneous
as 'grammatical (or lexical) critic' would be applied to a linguist. Syntactic
and morphological research cannot be supplanted by a normative grammar,
and likewise no manifesto, foisting a critic's own tastes and opinions on creative literature, may act as a substitute for an objective scholarly analysis of
verbal art" (33). We can see obvious formalistic tendencies in Jakobson's comments, for there is the phrase, "intrinsic values of literature," the phrase,
"objective scholarly analysis of verbal art" (which foreshadows New Criticism), and more generally, the comments voice a need for a specialized and
élitist grammar to deal with literature. This emphasis on the concept of pure
literature and specialized study of that literature is reflected once again in
Jakobson's argument when he gives a brief, but almost fetish-like analysis of
Poe's "The Raven" at a linguistic level that emphasizes the "literariness" of
words (particularly in poetry): "The perch of the raven, 'the pallid bust of Pallas,' is merged through the 'sonorous' paronomasia /páel*d/—/páel*s/ into one
organic whole (similar to Shelley's molded line 'Sculptured on alabaster obelisk'
/sk.lp/—/l.b.st/—/b.l.sk/). Both confronted words were blended earlier in
another epithet of the same bust—*placid* /pláesld/—a poetic portmanteau, and
the bond between the sitter and the seat was in turn fastened by a paronomasia: '*b*ird or *b*east upon the . . . *b*ust.' The bird 'is sitting // On the pallid
bust of Pallas just above my chamber door,' and the raven on his perch, despite
the lover's imperative 'take thy form from off my door,' is nailed to the place
by the words **st *b*v/, both of them blended in /b*st/" (50). A fascination
with words is quite obvious in this description, but equally so, we can sense
a strong linguistic/grammatical presence, in the sense that the thematic meaning of Poe's poem is being rejected in favor of an assessment of textual and
verbal structures; in this way, we can clearly see how Formalism goes beyond

the impressionistic and thematic, moral commentary of late nineteenth-century liberal humanist criticism. In Jakobson's article, there is a fascination with the mechanical nature and presence of words, and a need for ordered and structured, "objective" linguistic assessment, a need which can be felt in his other article as well, "The Metaphoric and Metonymic Poles," particularly near the conclusion, when Jakobson says that "there exist . . . grammatical and anti-grammatical but never agrammatical rhymes" (61).

While the early phase of Russian Formalism goes beyond the historical contextualism and obviously subjective, impressionistic commentary of nineteenth-century literary criticism, by returning to "the text" itself and to the presence of "the word" as an object, entity, and structure that defines certain things as being proper "literature," already in Mikhail Bakhtin's article, "From the Prehistory of Novelistic Discourse," we find the beginnings of a critique that is directed at the earlier, formalistic assumptions. While Bakhtin does not go so far as to deconstruct the concept of literature per se, and of self-sustaining art forms, he does do a subtle shift on the Jakobsonian-type argument by emphasizing the need for stylistic rather than linguistically/scientifically oriented studies, especially because "the distinctive features of novelistic discourse, the stylistic *specificum* of the novel as a genre, remained as before unexplained" (126). Bakhtin's emphasis on stylistic study seems to open the floor, so to speak, to larger social and/or historical questions, as exemplified when he cites Belinsky (who called Pushkin's *Evgenij Onegin* "an encyclopedia of Russian life") and then argues against the one-sidedness of Belinsky's comment. It is best to quote most of the passage in question, because the critique against certain aspects of Formalism (Shklovsky's *defamiliarization*, linguistic emphasis, aesthetic unity, etc.) is present to a great degree:

> But this is no inert encyclopedia that merely catalogues the things of everyday life. Here Russian life speaks in all its voices, in all the languages and styles of the era. Literary language is not represented in the novel as a unitary, completely finished-off and indisputable language—it is represented precisely as a living mix of varied and opposing forces [*raznorecivost'*], developing and renewing itself. The language of the author strives to overcome the superficial 'literariness' of moribund, outmoded styles and fashionable period-bound languages; it strives to renew itself by drawing on the fundamental elements of folk language . . . Pushkin's novel is a self-critique of the literary language of the era, a product of this

language's various strata . . . mutually illuminating one another. But
this interillumination is not of course accomplished at the level of
linguistic abstraction: images of language are inseparable from
images of various world views and from living beings who are their
agents—people who think, talk, and act in a setting that is social
and historically concrete. . . . The stylistic structure of *Evgenij One-*
gin is typical of all authentic novels. To a greater or lesser extent,
every novel is a dialogized system made up of the images of 'languages,' styles and consciousness that are concrete and inseparable
from language. Language in the novel not only represents, but itself
serves as the object of representation. Novelistic discourse is always
criticizing itself. (131)

While Bakhtin appears to set up a subtle critique of Formalism in order
to resurrect certain aspects of liberal humanist discourse, but in a more modern, socialized and polyphonic way, so as not to repeat the kind of humanism
that Formalism had itself critiqued, it is Jacques Derrida's seminal article,
"Structure, Sign, and Play in the Discourse of the Human Sciences," which
goes into a different gray area, so to speak, by exposing the fallacies of Lévi-
Strauss' work (as a structural anthropologist). One might initially expect that
Derrida, by arguing against Strauss' approach (which we might consider a mod-
ernized and refined humanism, as in Bakhtin's case), will eventually come back
to some sort of neo-Formalist position (with its emphasis on linguistics and
the word as a "sign"), but Derrida also critiques Formalism's position as an
alternative to humanistic and structural discourse, when he speaks of how if
we wish to extend "the domain or play of signification" infinitely, then we
must also reject "the concept and word 'sign' itself—which is precisely what
cannot be done," since we are also caught up in the metaphysics of presence
(395). Derrida becomes more specific in his argument when he speaks of two
notions of "totalization," where the classical explanation of why totalization
is impossible is because there are too many things to empirically circumscribe,
and the new explanation of why totality is impossible is because the field of
vision, the act of circumscription, is itself finite and totalization is outside the
field of "play," play being a concept which Derrida explains as the "movement of supplementarity" that is "permitted by the lack or absence of a center or origin," that is "no longer turned toward the origin" (like the classical
attempt at totalization) but rather is a new interpretation, "to which Nietzsche
pointed the way," which "tries to pass beyond man and humanism" and does

not seek the "inspiration of a new humanism" (404-08). Derrida's critique is therefore directed at the traditional concept of humanism (nineteenth-century mode), at the "new humanism" of Bakhtinian and Lévi-Strauss-like arguments (which is dispersed, polyphonic, difficult to detect, etc.), and at Formalism per se (with its love of the word-sign as a linguistic entity on which we build definitions of literariness, something that Derrida problematizes by destabilizing the Saussurian concept of sign).

This can-of-worms which deconstruction has opened up has of course created a larger split between theory and discipline (i.e., comparative literature) than was previously present. In fact, the literariness which Formalism was searching for, together with its division between poetry proper and other literary forms, and together with New Criticism's emphasis on the autonomous artifact (which we also sense in Shklovsky's article), was rather beneficial for the concept of institution, department, discipline, and so on. Since disciplines, especially as they grow, require stability and consensus, then Formalist and New Critical notions of literariness, which maintain the stability of the literary canon, also maintain the élitism and command-structure by which most departments and disciplines begin. In other words, the first step in destabilizing the boundaries of a discipline such as comparative literature, and even art history, etc., is to throw away such terms as artfulness and pure literature, which in turn destabilizes the boundaries of the canon (which may consist of books or paintings) and which defines the discipline in question, and is a marker by which the discipline measures itself. Needless to say, owing to deconstruction, definitions of literature have become more liberal and the canon more flexible, and yet, disciplines still exist, and many have neither collapsed nor fused with other disciplines. Part of the explanation for this anomaly is that, while deconstruction has problematized things, the very fact that deconstruction as a theoretical approach is "undefinable" in the traditional sense allows for institutionally and departmentally beneficial comments to circulate within it (however peculiar this may seem, it explains why institutions have not collapsed, but rather, deconstruction has itself become institutionalized).

One of the most interesting examples of such duplicity is in Paul de Man's article, "The Resistance to Theory," where, among other things, like arguing for a built-in duplicity within theory itself, de Man also, however post-structural his comments may be, seems to maintain, in a subtle fashion of course, that literature is still an autonomous and inherently "literary" entity (which echoes Formalist and New Critical tendencies): "Literature is fiction not because it somehow refuses to acknowledge 'reality,' but because it is not *a priori* certain that language functions according to principles which are those, or which are *like* those, of the phenomenal world. It is therefore not *a priori* certain that literature is a reliable source of information about anything but its own language" (362). However inverted de Man's comment may be, it once again, like Formalism, defines literature as a primarily linguistic and syntactic entity, and nothing more; of course, in de Man's case, rather than defining literature as successful if it attains fictive and aesthetic heights, he defines literature as inevitably failing since it inevitably is fictive and aesthetic, but in turn, this inevitable failure can be looked upon as a success, because in this context, literature that thinks it records reality would be a failure. This upholding of literariness, however pessimistic and inverted it may be, still maintains the stability (however hollow) of departments and disciplines, because the presence of a canon is now maintained; since the "best" texts are inevitably literary and aesthetic (through failure), the canon will forever be rejuvenated and maintained as a healthy entity, because these failed texts will be canonized as the "best texts," and so on, and because most texts fail in being mimetic, there is no chance that second-rate encyclopedias will ever be canonized. De Man's comments are even more complex than I have indicated, because while his inverted support of literariness may echo Formalism, he does say that "no grammatical decoding, however refined, could claim to reach the determining figural dimensions of a text" (367). Such complexities in argument allow de Man to maintain the stability of disciplines and institutions at the same time that he destabilizes them, so that it becomes difficult for us to assess the precise role of theory in institutions, or as he says regarding theory at the conclusion of his article: "What remains impossible to decide is whether this flourishing is a triumph or a fall" (371).

Perhaps it is because of such cases of undecidability that neo-humanist critics like M.H. Abrams and E.D. Hirsch Jr. have argued against deconstructive and duplicitous modes of thought. Abrams, in his article, "The Deconstructive Angel," appears to go back to a fundamentally humanist yet refined, and thematically-oriented position. He argues, with reference to Derrida, that his own "view of language, as it happens, is by and large functional and pragmatic: language, whether spoken or written, is the use of a great variety of speech-acts to accomplish a great diversity of human purposes; only one of these many purposes is to assert something about a state of affairs; and such a linguistic assertion does not mirror, but serves to direct attention to selected aspects of that state of affairs" (266). Hirsch, in his article, "Faulty Perspectives," concludes by saying that no matter how duplicitous and multi-layered one's perspective may be, there is no denying that behind such perspective rests an "empirical actuality," an actuality that is the source of perspective, maintains it, and will always "call in doubt a basic premise of hermeneutical relativism and, with it, most of the presently fashionable forms of cognitive atheism" (263).

This Pandora's Box—which we call theory—with its many antagonisms, variations, subtleties, and confusions, and with its potential to destabilize and threaten the presence of disciplines such as comparative literature, seems to have its modern origin, as it were, in the Jena-Berlin school of Romanticism, the first phase of the movement. The theorizing of the early Romantic phase also possesses inconsistencies, and antagonisms, and this discord may indeed have filtered down into modern theoretical debates between Humanism, Formalism, Deconstruction, and so on. Miroslav John Hanak, in his *A Guide to Romantic Poetry in Germany*, speaks of the high theorizing of the early Romantic school, and through his discussion, one sees the same discord and confusion that occurs when an Abrams or a Hirsch argues against a Derrida or a Paul de Man, or when a Bakhtin does a variation in thought on a Shklovsky or a Jakobson. Hanak's discussion of idealism and theory in early Romanticism can be split, I believe, into three phases, where each successive phase builds upon the discord and development of the previous phase. The three phases would be as follows: a) Hamann and Herder versus Kant; b) Fichte, Schelling, and Hegel versus Kant and each other; and c) Friedrich Schlegel attempts a reconciliation of contradictions (and may either parallel or precede Hegel in his endeavors). The problematic of theory and philosophy that still affect us start a bit earlier than the Jena-Berlin phase of Romanticism (1796–1803), but they lead up to this culminating phase, and thus deserve attention. Herder's *Ideas for the Philosophy of History and Mankind* (1784–91), which developed a philosophy of history and ethnic psychology, greatly inspired Kant, but in a negative way, to write his own interpretation of the historic process in *An Idea for a Universal History from the Cosmopolitan Point of View* (1784) (5). This work by Herder, considered his magnum opus, "brought up to date the principle of Aristotelian entelechy, the embodiment of the highest potentiality of a species, postulating a progressive ontology of all existence toward the production of ever more perfect specimens," and Herder, like Plato, "conceived the world as an organism; but rather than a static *zoon empsychon ennoun*, a creature endowed with soul and mind, Herder's universe was actually a dynamic evolutionary process from inanimate to animate nature, culminating in a graduated scale of cultures and individuals" (9).

Kant reacted against his student's views in his *An Idea for a Universal History from the Cosmopolitan point of View*, because Kant, as a man of the Enlightenment, regarded past history as a spectacle of human irrationality, and looked forward to a future Utopia of rational life (Hanak 12). The problematic aspect is that, as Hanak argues, while Kant reacted against Herder's interpretation, he simultaneously foreshadowed Hegel's own work, because "Kant's view of history as noumenally grounded reason progressing towards free self-embodiment in the world is already more of a Hegelian and hence, Romantic vision, than a Kantian principle of progress according to enlightened and enlightening reason" (13). The entire chain-of-influence is problematic, because by reacting against his student, Herder, Kant himself went beyond Enlightenment principles. Herder of course had another teacher, apart from Kant, Johann Georg Hamann, who influenced his student more so than Kant. Hamann, in his *Socratic Memorabilia* (1759), argued that the archrationalist Socrates realized that conceptual knowledge cannot penetrate the ultimate questions of being, and in this way, Hamann agreed with Kant's positing of an Ultimate Reality that had to be "assumed" and could not be detected, but instead of denying "absolute conceptual knowledge of any substance" in order to "make room for faith" (like Kant), Hamann, and Herder, kept seeking absolute knowledge, not through reason, but through the "affective faculties" (5–6). As Hanak argues, Hamann and Herder problematized Kant's notions by "radicalizing" the latter's idea of "intersubjectivity" that was developed in his *Third Critique* (1791), and by "glorifying as unique the bias toward sensibility, that paralleled along generally mystic paths the vaunted rationalism of eighteenth century Enlightenment. Hamann and Herder thus legitimized the nobility and cognitive force of the affects, bringing about an era which Rousseau and Voltaire had helped to prepare: the age of Revolution, of emotional, moral and aesthetic liberalism, and of Romantic Utopias" (6–7).

The second layer of theoretical and philosophical antagonism and subtlety occurs with Fichte, Schelling, and Hegel, and the variations in thought that arise between them (as a reaction to Kant). Hanak argues that Fichte departs from "Kant's fundamental premise that universal history is an unfolding of a plan," and that much like "Herder's endeavors to identify the Folk Spirit of each nation and race, Fichte sought to define the exact spirit of his own age" in works like

Doctrine of Science (1796–98) and *The Characteristics of the Present Age* (published in 1806) (14–15). In fact, Hanak goes so far as to state that the "Fichtean metaphysics of becoming reads like a blueprint for Hegel's *Phenomenology, Logic* and *Encyclopedia*" (15). Schelling is considered a disciple of Fichte, and through him, however remotely, of Kant (18–19). While Schelling's *Ideas for a Philosophy of Nature* (1797), *On the World Soul* (1798), and *System of Transcendental Idealism* (1800) may overlap with certain Hegelian concepts, through the use of phrases like "movement of nature," "Ultimate Truth," and "Universal Mind," Hanak is quick to point out that there is a subtle difference between Schelling's work and Hegel's: For Hegel, the point of departure is "spiritual-rationalist" while for Schelling the starting point is "aesthetical-naturalist," but this is all a matter of emphasis. For both, the Ground of Being is unconscious and universal, only for Schelling it is the Absolute as Nature, and for Hegel, the Absolute as Spirit; both agree that the real evolves through a process of reason" (19–21). The main difference between Hegel and Schelling is that in Hegel's *Phenomenology*, "the Kantian dualism between phenomena and noumena is *aufgehoben,* overcome in the broadest sense of the word" (23). In this way, while Fichte and Schelling may anticipate Hegel's work, it is only Hegel who fully breaks away from Kantian discourse.

Hanak's argument is interesting, particularly the way in which he sets up the various philosophers as offering polemic or non-polemic answers to Kant (as representative of the Enlightenment). His argument emphasizes the main point which Frederick C. Beiser is making in his article, "Early Romanticism and the *Aufklärung.*" Beiser argues that our difficulty in understanding the phase of early Romanticism stems from the fact that the representatives of the movement were "neither revolutionaries nor reactionaries. Rather, they were simply reformers, moderates in the classical tradition" (321). Beiser even looks upon the representatives as "nothing less than the Aufklärer of the 1790s. They seem to differ from the earlier generation of Aufklärer only in their disillusionment with enlightened absolutism and in their readiness to embrace republican ideals" (322). The main problem which the early Romantics had with the Enlightenment was that "two of its most basic ideals—radical criticism [which the early Romantics rejected] and Bildung [which they approved of]—were in conflict with one another. For if criticism ends in complete skepticism, then according to what moral, political, and religious principles should we educate the people" (324)? Beiser's question, which he believes the early Romantics raised, is the same question that we now raise when we look at the antagonism, rivalry, and fragmentation which contemporary theory instigates in relation to earlier, structuralist and pre-structuralist theories. The question which early Romanticism raises about the inconsistencies of the Enlightenment is the same question which we may raise about the inconsistencies in Derrida's or de Man's work (and more generally, about the end result of radical criticism). As Beiser says, the early Romantics did not solve the question through their program of "pure aesthetics," a program through which the Enlightenment was ironically "consumed by its own flames" (326), much like early Romanticism, I would add.

Friedrich Schlegel came closest, Hanak argues, to actually solving the contradictions which were inherent in the Enlightenment. Schlegel's speculations parallel closely the Hegelian system, but in the case of Hegel, the final solution-synthesis is expected to reveal itself as the "Absolute Spirit or Knowledge," while in Schlegel's case, the solution will come through "progressive universal poetry" (qtd. in Hanak 35). Friedrich Schlegel's attempt at resolution came in three phases. In the first phase (1795–96), he argued that the "flabbiness" and artificiality of modern literature could be rectified through an improvement on the "highest favor of nature," which, for him, was classical poetry, or in simpler terms, an improvement on classicism would simultaneously perfect the romantic program (37). In the second stage of Schlegel's speculation (1796–98), he defined the novel as the key "genre in literature" and a "Romantic life-style setter," by which the novel was viewed as a transcendentally-oriented "Christian poetry," a "symbol of the absolute ideal," the "poetic ideal *qua* God" (38). In this second phase, Schlegel later modified his views of the "absolute novel" by introducing the synthetic concept of "irony," through which one could see that "infinite representation" is still embodied in an "existential and aesthetic profile of clearly determined, finite outlines," whereby eternity and time are reconciled (40). In the third stage of his speculation (1799–1800), Schlegel expanded his earlier call for a Romantic "ideal" to include the creation of a new "mythology" which would "reflect the spiritual tendencies of the times," so that classical Greek art still remains prototypical for Schlegel, but rather than merely being surpassed in its "very classicism," it now becomes the prospect for a "limitless growth of classicism," as stipulated in his 116th *Athenäum Fragment* (43). As Hanak says, Schlegel's "bid for a modern mythology gravitates toward Platonic and Christian transcendentalism, rather than Kantian transcendentalism" (44). Needless to say, Schlegel's metaphysical sweeps did not solve the contradictions inherent in the Enlightenment, precisely because I now find myself in a rather Schlegelian position as I go on to the next part of my paper, all the while thinking how I will reconcile theory (with its discord) and discipline (which requires consensus).

BELATEDNESS, PERIOD STYLES, AND THE NATURE OF COMPARATIVE LITERATURE

Why does comparative literature as a discipline seem to be a product of the same Romanticism that gave birth to high theorizing but simultaneously seems to be divided and at odds with this "other," theoretical product? Is this an enigma? I personally do not think so. Romanticism as a movement is usually, broadly defined as extending from about 1797 to about 1840 or so, when it is overtaken by the Realist paradigm; these might be the dates for German Romanticism. In England, it is thought that Romanticism begins around the time of the French Revolution (1789), and extends to about Byron's death (1824). Examples can be given of other national literatures as well. However, it is precisely this over-generalization in period styles and literary movements that lead to ambiguities that I am attempting to elaborate on in this section of my argument. A shift in outlook, paradigm, whatever we wish to call it, seems to occur sometime within the period broadly defined as Romanticism. We can see the difference by looking at what various critics say. M.H. Abrams, in his article, "English Romanticism: The Spirit of the Age," speaks of how the Romantic poet of the 1790s, in dealing with current affairs, sets up a procedure which is often panoramic, where his stage is cosmic, "his agents quasi-mythological, and his logic of events apocalyptic. Typically this mode of Romantic vision fuses history, politics, philosophy, and religion into one grand design, by asserting Providence—or some form of natural teleology" (45–46). This is Abrams' view of the 1790s in England. Northrop Frye, in his article, "The Drunken Boat: The Revolutionary Element in Romanticism," speaks of how in "Romanticism proper a prominent place in sense experience is given to the ear, an excellent receiver of oracles but poor in locating things accurately in space . . . In later poetry, beginning with *symbolisme* in France . . . more emphasis is thrown on vision. In Rimbaud . . . the illuminations are thought of pictorially; even the vowels must be visually colored . . . Such an emphasis leads to a technique of fragmentation. Poe's attack on the long poem is not a Romantic but an anti-Romantic manifesto, as the direction of its influence indicates" (23–24).

Ali Behdad, in his *Belated Travelers: Orientalism in the Age of Colonial Dissolution*, speaks of how a "belated reading is not an orthodox reiteration or a reapplication of a previous theory; rather, it is an interventionary articulation of a new problematic through the detour—or, perhaps more accurately, retour—of an earlier practice" (3). He develops the concept of belatedness and of belated readings in order to account for the late "Orientalism of travelers such as Nerval, Flaubert, Loti, and Eberhardt [which] vacillates between an insatiable search for a counter experience in the Orient and the melancholic discovery of its impossibility" (15). Regarding Flaubert's *Notes de voyages* (1849–50), Behdad says that "Flaubert abandoned the idea of writing an organized travelogue like those of his orientalist precursors," that his work was "never intended" for publishing, and that the "belated orientalist's discourse [like Flaubert's] is thus an antinarrative, a discursive constellation without a shape, an ideological practice without a doctrine" (54). While Flaubert's belated orientalist discourse is considered by Behdad as a "constellation without a shape" and an "ideological practice without a doctrine," comparative literature as a discipline, and in order to remain a discipline, requires both shape and doctrine. However, if we exempt certain assumptions of belated Orientalism (as formulated by Behdad) from this discussion, but apply the concept of "belatedness" in general to comparative literature, we create a rather concise explanation for why comparative literature seems antagonistic to the theoretical discord of Romanticism, but also seems a product of the self-same Romanticism (as a movement or broad period). Put simply, comparative literature, together with the concept of national literatures and "specialization," came late in the game, late in the period known as Romanticism, and as such, it always seems a "step removed" from the high theorizing of Jena-Berlin Romanticism, and consequently, it appears to be threatened by the conflicts of modern theoretical discourse, which may indeed be an extension of the Jena-Berlin phase, in such figures as Derrida, de Man, Hirsch, and so on (where the contradictions of the Enlightenment have yet to be solved). Robert J. Clements, in his *Comparative Literature as Academic Discipline: A Statement of Principles, Praxis, Standards,* provides an outline of the modern origins of comparative literature which is best quoted in its entirety, since it implicitly emphasizes Behdad's concept of "belatedness" in relation to this discipline:

> "Fortunately in 1832, well after the fall of the Ancien Régime, Jean-Jacques Ampère condemned chauvinism as incompatible with liter-

ary cosmopolitanism, although it remained a hydra difficult to dispatch, as French historians of comparative literature acknowledge
. . . Between 1828 and 1840 the Sorbonne professor Abel-François Villemain not only employed the term 'comparative literature' in his writings, but led the pack by offering course work in this discipline. The influential Sainte-Beuve legitimized the term in the *Revue des deux mondes* (itself a comparative title) and his *Nouveaux lundis*, to be followed by an international company including Louis Betz, Max Koch, Joseph Texte, Longfellow, Georg Brandes, and others. In Italy Mazzini's *Scritti* (1865–67) declared that no literature could be nurtured by itself or could escape the influence of alien literatures . . . the first occurrence of the coinage 'vergleichende Literaturgeschichte' was in Moriz Carrière's book of 1854, *Das Wesen und die Formen der Poesie.*" (3–4)

The approximate dates for the origin of comparative literature, which Clements cites, become more significant when we turn to Virgil Nemoianu's *The Taming of Romanticism: European Literature and the Age of Biedermeier*, a work in which Nemoianu elaborates on the concept of a period called Biedermeier, which lasted from approximately 1815 to 1848 (1). Before giving characteristics of the Biedermeier, Nemoianu outlines the various scholarly endeavors which attempted to define this as a post-Romantic period over the years. The concept of Biedermeier as a literary-historical period was put forward in the 1920s by Paul Kluckhohn, Julius Wiegand, and others, but more systematically after 1931 by Günther Weydt and Wilhelm Bietak, who triggered an important scholarly debate in the 1930s (3–4). The participants agreed that the writings of the period they were discussing were marked by certain common features, such as an "inclination toward morality, a mixture of realism and idealism, peaceful domestic values, idyllic intimacy, lack of passion, coziness, contentedness, innocent drollery, conservatism, resignation," and so on (4). "The term 'Biedermeier' had originally been derogatory because of the character Gottlieb Biedermeier, who was invented by Adolf Kussmaul and Ludwig Eichrodt, and introduced to the public in the Munich *Fliegende Blätter* in 1855: "This smug and cozy philistine was a caricature of the old-fashioned petty bourgeois of southern Germany and Austria" (4). Already by 1900, art historians and fashion historians were using the term Biedermeier to describe the intimate, pretty, and quiet paintings of the 1815 to 1848 period (Carl Spitzweg, Ferdinand Georg Waldmüller, etc.) or even the furniture and dress styles (4). The term was also used to evoke the tone and color of an entire age by the nostalgic-ironic novelists Georg Hermann, in his *Jettchen Gebert* (1906), and Thomas Mann, in his *Buddenbrooks* (1901) (4). The debates of the 1930s concerning the Biedermeier did have their problems, among which is the contemporary suspicion that the reappraisal of the 1820s and 1830s was nationalistically motivated: Adolf Bartels, an anti-Semitic populist, tried using Austrian Biedermeier writers as a weapon against "degenerate" modernist writing of the pre-World War One period (4). The other suspicion was that the term Biedermeier is just a tedious concoction, a fruit of, as Nemoianu says, "the tireless *geistesgeschichtlich* urge to invent periodizations, define the spirit of an age, and multiply the breed of historical types" (5). The third objection was that the really important and dynamic force of the 1830s and 1840s is *Das junge Deutschland* (with figures like Karl Gutzkow, Heinrich Heine, Heinrich Laube, Ludwig Börne, etc.), which, like similar contemporary movements (*La giovine Italia,* etc.), represented national and radical tendencies, while the Biedermeier is merely a provincial and epigonic movement, limited to writers like Eduard Mörike, Franz Grillparzer, Jeremias Gotthelf, Anette von Droste-Hülshoff, and so on (5). Nonetheless, there were attempts to rescue the Biedermeier from such restrictions in scope; Hermann Pongs found that demonic and grotesque characters and situations abound in these writings, Rudolf Majut claimed that the Biedermeier could only be understood as a dialectical whole, covering "all the writing" of the period, and most importantly, Friedrich Sengle wrote his monumental three-volume *Biedermeierzeit,* in which he argued that the shifts in social psychology of the time, the objective historical conditions, and the agglomeration of contrasting literary developments, when combined, created a cultural climate that was different from both the early and high Romantic periods and from the post-1850 Realist age (5–6). According to Sengle, the term Biedermeier worked best as a traditional description of a particular "current" in German literature of the time, while "Biedermeierzeit" could be applied to the entire, Metternichian-Restoration period so as to accommodate even opposing literary trends, broadly united by a framework of socio-historical events (6).

It is within the framework of a Biedermeier, or should I say Biedermeierzeit paradigm, to use Sengle's term, that we can place the origins of comparative literature, if we remember the dates that Clements gives us for the beginning of the discipline. Behdad's concept of "belatedness" can in this way be seen as an explanation of how the Biedermeier arose in relation to Romanticism proper (which begins with the Jena-Berlin school around 1796 or 1797 and terminates around 1815, coinciding with Napoleon's defeat). The Biedermeier, together with its products (i.e., comparative literature, specializations, national literatures), was, to reintroduce Behdad's terminology again, not an orthodox reiteration or a reapplication of a previous theory, but rather, an interventionary articulation of a new problematic through the detour or, perhaps more accurately, retour, of an earlier practice. Comparative literature, as a belated product of what was once a high Jena-Berlin Romanticism, could not, at the moment of its modern inception, catch up historically and existentially with the discursive, theoretical components of Romanticism proper. As such, comparative literature, because it is a discipline, and more generally, the nature of disciplines per se, as Biedermeier products, would always be naturally and historically threatened by theory and the destabilizing character of such discourse, which, owing to the fact that the Jena-Berlin school preceded the Biedermeier by nearly a quarter-century, itself precedes the inception of disciplines per se, and thus, discipline follows theory, and is not necessarily Behdad's interventionary articulation of a new problematic, but is certainly Behdad's detour or retour around an earlier practice. With this notion in mind, that disciplines are created after theory and "detour" around earlier events, we can see how Comparative Literature absorbs, for better or worse, destabilizing elements that come before its inception (i.e. theory), but simultaneously, we can see it always maintaining a perhaps not-so-safe distance from the destabilizations inherent in theory, precisely by being historically tied to the Biedermeier period, which faces Romanticism proper, and can even be interpreted as sharing a "door" with Romanticism, through which, if the door is left open, theory will seep into discipline, and inevitably so.

Nemoianu seems well aware of this contamination that in part defines the Biedermeier, for when he defines its nature, its constitution, we can see the Biedermeier absorbing certain Romantic tendencies, but we can also see it struggling to define itself as an autonomous entity in relation to its "loftier" predecessor. The disciples of Friedrich Schiller, after 1815, as Nemoianu says, are "rare birds: few were inclined to accept play and aesthetic creation as privileged areas of humaneness" (6–7). The aesthetician J.F. Herbart was typical of the Biedermeier, because he was anti-Kantian and anti-Hegelian, a pragmatic idealist, who believed that art has some autonomy, but that it should not be regarded as a salvation and should be adapted to reality to "provide service" (7). Such utilitarian tendencies are represented by the first, modern network of "popularization," as well, as Nemoianu calls it (7). In the 1820s, 30s, and 40s, there were massive extensions of publishing houses, collections, libraries, and newspapers; Emile Girardin's *La Presse* (1836) is considered the first modern newspaper (7). In Germany, the number of publications hardly rose from 1800 to 1821, but tripled in the next two decades (7). Sensational literature and fairy tales flourished as never before; collections of the brothers Grimm appeared between 1812 and 1826, and England was hit slightly later, by translations of Hans Christian Andersen in 1846, and of F.E. Paget's *The Hope of the Katzekopfs,* in 1844 (8). Even in science, the lofty and visionary theories of earlier times were now empirically tested and directed toward practical application; André-Marie Ampère, Jöns Berzelius, Justus Liebig, Hans Christian Oersted, Georg Ohm, Farraday, and others, were characteristic of the age (8). There is even a Biedermeier age of medicine, characterized by an uneasy empiricism that tried to accommodate James Mill's empirical views with echoes of the earlier "organic vitality" theory; Samuel Hahnemann took the mystical principles of earlier Romanticism and gave them a practical twist by starting a curative industry, homeopathy (8–9). In historical study, the universal syntheses of Schelling and Hegel were replaced by the scruples of Barthold Niebuhr and Leopold von Ranke, and by Friedrich Karl von Savigny's attempts at objectivity; the *Monumenta Germaniae Historica,* directed by Georg Heinrich Pertz, got underway in 1823, August Böckh began the *Corpus Inscriptionum Graecorum* in 1828, and Georg Grotefend and Jean-François Champollion deciphered the texts of Persian and Egyptian civilization in the 1820s (9). The range of terms in the dictionary of the *Académie Française* was expanded, and dictionaries with 110,000 to 170,000 entries became popular (9). Eight of the major German museums (including the Glyptothek and what is now called the Alte Pinakothek in Munich) were initiated between 1815 and 1855 (10). The Biedermeier was also an age of caricature and ironic art, like that of the post-Hogarthians (George Cruikshank, Thomas Rowlandson, James Gillray, etc.) (10).

   Nemoianu's description of the Biedermeier age, or more broadly, of a Biedermeierzeit, takes into account the characteristics which were fruitful for the rise of comparative literature as a discipline, because the age's need for compartmentalization, orderliness, and concretization, as exemplified via the publishing of anthologies of literature, the proliferation of dictionaries and encyclopedias, the creation of museums, and more generally, the need for stability, can in itself be taken as a definition of the nature of disciplines per se, and of their common features, features which distinguish disciplinary endeavors from purely theoretical ones, which appear to gravitate toward meta-syntheses, panoramic, Schlegelian sweeps, and ideal, Platonic models. Nemoianu is not alone in his argument for a distinct Biedermeier age (that differs from early and high Romanticism and the post-1850 Realist period), and his views are echoed in the comments of others. On the website, *Bidermajer u Hrvatskoj* (*Biedermeier in Croatia*), Vladimir Malekovic, in his introductory article of the same title, gives the etymology for Biedermeier style as follows:

> "Its roots are in English Rococo furniture (Chippendale), in 'Gothic forms' which will experience their revival at the end of the eighteenth century, especially in Germanic lands; in classicism, from which it takes, among certain decorative elements, a tendency toward the functional; in the Empire style, to which it owes something that G. Semper describes as 'antike Formalismus.' Without a doubt the Biedermeier owes most to England, where already in the second half of the eighteenth century there was a search for unity between technology and art, and the beginnings of industrial technology use, especially in craft manufacture . . . Cultural differences aided the transition of classicism and Empire to Biedermeier, and the conflict of interest between countries which decisively influenced that process (England, France, Austria, Germanic lands), if anything, gave an ironic context to things . . . The doors to the Empire style were opened across Europe by Napoleon's victories, the doors to the Biedermeier were opened by his defeat . . . The history of art has already shown that those places receptive to classicism, particularly the Empire style, were ideal places for the development of a new style—Biedermeier. Among such places is Croatia, where classicist and Empire cultures penetrated directly: from the Sava in the north to the Adriatic in the south during the time of Napoleon's Illyria, notably, 'French Croatia'." (My translation; Malekovic <http://www.tel.hr/muo/bider/hrv/hmalek.htm>)

In his book on the Serbian Biedermeier poet, Jovan Sterija Popovic, who is described as a "humorist and parodist," Dragisa Zivkovic defines the Biedermeier as follows:

> The main characteristic of this epoch is the mixture of directions and trends, so that the Biedermeier appears as a stylistic complex in which come together Byronists, late classicists, and late Romantic

epigones, young German, liberally oriented revolutionaries and for-
malistically oriented novelists. And these 'feuding brothers' of the
Biedermeier, so similar in general worldly feeling and in melancholic mood, but then again so different in their literary orientations,
use parody as a general offensive tool. Parodied are the classicist
epic and Baroque novel, Romantic idealism and sentimental pathos,
enlightened treatises and moralistic writings. At the basis of all this
lies a strengthening of traditional consciousness and conservative
thoughts tied together with an ever growing historicism. Pushed out
of politics, the Biedermeier citizen turns to literature and cultural
works, hoping to become the equal of the nobility not only through
monetary wealth but also through cultivation and style of life. That
aristocratic-civic culture ('transforming of nobility to bourgeois' and
'aristocratization of civilians') slowly erases and dulls class boundaries; the satire which is intensively nursed in this period is directed
more toward human imperfections than toward social-class oppositions. From there, in that genre, we come upon a caricaturing of
banal and trivial occurrences in human behavior. (*Bidermajerski
Usamljenik Sterija* 10–11, my translation)

Such observations allow us to see comparative literature, as a discipline,
and the nature of disciplines per se, within the framework of a socio-historical milieu from which the origins of disciplinariness emanate. As I mentioned
earlier, when we speak of Romanticism in overly broad terms, we come to view
comparative literature as being some sort of "paradoxical" product of the self-
same Romanticism which also gave birth to modern theoretical debates that
still affect us, and which threaten to destabilize the concept of disciplinary studies in general, to break down the boundaries, as it were. Behdad's concept of
"belatedness," when coupled with Nemoianu's argument for a Biedermeier
milieu that comes after early and high Romanticism but before the later tur-
bulence of a post-1850 Realism, becomes a rather elaborate, but I believe satisfactory explanation for why comparative literature is not a parallel product
of Jena-Berlin theorizing on literature, literariness, aesthetics, and the contradictions of Enlightenment discourse (radical criticism versus Bildung), but is a
belated product of the concerns and problems which marked this earlier, more
idealistic and philosophical phase of Romanticism. When we think in terms
of a bi-part model, where Romanticism is followed by a Biedermeier phase
that attempts to put thought and idea into a practical, and serviceable con-

text, via the creation of disciplinary studies, the building of museums, the inception of national literatures, the making of specializations, and so on, we realize that comparative literature is not paradoxically tied to the potentially destabilizing discourse of Hegelian and Schlegelian sweeps, and more recently, Derridian discursiveness, but is a "step removed" from theory. Why do I say this? By "step removed," I mean to say that comparative literature, as a product of the Biedermeierzeit, is itself historically and spatially removed from theory originating around Jena and Berlin, or rather, separated by time and context (about a quarter-century). This removal, rather than cementing the impossibility of a reconciliation between theory and discipline-praxis, has its good points. By being a "step removed" from high theory in its own origin, comparative literature is guaranteed autonomy through historical and existential facts, and precisely because of this, because of its Biedermeier-originated existence as a "discipline," it can attempt to reconcile itself with the revolutionary and destabilizing nature of theory, because by looking at theory and theoretical concerns, it does not need to "fear consuming itself in its own flames," a phrase that Beiser uses to explain the collapse of the Enlightenment/early Romantic project. It does not need to fear that by looking at and trying to understand theory, it will recreate the Hegelian and Schlegelian attempt to understand and transcend Kant, an attempt that turns into a Phoenix. As Nemoianu says, wrapped around Biedermeier events was "Metternich's system, not the repressive ogre-like enclosure it was made out to be by partisan commentators, but rather a dialectical and sophisticated framework that could preserve stability by absorbing and particularly by expecting opposition from within and without" (12). There is no destructive paradox enacted when comparative literature glances at its preceding, Romantic period, because, to use Behdad's terminology again, it retours around earlier events, and, I will add, allows earlier events to pass through it, thereby maintaining the potential for reconciliation between theory and discipline.

RECONCILIATION THROUGH LITERARY HISTORY AND OTHER THINGS

I mentioned in the introduction that in this final part of the paper, I would attempt reconciling theory and discipline (i.e., comparative literature) by bringing in the notion of literary history as a medium through which antagonisms can be subsumed, and perhaps even cancelled out, by larger narrative accounts of literary and theoretical development, by meta-endeavors, as it were. To view literary history as a possible salvation, where theoretical destabilizations and disciplinary cohesions come together, is problematic in this day and age, to say the least.

David Perkins, in his work, *Is Literary History Possible?*, voices serious reservations about the possibility and accuracy of literary history, to do anything. Literary history, of the narrative type, was rather popular during the first three-quarters of the nineteenth century, and was guided by three main assumptions: a) that literary works are formed by their historical context b) that change in literature takes place developmentally c) that this change is the unfolding of an idea, principle, or suprapersonal entity (1–2). The assault on literary history was already evident by the end of the nineteenth century, with its *fin de siècle* aestheticism, because such critics as Edmond Scherer and Emile Faguet pointed out that historical contextualism can explain everything except what one most wants to explain, literary "genius" (7). Russian Formalism did not question the possibility of writing literary history, but argued that historical contextualism was ineffective, and that traces of development were to be found in the text itself (8). New Criticism programmatically rejected literary history, and eventually, deconstruction, by exposing the aporias of periods, movements, genres, classifications, and so on, made it difficult, probably impossible to generalize texts and frame them within meta-historical discussions (8–9). Perkins remains unconvinced that literary history can be written, because future criteria will demand different literary histories, and so on, but he still believes that it is a necessary endeavor (17). He remains unimpressed by the obvious artificiality of literary history; the chosen starting point of discussion in literary history has a strong impact on the way the past is represented, so that quite often, a phase of synthesis and homogeneity is said to precede the period which is the subject of the book, as in one article by Marshall Brown on nineteenth-century Realism, which stipulates that the eighteenth century was "more unified," or in the work of Ian Watt, where the divisions of the eighteenth century are juxtaposed to the homogenous Renaissance and seventeenth century, or in the work of Victorian specialists, who speak of Romanticism as the lost age of "universals" (36–37). Perkins argues that the ending of a literary history is equally artificial, set up for reasons of climax, as in Wilhelm Scherer's *History of German Literature* from 1883, which concludes with Goethe, saying that the latest 50 years will not be dealt with, since they will "spoil the study" (37). As far as the postmodern, "encyclopedic" literary history is concerned (examples of which are the *Columbia Literary History of the United States* from 1987 and *A New History of French Literature* from 1989), Perkins dismisses it as not being literary history per se because it establishes diversity and contradiction as structural principles, foregoes closure and consensus, and most importantly, does not organize the past into an entity (56–60).

Roland Champagne, in his work, *Literary History in the Wake of Roland Barthes,* echoes certain aspects of Perkins' comments, particularly the opinion that the concept of literary history has been problematized in our own day and age. Barthes in fact played a key role in bringing theoretical concerns into the arena of literary history, and through that gesture, he foreshadows what I may be said to be doing here, namely, setting up literary history as a bridge on which theoretical, meta-literary concerns meet up with disciplinary and empirically oriented concerns regarding the integrity of national literatures, specific genres, styles, and so on. Barthes enlarged the empirical-scientific view of literary history developed by Gustave Lanson to include "that 'impressionism' which Lanson had easily relegated to an activity called 'criticism.' By introducing the subject into history, Barthes advocated a new era for literary history wherein texts of previous historical moments would be re-examined in order to account for the complex threads of the subjective investigator in the assumptions of established literary traditions" (3). Barthes refuted the systematic ordering of what he called "classical texts" by literary history into a linear and temporal succession of one tradition after another, by advocating the "modern text" (like the works of Flaubert), as having an "historical self-awareness" that paradoxically makes it "ahistorical," whereby we can, by reading the modern text, understand the problematic of literary history through our contemplation of how these new texts generate meaning, rather than how they can be grouped into convenient literary movements (5). It is interesting that Barthes should define the modern text, which invites interpretation rather than periodization, as originating around 1850, and as having something to do with Flaubert, because, as we remember, Ali Behdad applies his concept of "belatedness" to the orientalism which operates in Flaubert's *Notes de voyages* of 1850, this being a concept which I found easily explains and parallels the relationship of the Biedermeier to Romanticism, even though Behdad and Barthes seem to be speaking of a post-Biedermeier, post-1850 phase. It is entirely possible that they may not even have a Biedermeier context or paradigm in mind, but are, however implicitly, elaborating their arguments in terms of the more traditional, simpler, and cleaner Romanticism-Realism "break" in literary periods.

Barthes' approach, which brought the "subject" into the question of literary history, seems to have rubbed off on Mario J. Valdés' article, "Rethinking Literary History—Comparatively," because here, Valdés, while attempting to break the confines of typical, national literary histories, advises caution. He believes that a shift has occurred from "validation to signification," whereby literary historians must now "reconceptualize historical process to include the relations between texts and the contexts of production and reception . . . The Foucaultian linking of power and knowledge points here . . . to an awareness that, while events did occur in the past, we give meaning to [them] . . . This is not a defeatist invalidation of the process of history-writing; it is merely a frank acknowledgment of a hermeneutic reality" (6). Valdés further speaks of how in order for a "comparative literary history" to take such things into account, it would have to "foreground . . . methodological frameworks (hermeneutic, post-structuralist, post-colonial, feminist, and so on) and directly address its own theoretical assumptions regarding both texts and contexts (socio-cultural, economic, political, aesthetic). How this might work *in practice* [remains to be seen]" (6).

Valdés' concept of the "comparative literary history," which I believe would have a greater chance of reconciling theoretical discord with comparative literature as a coherent body and disciplinary effort, precisely because of the comparative thrust of such a history, is more difficult to set up than a merely national literary history, that functions within smaller boundaries, and that does not offer as great a promise of reconciliation. Even the current *Comparative Literary History Series* (initiated and sponsored by the International Comparative Literature Association) which is published under the directorship of Valdés, does not necessarily set up a full and comprehensive analysis of literary and meta-literary concerns; *Romantic Irony*, edited by Frederick Garber, obviously gravitates (with most of the articles) toward German literature, and as far as I can remember, there are no articles on Romantic Irony in Far Eastern literatures; in the case of *Symbolist Movement*, edited by Anna Balakian, most articles obviously gravitate towards France, and so on. Needless to say, an assessment of literary movements is usually tied to their country of origin, so to speak, and besides, comparative literary histories, like the series just mentioned, are limited by practical concerns as well (they would be thousands of pages long if they dealt with literary periods in a fully international fashion, and there is always the risk that a "forced internationalism" of certain movements would result, creating an artificial and false assessment). We should also remember that the above mentioned series is published as individual collections of separate articles, in "postmodern encyclopedic" style (to use Perkins' phrase), on certain topics and movements, so that the very form gravitates toward fragmentation. An example of a comparative literary history that functions as a narrative, putting movements into chapters, would be Werner P. Friederich's *Outline of Comparative Literature from Dante Alighieri to Eugene O'Neill*, published in 1954, but such a format also has its limitations, and may be accused of being forced, overly general, and artificial. Indeed, such ultra-comprehensive endeavors do have an amateurish air about them. Valdés' point is thus well taken, that comparative literary histories would be difficult to set up, because both methodological frameworks and theoretical assumptions would have to be taken into account.

In his *An Analytical Approach to Comparative Literature*, Jintaro Kataoka also speculates on the potential for comparative, and world literary histories. Among several interesting points that he makes are three which stood out in my mind, and which seem crucial if one is to develop a truly comparative literary history: a) for a comparative literary history to emerge, dimensional restrictions need to be overcome b) for such a history to emerge, the intuitive factor of literary creation needs to be accommodated for c) for this history to emerge, the literary historian must recognize as his true audience the writers who are spoken of. The first point, of overcoming dimensional restrictions, Kataoka appears to derive from John Drinkwater's *The Outlines of Literature and Art* (1924), which attempted to give form to a history of world literature, and Kataoka elaborates by saying that if "there could exist a legitimate history of world literature very well adapted to the life [political, economic, cultural, climactic, etc.] in these two different worlds [East and West], then and then only would there be able to appear a real history of the Western Literature and a valid history of the Eastern Literature" (16). Regarding the second point, of accommodating intuition, which Kataoka also calls the "impetus of life" and the "feeling of existence," it is said that intuition, being our thought at some primordial level, "is not yet intellect and as such it is not concerned with the relations between things: it cannot err, as intellect can, by referring *things* to the wrong *concepts*" (65); Kataoka argues that such a purely aesthetic, unerring idea (which he seems to manufacture by mixing the ideas of

Kant, Schelling, Bergson, and others) must be accommodated for in world literary histories, primarily because art, that is to say, literature, is being dealt with, and he offers an equation which would accommodate for this creative principle, that is evocative of Keats' "Truth and Beauty": (L times S) L = SLsquare, where S stands for scientific factors which endorse intuition through experiment, and L is literature, and where S corresponds with Keats' "Truth" and L with his "Beauty" (65). Regarding the third point, Kataoka argues that for "a literary historian, the aim and the interest he seeks to find are just those the author tries to embody . . . In creation the author should, either consciously or unconsciously, appreciate the position of the literary historian, in whose work the former is to be represented exclusively by his own productions" (83). The reason I mention Kataoka's points is because they demonstrate how a comparative literary history, particularly in order somehow to reconcile and intermesh high theory with the disciplinary endeavor of writing a literary history, would have to juggle several concepts and needs simultaneously. Kataoka's proposition is a perfect example of the difficulty of such an endeavor, because while his first point is well taken, that dimensional restrictions need to be broken for such a literary history to emerge (which echoes Valdés' point in his article), the second point, dealing with intuition as a pure, unerring, and Keatsian principle that must be interwoven into a comparative literary history, while it sounds pretty, threatens, much like the early Romantic endeavor to solve Enlightenment contradictions, "to consume itself in its own flames." Kataoka's final point, that literary historians should write for authors as their true audience, I am sure, would be attacked for leaning too closely on Formalist principles (i.e., that readers when reading, and writing, should put themselves into the mind of a writer).

Setting up a comparative literary history that would somehow be aware of its own theoretical limitations and fallacies, but would simultaneously offer an effective and understandable assessment of the topic at hand (literary influence, period styles, revolutionary trends, etc.), and thereby, would reconcile the dangerous, and cautionary aspects of theory, with the need to maintain a disciplinary endeavor (the very writing of a literary history), is not simple. Valdés' comments, Perkins' grudges, and Kataoka's all-too-lofty machinations are obvious examples of the difficult position I find myself in: offering literary history as a salvation, where theory and discipline meet. I believe the best way to ensure for success in this venture is to remain modest, and aware of the subtleties that are involved in the very process of writing, which becomes a meta-writing when literary history is involved. Earl Miner, in his *Comparative Poetics: An Intercultural Essay on Theories of Literature,* almost seems to be apologizing for writing his work, when he concludes the first chapter by saying the following: "Nothing in the preceding, nothing in what follows, is meant to argue for a single conception of comparative poetics. All that is argued, and it is quite enough, is that comparative poetics requires two things: a satisfactory conception and practice of comparison along with an attention to poetics (conceptions of literature) that rest on historically sound evidence" (32).

Post-structuralism would of course ask the question, What is "historically sound evidence"?, so that Miner's comment itself falls apart, once again undermining the purpose behind literary history. As I have said, comparative literary history may reconcile theory and discipline, but only through a cautionary and modest approach. My proposal for success requires that we write a conceptual literary history, which is a sub-branch of narrative literary history, but is a more interesting variant, because it organizes and interconnects events in a powerful way, by exhibiting the interrelation of events as the logical relations of ideas; a possible example would be to view only a "section" of the eighteenth century as the "Age of Reason," and then to display certain texts as being not completely representative, but only representative of particular "sides" of the idea in question (Perkins 49). We would have to keep in mind two things while writing such a subtle and cautionary history. First, we would have to acknowledge Barthes' conception of the "subject" as being an active factor in the construction of a literary history, whereby we would have to argue that our analysis of certain literary-historical periods, rather than extracting the "essence" of a period, is juxtaposing our own notion of the "essence of a period" onto the period in question in order to attempt explaining our own contemporary period, in the act of "hypothetically" explaining an earlier historical period, whereby the "hypotheticality" of this latter maneuver, rather than being cancelled out through the act of bestowing significance on our own period (echoing the Hegelian dialectic), would itself be recognized as significant, in the sense that certain hypothetical explanations are useful (practical and beneficial). The second thing we would have to keep in mind (which is required for the above mechanism to work) while writing a conceptual, comparative literary history, is a comment uttered by Dilthey, that while he cannot accept the teleological/mystical ideas of Hegel in unmodified form, he is willing to accept that because of complex and specific circumstances, an idea may indeed have an historical moment of prevalence (qtd. in Perkins 134).

The other, perhaps final way to attempt reconciling theory and comparative literature as a discipline, which may be accommodated for most appro-
priately in a conceptual literary history, by the way, is through the use of
geometrical models of discourse. However unusual or perverse it may sound,
I was inspired to propose this as a possible solution by a section of Paul de
Man's article, "The Resistance to Theory," where he mentions the following:
"Seventeenth-century epistemology, for instance, at the moment when the relationship between philosophy and mathematics is particularly close, holds up
the language of what it calls geometry (*mos geometricus*), and which in fact
includes the homogenous concatenation between space, time and number, as
the sole model of coherence and economy. Reasoning *more geometrico* is said
to be almost the only mode of reasoning that is infallible, because it is the only
one to adhere to the true method, whereas all other ones are by natural necessity in a degree of confusion of which only geometrical minds can be aware"
(364–65). Geometrical models, precisely because of their three-dimensional
nature of representation, whether they be on paper or contemplated in the
mind, allow for a spatial analogy with the external world, outside of the "subject," and thereby, such models allow for bonding between theoretical concepts, literary/aesthetic styles, and architectural figures. This may be a possible
solution that brings together theory and comparative literature (as a discipline
requiring cohesion), via the representation of a conceptual-stylistic-figural continuum, through the three-dimensionality of geometrical models. I should mention a rather important point here, that while these geometrical models which
I am proposing do evoke and should evoke spatial constructs (architecture,
etc.), they are nonetheless and necessarily toned-down, by being *only* models,
and as such, they are subtle and fluid enough to function within a discipline,
such as ours, that deals with discourse, text, and the very notion of medium.

These geometrical models of discourse would, in their final stage, best work
within a conceptual, comparative literary history, because they themselves,
through their spatial analogy with the world, stand as comparative con-
cepts/constructs. The models would probably emerge from a subtle and historically self-conscious analysis, that may deal with literature per se, or certain
textual features, or even the notion and nature of medium and communication. The models might even emerge initially within the context of a rather
limited discussion, that may only deal with a few writers, or a few theoreticians, but would eventually, gradually, and cautiously, be verified or disproved
within larger contexts (literary histories, New Historical readings, political-

ideological discussions, etc.). It may be the case that a certain number of these proposed models of discourse would be rejected as inaccurate or incomplete, but that a few would be found to be rather effective in their potential for explanation within our discipline. To use the example of myself, I began playing with the concept of these geometrical models through my reading of the Lacan-Derrida-Johnson-Irwin debate on Poe's "The Purloined Letter," which is a rather focused topic, but gradually, after becoming acquainted with hermeneutics, I was further able to develop my views on geometrical models, and their potential to reconcile antagonisms, by looking at Gadamer's disapproval of Cartesian and Hegelian models of subjectivity, and his preference for Aristotle, who, unlike Plato, does not separate theory from praxis (qtd. in Hoy 60). This Platonic separation of theory from praxis is, at some fundamental level, what I have been contemplating throughout this paper. The geometrical models which I am proposing, that might crop up anywhere but would probably be used as tools in conceptual literary histories, are possible solutions to discord and fragmentation, and I assume, as with any such unusual proposal, modifications are both required and welcome.

The table is my own attempt at these geometrical (and numerical) models, and is merely offered to illustrate what I have been saying. In the table are various models that I have associated with certain types of discourse, and certain period styles. In the case of the Rococo model, I have left one side open, to emphasize that the Rococo was a "play of surfaces," via *chinoiserie* and other features, and not a closed system like Romanticism, which Frye compares to Greek architecture and says, citing Melville, that both showed "reverence for the Archetype" (25). In the case of the Hegelian dialectic, I set the model up as doubling the Aristotelian dialectic (which Gadamer prefers for its emphasis on "phronesis," i.e. practical wisdom, the recognition of man's finitude and historicity) (qtd. in Hoy 60). In this way, my model for the Hegelian dialectic accommodates for Romantic reflexivity, and for the Hegelian idea of "coming-to-self-consciousness," which gradually translates historical experience into a false absolute, giving the individual a sense of "being in a center," and other similar things. Such were the thoughts which went through my mind as I set these models up. In the case of the Derridian model, I set it up as framing the Hegelian model for reflexivity, because Derrida argues against "logocentrism" but is still forced to use the language he disdains. In the case of the Poe-Borges model, I set it up as framing the Platonic notion of an "ideal truth beyond reality," in order to account for the "dream within a dream" quality

Models of Discourse

Type	Value	Shape
Socratic-Platonic discourse	2 or 4	
Sophoclean-Aristotelian dialectic	1 or 3	
Rococo chatoyante-broderie	$1^1/_2$	
Hegelian dialectic	3	
Poesque-Borgesian discourse	4	
Derridian discursive dialectic	$3^1/_2$	
Hegelian dialectic doubled and self-framed	7	
Hegelian dialectic multiplied infinitely	n	

that is found in the work of these two writers. The last two models, the doubled, self-framed Hegelian dialectic and the infinitely multiplied one, have not yet been attained in discourse, and are my speculation on "future models," that might crop up in future literary-historical periods, and so on.

Even though these models require further elaboration, more discussion as to why particular geometrical shapes were chosen and as to how exactly such shapes would be used as disciplinary tools, a lengthy speech on these and similar issues would go beyond the immediate topic of this paper. Once again, I must stress that the views, particularly of the third part of this paper, are only possible solutions, and require further analysis, but I will venture to say that at least some of my opinions may be relevant. It is already evident in these models, even at a primarily visual level, that some faint reconciliation between literary theory and our discipline seems to have taken place. The models are, through their simple, reduced, and elegant lines, simultaneously reverential toward the Biedermeier smugness of disciplines and caricatural of the high Romantic endeavors of Derrida and company.

WORKS CITED

Abrams, M.H. "English Romanticism: The Spirit of the Age." *Romanticism Reconsidered*. Ed. Northrop Frye. New York: Columbia UP, 1963. 26–72.

Abrams, M.H. "The Deconstructive Angel." *Modern Criticism and Theory: A Reader*. Ed. David Lodge. London: Longman, 1988. 265–76.

Bakhtin, Mikhail. "From the Prehistory of Novelistic Discourse." *Modern Criticism and Theory: A Reader*. Ed. David Lodge. London: Longman, 1988. 125–56.

Balakian, Anna. Ed. *The Symbolist Movement in the Literature of the European Languages*. Budapest: Akadémiai, 1982.

Behdad, Ali. *Belated Travelers: Orientalism in the Age of Colonial Dissolution*. Durham: Duke UP, 1994.

Beiser, Frederick C. "Early Romanticism and the *Aufklärung*." *What is Enlightenment?: Eighteenth-Century Answers and Twentieth-Century Questions*. Ed. James Schmidt. Berkeley: U of California P, 1996. 317–29.

Champagne, Roland. *Literary History in the Wake of Roland Barthes: Re-Defining the Myths of Reading*. Birmingham: Summa, 1984.

Clements, Robert John. *Comparative Literature as Academic Discipline: A Statement of Principles, Praxis, Standards*. New York: Modern Language Association of America, 1978.

De Man, Paul. "The Resistance to Theory." *Modern Criticism and Theory: A Reader.* Ed. David Lodge. London: Longman, 1988. 355–71.

Derrida, Jacques. "Structure, Sign, and Play in the Discourse of the Human Sciences." *Literary Theories in Praxis.* Ed. Shirley Staton. Philadelphia: The U of Pennsylvania P, 1987. 390–409.

Friederich, Werner Paul. *Outline of Comparative Literature from Dante Alighieri to Eugene O'Neill.* Chapel Hill: U of North Carolina UP, 1954.

Frye, Northrop. "The Drunken Boat: The Revolutionary Element in Romanticism." *Romanticism Reconsidered.* Ed. Northrop Frye. New York: Columbia UP, 1963. 1–25.

Garber, Frederick, ed. *Romantic Irony.* Budapest: Akadémiai, 1988.

Hanak, Miroslav John. *A Guide to Romantic Poetry in Germany.* New York: Peter Lang, 1987.

Hirsch, E.D., Jr. "Faulty Perspectives." *Modern Criticism and Theory: A Reader.* Ed. David Lodge. London: Longman, 1988. 254–63.

Hoy, David Couzens. *The Critical Circle: Literature, History, and Philosophical Hermeneutics.* Los Angeles: U of California P, 1982.

Jakobson, Roman. "Linguistics and Poetics." *Modern Criticism and Theory: A Reader.* Ed. David Lodge. London: Longman, 1988. 32–57.

Jakobson, Roman. "The Metaphoric and Metonymic Poles." *Modern Criticism and Theory: A Reader.* Ed. David Lodge. London: Longman, 1988. 57–61.

Kataoka, Jintaro. *An Analytical Approach to Comparative Literature.* Tokyo: Shinozaki Shorin, 1970.

Malekovic, Vladimir. "Bidermajer u Hrvatskoj: Politicka, gospodarska i kulturna osnovica" ("Biedermeier in Croatia: Its Political, Economic and Cultural Foundations"). *Bidermajer u Hrvatskoj (Biedermeier in Croatia).* 1997. Zagreb: Muzej za umjetnost i obrt (4 November 1999): <http://www.tel.hr/muo/bider/hrv/hmalek.htm>.

Miner, Earl. *Comparative Poetics: An Intercultural Essay on Theories of Literature.* Princeton: Princeton UP, 1990.

Nemoianu, Virgil. *The Taming of Romanticism: European Literature and the Age of Biedermeier.* Cambridge: Harvard UP, 1984.

Perkins, David. *Is Literary History Possible?* Baltimore: The Johns Hopkins UP, 1992.

Selden, Raman. *A Reader's Guide to Contemporary Literary Theory.* London: Prentice Hall, 1997.

Shklovsky, Victor. "Art as Technique." *Modern Criticism and Theory: A Reader.* Ed. David Lodge. London: Longman, 1988. 16–30.

Valdés, Mario J. "Rethinking Literary History—Comparatively." *ACLS Occasional Paper, No. 27.* New York: American Council of Learned Societies, 1994.

Zivkovic, Dragisa. *Bidermajerski Usamljenik Sterija (Biedermeier Loner Sterija).* Novi Sad: Matica Srpska, 1983.

Popular and Highbrow Literature:
A Comparative View

Peter Swirski

Music historians record that when ardent admirers mobbed Verdi at the opening of one of his operas, brown-nosing him that it was sublime, the maestro said only, "Fine. What was the ticket sale?" Seconded by no less a champion of literary sense and sensibility than Doctor Johnson, famed for quipping that no man but a blockhead ever wrote except for money, Verdi's brazenly mercantile attitude challenges one of the most dogged myths about art. The Pure Art myth wants us to believe that high art abides in the realm of creation untainted by the cupidity of its lower caste cousins. Like Disney's Seven Dwarves, who typically hang out in a troop, this myth does not dwell alone in the forest of literary and cultural misconceptions. On most days it can be seen having cocktails atop the Ivory Tower with a small but influential coterie: the myth that the Novel Is Dead, the myth that People Don't Read Books Anymore, the myth that the Paperback Is a New Kid on the Block, the myth that Reading Pulp Fiction Is Bad For You, and the grand myth that We Can Ignore Popular Literature.

In what follows I would like to take a closer look at some of the ways in which highbrow literature and popular fiction relate to each other. My aim is to take stock of select sociological data and aesthetic arguments that have accrued between the birth of popular literature—the term I will use interchangeably with fiction—in the eighteenth century and its *drosophila*-like explosion in the twentieth century. Its career may be all the more remarkable in that, for the most part, it has taken place without the sanction of the "eliterati" or literary scholarship in general. Like a backyard fungus, mass fiction conquered the world without the benefit of a gardener's pruning knife (in the shape of systematic criticism) or clods of fertilizer (art grants, writer in residence funds, poet laureate stipends, government subsidies, etc.) which midwife the efforts of highbrow *littérateurs*. More than two hundred years of fruition in all corners of the world warrants the examination of popular literature as a *literary* phenomenon, rather than as a mere cultural nuisance.

In one of his inspired cartoons, Gary Larson depicted a bunch of hyperactive animals in a jungle clearing, all swaying and dancing to a blasting transistor radio. The caption read: "What Sloths Do When No One Is Around." I suspect that being at once an aficionado of "serious" literature and a buff of pulp fiction may be the lot of many scholars, students, and critics of literature. Professing the classics and, when no one is around, languishing over a wellthumbed copy of a Simenon, LaPlante (of *Prime Suspect* fame), or a McMurtry, may be typical symptoms of a literary split-personality syndrome. One is reminded of a playful scene from Walker Percy's *The Moviegoer,* in which a small-time stockbroker, Binx Bolling, tries to conceal the book he reads at work from the eyes of his secretary (for Percy, see Mills <http://metalab.unc.edu/wpercy>). With a full professional mien, he thus buries himself in *Arabia Deserta* enclosed in a Standard & Poor binder. In another incarnation, it seems, he might be reading Tom Wolfe's new (old) social novel *A Man in Full* inside the covers of Thomas Wolfe's *You Can't Go Home Again* (for Wolfe, see Farrar et al. <http://www.tomwolfe.com>; for background, see, e.g., Varsava).

Such professional dereliction/curiosity/openness (choose one) is not too likely, however, to be tolerated/accepted/encouraged in contemporary departments of literature. Many appear not to have heard of the large corpus of scholarship about *Trivialliteratur* or *paralittérature* in German and French scholarship, let alone the existence of such studies in comparative literature. The sentiment expressed to me by a senior English professor at a major North American university may be typical in this regard. Asked why *literary* scholars by and large ignore popular *literature,* he replied that this is not really the domain of departments of literature but of cultural studies. This strikes me as a grave abdication of professional responsibility. Any demarcation of a field of study that leaves 97% of its subjects camping outside the city gates must be regarded as methodologically suspect. A chemist contending that the proper domain of chemistry is only one element, even one as valuable as gold, would surely not be worth his NaCl. A botanist who identified all flora with a wellmanicured hibiscus garden, ignoring the leaves of grass which surround it on all sides, would not be likely to have the fruits of his studies accepted in any self-respecting journal.

And yet the opinion persists, often as part of an unarticulated and thus unexamined set of background beliefs, that popular fiction has no merit and thus no place in literary studies. In the absence of an authentic axiological theory, backed with rigorous analysis and systematic evidence, such a sweeping verdict sounds more like wishful thinking than a viable research position. A scientist who declares a compound worthless just because it smells funny is as misguided as a literary scholar who a priori limits himself/herself to the study of what other scholars study, while ignoring what the rest of society depends on for its daily cultural bread. It remains to be examined if a given set of cultural perceptions, no matter how widely shared or deeply entrenched, can be relied upon to check with available data. Indeed, as I will try to show, many of the perceptions favored in academic circles and in society at large are but distant shadows of reality outside the highbrow cave.

I begin with a careful look at the statistical and sociological data which sheds light on many of the myths accepted as part of our cultural subconscious, among them the death of the novel, the decline of the reading public, and the impact of paperback publishing and commercial pressures in shaping literary output. All of them have been used as argumentative spades to dig literary trench lines, or quarried for rhetorical stones with which a Great Wall of China has been built around a handful of perennial literary classics. I will also discuss many of the aesthetic arguments used to divert traffic away from the teeming ocean of popular literature to the literary corner-store, with its carefully labeled, safe-to-drink bottles of filtered water. Both parts of my discussion are, in effect, extended arguments for greater literary democracy. As such, they conclude with a few recommendations for the type of critical response to popular fiction more compatible with its actual socio-aesthetic status. Further, the comparative character of this study is a direct reflection of its focus on *both* popular and highbrow literatures, including the nature of their more or less uneasy cohabitation. Quite apart from this intrinsic reason, the fact that popular fiction is by now a truly international cultural and business phenomenon which transcends all national, political, or language barriers, demands a nonsectarian comparative approach. Given this situation, wherever possible I have tried to include statistics on global and select European trends in addition to the homegrown market. The fact that much of my data comes from the North

American continent is a simple reflection of the availability of resources and the sheer size of its market which renders it one of the global trend-setters.

POPULAR AND HIGHBROW LITERATURE: A SOCIOLOGICAL VIEW

The novel is dead. The author is dead. So hail two dicta which have gained much currency in contemporary culture. Browbeaten by their air of finality, one might indeed be inclined to accept them at face value. And yet, authors Barthes and Foucault notwithstanding, other authors seems to be doing fine, despite the poststructuralist campaign to drop them from the curriculum (for a trenchant critique, see Livingston). After the tragic executions in Nigeria and the lifting of the *fatwa* which hung for years over Rushdie (for Rushdie, see <http://landow.stg.brown.edu/post/rushdie/rushdieov.html>) and who is now free to appear for photo-ops with ex-Playboy bunnies at high-profile West Coast book fairs (see *Playboy Magazine* <http://www.playboy.com>), the quantity of authors on the endangered list has grown scarce. In fact, the real challenges to authorship seem to be coming from the directions so far overlooked by critics: fiction "factories," novelizations, direct mail-order publishing, or multimedia-packaging. But what about the death of the novel? Somehow the myth refuses to crawl into a dark hole and say uncle. The novel is dead, we hear, slain by the twin dragon of TV and Hollywood films. But, as Patricia Holt reports in 1979 in the *Publishers Weekly,* a full one third of all movies made annually in America are based on published novels. "People don't read any more," we read in the print media. Yet the postwar decades have witnessed a runaway boom in publishing (see below), so much so that the book industry keeps sending red flares calling for some form of reduction in numbers. Books are going the way of the dodo, chip in the tekkies, clipping to their belts, next to the pager and the cell-phone, the electronic book (a hand-held computer that uses plastic cards holding the entire contents of a novel and even provides the illusion of page turning). Yet, although such reading devices have been around for some time now, the paper-bound, dog-eared book refuses to throw in the towel—and for a good reason. After all, as John Tebbel observes in his short history of book publishing in the United States, "Who wants to go to bed with a floppy disk—or with a microfilm projector?" (155).

Let us examine, then, the facts behind the "decline" of the novel. Despite all forecasts and most people's media-fed impressions, book publishing has flourished since 1950 and the dawn of the TV era. UNESCO and other sources (e.g., Curwen; Escarpit) report that worldwide book production, as expressed in number of titles, has increased more than threefold in the decades between 1950 and 1980 (see UNESCO <http://www.unesco.org/general/eng/publish/index.html>). The accepted estimate for 1950 is 230,000 titles, with the total climbing to 725,000 titles in 1980. This rate of increase is much higher than that of the world's population which, during the same period, grew from 2.5 billion to 4.5 billion. The number of book copies printed is estimated as 2.5 billion in 1950, and a whopping 9 billion in 1980. In other words, where there was one book per person worldwide in 1950, thirty years later there were two—a 100% increase in little more than one generation. It may be worth noting that during the same three decades the global literacy level has risen from 1.2 billion to 2.5, which puts is (regrettably) at a rate far below that of book production.

The numbers closer to home are even more impressive. It is hard to square the myth that people do not read books anymore with the fact that book production, the quantity of bookstores, or total sales fail to display any signs of decline. Quite the contrary. The number of new titles released each year in the United States, for example, more than quadrupled between 1950 and 1991, with the respective figures of roughly 11,000 and 49,000 (after peaking at 50,000 in 1985). In the same period the number of bookstores shot up from over 8,000 to more than 25,000. And, driving a symbolic stake through the heart of the myth of a non-reading public, the total 1991 book sales were 35 times greater than in 1950, ballooning from under $0.5 billion to $16.1 billion. These trends are, needless to say, not confined to the US. As reported in the 1996 edition of *Five Hundred Years of Printing,* the approximate number of new titles released in Great Britain in 1955 and 1995 was, respectively, 14,000 and 90,000 (Steinberg 243).

In North America, a sure sign of the publishing industry's vitality is the keen interest that the Wall Street has evinced in its operations over the last three decades. The 1960s, with skyrocketing college enrollments and post-Sputnik investment in education, research and libraries, were boom years for publishing. The key players thrived by becoming public stock companies to fund a tsunami wave of expansion (e.g., Random House, Houghton Mifflin), diversifying into other fields (e.g., Macmillan, Harcourt), swallowing its smaller brethren (e.g., Harper & Row buying out J.B. Lippincott, the Hearst syndicate adding the hardcover Arbor House to their softcover Avon Books), or succumbing to the widely publicized "urge to merge" (e.g. Doubleday and Dell, Viking and Penguin). The clearest index of how profitable book publishing has become is the speed with which the movie industry got into the act. MCA, Filmway Pictures, Gulf & Western, and others, all now own reputable publishing houses (Gulf & Western, for instance, boasts Paramount, Simon & Schuster, and Pocket Books in its entertainment division), with Warner Communications having founded its own Warner Books (see Warner <http://www.warnerbooks.com>). In the long run, the emergence of such multimedia octopi, with tentacles in film, TV, cable TV, video, magazines, newspapers, and book publishing, is likely to be one of the more significant cultural trend-setters for the future.

Besides establishing beyond reasonable doubt that book reading is *not* in decline, what else can recent statistics tell us? Two things may be worth singling out. One is the negligible percentage of books traditionally accorded attention by literary critics and scholars—time-tried classics, poetry, and new literary fiction—among this renaissance of reading. The estimates for book distribution through US general retailers reveal that, for the four most relevant categories of fiction, their respective shares of the 1985 market were: popular fiction (31.5%), best-sellers (12.1%), classics (0.9%), literary fiction and poetry (0.3%). In relative numbers, the situation is even more lopsided, with the classics, literary fiction and poetry amounting to less than 3% of all four fiction categories under discussion. Let us face it. The sea of literature that washes daily over our society, the type of ideas it disseminates, the nature of values it feeds back into public opinion and political decision making, the range of subjects and concerns it touches on, and the level of cultural awareness it shapes, dwarfes the Ivory Tower into a check-threatened ivory castle on a busy cultural chessboard.

It is true that, in terms of titles released annually, highbrow fiction commands a much greater share of the market than distribution figures allow. On the other hand, there is little doubt that there yawns a gulf the size of Norman Mailer's ego between the public and the academic custodians of letters in what they buy, read, and peg their cultural literacy on. The knee-jerk defense that the highbrow 3% forms the cream of the literary crop must contend with several obvious rejoinders. Quite apart from the accuracy of such claims—as I show below—such aesthetic elitism seems misplaced in the consideration of literature in its socio-cultural context. Moreover, a defense of this kind could hold fort to the extent that popular novels routinely ranked a level of critical analysis comparable to the classics, which they manifestly do not. When occasional pulp writers are pulled out of the literary cellar, however, with their jackets dusted and their pedigrees suppressed, they are discovered to be not so shabby at all, as evidenced by the recent MLA convention panels on Raymond Chandler, Stephen King, or Bram Stoker.

Outside of allegations of popular literature's inferiority or its inability to pollinate culture with commendable ideas and attitudes, there may be quantitative reasons for critical inattention to popular fiction. More books have seen the light of day since 1950 than in all previous stages of history combined. "The point has long since passed," conclude the editors of *Five Hundred Years of Printing*, "when any library or bookseller can stock more than a fraction of the books in print, or when every book which merits reviews receives any" (Steinberg 243). Noting the "enormous number of manuscripts received by any editor," the authors of *Books: The Culture and Commerce of Publishing* opine that, "Were editors to rely solely on formal means of manuscript submission. . . . publishers would soon go out of business" (Coser 73). Doubleday, for one, estimates that each year it receives an average of 10,000 manuscripts "over the transom" (the industry's term for "unsolicited") alone, of which only a few may be signed on (see Balkin 6).

At the threshold of the new millennium, the estimated number of new titles published worldwide in a given year approaches 1,000,000. The number of books in print in Great Britain alone is today well in excess of 700,000. More than 300 paperback titles are released *monthly* in the United States. The number of pulp-fiction booklets (cheap 64-page popular fiction novelettes) which flood the German market is over 200 million a year. And so on, and so forth. More than ever before in the history Western civilization, the production, and consumption of books has reached inflationary proportions. Neither the market, nor the critical superstructure can sustain such a "Honey, I Blew Up the Book" tempo of growth. The volume of words deposited daily on library bookshelves, already sardined to the point of bursting, is staggering. An instructive metonymy of this state of affairs may be the micro world of scholarly and scientific publishing. Before the formation of the Association of American University Presses in 1932, only 8 presses were reported at an informal meeting of directors; fifty years later there were more than 70. The flood of publications in learned journals and conference proceedings is so urgent that most institutional libraries have been forced to impose draconian limits on book acquisition. In the 1980s it gradually became necessary to publish indices to indices of publication titles as a measure of coping with this deluge of information. One can only wonder how much time such meta-indices can buy, and how many years away we are from having to resort to publishing indices of indices of indices.

With the volume of writing growing at a head-spinning rate, the literary culture loses its ability to function critically, buried under pyramids of books that no one will ever have time to read. The critical community has traditionally followed a strategy inherited from the days when books were scarce enough to command individual attention and attract universal response. Out of what for centuries has been a genteel trickle, then a middle-class river, finally a modern deluge of print, critics filter out a manageable and increasingly smaller fraction. This select group, its aesthetic status bolstered by the virtue of having been separated from a field so large, is subsequently awarded the luxury of in-depth analysis and critique. There is not much talk about the literary detritus which does not make it to the tip of the critical Ararat since, as everyone knows, it is inherently inferior to the anointed sample. The elitist nature of this process is satirized by the folksy aphorism about two kinds of literature: that which is read and that which is studied by critics and literary scholars. One can detect behind this polarity the capricious shadow of the machinery of canon selection. During his career, few writers could rival Ring Lardner in popular *and* critical acclaim, with Hemingway among the cognoscenti who lauded and applauded his popular style (for Lardner and Hemingway, see Topping, <http://www.tridget.com/lardnermania/>; Joedaisy, <http://www.ernest.hemingway.com>). Lardner's syndicated sales exceeded Hemingway's, and his best fiction, such as the celebrated "You Know Me Al" series, earned him critical accolades around the country.

Yet, today, the posthumous author of *True at First Light: A Fictional Memoir* (1999) is a bull of a classic, while Lardner's stories are buried at the "sematary" labeled "popular fiction." Is it because Lardner was a humorist writing in the hale, low fallutin' vernacular he knew from years as an itinerant sportswriter? But that should place him squarely in the populist tradition of Dickens or Twain. Is it the lowbrow stigma of baseball as his first subject matter that cost him the laurels lavished on writers on proper literary subjects, such as bull-fighting, rum-running, or marlin fishing? But then, how could Bernard Malamud attain the first rank in American letters, having inaugurated his career in 1952 with a novel about baseball (*The Natural*)? Such questions about canon formation are worth deliberating inasmuch as the answers to them may have far-reaching critical consequences. A prior verdict about the blood-line of a given novel (popular or "literary") may affect the verdict about its aesthetic attributes, given that highbrow fiction is for the most part approached in a symptomatically a-generic fashion. It would be iconoclastic and contrary to established critical practice to approach works from the top of the big literary pile in terms of popular genre novels. Few connoisseurs could be induced to interpret Dostoyevsky's *Crime and Punishment* as an inferior (because suspense-less) murder mystery, Mann's *Doctor Faustus* as an inferior (because unscarifying) satanic fantasy, or Malamud's *The Assistant* as an inferior—because failed—Harlequin romance. Yet no such categorical benefit of a doubt is granted to works booted to the other end of the literary spectrum.

The typical view of popular fiction may be summarized by two tacit equations: Popular Literature=Bad Literature (if it were good, it would not be popular in the first place), and Popular Literature=Genre Literature (it appeals to many by being simplistic, schematic, and repetitive—in other words, by amply betraying its heritage). Given such premises, it is hardly surprising that many studies of contemporary fiction continue to subscribe to the myth of a categorical disunity between "serious" literature and mass entertainment. When popular fiction enters the picture at all, it is mostly in case studies which exemplify and buttress the same hierarchical system which can accept the literature of entertainment in the past, but only the literature of enlightenment from the present. My point here is not that all popular fiction is good literature, because much of the time it manifestly is not. There are good reasons to believe that a great deal of popular fiction goes in one eye and out the other, and that many a novel is no more than a short-lived and forgettable experience for its readers. Granting all that, popular fiction is by now a ubiquitous phenomenon which refers to and comments on many aspects of contemporary life, in the end informing (and in some cases perhaps even forming) the background of many popular values and beliefs. Moreover, it bears reminding ourselves that among its offerings, almost a priori destined for the cultural trash can, are literary works as worthy of notice as anything in the canon. The charge that genre fiction has no aesthetic merit could only be parroted by someone ignorant of the quirky horror novels of Thomas M. Disch, the ground-breaking police procedurals of Maj Sjöwall and Per Wahlöo, the neo-noir trilogy of Philip Kerr, the literate spy fiction of David Cornwell (alias John Le Carré), the revisionist westerns of Larry McMurtry, the scientific fiction of Stanislaw Lem (see Swirski 1997, 1999), the tragicomic fantasies of Karel Čapek, or the stylish erotica of Erica Jong. For that matter, one of the funniest and brainiest comedies of the recent years was the madcap *The Road to Omaha*, from the writer touted as incapable of writing anything but *ludlums* (espionage thrillers of the tritest and most repetitive sort)—Robert Ludlum.

But what about the much deplored invasion of paperbacks and their commercial threat to the noble art of writing in the post-war years of this century? As documented in the *International Book Publishing: An Encyclopedia*, between the arrival of the first printing press in the Massachusetts Bay colony in 1638 and the end of the eighteenth century, about 50,000 books, pamphlets, broadsheets, and newspapers were printed. Most were paperbacks. In fact, the first clothbound book, Charlotte A. Eaton's *Rome in the Nineteenth Century*, did not appear until 1827. While in the eighteenth century, we may also set the record straight on other supposedly twentieth-century bogeymen: the bestseller and formula fiction. Susanna Rowson's *Charlotte Temple*, published in 1793, was *the* best selling book of the century, continuing to retail for another 100 years and becoming one of the best-selling books of the nineteenth century as well. Combining illicit sex and melodramatic characters, and alluding to well-known national events, the novel mined a recipe which is proving its selling power to this day.

The next wave of paperbound books arrived between 1830 and 1845, triggered off by the replacement of the Gutenberg screw press by the high-speed cylinder press which for the first time allowed publishers to reach a mass market. These modern paperbacks were, for the most part, pirated popular British novels, sold for a quarter in peacetime, or shipped in bales to the front lines during the Civil War. After the paperback fiction boom of the 1890s, the 1920s saw yet another paperback revolution when E. Haldeman-Julius launched the cheapest of all mass market lines, the Little Blue Books, marketed with the aid of full-page newspaper ads. Priced at a nickel, and with hundreds of numbered titles to be ordered simply by circling, these books became an American institution. The paperback novel received another boost in 1939 when Robert F. de Graff created Pocket Books, alchemizing the quickly yellowing (owing to a high acid content) pulp paper into gold. Packing racy, modern content in catchy, multicolored covers, mass-printed by rotary presses, and sold through newsstands and outlets run by print-media wholesalers, these 25-cent book-wonders sold in the millions. Available during World War II through the

Armed Services Editions, they offered countless soldiers reading material, laying the groundwork for the vast expansion of the postwar market.

It may be true that nineteenth-century publishers thought of themselves not as merchandisers but business men of letters, intent on promoting good literature. It did not save them, however, from charges of commercialization and sellout which, if anything, show that the cultural battle lines of today were drawn much earlier than commonly supposed (a good source on the origins of popular fiction critique is Lowenthal and Fiske's "The Debate Over Art and Popular Culture in Eighteenth-Century England"). The well-known *North American Review* bemoaned in 1843: "Literature begins to assume the aspect and undergo the mutations of trade. The author's profession is becoming as mechanical as that of the printer and the bookseller, being created by the same causes and subject to the same laws" (Douglas 82). As early as 1890, *Publisher's Weekly* thundered at the creeping commercialism: "This is an age of ambition. . . . If literature and art are to be treated as common merchandise . . . it will make commonplace the manners of our people and their intelligence restricted to the counting-room" (qtd. in Coser 17–18). Such sentiments reached crescendo in the clerical and political anti-fiction crusade of the 1890s, in the heyday of a fiction boom which swept America between 1890 and 1920. With publishers devoting up to 70% of their advertising budgets to popular literature and the public clamoring for more, popular novels were accused of depleting the moral fiber of the country, with calls for curbing the production of novels by law. Clearly, today's publishing trends are *nihil novi sub sole*— the fact apparent once again from Henry Holt in "The Commercialization of Literature," published in 1905 in the prestigious *Atlantic Monthly*. "The more authors seek publishers solely with reference to what they will pay in the day's market, the more publishers bid against one another as stock brokers do, and the more they market their wares as the soulless articles of ordinary commerce are marketed, the more books become soulless things" (578), remonstrated Holt, the dean of American publishers.

As I examine these and related charges below, we should keep in mind that, while in absolute numbers popular fiction may indeed contain more inferior prose than its highbrow counterpart; it is not at all certain that this relation can be sustained in *relative* terms. For all we know, the percentage of intelligent prose against the total volume of output may be no different for popular and highbrow fiction. If so, it would mean that in real terms there is *more* good writing coming out of the popular, rather than the highbrow region of the literary spectrum. Chandler, at once a purveyor of hardboiled mysteries and one of the most accomplished authors of his time, demurred in the introduction to *The Simple Art of Murder:* "The average critic never recognizes achievement when it happens. He explains it after it has become respectable" (*Later Novels* 1016; for Chandler, see Moss <http://www.geocities.com/athens/parthenon/3224/>). It might thus be worth the while of Chandler's better-than-average critic to prospect the less charted regions of the literary country to see if we have not lost anything by sticking to the well-trodden highways.

POPULAR AND HIGHBROW LITERATURE: AN AESTHETIC VIEW

Below I will outline and discuss some of the most persistent criticisms brought to bear on popular fiction. I will follow the analysis developed by Herbert J. Gans in his ground-breaking study of contemporary taste cultures, *Popular Culture and High Culture*. In the process I will update and refine his insights to reflect what is distinctive about the contemporary American literary market. In a break from Gans, I focus exclusively on the literary domain both in my theoretical remarks and in my choice of examples. Also, while not shying away from sociological data when available, I will extend my discussion to some of the structural and aesthetic aspects of popular novels. Finally, while I will examine each of the charges in some detail, for reasons of space and focus I will largely refrain from elaborating the separate arguments or nuances of opinion among individual critics that go into these censures.

Broadly speaking, the critique of popular fiction can be separated into four related charges: 1) the negative character of popular literature creation: popular fiction is objectionable because, unlike high literature, it is mass-produced by profit-oriented hacks whose sole aim is to gratify the base tastes of a paying audience; 2) its negative effects on high literary culture: popular literature steals from highbrow literature, thus debasing it, and it lures away potential contributors, thus depleting the latter's pool of talent; 3) its negative effects on the audience (readership): the consumption of popular fiction at best produces spurious gratification, and at worst can be emotionally and cognitively harmful to the reader; 4) its negative effects on the society at large: the mass distribution and wide appeal of popular fiction lower the cultural level of the reading public and encourage political, social and cultural dictatorship by creating a passive and apathetic audience rendered highly responsive to the techniques of mass demagoguery and propaganda. Let us look more closely at the first indictment. It consists of three causally related charges: 1a) commercialism: popular literature is just another profit-oriented industry; 1b) uniformity: in order to be profitable, this industry must create a homogenous product with the lowest common denominator; 1c) alienation: this implicit or explicit transaction turns creators of popular literature into assembly line drones who surrender the individual expression of their skills, emotions, and values.

In a partial response, let us consider the following: Popular literature naturally operates on the premise of maximizing audiences and turning a profit, but so does much of highbrow fiction, especially in the contemporary climate in which government subsidies have become scarce and wealthy patrons few. It is true that one cannot yet buy books by Calvino or Eco printed on rolls of toilet paper, as is the case with some homegrown popular novels (e.g., William Morrow's *The Book of Lists*) for a nominal price of $3 (1980s' price). Oh, Dawn, a New York company promotes its publication list in this way in the hope that people, after having used the toilet paper in the standard fashion, will remove to the bookstore and get the paperback for more leisurely reading. Yet, the same processes are at work in the case of renowned highbrow writers whose names function precisely as trademarks which are used to promote their marketability. Who would ever dream of purchasing a bad first draft of a self-aggrandizing safari memoir (*True at First Light*) if the name of Hemingway was not attached to it? As a matter of fact, the bottom-line pressures may be, if anything, more acute for high literature, if only because its limited market makes the struggle to make a living much harder. The fact is that ambitious writers frequently turn to popular genres or techniques, as Walker Percy did in his detective cum medical cum philosophical thriller, *The Thanatos Syndrome*, to broaden their appeal and score a best-seller (see Mills <http:// metalab.unc.edu/wpercy>). In general, the Pure Art myth which lies behind the anti-commercial bias of this critique, fails to explain adequately why so many writers of Pinter's or Faulkner's stature should be drawn to the greenback pastures of Hollywood.

With regard to uniformity (above), although academic readers pride themselves on the high individuality of their tastes, just because as a group they form such a small and select audience, highbrow literature which appeals to them is, in fact, often *more* homogenous and uniform than popular fiction. Furthermore, imitation and formulaic solutions are no less common in highbrow than in mass literature. Mailer's *The Naked and the Dead,* by all accounts a fine novel, is in numerous ways derivative of other works. In structure, for example, it clearly imitates Erich Maria Remarque's *All Quiet on the Western Front* and Henri Barbusse's *Under Fire,* two trend-setting World War I novels which focus on a typical platoon of men of diverse backgrounds to document individual reactions to combat conditions. In narrative technique, Mailer mimics Dos Passos's *U.S.A.* in its flashback vignettes. For example, Dos Passos's "Camera Eye" becomes Mailer's "Time Machine" and even in the more innovative "Chorus"' parts he is indebted to Dos Passos's experiments with montage. There are, of course, countless other examples of this kind. Some of them are obvious even to a sociologist like Gans who points out: "many recent 'serious' novels have made the theme of the artist as a young man, borrowed originally from Joyce and D.H. Lawrence, into a formula, featuring a stereotypical young man striving to develop his identity as an artist" (1974; 22). The stream of consciousness technique, another *bona fide* highbrow invention, became at one point so heavily imitated among the literati that it began to be ranked as a separate sub-genre: the stream of consciousness novel. A highbrow reader who reaches for a self-reflexive or minimalist piece of writing knows in advance what formula was conformed to in its design, in a manner comparable to popular genres and categories. So much for the myth of highbrow uniqueness and originality.

As for homogeneity on the popular front, we may begin by observing that in some ways the sheer magnitude of the field determines some of its structural and even aesthetic qualities, such as originality and diversity. Given the size of its cultural environment—of continental, if not global proportions—popular fiction invades and explores every niche available as part of a self-organizing process known to evolutionary biologists as adaptive radiation. Competing to stand out from the crowd, popular writers diversify to a possibly far greater extent than their highbrow counterparts (this conjecture is open to empirical verification). Because the competition is so numerous and so fierce, there is pressure on adding to and transforming the winning formula of any successful theme/technique/genre, much as the sonnet underwent its metric, thematic, and rhyming transformations while remaining bound to the genre. Sustained by numbers unheard of in the canonical kingdom of Lilliput, such an adaptive process produces a variety which appears homogenous or static only from the top of Mount Brobdingnag. The charge that popular fiction is blandly homogenous, that it erases distinction between one novel and another, is in many cases simply false. A connoisseur of a popular genre finds significant differences between books and writers who contribute to it, much as a highbrow critic differentiates between the (anti)novels of Alain Robbe-Grillet and Jean Genet or the stories of John Cheever and Raymond Carver. This is not to dispute the existence of fiction "factories," such as Lyle Kenyon Engel's Book Creations Inc., whose 80 authors "manufacture" up to 3,000 titles a year by filling out story outlines provided by the Engel enterprise. But the fact remains that, just like highbrow literature, popular fiction mutates, radiates, and diversifies constantly, in the course of the last several decades giving us such new types of writing as science fiction, the hardboiled novel, the police procedural, or the techno-thriller, and their countless thematic and structural sub-categories.

As far as the charge of alienation is concerned (1c above), all available data indicates that the proverbial image of a highbrow *littérateur* who does not care to communicate with his/her readers but creates only for himself/herself, and of a popular hack who suppresses his/her own values and caters only to the appetites of the audience, is simply false (for a good analysis of the problem, see Bauer). From the innumerable examples which belie this picture I singled out Robert Ludlum who, with almost a quarter *billion* copies sold to his credit, single-handedly defines the popular in contemporary fiction. In the Iran-Gate era (1989) introduction to *Trevayne,* a novel written in the direct aftermath of the Watergate scandal, Ludlum summed up his feelings in this way: "For me, one of the truly great achievements of man is open, representative democracy. . . . But wait. Someone is always trying to louse it up. That's why I wrote *Trevayne* nearly two decades ago. It was the time of Watergate, and my pencil flew across the pages in outrage. Younger—not youthful—intemperance made my head explode with such words and phrases as *Mendacity! Abuse of Power! Corruption! Police State!*" (v).

Are these the words of a browbeaten hack who relinquishes what is dear to his heart in order to pander to the big boob of popular readership? Hardly. In fact, popular and financial success may allow writers precisely to swim *against* the current, liberating them from prevalent tastes and fashions. Between Ludlum, assured of mega-sales no matter how much he *expresses* rather than *suppresses* his own values, and a postmodern deconstructionist fashioning his art with the aim of making a splash on the minimalist market, it may well be that it is the popular writer who enjoys more creative space in which to maneuver. Neither is it true that canonical writer do not defer to their audience's tastes. After the critical success and total financial failure of *The Sound and the Fury* (1929), the newly married Faulkner conceived to make a bundle by writing a pot-boiler. Anticipating what the audience expected from a best-seller, he wrote *Sanctuary* (1931) in an almost conventional style, and packed it with lurid content, including a car wreck, forceful confinement, sadism, impotence, rape, vicarious sexual gratification, wanton murder, brothels, lynching, perjury and hanging. Creating only for himself in a haughty disregard for his audience and the remuneration for his labors? Hardly.

The second charge against popular literature, which singles out its alleged negative effects on high literary culture, falls into two types: popular fiction borrows much (in another version, only some) content from highbrow fiction, thereby debasing it and by offering powerful economic incentives, popular literature diverts talent away from highbrow literature and thus lowers the latter's overall quality. What could be the answer to these indictments? To begin, one could ask what is wrong with popular literature borrowing from highbrow fiction? It seems that such borrowings ought to be lauded rather than deplored, inasmuch as they introduce valuable aspects of high culture to readers who would otherwise remain outside its influence. In other words, instead of decrying the glass as half empty, one should rejoice in it being half-full, given that such cross-pollination diffuses the techniques and contents of high literature among its popular counterpart, ennobling the latter rather than debasing the former.

Moreover, once again this critique is compromised by selective bias. Borrowing and imitation has always been a two-way street, and many writers of highbrow fiction have been known to freely imitate their popular cousins. It was not for nothing that an anonymous reviewer of the Memphis *Evening Appeal* called *Sanctuary* a "devastating, inhuman monstrosity of a book that leaves one with the impression of having been vomited bodily from the sensual cruelty of its pages" (26 March 1931 edition). The novel caused this kind of stir precisely to the extent that it galvanized the public with its sensationalist and trashy content. Besides, if popular literature borrows more from highbrow fiction—by no means a proven fact—it may be because its audience is larger and requires more literary production. As I mentioned before, authors who want to reach a wider audience frequently resort to borrowing from popular genres, as Art Spiegelman did in his Book Critic's Circle Award and Pulitzer winning non-fictional comics, *Maus* and *Maus II*. In any case, mutual borrowing and interpenetration have been going on for long enough that, if the charge of debasement was indeed true, highbrow literature would not exist today any more—it would be by now thoroughly debased. Clearly, this particular critique is trapped by its own logic: either the charge of debasement is wrong, or serious fiction written by serious writers and dissected by serious critics is by now nothing but debased popular literature anyway: *quod erat demonstrandum.*

The charge that popular literature lures away talented writers is correct to the extent that we overlook the fact that popular writers try their hand at more ambitious projects (or in any case, designs), lured by the cultural prestige attached to highbrow fiction. A good example may be Disch's *Neighboring Lives,* a Victorian era drama penned by a writer celebrated for his science fiction and horror novels. Besides, highbrow writers who might score an occasional bestseller, need not be automatically less inclined to write serious fiction afterwards. After the success of *The Merchants of Yonkers* (better known as a 1964 smash-hit musical, *Hello Dolly*), Thornton Wilder embarked on another of his ambitious literary endeavors, the epic *The Eighth Day* (for Wilder, see Parris <http://www.sky.net/~emily/thornton.html>). More important, it is not at all clear that, if we were to abolish popular fiction, highbrow writers would immediately rush in to take its place. Not all critically acclaimed creators can write successfully for popular audiences, as the repeated failure of serious novelists (e.g., Fitzgerald) in Hollywood has amply demonstrated. Last of all, popular success may provide ambitious artists with the means to pursue more esoteric projects which might never be written if they had to seek regular employment in order to put food on their tables. The financial precariousness of the literary profession is a byword, and it is no secret that most good authors, from Shakespeare down, had other resources to pull them through.

The charge that popular literature's allegedly deleterious effect on society assumes a number of incarnations such popular literature is emotionally debilitating because it provides nothing but spurious gratifications and because it brutalizes readers by feeding them gratuitous sex and violence. This is the qualitative version of this critique; the quantitative version abandons the charge of wantonness and argues simply that mass fiction is inundated by sex and violence (in implicit contrast, presumably, to canonical literature), that popular literature is intellectually debilitating because of its emphasis on escapist content which inhibits its readers' ability to cope with reality, and that popular literature is culturally debilitating because it prevents readers from partaking of more serious and difficult types of writing. These charges are predicated on the assumption that the behavior postulated by the critics of popular literature actually exists, that the content of popular fiction actually contains models of such behavior, and that there is a direct causal link between the two.

These three assumptions are contradicted by all available data (the reader may begin with chapter nine in Gans's own *Urban Villagers* and Steven Tötösy and Philip Kreisel's pilot study of English-Canadian urban readership). Of particular interest here may be Achim Barsch's recent study of the status and reception—in Germany—of the typically German popular fiction phenomenon, the already mentioned 64-page pulp fiction booklet (*Heftroman*). There is little doubt that the findings Barsch reports squarely contradict almost all of the vices traditionally attributed to readers of popular fictions. Not only is there no "typical" reader of popular/commercial fiction, i.e., readership is distributed more or less evenly across the income, social and educational spectrum, but pulp fiction buffs are quite simply avid *readers* who, in addition to *Heftromans*, often consume vast quantities of highbrow fiction as well as nonfiction (for similar findings elsewhere, for example in Brazil, see Serra). They make complex and differentiating judgments about the contents of what they read and about the distance between fiction and their personal lives, and are emphatically not pathological escapists. Although an escape from everyday stresses and sorrows is an important reason for turning to popular/commercial fiction, numerous multi-layered and sophisticated motivations were found to come into play in readers' contacts with the booklets. A relatively high incidence of repeated reading was another unexpected result of the study, linking the reading patterns of popular literature aficionados even closer to those of highbrow consumers.

In general, with regard to the charge that popular literature is emotionally debilitating (3a above), there is no empirical evidence that the majority of North Americans—the majority who, like myself, regularly indulge in pulp fiction—are indeed brutalized, animalized, atomized, escapist, narcotized, or incapable of dealing with reality. In fact, what scant data exists—particularly from community and leisure studies (see Katz and Lazarsfeld)—indicates that most people from the lower middle and middle middle class, i.e. the group most "at risk," are not isolated brutes living out escapist and violent fantasies, but rather active members of family, peer and social groups. This is not to deny that some popular novels betray the characteristics of which they are accused. My only point is that content attribution, the standard critical practice of inferring effects and attitudes from literary content, is a singularly unreliable and demonstrably fallible method. In fact, the very same method of content attribution would find a lot amiss with most of highbrow fiction. No one, however, pillories Updike for brutalizing the sensibilities of literature professors with tediously endless descriptions of anal sex in *Roger's Version,* or denounces Percy for describing

systematic pedophilia in *The Thanatos Syndrome,* or critiques Malamud for
making his protagonist copulate with a beast in *God's Grace,* or . . . but I think
the point has been made. In general, we should keep in mind that popular fiction, which mainly addresses itself to its widest consumer, the middle class, is
frequently more conservative and puritanical than its highbrow relative because
it strives to reflect and cater to the middle class social and sexual ethos.

People choose literary content to fit their individual and social preferences,
rather than adapting their emotional and intellectual lives to what popular fictions describe. Most readers of popular fiction have a crassly pragmatic attitude to what they read: they do not generally pick up whatever lies on the
best-sellers' rack, but instead select literature that satisfies their individual and
group goals, needs and values. In addition, they are as a rule less attuned to
the verbal and symbolic content of what they read, making them if anything
less susceptible to the "trash" they consume. Indeed, if my own experience is
typical in this respect, readers often use popular fiction for pleasure and diver-
sion and would never dream of styling their lives after the patterns depicted
in the books they read with such passion. There are few Mmes Bovarys in real
life, and for the people who enjoy popular literature as a breather from everyday life, a dose of fantasy serves this purpose better than gritty realism.

Popular fiction readers taken as a social group form a taste culture inasmuch as popular fiction expresses and reflects their aesthetic and social values. As such, their decision to participate in popular culture is at least in part
a matter of *choice* and not mere cultural and ideological brainwashing (see,
e.g., H-Net <http://www.h-net.msu.edu/~pcaaca/popindex.html>). Those who
are willing to pay for popular novels must find value and satisfaction in them;
for them popular fiction performs an appreciable cultural role. Moreover, as
Nöel Carroll brilliantly argues in "The Nature of Mass Art," popular (or what
he calls "junk") fiction evokes the same processes of emotional and intellectual (erotetic) involvement that high literature does, albeit using different
themes and methods. Once again, this shows a high degree of cultural value
in popular fiction and an appreciable degree of discrimination in its consumers. Recipients of popular literature, or more generally, mass culture, are
not all passive trashbins, as the failure of some hyped-up H-wood money guz-
zlers (e.g., Costner's *Waterworld*) demonstrate.

The only model that can accurately describe the functioning of the literary
marketplace must be of cybernetic nature. Literary supply and demand are feed-
back-linked, and there are good reasons to believe that popular fiction, instead

of luring gullible readers away from serious art, responds to the demands of the reading public, or at least to what the popular writers and their publishers perceive these demands to be. If my arguments are correct, i.e. if turning to popular literature is a matter of choice instead of a Pavlovian response, the charge that Even Hunter (better known under his pen name, Ed McBain is the only obstacle between an average reader and *Crime and Punishment* is simply not true (see Maria <http://www.geocities.com/SoHo/Den/7417/>). Besides, as previously mentioned, some elements of highbrow literature become accessible to mass readership through the mediation of popular fiction, giving the latter a constructive role to play in the broadly conceived cultural education. Speaking of the latter, we should mention that some of popular literature's apparent vices, such as predilection for well-tried techniques and formulas, make it culturally valuable as a medium of literary tradition and continuity, as opposed to highbrow fiction whose avant-garde constantly tries to break away from the mould. Contrary to common wisdom, it may actually be popular fiction that preserves and perpetuates the literary achievements of the past, on top of doing so not via a suspended animation of the canon, but through the popular vitality of mass readership.

The fourth and last charge against popular literature takes two forms. On the one hand, it is argued that the mass presence and appeal of popular literature lowers the general cultural level of the reading public. Its other ill-effect on society is that it is said to pave the way for political, social and cultural dictatorship by creating a passive audience which can easily fall victim to totalitarianism—essentially a variant on the charge. In a brief answer to both parts of this indictment, we should note that within the last fifty years, popular culture in America has gradually changed from that of lower middle class to middle middle class. So much for the debasing and lowering of the cultural standards of the society by popular literature which, needless to remind, flourished during the period in question.

Since all previous arguments in defense of popular literature are an *en masse* refutation of the fourth charge, here I will only add that there is often a great deal of tendentiousness evident in comparisons of literary productions from the past and present. Critics who argue that popular literature leads to a decline in literary standards tend to contrast the highest achievements of the past with the mediocre of the present. Similarly, the argument that the literary culture would immediately improve if only pulp fiction was not in the way, does not convince. My personal experience from then-communist Poland, in which the government promoted an official highbrow fiction against the grass-roots demand for domestic equivalents of American popular literature, persuades me that things are not as simple as some would have us believe. My favorite example is that of Andrzej Sonimski, the Polish writer and esteemed translator of Shakespeare, who decided to apply his ample talents to the detective novel, becoming a best-selling author under a pen name Joe Alex.

CONCLUSION

Having examined some of the most persistent misconceptions about and critiques of popular literature, I conclude that almost all of them are groundless. Contrary to most people's impressions, the available data indicates that popular fiction has had no appreciable harmful effect either on highbrow literature, on its intellectually refined consumers, or on the society as a whole. My orientation, socio-aesthetic for the most part, was predicated on a value judgment that popular literature reflects and gives voice to the cultural needs of many people. For these reasons we need to recognize and acknowledge that popular fiction performs a valuable socio-aesthetic role rather than constitutes a cultural menace.

From the many arguments dispersed throughout this article it should be clear that we have little to gain by continuing to ignore it, except a further degree of critical isolation from and irrelevance in the society. The apparently unstoppable popularity and omnipresence of popular literature demand serious and sympathetic analysis, free of prejudice and unexamined impressions on the one hand, and of radical anti-canonical backlash on the other. Much of popular fiction can stand on its own feet next to many works hailed as lasting triumphs of Western literature. Much more deserves to be treated as the only thing it tries to be: gripping but ephemeral entertainment without aspirations to bowl over the literary establishment. Some of it is demonstrable shlock, which makes the task of educating the readers who persist in buying it all the more worthwhile. But to tell a good popular novel from a bad one, or a good popular novel from a bad classic, we need to approach contemporary literature—in whatever form or genre it chooses to manifest itself—with an un-jaundiced eye and a critical apparatus of sufficient refinement.

WORKS CITED

Barsch, Achim. "Young People Reading Popular/Commercial Fiction." *Systemic and Empirical Approach to Literature and Culture as Theory and Application.* Ed. Steven Tötösy de Zepetnek and Irene Sywenky. Edmonton: Research Institute for Comparative Literature, U of Alberta and Siegen: Institute for Empirical Literature and Media Research, 1997. 371–83.

Bauer, Raymond A. "The Communicator and His Audience." *People, Society and Mass Communications.* Ed. Lewis A. Dexter and David M. White. New York: Free Press, 1964. 125–40.

Balkin, Richard. *A Writer's Guide to Book Publishing.* New York: Hawthorne, 1977.

Carroll, Nöel. "The Nature of Mass Art." *Philosophic Exchange* 23 (1992): 5–37.

Chandler, Raymond. *Later Novels and Other Writings.* New York: Library of America, 1995.

Coser, Lewis A., et al. *Books: The Culture and Commerce of Publishing.* Chicago and London: U of Chicago P, 1982.

Curwen, Peter. *The World Book Industry.* New York and Oxford: Fact On File Publications, 1986.

Dennis, Everette E., et al., eds. *Publishing Books.* New Brunswick: Transaction Publishers, 1997.

Douglas, Ann. *The Feminization of American Literature.* New York: Knopf, 1977.

Escarpit, Robert. *Trends in Worldwide Book Development 1970–1978.* New York: UNESCO, 1982.

Farrar, Straus and Giroux, Publishers. "Tom Wolfe: A Man in Full." (1999–): <http://www.tomwolfe.com>.

Gans, Herbert J. *The Urban Villagers.* New York: Free P of Glencoe, 1962.

Gans, Herbert J. *Popular Culture and High Culture: An Analysis and Evaluation of Taste.* New York: Basic Books, 1974.

H-Net: Humanities, and Social Sciences OnLine. "The Popular Culture Association and the American Culture Association: Home Page." (1999–): <http://www.h-net.msu.edu/~pcaaca/popindex.html>.

Holt, Henry. "The Commercialization of Literature." *Atlantic Monthly* 96 (1905): 578–600.

Holt, Patricia. "Turning Best Sellers Into Movies." *Publishers Weekly* (22 October 1979): 36–40.

Joedaisy Studio. *Ernest Hemingway: Front Page* (1999–): <http://www.ernest.hemingway.com>.

Katz, Elihu, and Paul Lazarsfeld. *Personal Influence.* Glencoe: Free P, 1955.

Livingston, Paisley. "From Text to Work." *After Poststructuralism: Interdisciplinarity and Literary Theory.* Ed. Nancy Easterlin and Barbara Riebling. Evanston: Northwestern UP, 1993. 91–104.

Lowenthal, Leo, and Marjorie Fiske. "The Debate Over Art and Popular Culture in Eighteenth-Century England." *Common Frontiers of the Social Sciences.* Ed. Mirra Komarovsky. Glencoe: Free P, 1957. 33–96.

Maria. "Ed McBain Discussion List." (1999–): <http://www.geocities.com/SoHo/Den/7417/>.

Mills, Henry P. "The Walker Percy Project." (1999–): <http://metalab.unc.edu/wpercy>.

Moss, Robert F. *The Raymond Chandler Web Site*." (1999–): <http://www.geocities.com/athens/parthenon/3224/>.

Playboy Magazine Home Page. (1999–): <http://www.playboy.com>.

Parris, Emily M. "Thornton Wilder (1897–1975)." (1999–): <http://www.sky.net/~emily/thornton.html>.

Rosenberg, Bernard, and David Manning White. *Mass Culture: The Popular Arts in America*. Glencoe: Free P, 1957.

"Rushdie, Salman." (1999–): <http://landow.stg.brown.edu/post/rushdie/rushdieov.html>.

Serra, Tania. "Humanism and Romanticisms in Brazilian Literature: The First and the Last Best-Seller Novels." *Humanism and the Good Life*. Ed. Peter Horwath, William L. Hendrickson, L. Teresa Valdivieso, and Eric. P. Thor. New York: Peter Lang, 1998. 555–61.

Steinberg, S.H. *Five Hundred Years of Printing*. New Edition. Rev. John Trevitt. London: The British Library and Oak Knoll P, 1996.

Swirski, Peter. "Critical Mass: Mass Literature and Genre Criticism." *Les Problèmes des genres littéraires / Zagadnienia rodzajów literackich* 37 (1994): 97–107.

Swirski, Peter. *A Stanislaw Lem Reader*. Evanston: Northwestern UP, 1997a.

Swirski, Peter. "Genres in Action: the Pragmatics of Literary Interpretation." *Orbis Litterarum: International Review of Literary Studies* 52 (1997b): 141–56.

Swirski, Peter. "Robert Ludlum: *The Cry of the Halidon*." *The Encyclopedia of Popular Fiction*. Ed. Kirk Beetz. Osprey: Beacham, 1998a. Vol. 11, 5343–354.

Swirski, Peter. "Bernard Malamud: *God's Grace*." *The Encyclopedia of Popular Fiction*. Ed. Kirk Beetz. Osprey: Beacham, 1998b. Vol. 11, 5592–601.

Swirski, Peter. "Stanislaw Lem." *Science Fiction Writers*. Ed. Richard Bleiler. New York: Charles Scribner's Sons, 1999. 453–66.

Tebbel, John. "The History of Book Publishing in the United States." *International Book Publishing: An Encyclopedia*. Ed. Philip G. Altbach and Edith S. Hoshino. New York: Garland, 1995. 147–55.

Topping, Scott. *Lardnermania*. (1999–): <http://www.tridget.com/lardnermania/>.

Tötösy de Zepetnek, Steven, and Philip Kreisel. "Urban English-Speaking Canadian Literary Readership: Results of a Pilot Study." *Poetics: Journal of Empirical Research on Literature, The Media and the Arts* 21 (1992): 211–38.

UNESCO Publications. *UNESCO Publishing: English Page*. (1999–): <http://www.unesco.org/general/eng/publish/index.html>.

Varsava, Jerry A. "Tom Wolfe's Defense of the New (Old) Social Novel; or, the Perils of the Great White-Suited Hunter." *Journal of American Culture* 14 (1991): 35–41.

Warner Books. *Time Warner Bookmark*. (1999–): <http://www.warnerbooks.com>.

Comparative Literature as Textual Anthropology

Antony Tatlow

In his study, "Why Look at Animals?," John Berger observes: "The animal has secrets which, unlike the secrets of caves, mountains, seas, are specifically addressed to man" (3) and he asks:

> What were the secrets of the animal's likeness with and unlikeness from man? The secrets whose existence man recognized as soon as he intercepted the animal's look. In one sense the whole of anthropology, concerned with the passage from nature to culture, is the answer to that question. But there is also a general answer. All the secrets were about animals as an intercession between man and his origin. . . . Animals interceded between man and his origin because they were both like and unlike man. Animals came from over the horizon. They belonged there and here. Likewise they were both mortal and immortal. An animal's blood flowed like human blood, but its species was undying and each lion was Lion, each ox was Ox. This—maybe the first existential dualism—was reflected in the treatment of animals. They were subjected and worshiped, bred and sacrificed. . . . All theories of ultimate origin are only ways of better defining what followed. . . . What we are trying to define, because the experience is almost lost, is the universal use of animal signs for charting the experience of the world. (4–6)

Brecht's *Auf einen chinesischen Theewurzellöwen* (*On a Chinese Tea Root Lion*), a private totem, descends from the animals described by Berger (I draw on a discussion of animal signs in art in an earlier study; see Tatlow 1990).

The *Tea Root Lion* also illustrates the universal use of animal signs for charting the experience of the world: "Die Schlechten fürchten deine Klaue./ Die Guten freuen sich deiner Grazie./ Derlei/ Hörte ich gern/ Von meinem Vers" (1967, 997). At first glance, the *Tea Root Lion* may appear to domesticate the consternation embodied in the earlier animal figures but in its own way this figure speaks to Berger's anthropological question. We should not be misled by the apparently emblematic figure or by what first looks like the flatly allegorical function of the verse, by the supposition of a one-to-one correspondence in what may then seem an only too easy moral equation, the good and the bad neatly divided from each other like the sheep and the goats. This verse should never be, but invariably is, separated from the artefact to which it is conjoined and such separation greatly facilitates these simplifications.

Everything depends upon the level on which we choose to conduct our enquiry. Brecht's work has suffered enough from being reduced to, and then constrained within, those superficial and convenient perspectives from which its meaning was once socially authorized. It is, therefore, necessary to explore the possibility of further connections between totemic and utopian thought. When the animal's look is transformed into an animal sign, into an imagined alien Other and located within the structure of a work of art, hidden forces undergo a process of externalization. We therefore approach a potential self-encounter as we are drawn into an interrogation of the work. When representation separates layers of perception, whilst presenting them with visual immediacy, every more or less adequate act of interpretation must put our sense of self into jeopardy or, at the very least, draw attention to how we are engendered and positioned by our culture. In this particular case the utopian reflection contained within the verse cannot dispense with, therefore in some sense derives from and is interwoven with, an engagement with the anthropological other in the form of an intriguing artefact, the representation of an imagined animal from that other culture. This animal sign undergoes, in the newly established juxtaposition that playfully echoes and develops the aesthetics of Chinese painting, a process of acculturation, even as such repositioning provokes, like all anthropological engagements, a potential self-encounter or, to be more accurate, cannot really be interpreted unless such an encounter takes place.

"In grasping these truths," Lévi-Strauss observed of the wider consequences of the anthropological encounter, we are "ramenés à nous-mêmes par cette confrontation" (1955, 354). The discerning anthropologist can be sure of at least one thing: that he will have to face up to himself if his work is to have any

descriptive cogency. Much has been said in recent years about the interpenetration of the disciplines of anthropology and literary criticism. (Here I am thinking primarily of studies by Clifford Geertz, James Clifford, George Marcus, and
James Boon. The way these disciplines now learn from, adjust to and change
each other is itself a subject for anthropological reflection and an example of
the dialectics of acculturation in thought.) Ethnographic anthropology is always,
finally, writing about culture and hence, in some degree, invents the culture which
it studies as criticism creates the work it interprets. Both activities respond to
cultural demands and these both fashion the ethnographer and select the perspectives he must transcend in choosing what he wants to see. At the end of
Tristes Tropiques, Lévi-Strauss speaks of the anthropologist as someone in
flight from his own culture, searching abroad for what he lacks at home. Of
course this can involve a form of escape, but this search and the activity of writing which brings it to a temporary conclusion should not be confused with that
fearful, blind or arrogant avoidance of the self which escapism usually connotes.
We can surmise that the anthropologist or artist or critic will be predisposed to
discover and fashion in the object of his attention what is neglected or denied
in, and what we can therefore describe as the unconscious of, his own culture.
The new narratives arise, according to Foucault, out of the silences of the previous episteme. If anthropology, for Clifford Geertz, can be termed "behavioral
hermeneutics" (1986, 379), with all that this implies in respect of self-reflexivity,
then criticism can surely be thought of as a form of textual anthropology, inter-
rogating texts as functions of the culturally necessary and culturally possible.
Geertz also calls this form of writing "faction" (1988, 144). The best account
I have seen of the changing status of anthropology in cultural studies and the
various positions from which its discourse may be determined is offered by Marcus and Fischer. (1986).

To my mind, some of the most interesting recent comparative literary criticism has been written by anthropologists who have applied the insights of literary theory to their own discipline, thus helping us all to understand better
the nature of creative and communicative processes. Geertz and James Clifford have shown how Malinowski created cultural order in the unified narrative of his anthropological descriptions of the Western Pacific, a practice of
writing long equated with the totality of the discipline, by rigorously excising
the self of the investigator whose troubled reflections he confined to the pages
of his diaries (Geertz 1988, 73). This scientific "objectivity," therefore, depended
on a form of perceptual schizophrenia, required by the larger political strategies of his own culture, since it enabled him to pin down the Trobrianders in

a rhetorical power game, placing them where they belonged in the Western disposition of knowledge (see Clifford; Clifford shows how Malinowski and Conrad negotiated languages and their own identities as they created or occupied various narrative positions in relation to their description/invention of remote and exotic places; see also Tatlow 1995).

As auto-anthropologist, the artist "invents," instead of "describing," the Other. The work both investigates and is itself the object of investigation. Gauguin's invention of the Pacific fascinated Brecht and had numerous consequences for his own work. Gauguin reached Tahiti, only to discover that "Tahiti" had already vanished. And so the "savage," in flight from a rotten European civilization, and probably bringing his syphilis with him, re-invented what had disappeared. The process is fascinating and I can only refer obliquely to it. He constructed his own "oceanic character" by reading Moerenhout. He then invented a mistress who tells him stories of the gods. He borrowed from everywhere. His disdain of originality, constantly and almost literally drawing on the work of others, just as Brecht did, was also his mark of it. Out of Gauguin's incompatible narratives emerge his extraordinary paintings. In *Noa Noa*, he bids goodbye to the hospitable soil, imperative family duties call him back, his lover is in tears. He leaves behind on the quay-side legend, fragrance, love, natural innocence and dignity (see Gauguin 1985, 42). But the unprinted Appendix, like Malinowski's diary, tells a different story: "After the work of art—The truth, the dirty truth" (Gauguin 1985, 43; "work of art" here means the text of *Noa Noa*). He is shipped back as a pauper in third class, with 50 square centimeters of space among sheep and cattle, longing to escape the actual Tahitians he viewed as primitive thieves and to be "among my own people and my friends." Identity is a function of stylization, pure artifice. Most of his provocatively Tahitian paintings were structured on Western models, Cranach, Manet, among others, and the most famous of them all, *D'Où venons-nous? Que sommes-nous? Où allons-nous?* even echoes—and there is more to this than parody—the nineteenth-century allegorists Signac, Sérusier, and Puvis de Chavannes (see Thomson 196). Even in his last and remotest retreat on Hivaoa in the Marquesas, he had fixed a print of Botticelli's *Primavera* to his wall.

In this context it is instructive to observe how *Te arii vahine* recapitulates virtually all the body postures of Cranach's *Diana Reclining*, except that Gauguin has retained the hand which covers the sex of the naked woman, as if from the more overtly repressive gesture of Manet's *Olympia*, which he had copied in 1891 and where the Western women displays herself in this contradictory posture beside the fully clothed black servant. Gauguin did not paint

the natural, or the exotic, he painted his dreams and the repressions of his culture: "You drag your double along with you and yet the two contrive to get
on together" (Gauguin 1921, 240). These paintings reach deep into himself
and his experience of the obsessions of his culture and so transcend the natu-
ralist allegories, the politically anarchist idylls which helped him paint them.
He was not interested in what could be seen in Tahiti but in what was no longer
visible. He did not fantasize a Tahitian unconscious but he did reinvent it by
passing it through the practice of his own imagination, giving his shape to their
fears. Take, for example, *Manao tupapau*. This is how Gauguin describes the
experience that led to the notorious painting which mixes fear and the erotic:

> Tehura lay motionless, naked, belly down on the bed: She stared up
> at me, her eyes wide with fear, and she seemed not to know who I
> was. For a moment I too felt a strange uncertainty. Tehura's dread
> was contagious: it seemed to me that a phosphorescent light poured
> from her staring eyes. I had never seen her so lovely; above all, I had
> never seen her beauty so moving . . . Did I know what she thought
> I was in that instant? Perhaps she took me, with my anguished face,
> for one of those legendary demons or specters, the Tupapaus that
> filled the sleepless night of her people (Gauguin 1988, 280).

And yet the dispositions in his paintings, a form of communication
unknown to Tahiti, are nevertheless akin to the function of totemic thought
which metaphorizes relations and organizes perception in a productive and pro-
tective relationship to the forces man contends with, offering, like works of
art, conceptual models in the form of metaphor. The anarchist idylls domesticate nature, as the Neoplatonist idealizes perception, in a projection of
untroubled utopian control, and even here we can see a tenuous link with
totemic thought, but Gauguin's project energized, and was energized by, deeper
dispositions, searching for the self in the other, seeking an arrangement with
what cannot be so easily controlled yet must be lived with.

In *The Savage Mind*, Lévi-Strauss offers an account of how totemic thought
establishes codes for discriminating relationships, establishing dispositions
between phenomena through the organization of perceptual space and of the
correspondences which enable us to make imaginative and practical sense of
the world. He recounts a practice among the Hidatsa Indians in America who
developed a particular technique for catching the elusive eagle, lord of the sky
and metaphor of their aspirations. They would dig a pit, a trap, and lie in it,
waiting for the eagle to descend upon them. They were, observes Lévi-Strauss,

"both hunter and hunted at the same time" (1966, 50). He uses this to exemplify the binary—high/low—and triadic—sky/earth/underworld—patterns that organized their totemic thought and tribal life.

Brecht's early plays constitute an iconographical zoo, they teem with animal metaphors. They are constructed as mythologies of the unconscious, and consequently their plots are labyrinthic. They do not move logically, like the well-made play, from incident to incident but wind erratically through uncharted psychographic territory. The other or exotic, no matter how far this mental territory may be placed beyond the Berlin/Bavarian borders, whether in Africa, Tahiti, China, or America, is not a geographical but a methodological concept, an ethnography of the imagination, a proto-surrealist psycho-collage, rhetorical exploration, all designed to one end: combating the insanity which was that positivist normalization of the actual. Normality in 1918, when he was writing Baal, was monstrous. It had to be re-invented. It is noticeable how the scene titles of this play echo the apparently inconsequential titles of paintings like those of van Gogh—*Nachtcafé, Green Field, Blue Plum Trees, Maple Trees in the Wind*—and how the language appears to paint scenes in strong Gauguinesque colors. Like the Hidatsa Indians, Baal, in the provocative song that starts the play, tells how he hunted vultures by personifying their prey, and this passage occurs again within the play, in the scene *10 Degrees East of Greenwich* (Brecht 1970, 56) He does so, just as they did, to absorb into himself their soaring immortality. Baal consumes them, swallowing the light of their skies, light enough to hold off the death he embraces, for his whole trajectory is a descent into materiality, the obverse of the Christian and Neoplatonic topography which structured the conventions of Brecht's culture.

Nothing is more savage than normality. The imagination resists its own obliteration by proposing a counter reality that now radically undermines, is simply incompatible with, the whole industrializing post-Enlightenment cultural paradigm, drawing on the metaphorical dispositions of totemic thought because it allows you to reconceive all relationships. But this is no abstract reaction, no simple rejection of indefensible instrumentalization, for it also anticipates realignments of individual positions which refuse the spaces available in modern industrial culture, and this is a constant counter-theme in Brecht. Sartre once observed that Racine and Brecht have something in common—the savage dreams and emotions in their distanced characters: "on nous les montres à froid, séparés de nous, inaccessibles et terribles . . . et nous nous retrouvons en eux sans que notre stupeur diminue" (1973, 82).

In fact many of my themes are anticipated by Sartre, though without the vital exploration of the relational models in totemic thought, when he writes of that moment of consternation produced by Brecht's dramaturgy:

> L'idéal du théâtre brechtien, ce serait que le public fût comme un groupe d'ethnographes rencontrant tout à coup une peuplade sauvage. S'approchant et se disant, dans la stupeur: ces sauvages, c'est nous. C'est à ce moment que le public devient lui-même un collaborateur de l'auteur: en se reconnaisant, mais dans l'étrangeté, comme s'il était un autre, il se fait exister en face de lui-même comme objet et il se voit sans s'incarner, donc en se comprenant (qtd. in Contat and Rybalka 327).

The audience comes face to face with itself, it produces itself—se fait exister—in that auto-ethnographic experience enabled through the interpretation of a work of art. Here, of course, lies the anthropological value of the so-called "alienation effect." Brecht consistently strove in his dramaturgic practice to provoke that experience of consternation which turns in upon the self, though people still confuse the socially-authorized trivial rationalizations, in what can only be repressive interpretations, with the capacity of his plays. These parallels between Racine and Brecht may seem superficially surprising but we have seen where they exist, if we can escape the comforting critical clichés, as their texts construct and plot the monstrous unconscious of their cultures. "Exploration," observes Lévi-Strauss, "is not so much a matter of covering ground as of digging beneath the surface" (1961, 50).

The Chinese associations in Brecht's work have almost invariably been read in terms of quietism, underlying all superficial politics (in my opinion, Martin Esslin gives the most intelligent account of this position) but when they are most interesting they represent precisely the opposite of any quietist retraction into the isolated self, because the models are all relational, figures for interconnectedness, and so can be seen in terms of the metaphors of totemic thought. This "other" Brecht of course does not stand for the totality of his positions, but is the one that matters now. Even the Buddhist associations have their activating moment. They do not represent, as has been suggested, any denial of the will to live, and hence an unflinching Schopenhauerian refusal or any intensification of "Nietzschean" existential despair but rather a rejection of the possibility of continuing to live as heretofore (see Dieckmann 92; see also Tatlow 1998). If On a Chinese Tea Root Lion appears to make easy reading, we need to remember its context, where the picture-poem was devised as an affront to Stalinist aesthetics. This animal is also another self-questioning self-portrait because the meaning of its third sentence is uncertain: "Derlei/ hörte ich gern/ von meinem Vers" (That's what/ I'd like to hear/ About my verse") is strictly ambiguous, capable of two diverging readings. Brecht's late poetry in Stalinist Berlin continuously interrogates his own positioning and seeks relational figures, exploring other dimensions, as in that discussion of the aesthetics of Soviet painting, tracing filaments, webs of meaning in the small space then available. In a public discussion in February 1955 Brecht described the official aesthetic criteria as: "inhuman, barbaric, superficial, bourgeois, that is to say petit-bourgeois, slipshod, irresponsible, corrupt, etc., etc." (1983, 213).

Geertz finds particularly the later accounts that Lévi-Strauss gives of primitive thought too coherent, lacking the difficult and empirically unassimilable facticity of his earlier studies. Geertz reads the narrative of *Tristes Tropiques* in terms of the mythical quest, of that search for the labyrinthic other: "the journey . . . into another, darker world, full of phantasms and odd revelations; the culminating mystery; the absolute other, sequestered and opaque, confronted deep down in the sertao" (1988, 45). But this "other," how could it be otherwise, not only locates the self, it is the self: "The book is a record of a symbolist mentality (French) encountering other symbolist mentalities (Bororo, Caduveo, Nambikwara) and seeking to penetrate their wholly interior coherence in order to find in them the replication of itself—'the most fundamental form' of thought" (1988, 43) This mytho-logic seeks "the foundations of social life, and . . . of human existence" (1988, 45). Yet to position yourself thus would surely be, not to discover the self that has been hidden from you but, in reality, to forget yourself and how you have been positioned. It should, however, be possible—although obviously not completely, that is out of the question—to take something of these mutual placings into account. And if that happens, they defamiliarize each other in the process I call "dialectics of acculturation," although only because of the points of contact between them. If that is so, then I do not see how we then necessarily inhabit what Geertz attributes to the thought of Lévi-Strauss which developed out of his reflections on these encounters, namely that "closed-world view of meaning that results from it all" (1988, 44).

Surely the point is that "their" horizons appear fixed and delimited only because "we" set them. And "our" horizons are opening up, after a relatively long period of closure and certainty, in part because we now understand how "theirs" encode paradigms that are not exhausted, that are capable of re-examination. If we feel uncomfortable with the rigorous formalism of structuralist anthropology, it is because it apes our totalizing, or even totalitarian, desire to possess the world. Totemic thought knew no such attitude. In *Tristes Tropiques* Lévi-Strauss undoes the power of absolute signs and this is certainly true of Brecht. To envisage this, they both employ Buddhist or Daoist associations, and Daoist or Buddhist models fit very well with a Marxist philosophy of process. It cannot be a coincidence, though Brecht knew nothing of Lévi-Strauss, that we can discern this parallel in their thought (see Tatlow 1998).

The Popperian reduction of science now seems almost as unproductive as the vulgar Marxist models he so caustically, and rightly, rejected. Scientific thought is rediscovering how understanding grows from the exploration of intuitive and poetic metaphors. When most suggestive, scientific like totemic thought is perhaps analogical. There is indeed a Dao of physics. Science depends on understanding how the imagination works and will be most productive when intuiting a wholeness that will always remain "unknowable" (see the cited texts; Capra 1975, 1982; Tolstoy 1990). We need to explore every avenue of escape from closed totalities into the openness of holistic thought. Closure will be global, absolute, and irreversible unless we confront the monsters engendered in ourselves. In the conclusion to *Tristes Tropiques*, Lévi-Strauss reflects on Buddhist meditations, on "the mutual exclusiveness of being and knowing" (1961, 395). Such a refusal of "knowledge" in favor of "being" should not be thought of as a Heideggerian metaphysic or as a blanket abstraction, denying material and intellectual life, even if Lévi-Strauss plays with the anthropology/entropology pun, (1961, 397) but rather as welcoming that "emptiness" which is the metaphorical figure for relationality. In Chinese terms, there is no *you* (having) without *wu* (nothing), "having" depends on "not having," on being content with "nothing" because, like fullness and emptiness, they interpenetrate, one cannot be thought, or had, without the other. The same is true for totemic and utopian thought. Both arrive at their figurations through a process that draws on and is energised by the repressions lodged in what we call the social or cultural unconscious.

WORKS CITED

Berger, John. *About Looking*. London: Readers and Writers Publishing, 1980.
Brecht, Bertolt. *Collected Plays*. London: Methuen, 1970. Vol. 1.
Brecht, Bertolt. *Gesammelte Werke*. Frankfurt: Suhrkamp, 1967. Vol. 10.
Brecht, Bertolt. *Über die bildenden Künste*. Frankfurt: Suhrkamp, 1983.
Capra, Fritjof. *The Tao of Physics*. London: Wildwood House, 1975.

Capra, Fritjof. *The Turning Point*. New York: Simon & Schuster, 1982.

Clifford, James. "On Ethnographic Self-Fashioning." *Reconstructing Individualism: Autonomy, Individuality, and the Self in Western Thought*. Ed. T.C. Heller. Stanford: Stanford UP, 1986. 140–62.

Dieckmann, Friedrich. "Brechts Utopia." *Brecht 88. Anregungen zum Dialog über die Vernunft am Jahrtausendende*. Ed. Wolfgang Heise. Berlin: Henschel, 1987. 373–80.

Esslin, Martin. *Brecht: A Choice of Evils. A Critical Study of the Man, His Work and His Opinions*. London: Methuen, 1959.

Gauguin, Paul. *Noa Noa: Gauguin's Tahiti*. Ed. Nicholas Wadley. Salem: Salem House, 1985.

Gauguin, Paul. *Paul Gauguin's Intimate Journals*. Trans. Van Wyck Brooks. New York: Liveright, 1921.

Gauguin, Paul. *The Art of Paul Gauguin*. Washington: National Gallery of Art Catalogue, 1988.

Geertz, Clifford. "Making Experiences, Authoring Selves." *The Anthropology of Experience*. Ed. Victor W. Turner and Edward M. Bruner. Urbana: U of Illinois P, 1986. 373–80.

Geertz, Clifford. *Works and Lives: The Anthropologist as Author*. Stanford: Polity, 1988.

Lévi-Strauss, Claude. *A World on the Wane*. Trans. John Russell. London: Hutchinson, 1961.

Lévi-Strauss, Claude. *The Savage Mind*. London: Weidenfeld & Nicolsson, 1966.

Lévi-Strauss, Claude. *Tristes Tropiques*. Paris: Plon, 1955.

Marcus, George E., and Michael M.J. Fischer. *Anthropology as Cultural Critique: An Experimental Moment in the Human Sciences*. Chicago: U of Chicago P, 1986.

Moerenhout, J.A. *Voyages aux îles du Grand Océan*. Paris: A. Bertrand, 1873.

Sartre, Jean-Paul. "Brecht et les classiques." *Un Théâtre de Situations*. By Jean-Paul Sartre. Paris: Gallimard, 1973.

Sartre, Jean-Paul. "Deux heures avec Sartre." *L'Express 431* (14 September 1959).

Tatlow, Antony. *Repression and Figuration: From Totem to Utopia*. Hong Kong: Department of Comparative Literature, U of Hong Kong, 1990.

Tatlow, Antony. "The Repressive Anthropologist: Another Look at Malinowski and Conrad." *New Perspectives: A Comparative Literature Yearbook*. Hong Kong: Department of Comparative Literature, University of Hong Kong, 1995. 155–84.

Tatlow, Antony. *Brechts Ost Asien*. Berlin: Parthas, 1998.

Thomson, Belinda. *Gauguin*. London: Thames & Hudson, 1987.

Tolstoy, Ivan. *The Knowledge and the Power: Reflections on the History of Science*. London: Canongate, 1990

Analyzing East/West Power Politics in Comparative Cultural Studies

William H. Thornton

HUNTINGTON AND CULTURAL REALISM

In the post-Cold War thought of Samuel Huntington, culture has supplanted ideology as the shaping force of global politics ("Erosion" 39). Unlike the postmodern culturalist, who celebrates "difference" as an unequivocal virtue, Huntington's cultural politics is marked by multipolar and multicivilizational strife (*Clash* 21). Nevertheless he partakes in the cultural imperative that has become almost synonymous with postmodernism in foreign affairs: international relations, security studies, and international economics (Mazarr 177). Political realists find themselves in a bind, for it was on their watch that culture was strictly marginalized (Lapid 3).

Drawing on comparative cultural studies (see Tötösy in this volume), in this paper I explore the place of culture in East/West power politics and I argue to preserve the strategic potency of political realism while putting culture back on Asia's geopolitical map. This requires that "classical" and "neo-" realism alike be revised in favor of a new "cultural realism": a post-Cold War melding of geopolitical strategy and geocultural negotiation, or what Joseph Nye has called "hard power" and "soft power" (181). As here employed, the term "cultural realism" carries a double meaning, tied at once to geopolitical and literary/cultural discourses. Its concern with the emic channels of local knowledge owes much to postmodern realism in cultural theory. The politics of postmodern realism—as developed in my *Cultural Prosaics: The Second Postmodern Turn* and previous studies such as "Cultural Prosaics" and "Cross-

216

Cultural"—is congruent with Bakhtinian cultural dialogics rather than the epistemological anarchy of deconstructionist or Foucauldian theory (see Thornton *Cultural,* Chapter Six). The latter school of thought powerfully influenced Edward Said, but could not be sustained where Said turned his attention to the particulars of cultural politics. His *Covering Islam,* as Bryan Turner points out, is built upon a solidly realist epistemology (6).

On its geopolitical side, cultural realism is a manifestation of what Yosef Lapid and Friedrich Kratochwil call, in their anthology of that title, *The Return of Culture and Identity in IR Theory* (1996). The term "cultural realism" has been applied specifically to Chinese cultural politics by Alastair Johnston (1995), who argues that a tradition of realpolitik lies beneath China's cloak of Confucian-Mencian moderation. This inclines China to be much faster than most states to use force in territorial disputes. Johnston considers this cultural proclivity to be heightened by improvements in China's military capabilities. Here I broaden the application of "cultural realism" to the whole question of East/West geopolitics, qualifying rather than replacing the standard realist concern with balance of power relations. Johnston's insights, for example, lend cultural depth to the realist admonitions of Bernstein and Munro (1997) concerning China's destabilizing impact on the current Asian balance of power. Globalists tend to overlook the inertia of the bureaucratic and authoritarian tradition that traces to the Qin dynasty, and the isolationism that traces to the Ming (builders of the Great Wall). In this study, however, cultural realism is equally concerned with traditional and emerging relations between political cultures, e.g., the Chinese and the Vietnamese. It is thus the perfect medium for "soft power" analysis.

This "soft" realism offers a timely corrective to the cultural tunnel vision of both globalism and classical realism. The latter, according to Hans Morgenthau, has been distinguished by the subordination of all factors that lie outside a rational calculation of "interest defined in terms of power" (Morgenthau 5). This is supposed to render politics "autonomous" by purging realism of "irrational" elements such as religion and moral valuations. "Neo-" or "structural" realism, as developed by Kenneth Waltz (1979), begins with that same purgation but moves farther toward what is considered a scientific geopolitics, one in which the basic balancing act of realism operates systemically and without any necessary conscious intent (see Sheehan 194; Forde 142). Francis Fukuyama denigrates realism for treating:

nation-states like billiard balls, whose internal contents, hidden by opaque shells, are irrelevant in predicting their behavior. . . . International politics, then, is not about the interaction of complex and historically developing human societies, nor are wars about clashes of values. . . . [Nonetheless the] earlier generation of realists like Morgenthau, Kennan, Niebuhr, and Kissinger allowed some consideration of the internal character of states to enter into their analyses, and could therefore give a better account of the reasons for international conflict than the later academic school of "structural" realists. The former at least recognized that conflict had to be driven by a *human* desire for domination, rather than from the mechanical interaction of a system of billiard balls. (*End* 248 and 256).

In *The Clash of Civilizations* (1996), Huntington likewise points the way towards a revised realism where "internal contents" count as much or more than external mechanics. Thus Huntington implants culture or "civilization" in the very heart of realism—if only negatively, by way of a sweeping cultural agonistics. The stress he gives to intractable conflict undermines the democratic trajectory of his previous book, *The Third Wave* (1991), where he granted the problem of a geopolitical rent between East and West, yet clung to his modernist optimism (310). As late as 1991, then, it could still be said that he broadly concurred with democratic optimists such as Fukuyama, Rueschemeyer, and Di Palma (see works cited) on the thrust of liberal democratic globalization. By 1995, however, Malcolm Waters should have qualified his linkage of Huntington with Fukuyama's liberal democratic teleology (Waters 118–19); for Huntington's *Foreign Affairs* article of 1993 had clearly marked his cultural turn. This shift is all the more dramatic because his previous work was so often the epitome of cultural myopia. Thirty years before, in *Political Order in Changing Societies,* he famously overlooked the moral and cultural weaknesses of Soviet modernism, viz., the destabilization that was sure to erupt in a system built on the hard politics of lies, militarism, and ethnic repression (see Lane <http://www.tnr.com/archive/11/112497/trb112497.html>).

Just as he had been too pessimistic regarding the staying power of the Soviet system, he was now too trusting of the new democratic teleology. That optimism, however, was nowhere to be found in his incendiary *Foreign Affairs* article, "The Clash of Civilizations?" His subsequent book, which dropped the question mark in the title, details the ethnic and civilizational factors that fracture nations even as they threaten to culturally fuse whole regions, such as East

Asia, against the West. Although Huntington's credentials as a realist are a solid fixture of Cold War history, the germ of his cultural turn can be traced to his 1968 classic, *Political Order in Changing Societies*. There he argued that it was simply unrealistic to press developing countries to become instant democracies when they lacked any semblance of democratic traditions. Hence, given the grim realities of Third World cultural politics, strong central authority must first be established. Whatever its intent, *Political Order* was widely read as a case for the realist suspension of Wilsonian idealism in foreign affairs. Walden Bello points out that it quickly became the handbook for a whole generation of development-minded officials in organizations such as the State Department, the Agency for International Development, and the U.S. dominated World Bank (33). In *Clash*, Huntington easily disposes of the non-cultural competition within realism by noting that by their pristine logic Western Europe (either by classical realist design or neorealist structural reflex) would have coalesced with the Soviet Union against the U.S. in the late 1940s (24). Likewise, in the post-Cold War world, the core states of non-Western regions should logically unite against America and the West. This has been attempted, but its force is limited by the constant factionalism that stems from deep cultural/civilizational distrust (185).

One can credit the cultural turn of Huntington's realism while rejecting the fatalism of his "Atlanticist" retreat from Asian cultural politics (see Huntington, *Clash* 312)—a retreat that would leave as little room for the art of diplomacy as does neorealism. By rejecting that retreat and neorealist positivism alike, this study keeps diplomacy in the geopolitical game and in that respect moves closer to classical realism. Where it profoundly differs is in its focus on culture as a vital element of political reality. In the tradition of Vico's verum-factum principle (whereby we know history or culture far better than nature, insofar as we create the former), cultural realism makes no apology for not being "scientific." The one element that will be salvaged from Huntington's cultural retreat is his recoil from any attempt to impose Western values and institutions as a blueprint for global development. Since most "globalism"—here defined as the ideology of those who "are in the habit of *praising* the current process of globalization" (Salih 137; my emphasis)—follows that Orientalist blueprint in all but name (see Waters 3), this study is in that sense anti-globalist. Especially it opposes what Huntington calls "Davos Culture": The convergent interests and values of the small global elite that controls virtually all of the world's dominant international institutions (Huntington, *Clash*

57). However, in place of Huntington's cultural agonistics, my weapon of choice against Davos Globalism is a realism built on cultural dialogics. For me this involves a post-Bakhtinian commitment to crosscultural engagement, including political engagement. In such a dialogics, cultural identities take shape very much as do individual voices: "in response to and in anticipation of other voices" (Bialostosky 214). This makes for a fluid identity, but hardly a vacuous one. As Caryl Emerson convincingly argues, Bakhtin's dialogics kept the self intact, since it is only by asserting one's own uniqueness that one can hope to engage a unique Other dialogically (110). Thus the twin acts of taking a stand and interacting become integral to the twin processes of identity formation and political action. I therefore depart from Emerson, in *Cultural Prosaics* and elsewhere, by extracting from Bakhtin the ingredients of a political counterdiscourse that she would not countenance. This political grounding avoids the cultural relativist trap of holding that on all issues one cultural perspective is as good or just as another—an attitude that has permitted such pressing global issues as human rights and the environment to be labeled "Western" and hence "imperialist." These agonistic labels are designed to block communication and freeze geopolitical discourse in an East/West or South/North mode. The dialogic reach of cultural realism equips it to cross those agonistic lines to deal with vital transnational issues that have no place in classical realism or neorealism.

One such issue is global environmentalism. The rise of environmental consciousness has given "Third World countries an important potential source of blackmail, with countries (not all of them very poor) demanding to be paid to carry out environmental measures which are actually in their own interest as well as everyone else's" (Beloff 5). Insofar as global ecology is a moral or in any case a transnational concern, neither classical realism nor neorealism is equipped to handle it; whereas cultural realism is perfectly suited to the task. As with all realism (Lentner 39), one of cultural realism's primary concerns is assuring security. But in an increasingly global age, security can no longer be restricted to "national interest" in the limited sense. And just as there is now a place for "green" issues within realism, so too there is a growing "realo" wing within Green parties. These groups recognize that although the state has often worked against the environment, its powers are "needed to match the scale of ecological problems. . . . [and to] counter corporate power" (Dryzek 35–36). The environmental recklessness of international organizations like the World Bank and General Agreement on Tariffs and Trade (GATT) is a matter of record. Between 1976 and 1986, for example, the World Bank funneled $600 million into deforestation/resettlement programs in Indonesia alone. The result was massive erosion that "degraded the soil to the point where it could not sustain subsistence agriculture or even absorb water" (Bello 53). John Dryzek points out that in 1991 "a GATT committee declared that the United States' ban on imported tuna caught in ways that caused the deaths of large numbers of dolphins contravened the GATT. If a state wishes to guarantee by law or regulation that its food imports do not contain unsafe levels of pesticides, then that, too, will be a violation of free trade" (81).

Meanwhile, environmentalism has taken a postmodern turn in the direction of a new moral/cultural realism. Its goals are no longer tied so closely to an empirical and hence material frame of reference, exclusive of the moral and aesthetic concerns that are now embraced by "post-environmentalism" (Eder 214–15). The result of these various trends is a remarkable fit between the new (as opposed to "neo") realism and the new ecology, including the new literary eco-criticism. Clearly this is part of a broad postmodern shift from mere survival values to well-being values, and from achievement motivation to post-material motivation (see Inglehart 77). Once realism takes this postmodern turn, however, it confronts the agonistic realities that killed the "New World Order" in its infancy. At that point it faces a stark choice: Huntingtonesque retreat into cultural insularity or the development of a more "engaged" moral realism (as explored in my "Back to Basics"). What Huntington's *Clash* gives us is negative realism. In the post-Cold War world that *Clash* so well describes, but declines to fully engage, affirmative realism requires that cultural agonistics be tempered by cultural dialogics.

CONFRONTING EAST/WEST AGONISTICS

Cultural realism bypasses both sides of the East/West incommensurability argument, as propounded by Huntington on the Western side and Singapore's Lee Kuan Yew on the side of "Asian values." Fortunately there are dialogic alternatives to both. Elsewhere, as part of my case against East Asian exceptionalism, I have contrasted the "Singapore model" of authoritarianism with the democratic voice of Kim Dae Jung, Korea's inveterate dissident-turned-president (see Thornton, "Korea"). The coexistence of economic and political development in Kim's "Korean model" would free American foreign policy from the burden of choosing between the false antipodes of stability and social justice. That blighted choice was thought necessary during the Cold War, when the West hesitated to advance its own values for fear of driving developing countries into Moscow's camp (see Kausikan 27).

The always dubious rationale for treating oppressive regimes as full strategic partners died with the Cold War. With it died, also, the rationale for a virulent strain of realism that helped produce—in terms of genocide, ethnocide, and environmental apocalypse (see Bello, Chapter 7)—the most destructive century in recorded history. Many, unfortunately, did not get the message. On 9 March 1991, in the wake of the Gulf War, President Bush declared, "By God! We've kicked the Vietnam Syndrome once and for all. . . . The specter of Vietnam has been forever buried in the desert sands of the Arabian peninsula" (qtd. in Long 397). By retreating from post-Cold War global imperatives, the "Vietnam syndrome" was indeed an invitation to trouble, and no realist should lament its passing. Unfortunately, the cultural sensitivity that attended that syndrome is also put at risk by the return of the old power politics. What is needed, in the absence of a new world order, is a *via media* between Fukuyama's dialogic liberalism and Huntington's undialogic realism. Huntington's agonistics stems from his still-modernist habit of treating whole cultures as reified systems. It must be granted that the agonistic worldviews of Hobbes and Huntington are in many ways closer to global reality, and especially Asian reality, than are dialogic alternatives such as the Grotian notion of a salutary society of nations (see Sheehan 11–12). Here my objective is simply to keep dialogics in the game by charting a course that is "in but not of" agonistics. The last effective metatheory of global peace—based largely on a nuclear balance of terror—could not survive the passing of the Cold War. Its heir apparent, Fukuyama's posthistorical vision of a New World Order, never materialized. History refused to go away. That is not to say that Fukuyama's liberal globalism is a feckless illusion. Rather, it is intertwined with its theoretical opposite, realism. Too often globalism turns out to be little more than a front for vested interests, while "realism" is but a euphemism for the purchase of stability or geopolitical advantage at any price. Theoretical distinctions between the two then evaporate. For example, the opposition one would expect between Clinton's manifest globalism and Kissinger's nominal realism all but vanishes where China is concerned.

The operative theory behind Clinton's China policy has been a market-obsessed economism that even Fukayama could not endorse (see *Trust* 34).

This vision of unproblematic economic growth rests on the expansion and empowerment of the middle classes, which are expected in turn to demand political reform. Proponents of such economic prioritization often point to the development patterns of South Korea and Taiwan. However, as Kanishka Jayasuriya counters, Singapore and Malaysia could just as well be spotlighted in support of the opposite case. Both sing the praises of authoritarian "Asian values," despite the fact that each is "dominated by a party with strong middle class support . . . Hence, those who suggest that Asian middle classes will demand greater liberalization are likely to be sorely disappointed. The Asian values ideology serves only to provide a comfortable canopy for this middle class" (Jayasuriya 88).

The unilateral privileging of economic over political liberalization in the Singapore model differs from Japanese economism in that the Japanese people have clearly given their consent to these priorities. In that sense the authority behind the Japanese model could be called, if not quite bilateral, then at least top-down by consent. It is the more forceful removal or manipulation of consent which distinguishes the "Asian values" model from the Japanese. In Singapore's case this hegemonic turn had its debut in 1963 with the PAP (People's Action Party) Operation Cold Store: The arrest of one hundred opposition leaders. Since that time all Singaporeans have been subject to constant political surveillance (see Chua 16 and 44). But for the most part PAP has operated through the less direct means of intense media control and a unilateral scripting of tradition. If "other" Asian values have been politically dormant in Japan, they have been forcefully suppressed in Singapore, Malaysia, and Indonesia, and virtually crushed in Myanmar and the People's Republic of China. Here the de facto motto might go beyond "growth first" to "growth only." This dictum was spelled out by Deng Xiaopeng, and its place in post-Deng CCP ideology is hardly less secure. By no means, however, does this development strategy stop at the boundary of "Asian values." It is a potent factor throughout the Third World, or what is increasingly—metaphorically more than geographically—called the South, where authoritarianism is primarily an instrument for suppressing the unrest that is bound to erupt from gross inequality in distribution. Speaking before the United Nations General Assembly in 1974, Secretary of State Henry Kissinger asserted that the "notion of the Northern rich and the Southern poor has been shattered" ("Common Response" 3). Indeed, many countries that fall under this "Southern" rubric did make impressive gains prior to the 1980s in terms of GDP per capita. Only on closer analysis, with attention shifted to the actual distribution of gains, does the "Southern" argument strike home. As the South Commission reported in 1990, inequalities "tended to widen as the economy grew and became more industrialized. . . . Increasingly, the rich and powerful in countries of the South were able to enjoy the life-style and consumption patterns of developed countries of the North. But large segments of the population experienced no significant improvement in their standard of living, while being able to see the growing affluence of the few" (qtd. in Thomas 5).

Consequently, the stage is set for what Jayasuriya—generalizing a term that Jeffrey Herf applied to Nazi Germany—calls "reactionary modernism" (82–84)—a condition of radical divorce between economic and technical modernization, on the one hand, and political (liberal democratic) modernization on the other. Where cultural or civilizational friction reaches the proportions described by Huntington's *Clash,* we can expect reactionary modernism to be the rule rather than the exception in developing countries. In India, for example, Hindu fundamentalism is less a threat to material modernization than to the secular state and the whole democratic apparatus. Countries such as Algeria, Nigeria, and Sudan have reverted to military authoritarianism, while Egypt, Peru, and Russia have shifted to repressive state controls. Elsewhere, as in Guatemala, Argentina, Uruguay, and (until very recently) Chile, the ongoing veto power of the military has reduced democracy to a stage prop (Shaw and Quadir 49).

THE NEW SINO-GLOBALISM

It is no accident that former US president Clinton's development strategy— built on the assumptions of vintage modernization theory—bears remarkable resemblance to Kennedy's Alliance for Progress. Both lay stress on the cultivation of the middle classes as the alpha and omega of development. This class/ic error—a naive faith in class alone as the engine of progress—had its first incarnation in the Old Left notion of the proletariat's innate progressivism. After the German working class threw its support behind Nazism and the war, Frankfurt School critical theory laid that class/ic blunder to rest. Soon, however, it had a second, liberal incarnation in the American vision of the middle class as the "vital center" (as Arthur Schlesinger called it) not only of American political culture but of global development.

Castro believed that insofar as Kennedy's Alliance for Progress rose above the vested interests of corporations, foreign regimes and the Pentagon, it was doomed to fail (Schlesinger 147). And Castro was right. At least Kennedy's naiveté can be defended on the grounds that—apart from the experience of fascism, which could be dismissed as a twentieth-century aberration—reactionary modernization had not yet made its full global debut. Clinton has no such excuse. Indeed, as Richard Rorty argues in *Achieving our Country* (1988), American society is itself being split into a cosmopolitan upper crust and a downwardly mobile remainder. America's own "vital center" is decomposing even as American foreign policy strives to create new "vital centers" around the world. This might be a harmlessly quixotic enterprise except that extant power elites are imagined to be the vanguard of these proto-democratic "centers." Likewise, growth of any kind is imagined to be progress. One of the chief architects of Clinton's China policy, Anthony Lake, a self-described "centrist," so closely equates U.S. interest with Chinese economic growth that he has pressed the U.S. not to expose Chinese exports of nuclear materials to Third World clients (see Heilbrunn <http://www.tnr.com/textonly/032497/txtheilbrunn032497.html>).

Whether judged by a Wilsonian or realist standard, Kissinger's current stance on China is no less odious. In 1987 he was encouraged by China's ambassador to the U.S. to found the American China Society, through which he has become one of the Chinese government's most powerful defenders. He is credited with personally persuading former House Speaker Newt Gingrich to drop his support for Taiwan independence, and for convincing the Clinton administration to disconnect the issues of trade and human rights (see Judis <http://www.tnr.com/textonly/031097/txtjudis031097.html>). Whatever argument might be made for these policies from a globalist perspective, there is no reconciling them with any form of realism—not at a time when China is the paramount source of Asia's growing *im*balance of power—a fact that is only compounded by the prospect of Korea's reunification (see "Japan"). This raises the question of the purity of Kissinger's realist credentials even during the Cold War. Legend has it that his policies dislodged the illusion of monolithic communism from American foreign policy. In fact, Kissinger was inclined toward a highly ideological reading of world affairs. Daniel Patrick Moynihan points out that, as Secretary of State, Kissinger warned that America must "face the stark reality that the [Communist] challenge is unending" (qtd. in Moynihan 145). The context of this almost eschatological utterance was America's by then obvious failure in the Vietnam War. The domino theory, the most commonly stated rationale for escalating the war in the first place (Kolko 75), was being justly discredited by a new brand of culturalism, as in, for example, Walker Conner's case for the vital political role of ethnic heterogeneity in Asian political cultures (see Conner; and, specific to Vietnam, FitzGerald, *Fire in the Lake*). At this of all times, Kissinger blew second wind into America's Cold War ideology by naturalizing its communist adversary.

Nonetheless Kissinger recognized the limits of the domino theory as applied to Vietnam (Kissinger, *Years* 82) and China, which he perceived as a nationalistic entity vis-a-vis the Soviet Union and North Vietnam alike. Kissinger was aware that China secretly condoned U.S. operations in Laos, despite (or even because of) its negative impact on North Vietnam (Kissinger, *Years* 58). He favorably cites André Malraux's belief that China's support of North Vietnam was an "imposture," for the historical animosities between China and North Vietnam ran too deep (Kissinger, *White House* 1052). In global balance of power terms, it was no secret that China feared the possibility of Vietnam becoming a Soviet satellite state, thus completing the encirclement of China (Kolko 419). If Kissinger's early China policy can be credited with promoting a global balance of power, it now lives on as an effete mockery of realism; for China is fast becoming the major agent of Asian instability. By any "realist" logic, the fall of the Soviet Union and the concomitant rise of China should have prompted an immediate shift in Kissinger's position on China. This naturally raises suspicions that his refusal to budge an inch in that direction is directly related to the operations of the firm he founded, Kissinger Associates, which assists corporate clients in setting up business ties in China. Thus Kissinger the arch-realist has become, in actual practice, a closet globalist.

Having served as president of Kissinger Associates, former Secretary of State Lawrence Eagleburger now works for a law firm that likewise helps businesses to obtain contracts in China; and another president of Kissinger Associates, former National Security Advisor Brent Snowcroft, freely mixes public policy advice with private business connections via his consulting firm, the Scowcroft Group, which operates out of the same office complex as the nonprofit policy group he founded: The Forum for International Policy. In 1996 he helped Dean O'Hare, chairman of the Chubb insurance group, secure a meeting with Chinese Premier Li Peng. All the while, not surprisingly, he has defended China assiduously on issues such as MFN and Chinese sales of nuclear material to Pakistan, which he has publicly blamed—through a bizarre twist of logic—on U.S. non-proliferation legislation (see Judis), as if China did it to save face when confronted with evil imperialist pressures. Next to Kissinger himself, however, the most egregious China-card player is former Secretary of State Alexander Haig, Kissinger's aide during the opening of China. Haig has the distinction of having been the only prominent American to join the October 1989 celebration of the fortieth anniversary of the PRC—i.e., to join Deng Xiaoping in Tiananmen Square just four months after the Tiananmen massacre. His continuing role in the defense of MFN and as a critic of anyone who defends Taiwan has earned him a good deal more than praise from the Chinese. Deng saluted his "courage," but what counts are the contracts: One of the major clients of his consulting group, Worldwide Associates, has hauled in billions of dollars in business deals with the Chinese (see Judis). Haig is not one to be concerned about theoretical contradictions, but more might be expected from his realist mentor, Kissinger.

THE POST-COLD WAR CULTURAL IMPERATIVE

With the end of the Cold War, the brutal amorality of Kissingeresque realism has lost whatever justification it could ever claim. So too, its cultural indifference renders it obsolete, for culture has emerged as a prime mover of world affairs (see Kahn x). Fukuyama has managed to keep his version of globalism in the game by taking a modest cultural turn, blurring the stock association of economism with rationality and culture with irrationality (see *Trust* 37–38). Perhaps it would be fair to call his position a cultural globalism, as far removed from unalloyed globalism as cultural realism is from traditional realism. Kissinger, however, holds fast to the tablets he brought down from the mountain. His hard line realism treats culture as local color, style, or sentiment rather than political substance. In his Washington years he perpetuated Cold War logic by putting containment in an older realist package: The classic balance of power that tries to reduce international relations to a cold calculation of interest. Moynihan wryly notes that Kissinger's "realism" put him out of touch with the inner substance of political reality (145–46). It certainly obscured the cultural and civilizational realities that suffuse Moynihan's *Pandaemonium* (1993) and Huntington's *Clash*. Where East Asia is concerned, responses to this cultural challenge range from globalist denial, on the one hand, to militant agonistics on the other. Huntington's thesis, for example, receives a concerted challenge from the collection of papers contained in *Techno-Security in an Age of Globalization: Perspectives from the Pacific Rim,* edited by Denis Simon (1997). One reviewer, Steven Rosefield, points out that these papers collectively comprise a national security paradigm consistent with "Lester Thurow's and Francis Fukuyama's notions about the global triumph of capitalism and the end of history. . . . Traditional international security concerns, it is intimated, have become obsolete. Imperialism is dead, great nations are war averse, economic systems don't matter (because there is only capitalism), and Huntington's clash of civilizations is a mirage. What really matters today, the authors variously contend, are technological threats . . . and other lower intensity quarrels" (751).

At the opposite pole there is the all-too-cogent realist manifesto of Richard Bernstein and Ross Munro (*The Coming Conflict with China*). In a recent *Foreign Affairs* article, Bernstein and Munro attempt to distinguish their approach from that of Huntington, on the ground that theirs is strictly geopolitical rather than cultural or civilizational ("Coming" 21). That distinction, however, runs aground on several points. First, it is granted that part of the reason for China's new assertiveness is its traditional view of itself as Asia's preeminent power (22). That is a deeply ingrained *cultural* viewpoint, entirely consistent with Huntington's thesis. Second, Bernstein and Munro's working assumption that China will not readily go the route of democracy, despite its rising affluence, is based on the absence of such key ingredients as a tradition of limited government, individual rights, independent judiciary, etc. (26–27). Are these absences not part of China's political *culture?* Notions such as the consent of the governed and the will of the majority are not just ideas, but deeply rooted cultural institutions. A thriving market economy can be conducive to the formation of such institutions. Perhaps it is a necessary but insufficient prerequisite for their development. The bottom line, as Bernstein and Munro point out, is that China treats opposition as treason. So far that *cultural* fact has not proved incompatible with China's new techno-nationalism. Bernstein and Munro, in any case, have the good fortune of not being the classical realists they imagine themselves to be.

One reason why their warning is not being heeded is likewise culture-related. Americans view Asia as a far more alien place than Europe. Even if they see China as a budding superpower, they are not inclined to see her regional power as posing so serious a threat to their culturally defined interests as would an equivalent military threat on the European side. This bias skews Americans' sense of shifting global priorities. As Fareed Zakaria argues, two simple facts define today's geopolitics: "Russian weakness and Chinese strength. . . . Yet increasingly the Clinton Administration's foreign policy looks as if it were intended to meet precisely the opposite challenges. . . . the Administration is spending vast amounts of time, energy, money and political capital to deter [Russia] from launching an invasion of Central Europe. China, on the other hand, is surging economically, bulking up its armed forces and becoming more assertive by the day" (Zakaria <http://www.mtholyoke.edu/acad/intrel/zakaria.htm>). Early in May, 1998 India shocked the world by conducting three nuclear tests. It was generally assumed that this breach of nuclear nonproliferation was aimed almost exclusively at Pakistan; but for Henry Sokolski—the Bush Defense Department's top official for nuclear nonproliferation issues—it amounted to "an act of impatience with failed American efforts to stop China and North Korea from developing and spreading strategic weapons": Sokolski quotes *The Times of India*'s comment that "by the time the Clinton Administration wakes up to the danger posed by the China-Pakistan-North Korean axis, it will be too late for India" (Sokolski <http://www.mtholyoke.edu/acad/intrel/sokolski.htm>). This view gains credibility in the light of India's former conciliation towards Pakistan. Despite friction over Kashmir, the two antagonists had renewed ministerial contacts and, guided by Indian Prime Minister Inder Kumar Gujral, were seeking more economic cooperation (*International Institute for Strategic Studies* 146). The U.S., however, was sluggish in revising policies formed when Pakistan was a Cold War ally and India a leader of "nonaligned" nations and a major recipient of Soviet economic and military aid (Kennedy 507). By the 1990s, if not before, that Cold War mindset was worse than obsolete. In combination with Clinton's China policy it contributed to renewed militarism in the region. Likewise, the perpetuation of a Cold War China policy is aggravating an already dangerous imbalance in Northeast Asian (NEA) geopolitics. Even as the Cold War abates between the two Koreas, new power configurations must be taken into account. By the early 1990s, thought was being given to an ASEAN-type NEA unity. Like AFTA in the south, one goal of this accord was a trade bloc that would exclude the U.S., Australia, and Canada.

From 1967 to 1989 ASEAN (the Association of South-East Asian Nations: Indonesia, Singapore, Malaysia, the Philippines, and Thailand, plus Brunei in 1984 and Vietnam in 1995) was the only regional political organization in Asia (Godement 281). A first step toward a more globally attuned regionalism was taken by APEC (Asia Pacific Economic Cooperation), which was founded in 1989 under Western auspices. The U.S. and Australia sought to circumvent trade barriers by transforming APEC from a mere consultive group into a formal trading bloc. Asian governments immediately perceived this as an attempt to saddle them with a U.S. free-trade package. Indeed, a key figure in the U.S. strategy was Fred Bergsten, who by no accident had also been a lobbyist for GATT and NAFTA (North American Free Trade Area). ASEAN, which leaned heavily toward state-assisted capitalism rather than free trade, reacted to this Western initiative by shortening the timetable for their own AFTA (ASEAN Free Trade Area) trade bloc. Another anti-Western shock wave erupted when Mahathir Mohamad, Malaysia's prime minister, proposed an East Asia Economic Group (EAEG) under the aegis of Japan, with China and Korea invited but with the U.S., Australia, and Canada strictly excluded. Still another shock came when the Philippines shut down the American naval base at Subic Bay, to the tune of an anti-Western diatribe from the Philippine Senate president, Jovito Salonga: "Today we have summoned the political will to stand up and end 470 years of foreign military presence in the Philippines" (Bello 3). Meanwhile the potential for a Northeast Asian (NEA) accord was being explored. The idea had obvious economic merit: Coupled with China's huge and affordable work force and Russia's abundant natural resources, the capital and technology of Japan and South Korea could be expected to turn the NEA region as a whole into an Asian "mega-tiger." By 1994, however, this dream had all but disintegrated (see Rozman 1, 4). Gilbert Rozman points out that the prospect of NEA regionalism "brought to the forefront true civilizational divides" (22).

Fearing that Japan would turn NEA cooperation into its own "flying-goose" cartel, China upgraded her diplomatic relations with Moscow, thus putting both Tokyo and Washington on edge. Increasingly, however, the U.S. took the brunt of Chinese invective (Rozman 20). Since NEA multilateralism tends to vary inversely with U.S. diplomatic strength in the region, it was not good news for the U.S. when, in the middle of Clinton's first term, China's Vice-Premier Zhu Rongji got a warm reception on his trip to Tokyo, when Japan's Hosokawa reciprocated with a visit to Beijing, or when President Kim Young Sam of Korea visited both ("Time" 19). An even worse omen was the April 1997 Moscow summit between Jiang Zemin and Boris Yeltsin, both of whom pledged support for a multilateral world order to block the hegemony of any state—meaning, obviously, the U.S. (Wishnick 1049).

What kept the U.S. in the game was the enormous distrust that every NEA power feels towards every other. This same distrust makes the June 2000 summit between North Korea's Kim Jung Il and the South's Kim Dae Jung a dubious blessing so far as regional stability is concerned. Reunification would revive the centuries-old competition for hegemony over Korea (see "Japan").

Given the region's culturally ingrained distrust, the U.S. has a vital role to play as a counterbalance to resurgent Sino-centricism. This strategy, however, requires close attention to the minutia of cultural realism. To follow Huntington in his concentration on "civilizational" fault lines is already to miss those details: This would reproduce in cultural geopolitics the monolithic scale that encumbered domino theory logic, and with the same catastrophic results. Not only would it do a disservice to legitimate U.S. security concerns, but to the interests of all Asian nations under China's hegemonic shadow. Without outside support, weaker Rim countries will be pushed into a politics of accommodation where the center holds all too well, while stronger countries will be forced into a costly and perilous arms race.

By grounding balance-of-power politics in national and local (not just civilizational) social reality, the cultural realism of this article moves beyond Huntington and Fukuyama alike. It avoids the monolithic fallacies of political realism on the one hand and "reverse domino" globalization on the other. This affords a more effective realism, but, it must be granted, one that is still but a tool in a larger foreign policy schema. In terms of means and ends, it is still only a strategy—a means in search of a suitable end (suitable, that is, to both poles of a given cultural dialogue). In forthcoming work I argue that the end most commensurate with cultural realism—which I term "moral realism"—gets past Huntington's negative, retreatist realism by re-engaging other political cultures on an ethical plane. In the spirit of post-Bakhtinian dialogics, rather than any neo-imperialism (including, most emphatically, that of corporate globalization), this cultural realism turns Huntington's cultural isolationism on its head.

WORKS CITED

Bello, Walden. *People and Power in the Pacific: The Struggle for the Post-Cold War Order.* London: Pluto, 1992.

Beloff, Max. "Utopia Undone." *Times Literary Supplement* (26 January 1996): 5–6.

Bernstein, Richard, and Ross H. Munro. "The Coming Conflict with America." *Foreign Affairs* 76.2 (1997): 19–32.

Bernstein, Richard, and Ross H. Munro. *The Coming Conflict with China.* New York: Alfred A. Knopf, 1997.

Bialostosky, Don. "Dialogic Criticism." *Contemporary Literary Theory.* Ed. G. Douglas Atkins and Laura Morrow. Amherst: The U of Massachusetts P, 1989. 214–28.

Chua, Beng-Huat. *Communications Ideology and Democracy in Singapore*. London: Routledge, 1995.

Conner, Frank. "Ethnology and the Peace of South Asia." *World Politics* 22.1 (1969): 51–86.

Di Palma, Giuseppe. *To Craft Democracies: An Essay on Democratic Transitions*. Berkeley: U of California P, 1990.

Dryzek, John S. *Democracy in Capitalist Times: Ideals, Limits, and Struggles*. New York: Oxford UP, 1996.

Eder, Klaus. "The Institutionalisation of Environmentalism: Ecological Discourse and the Second Transformation of the Public Sphere." *Risk, Environment and Modernity: Towards a New Ecology*. Ed. Scott Lash, Bronislaw Szerszynski, and Brian Wynne. London: Sage, 1996. 203–23.

Emerson, Caryl. "Keeping the Self Intact During the Culture Wars: A Centennial Essay for Mikhail Bakhtin." *New Literary History: A Journal of Theory and Interpretation* 27.1 (1996): 107–26.

FitzGerald, Frances. *Fire in the Lake: The Vietnamese and the Americans in Vietnam*. New York: Vintage, 1972.

Forde, Steven. "International Realism and the Science of Politics: Thucidides, Machiavelli, and Neorealism." *International Studies Quarterly* 39.2 (1995): 141–60.

Fukuyama, Francis. *Trust: The Social Virtues and the Creation of Prosperity*. New York: The Free Press, 1995.

Fukuyama, Francis. *The End of History and the Last Man*. New York: Avon, 1992.

Godement, François. *The New Asian Renaissance: From Colonialism to the Post-Cold War*. Trans. Elisabeth J. Parcell. London: Routledge, 1997.

Heilbrunn, Jacob. "The Great Equivocator." *The New Republic* (24 March 1997): <http://www.tnr.com/textonly/032497/txtheilbrunn032497.html>.

Huntington, Samuel P. "The Erosion of American National Interests." *Foreign Affairs* 76.5 (1997): 28–49.

Huntington, Samuel P. *The Clash of Civilizations and the Remaking of World Order*. New York: Simon and Schuster, 1996.

Huntington, Samuel P. *The Third Wave: Democratization in the Late Twentieth Century*. Norman: U of Oklahoma P, 1991.

Huntington, Samuel P. *Political Order in Changing Societies*. New Haven: Yale UP, 1968.

Inglehart, Ronald. *Modernization and Postmodernization: Cultural, Economic, and Political Change in 43 Societies*. Princeton: Princeton UP, 1997.

International Institute for Strategic Studies: The Military Balance. 1997/98. London: Oxford UP, 1997.

"Japan and China Eye Each Other Warily—As Usual." *The Economist* (2–8 September 2000): Editorial.

Jayasuriya, Kanishka. "Understanding 'Asian Values' as a Form of Reactionary Modernization." *Contemporary Politics* 4.1 (1998): 77–91.

Johnston, Alastair Iain. *Cultural Realism: Strategic Culture and Grand Strategy in Chinese History.* Princeton: Princeton UP, 1995.

Judis, John B. "China Town." *The New Republic* (10 March 1997): <http://www.tnr.com/textonly/031097/txtjudis031097.html>.

Kahn, Joel S. *Culture, Multiculture, Postculture.* London: Sage, 1995.

Kausikan, Bilahari. "Asia's Different Standard." *Foreign Policy* 92 (1993): 24–41.

Kennedy, Paul. *The Rise and Fall of the Great Powers: Economic Change and Military Conflict from 1500 to 2000.* London: Fontana, 1989.

Kissinger, Henry A. *White House Years.* Boston: Little, Brown and Co., 1979.

Kissinger, Henry A. *A Common Response to the Challenge of Development.* An Address by U.S. Secretary of State, Henry A. Kissinger, To the Sixth Special Session of the U.N. General Assembly on 15 April 1974. Washington: U.S. Policy Statement Series, 1974.

Kissinger, Henry A. *Years of Upheaval.* Boston: Little, Brown and Co., 1982.

Kolko, Gabriel. *Anatomy of a War: Vietnam, the United States, and the Modern Historical Experience.* New York: The New Press, 1985.

Lane, Charles. "TRB from Washington: Disorderly Conduct." *The New Republic* (24 November 1997): <http://www.tnr.com/archive/11/112497/trb112497.html>.

Lapid, Yosef. "Culture's Ship: Returns and Departures in International Relations Theory." *The Return of Culture and Identity in IR Theory.* Ed. Yosef Lapid and Friedrich Kratochwil. Boulder: Lynne Rienner, 1996. 3–20.

Lentner, Howard H. *International Politics: Theory and Practice.* Minneapolis: Paul: West Publishing Co., 1997.

Long, Ngô Viñh. "Vietnam in the New World Order." *Altered States: A Reader in the New World Order.* Ed. Phyllis Bennis and Michel Moushabeck. New York: Olive Branch, 1993: 397–406.

Mazarr, Michael J. "Culture and International Relations: A Review Essay." *The Washington Quarterly* 19.2 (1996): 177–97.

Morgenthau, Hans, and Kenneth W. Thompson. *Politics Among Nations: The Struggle for Power and Peace.* 6th ed. New York: Alfred A. Knopf, 1985.

Moynihan, Daniel Patrick. *Pandaemonium: Ethnicity in International Politics.* Oxford: Oxford UP, 1993.

Nye, Joseph S. "The Changing Nature of World Power." *Political Science Quarterly* 105.2 (1990): 177–92.

Rorty, Richard. *Achieving our Country: Leftist Thought in Twentieth-Century America.* Cambridge: Harvard UP, 1998.

Rosefielde, Steven. Review of *Techno-Security in an Age of Globalization: Perspectives from the Pacific Rim.* Ed. Denis Fred Simon (Armonk: Sharpe, 1997). *The Journal of Asian Studies* 56.3 (1997): 750–51.

Rozman, Gilbert. "Flawed Regionalism: Reconceptionalizing Northeast Asia in the 1990s." *The Pacific Review* 11.1 (1998): 1–27.

Rueschemeyer, Dietrich, Evelyn Huber Stephens, and John D. Stephens. *Capitalist Development and Democracy.* Chicago: U of Chicago P, 1992.

Salih, Mohamed A. Mohamed. "Global Ecologism and its Critics." *Globalization and the South*. Ed. Caroline Thomas and Peter Wilkin. New York: St. Martin's, 1997. 124–42.

Schlesinger, Arthur M. *The Cycles of American History*. Boston: Houghton Mifflin Co., 1986.

Shaw, Timothy M., and Fahimul Quadir. "Democratic Development in the South in the Next Millenium: What Prospects for Avoiding Anarchy and Authoritarianism?" *Globalization and the South*. Ed. Caroline Thomas and Peter Wilkin. New York: St. Martin's, 1997. 36–59.

Sheehan, Michael. *The Balance of Power: History and Theory*. London: Routledge, 1996.

Sokolski, Henry. "A Blast of Reality." *New York Times Op-Ed* (13 May 1998): Mount Holyoke College: <http://www.mtholyoke.edu/acad/intrel/sokolski.htm>.

Thomas, Caroline. "Globalization and the South." *Globalization and the South*. Ed. Caroline Thomas and Peter Wilkin. New York: St. Martin's, 1997. 1–17.

Thornton, William H. "Korea and East Asian Exceptionalism." *Theory, Culture and Society* 15.2 (1998): 137–54.

Thornton, William H. *Cultural Prosaics: The Second Postmodern Turn*. Edmonton: Research Institute for Comparative Literature, U of Alberta, 1998.

Thornton, William H. "Cross-Cultural Prosaics: Renegotiating the Postostmodern/Postcolonial Gap in Cultural Studies." *Prose Studies: History, Theory, Criticism* 20.2 (1997): 108–24.

Thornton, William H. "Cultural Prosaics as Counterdiscourse: A Direction for Cultural Studies After Bakhtin." *Prose Studies: History, Theory, Criticism* 17.2 (1995): 74–97.

"Time for Focus: America Needs to Attune Its Interests to Asia's." *Asiaweek* (20 April 1994): 18–19.

Tötösy de Zepetnek, Steven. "From Comparative Literature Today Toward Comparative Cultural Studies." *Comparative Literature and Comparative Cultural Studies*. Ed. Steven Tötösy de Zepetnek. West Lafayette: Purdue UP, 2002. 235–67.

Turner, Brian S. *Orientalism, Postmodernism and Globalism*. London: Routledge, 1994.

Waltz, Kenneth. *Theory of International Politics*. New York: McGraw-Hill, 1979.

Waters, Malcolm. *Globalization*. London: Routledge, 1995.

Wheeler, Nicholas J., and Tim Dunne. "Good International Citizenship: A Third Way for British Foreign Policy." International Affairs. 74/4 (October 1998), 847–70.

Wishnick, Elizabeth. Review of *The Roles of the United States, Russia, and China in the New World Order* (1994). Ed. Hafeez Malik. *The Journal of Asian Studies* 56.4 (1997): 1049–50.

Zakaria, Fareed. "Let's Get Our Superpowers Straight." *New York Times Op-Ed* (26 March 1997): <http://www.mtholyoke.edu/acad/intrel/zakaria.htm>.

From Comparative Literature Today Toward Comparative Cultural Studies

Steven Tötösy de Zepetnek

Historically, the comparative perspective and method has proven itself indispensable in many disciplines and established itself, accordingly, intellectually as well as institutionally. For example, in a review of the George M. Fredrickson's *The Comparative Imagination: On the History of Racism, Nationalism, and Social Movements* (1997), the reviewer argues that the comparative perspective "give[s] us a good opportunity for assessing how comparative history can contribute to modern knowledge . . . in *The Comparative Imagination*, Fredrickson welcomes the increasing tendency of historians of the United States to write from a "comparative perspective . . . by using foreign examples to explain what is distinctive about American society" (Thompson 48; incidentally, Fredrickson explains that before his turn to history, he pursued the study of comparative literature [Fredrickson 8]). In the humanities, it has been established sufficiently and often enough that the discipline of comparative literature has intrinsically a content and form that facilitate the cross-cultural and interdisciplinary study of literature and culture. As well, it is generally accepted in scholarship that the discipline has a history that substantiated its intrinsic aims and objectives in content and in practice. Predicated on the borrowing of methods from other disciplines and on the application of the appropriated method to areas of study single-language literary study more often than not tends to neglect, the discipline is difficult to define however, because it is fragmented and pluralistic, non-self-referential and inclusive.

In US cultural studies in particular—and it is US cultural studies that made the strongest and most wide-spread impact in the humanities including the study of literature—it often happens that an idea, notion, or postulate is presented as innovative when in fact the same areas have been studied under similar terms in comparative literature (for the argument that comparative literature historically included many aspects of current cultural studies, see, for example, Daniel and Peck 16–17; Straw 89; Tötösy 1994). It is argued among comparatists and among a critical mass of scholars in the humanities—although rarely acknowledged—that the discipline of comparative literature is rich in its history with regard to both theory and practice of much of what cultural studies is about as practiced in the US today. Areas of study such as popular culture or film and literature have a long history of incisive work in comparative literature, for example. It is true, however, that cultural studies often presents new theoretical approaches (more often than not borrowed from other fields, similarly to comparative literature), methods, terminologies, and rhetorical content which when applied result in innovative work in the study of culture. In consequence, I accept the currency of cultural studies and I am aware of the intellectual and institutional difficulties comparative literature, in contrast, is experiencing globally while cultural studies has acquired both intellectual and institutional standing, arguably on a wider scale than comparative literature. Thus, for political reasons but which are at the same time parallel to intellectual bases and considerations, I intend to explore the viability of enriching and developing both fields of study, that of comparative literature and that of cultural studies. This theory construction involves the merger of aspects of comparative literature and cultural studies into a new approach I designate as "comparative cultural studies." In this paper, for reasons implicit in my statement above, namely that comparative literature has contributed significantly to literary studies, I argue that it also has much to offer to cultural studies.

I begin with a description of some aspects of the current situation of comparative literature from which I then proceed to a draft proposal of a framework for "comparative cultural studies." In principle, comparative cultural studies is conceived as an approach—to be developed eventually to a full-fledged framework—containing (for now) three areas of theoretical content: 1) To study literature (text and/or literary system) with and in the context of culture and the discipline of cultural studies; 2) In cultural studies itself to study literature with borrowed elements (theories and methods) from comparative literature; and 3) To study culture and its composite parts and aspects in the mode of the proposed "comparative cultural studies" approach instead of the currently reigning single-language approach dealing with a topic with regard to its nature and problematics in one culture only. In this schema of theoretical components the study of literature is not privileged, however, although for now because of my own interests I confer focus on literature. In other words, the discipline of comparative cultural studies would implicitly and explicitly disrupt the established hierarchy of cultural products and production similarly to the disruption cultural studies itself has performed. Among others, the suggestion is to pluralize and parallelize the study of culture without hierarchization.

AN INTERNATIONAL HISTORY OF THE DISCIPLINE OF COMPARATIVE LITERATURE

With regard to the history of the discipline of comparative literature, it is surprising that a truly international and synthetic history of the discipline—a description of its history within the larger field of literary studies as well as the history of theories and methodologies within comparative literature and with a description of the discipline's institutional history and making—is yet to be written. Curiously, apart from usually short descriptive studies such as chapter two in the early volume by Ulrich Weisstein, *Einführung in die Vergleichende Literaturwissenschaft* (1968) or chapter one in Claudio Guillén's *The Challenge of Comparative Literature* (1993), or, in German, the chapter "Zu Wissenschaftsgeschichte der Komparatistik," in Peter V. Zima and Johann Strutz's *Komparatistik: Einführung in die Vergleichende Literaturwissenschaft* (1992) or brief descriptions of comparative literature within national borders such as those in the recent collected volume of Tania Franco Carvalhal, ed., *Comparative Literature World Wide: Issues and Methods* (1997) or as in the Italian volume by Armando Gnisci and Francesca Sinopoli, eds., *Comparare i comparatismi. La comparatistica letteraria oggo in Europa e nel mondo* (1995), the history of the discipline is available only in this fragmented form. There are also some volumes such as Arno Kappler's *Der literarische Vergleich. Beiträge zu einer Vorgeschichte der Komparatistik* (1976) or specific histories such as Peter Theodor Leithmann's *Moriz Carriere and the Development of Comparative Literature* (1977). However, these studies, similar to the article-length type I mentioned above, offer a partial and limited view of the history of the discipline at best (for a selected international bibliography of histories and theories of comparative literature, see Tötösy, 1999– <http://clcwebjournal.lib.purdue.edu/library/clitbib1-99.html>; for a shortlist of recently published volumes in

comparative literature, see Tötösy, 1999– <http://clcwebjournal.lib.purdue.edu/
library/booklist.html>; for a long list of works in comparative literature, see
Tötösy, 1999– <http://clcwebjournal.lib.purdue.edu/library/clitbib2–99.html>;
for a selected bibliography of comparative literature and cultural studies, see
Tötösy, Aoun, and Nielsen in this volume).

There are "supplementary" types of material which would also be important for a synthetic international history of comparative literature. For example, personal histories such as in Lionel Gossmann and Mihail I. Spariosu, eds.,
*Building a Profession: Autobiographical Perspectives on the Beginnings of
Comparative Literature in the United States* (1994); or descriptions of various
conferences in comparative literature such as Marko Juvan's "Thematics and
Intellectual Content: The XVth Triennial Congress of the International Comparative Literature Association in Leiden" (see Juvan at <http://clcwebjournal.
lib.purdue.edu/clcweb99–1/juvan99.html>) or my own "Comparative Literature
and *Applied Cultural Studies*, Or, a Report About the XIVth Triennial Congress of the ICLA/AILC (University of Alberta, August 1994)" (Tötösy 1994).
As well, here is a marked need of institutional histories of comparative literature in both national and international contexts (for a selection of sources, see
Kirby 197–203; see also Tötösy, Aoun, and Nielsen in this volume).

The usual process of presenting histories of comparative literature in all of
the above mentioned volumes and in all others is in the context of and limited
to national borders, that is, comparative literature in Germany, in France, in
the United States, in China, etc. While this is the approach I would like to circumvent in an international history of comparative literature I am working on
now, I realize that it is indeed easier to proceed in the national model. And when
I myself, in this article, present examples of a renaissance of comparative literature in various "peripheral" countries (see below), I present these examples by
listing countries (because it is easier to do so). However, I would like to point
out with utmost conviction that this is not the best approach. A more "comparatist" model would be to discuss the histories of comparative literature with
regard to their cultural and regional settings, their sources of theory and method,
and so on. One useful approach would be, I propose, to present a description
of the history of the discipline based on a regional approach where "region" is
understood as a specific cultural environment, a system of communication
including a specific environment of scholarship historically and linguistically
determined (and I hope to be able to present such an international and synthetic history of the discipline in my forthcoming work).

COMPARATIVE LITERATURE TODAY

In my observation, compressed here in a brief overview, the following developments can be observed in comparative literature from a global perspective of the last ten to fifteen years: 1) The recognition of the importance of theory, and, occasionally, of method, by cultural studies and English and the consequent reduction of the area in activity by comparative literature, tied to the diminishing institutional stability of the discipline of comparative literature in the traditional centers of the discipline (USA and Europe); 2) The development of a comparative European literature; 3) The emerging of comparative literature in "peripheral" geo-cultural loci of scholarship; 4) The "Americanization" of comparative literature; and 5) The potential development of comparative literature with/within new media. In the following, I proceed in my discussion with a focus on selected points from the above five points, with the plan to develop, eventually, my discussion and proposals in forthcoming publications. With regard to my second observation, namely the development of a comparative European literature, I take my point of departure with George Steiner. When Steiner gave his inaugural lecture as Lord Widenfeld Professor of European Comparative Literature at Oxford University in 1994, he presented a paper entitled "What is Comparative Literature?" First, Steiner described how "every act of reception of significant form, in language, in art, in music, is comparative" (1) and he argued that "from their inception, literary studies and the arts of interpretation have been comparative" (3). True, especially today, after literary theory has become mainstream and in the era of cultural studies, this position is hard to refute. Steiner proceeds to say that "I take comparative literature to be, at best, an exact and exacting art of reading, a style of listening to oral and written acts of language which privileges certain components in these acts. Such components are not neglected in any mode of literary study, but they are, in comparative literature, privileged" (9). If I understand Steiner correctly, he is referring here to that traditional form of comparative literature where the knowledge of foreign languages for the scholar of comparative literature is an essential factor. Fair enough and I agree with him. He then outlines three specific areas which are essential features of the discipline in his opinion: 1) "It aims to elucidate the quiddity, the autonomous core of historical and present 'sense of the world' (Husserl's *Weltsinn*) in the language and to clarify, so far as is possible, the conditions, the strategies, the limits of reciprocal understanding and misunderstanding as between languages. In brief, comparative literature is an art of understanding centered in the eventuality and defeats of translation" (10), 2) the "primacy of the matter of translation in comparative literature relates directly to what I take to be the second focus" (11), and 3) "Thematic studies form a third 'center of gravity' in comparative literature" (13). Steiner's argument, clearly, hinges on the knowledge of foreign languages and on the matter of subject matter, that is, themes, which are universal, at least in principle.

While I agree with Steiner that this knowledge is an essential and basic aspect of the discipline, I find his argument seriously lacking. For, as we know, the knowledge of foreign languages is not necessarily a privilege of comparatists, i.e., there are many scholars in literary studies in English departments or in other national language departments who do speak and work with other languages. In my opinion, the distinctive feature of comparative literature is *cumulative*, that is, including interlinked factors such as the knowledge of foreign languages with an inclusionary ideology (the attention to *alterité*) tied to precise methodology (for an elaboration, see Tötösy, *Comparative Literature* 13–23). Curiously, Steiner does not mention methodology either explicitly or implicitly in his argumentation and thus this part of his position is hardly defendable in the present situation of the discipline.

In the USA, the much discussed volume of collected articles in *Comparative Literature in the Age of Multiculturalism* (Ed. Bernheimer, 1995; see, e.g., Mourão in the present volume) is in several ways similar to Steiner's arguments. With particular attention to what I find of importance, namely theory and methodology, the vast majority of contributors to the volume do not mention methodology either implicitly or explicitly. Of course, the main and most important feature of the volume is its aspects of and call for politically based ideology of inclusion. And the question of methodology does not appear in most comparative literature textbooks or works of today either. Perhaps this is for the reason that comparative literature, either as the translation of literatures and cultures (as in a conceptual and ideological translation and/or as actual translation) or as a cross-cultural inclusive ideology and practice is assumed to be a methodology per se. While I accept this as a historical argument and as an essential characteristic in the same historical context, I propose that this is not enough to justify the discipline today. And the fact that the comparative approach without explicit methodology is not enough to convince scholars today is evident, for instance, in an article entitled "Why Comparisons Are Odious" by the editor of *Critical Inquiry*, W.J.T. Mitchell, in 1996, in his response to the 1995 topical issue of *World Literature Today, Comparative Literature: States of the Art*. I would even argue that Steiner's proposal of a comparative European literature—as coming from an internationally reputed scholar whose work otherwise without doubt has been influential—manifests in some ways a certain regression. In contrast, Hugo Dyserinck situated comparative literature a decade earlier, in 1985, in two major areas, "1) A comparative history of literature, involving the mutual relations, as well as the similarities and differences, between individual literatures" and "2) A comparative theory and methodology of literature, dealing with literary theories developed in individual countries (or linguistic areas) and with corresponding methods of literary criticism" (xvii). In principle, the second point is closer to my own contention that in comparative literature one ought to state at all times a clearly and precisely described method which then is applied. And there are of course some good examples of such as in Dyserinck's theoretical and applied work, imagology, which has evolved since its early days in the 1960s and 1970s into a full-blown field of imagology with many studies where the framework has been applied successfully (see Joep Leersen's imagology material and bibliography at <http://www.hum.uva.nl/images>). There are some areas, however, where Steiner's argumentation corresponds to both Dyserinck's first area of comparative literature (literary history) and to Susan Bassnett's or André Lefevere's proposal that the discipline may be saved by such areas of study, among others, as the study of translation: see Bassnett's *Comparative Literature: A Critical Introduction* (1993) and Lefevere's *Translating Literature: Practice and Theory in a Comparative Literature Context* (1992).

In Steiner's proposal this is located in the "dissemination and reception of literary works across time and place" (11), further specified in the study of "who reads, who could read what and when? (12). This area of scholarship, indeed, I find promising, especially when defined as the area of "sociology and history of reading and readership" I propose in my own work (see, for example, Tötösy, *Comparative Literature* 43–78).

The notion of a comparative European literature is also prominent in French comparative literature. Among the publications of recent years, in particular the collected volume of Béatrice Didier, ed., *Précis de Littérature Européenne* (1998) and Didier Souiller and Wladimir Troubetzkoy, eds., *Littérature comparée* (1997) propagate the said notion championed by Steiner. The *Précis de Littérature Européenne* is divided into sections of methods, space, periods, and genres. In the first section, methods, the volume contains several articles discussing in various ways and from several points of view the notion of a the theory of comparative European literature and the topics range from the problematics of the study of European literature, the history of a European literature, the comparative history of myth in European literature, the question of European literature and social classes, European cultures and interdisciplinarity, the publishing history, libraries, and the reading of literature in Europe, and the history of the teaching of literatures in Europe. As the editor of the volume, Didier, announces and argues for, the volume is about comparative European literature. However, the definition of a European literature encompasses mainstream literatures and cultures (which I would call canonization one) and within the mainstream canonized texts and authors (which I would call canonization two). There are a few articles which deal with marginal, minor, or peripheral literatures and cultures in Europe, such as Yiddish and Arabic and there are two articles which argue "pour une littérature qui ne se limite pas à celle des 'langues courantes'" (185–89) and for the "place des littératures régionales en Europe" (191–98). Overall however, the general tone of the articles emanates from a national approach to literatures and cultures and the notion that in a unified Europe each literature and culture becomes "regional" is untouched and implicitly rejected. The approach and tone in the Souiller and Troubetzkoy volume is similar. In other words, there is an implicit and at times explicit hierarchy in the approach, which then stretches also to the methodologies discussed and presented. Here, comparative literature is based on the premise of national literatures which then can be and should be compared to each other and that the comparisons rest on the canon of mainstream literatures and cultures as well as on the canon of specific authors writing in the mainstream languages and cultures. Granted, it is difficult to argue for a divorce of literature from national bases and it takes some work to do this: Souiller and Troubetzkoy and the contributors to the Didier volume offer studies where the focus on national literatures—compared or not—is mediated by attention to genres or themes, for instance. However, overall both volumes are in a traditional mode of literary study and they do not take into account the newer developments of cultural studies, feminism, multiculturalism, or any such. There are also a number of programs in comparative literature where the notion of comparative European literature is established. For example, there is multimedia graduate course in distance education at the University of Granada (Spain) with the designation "Curso multimedia de literaturas europeas (Proyecto Euroliteratura)" <http://www.ugr.es/15700/europrogram.htm>.

With regard to my observation that comparative European literature is, in principle, based on the premise of national literatures despite various claims that the discipline is global and inclusive and that this represents anew an entrapment in the national paradigm, there is a further aspect I would like to mention briefly. This is the problem of national self-referentiality within the scholarship of comparative European literature. For example, in the above mentioned volumes of Souiller and Troubetzkoy and Didier, such volumes as Margaret R. Higonnet's collected volume *Borderwork: Feminist Engagements with Comparative Literature* (1994) are not often enough cited and referred to thus indicating limited attention (a similar "by-passing," at least in my observation, happens to Marie Francoeur's *Confrontations. Jalons pour une sémiosis comparative des textes littéraires* (1985), a volume that would deserve attention by comparatists and scholars in the humanities in general). I am not criticizing the fact that a particular text was not cited; rather, my observation brings me to the following additional factor with regard to national self-referentiality in scholarship, comparative European or other. Whether it is German or French oriented comparative literature, all too many scholars concentrate on "home-grown" sources, that is, in the case of French works on French sources and in the case of German works on German sources and in the case of the US (and Canada) scholars pay attention to mainstream French and German sources (although rarely to any other). I think it is precisely in comparative literature where the notion of "theory approximation" ought to be a standard, that is, when a theoretical framework, method, or theme is discussed, attention must be paid to similar and/or analogous frameworks in a range of languages and cultures (see Tötösy, *Comparative Literature* 215–20). In principle, I do not object to a comparative European literature if it constitutes method but I do object to it if it is implicitly or explicitly ideological and based on perceived or real hierarchies and by keeping to the "national" agenda. At the same time, in a curious twist, there is potential in comparative European literature and that is to counteract the often criticized Eurocentrism of comparative literature itself. Although I did not find any reference to this most obvious aspect of a comparative European literature, I assume that the focus on a truly inclusive study of all European literatures would make the criticism of Eurocentrism in this specific new designation redundant and paradoxical. And as to what I said above about national self-referentiality in scholarship and the national bases of comparative literature and comparative European literature, a new geo-political focus no matter how much on the surface aesthetically oriented would also include the lapsus with regard to the established parameters of comparative literature; regardless of the truth of the criticism that the discipline—or rather some of its practitioners—have indeed often been and are Eurocentric.

Next, I would like to briefly elaborate on my third observation of comparative literature today, namely that there is an emerging of comparative literature in some corners of the globe, geo-cultural spaces which in the politics of education and scholarship one would understand as "peripheral" areas. I would like to note that in some but not all cases this "peripheral" situation of education and scholarship overlaps with economics and technology while in some it does not. The said emerging of comparative literature is of some interest from several points of view, such as the sociology of knowledge, the current situation and history of literary studies, and the general status and situation of the humanities, etc., and including for and in the history of the discipline itself. This emerging appears to take place despite Bassnett's statement in her *Comparative Literature: A Critical Introduction* that "today, comparative literature in one sense is dead" (47). This development—perhaps as a quasi implicit structural response to the Anglo-American situation as perceived by Bassnett—is not occurring in the traditional geographical and cultural loci and mainstream of the discipline such as the United States, France, or Germany (although, I should add in a context of differentiation and with an eye on the particular that disrupts generalizations, some universities in states of the former East Germany such as Halle-Wittenberg and Erfurt, and in Frankfurt in the former West Germany appear to be interested in establishing new chairs of comparative literature). While Bassnett may be right that comparative literature in the traditional centers—France, Germany, the United States—is undergoing both intellectual and institutional changes and a certain loss of intellectual as well as institutional position owing to factors such as the takeover of theory by English, the impact of cultural studies, the diminishing number of comparative literature professorships, etc., this loss of presence is occurring in the *centers* of the discipline and with regard to its own natural context of Eurocentrism and Euro-American center. Clearly, Bassnett's pronouncement of the death of comparative literature is exactly from that Eurocentrism she otherwise attempts to subvert and to oppose in her work. And thus, curiously, Bassnett pays no attention to the strong development of the discipline and the promise its holds outside of the discipline's traditional centers: in the last two decades comparative literature has shown much promise in some countries and cultures where the discipline has not been very strong or, in some cases, in existence at all before. As I mentioned earlier, interestingly, while the traditional centers of the discipline—the *ménage-à-trois* of France, Germany, and the United States—are at best able to maintain a status quo of the discipline, in Mainland China, Taiwan, Japan, Brazil, Argentina, Mexico, Spain, Portugal, Italy, Greece, universities in the states of the former East Germany, etc., the discipline is emerging and developing strongly and this can be gauged by the emergence of new comparative literature journals, new chairs in comparative literature, a marked increase in publications, etc. And it is not without reason that colleagues from Spain and Italy, for example, write to me that in their view the insistence of the International Comparative Literature Association to maintain English and French as the official languages of the association is wrong, colonial, outdated, etc., because if French than why not Spanish, German, Chinese, and ALL the other languages. Consequently, they argue, only English should be the official language—as our present lingua franca—with many other languages allowed for presentation if there is an audience and interest.

Following my argument—in relation to my above third observation of the current situation of comparative literature—namely that we must pay attention to the situation of the discipline of comparative literature not only in the centers but also (or perhaps mainly) in the "peripheries," here are a few examples of recent work published in comparative literature in the "peripheries": in Portugal, the Portuguese Comparative Literature Association brought out several series of publications emanating from the annual conferences of the association, for example, Margarida L. Losa, Isménia de Sousa, and Gonçalo Vilas-Boas, eds., *Literatura Comparada: Os Novos Paradigmas* (1996). In Brazil, we have the collected volume of Tania Franco Carvalhal, ed., *Comparative Literature World Wide: Issues and Methods* (1997). In Spain—a particularly active area of comparative literature today—several books and manuals of comparative literature are of note. There are, for example, Dolores Romero López, ed., *Orientaciones em literatura comparada* (1997), Maria José Vega and Neus Carbonell, eds., *Literatura comparada. Principios y métodos* (1998), Dolores Romero López's *Una relectura del "fin de siglo" en el marco de la litteratura comparade" teoría y praxis* (1998), Claudio Guillén's *Múltiples moradas. Ensayo de literatura comparada* (1998) (for a review of these volumes, see Zambrano at <http://clcwebjournal.lib.purdue.edu/clcweb99-2/zambrano99.html>), and Darío Villanueva's collected volume, *Avances en . . . teoría de la literature* (1994). Although not specifically comparative literature, most material in Montserrat Iglesias Santos's *Teoría de los Polisistemas*

(1999) is comparative. As well, the University of Huelva publishes a new comparative literature journal since 1997, *Exemplaria: Revista Internacional de Literatura Comparada*. In Argentina, we have the special issue of *Filología* 30.2 (1997), *Literaturas comparadas*; the latter volume is interesting because it contains a mixture of foreign and domestic authors while most other such volumes I cited above contain translated work. Further, there are the volumes with selected papers from the second and third conferences of the AALC: Asociacion Argentina de Literature Comparada of 1997 and 1998.

In Italy we have the collected volumes of Armando Gnisci and Franca Sinopoli, *Comparare i comparatismi. La comparatistica letteraria oggi in Europa e nel mondo* (1995) and *Manuale storico di letteratura comparata* (1997). The 1995 Italian volume is also of some interest for the following reason. It is common knowledge that in Italy the mastery or even interest in foreign languages is limited (perhaps even more than in the United States) and thus the publication of anthologies of comparatist texts serves at least two purposes: it supports the suggestion that the interest in comparativism as an international discipline in the age of globalization makes sense and it suggests—via the presentation of the texts in Italian—that the local aspect of scholarship, that is, the study of the international via the local is also with purpose and of intellectual and pragmatic content and potential results. As to the pragmatically important genre of manuals for the teaching of comparative literature, Gnisci and Sinopoli's other collected volume, *Manuale storico di letteratura comparata* (1997) is of note. The editors provide their Italian readership with a historical perspective of comparative literature from the earliest times through the discipline's golden age through its present tense. The volume contains also a list of comparative literature handbooks and incisive articles since 1931 to the present, a list of the proceedings of International Comparative Literature Association congresses, a list of published volumes of the International Comparative Literature's *A Comparative History of Literatures in European Languages*, a list of major comparative literature learned journals, and a list of bibliographies of comparative literature. Similarly to Iglesias Santos volume in Spanish, *Teoría de los Polisistemas*, cited above, Aldo Nemesio's collected volume, *L'esperienza del testo* (1990), too, contains much comparative literature material.

In the German-language area, in Austria—a country where in recent years substantial efforts have been made in educational policy, university restructuring, funding, etc., to internationalize its scholarship—a volume of interest is the collected volume of Norbert Bachleitner, Alfred Noe, and Hans-Gert Roloff, eds., *Beträge zu Komparatistik und Sozialgeschichte der Literatur* (1997). We also have Peter V. Zima and Johann Strutz's volume *Komparatistik: Einführung in die Vergleichende Literaturwissenschaft* (1992). Note: It is somewhat difficult to classify Zima and Strutz's volume as "Austrian" as the volume was published in Germany for a German readership and predicated on the fact that it is in Germany where there are a good number of comparative literature programs while in Austria only in Vienna and Innsbruck; the *Lehrstuhl* (chair) in comparative literature has no degree program in the discipline; however, what is interesting at Klagenfurt is that there is a Faculty of "Kulturwissenschaften." At the same time, since both authors teach at the University of Klagenfurt, we are dealing with, obviously, a different cultural source than that of Germany. Strutz and Zima published a collected volume previously, *Komparatistik als Dialog* (1991), a precursor of their 1992 volume (above) in that the volume deals with questions relating to the triangle of the cultures of Southern Austria, Slovenia, Switzerland, and Italy. There is also the recent volume by the doyen of Austrian comparative Literature, Zoran Konstantinović, his *Grundlagentexte der Vergleichenden Literaturwissenschaft aus drei Jahrzehnten*, selected and edited by Beate Burtscher-Bechter et al. (2000). In Germany proper, there is Reinhold Görling's *Heterotopia: Lektüren einer interkulturellen Literaturwissenschaft* (1997). The volume is interesting because while the author refrains from naming comparative literature—there are brief references to the discipline on pages 27, 34, 53, and 65—the general concept of the book as well as the applications to primary texts of the proposed approach are comparativist. Perhaps the reason for the author's understated references to comparative literature is a result of his acute observation of the discipline's often preoccupation of doing comparative literature by default only. That is, the situation when the framework and its applications are based on and in the bases on national literatures, one would have better success in the academe. And there are some more recent volumes such as Carsten Zelle's *Kurze Bücherkunde für Literaturwissenschaftler* (1998) and *Allgemeine Literaturwissenschaft* (1999). The former contains a good section on comparative literature as well as it contains material about new media and the study of literature; the latter is a collection of selected articles about the history and contemporary situation of the specifically German *Allgemeine Literaturwissenschaft* (general literature) including specific examples of the subject matter taught at the universities of Essen and Siegen but also extending, briefly, to the example of Vanderbilt University. Interestingly, one author discusses the question of the study of general literature in the context of new media and technology in more detail. Angelika Corbineau-Hoffmann's *Einführung in die Komparatistik* (2000) is an example of traditional Eurocentric comparative literature and contains few newer sources and relies, instead, on older, although not necessarily outdated material. An interesting volume is, although presented very much in the tradition of German *Philologie*, Emer O'Sullivan's *Kinderliterarische Komparatistik* (2000). Further in Europe, in Holland—a traditionally strong area of comparative literature—we have the *Festschrift* in honor of Douwe Fokkema by Harald Hendrix, Joost Kloek, Sophie Levie, and Will van Peer, eds. *The Search for a New Alphabet: Literary Studies in a Changing World* (1996) and in Hungary—perhaps the strongest proponent of comparative literature, traditionally, in Central Europe—we have *neohelicon: acta comparationis litterarum unversarum*, a journal that over the last two decades issued several state-of-the-art volumes about the discipline of comparative literature. A good example of journal's interest in the history and theory of comparative literature is the more recent issue of 24.2 (1997).

Although a "periphery" from the standard Eurocentric point of view (but not otherwise as I am arguing here) in Mainland China including Hong Kong and Taiwan—among publications in Western languages—we have Yue Daiyun and Alain Le Pichon, eds. *La Licorne et le dragon. Les Malentendus dans la recherche de l'universel* (1995) and the volume *New Perspectives: A Comparative Literature Yearbook* (1995; for a more recent description of the situation of comparative literature in Taiwan and the Mainland today, see also Tötösy 1997; for a selection of studies in comparative literature published recently in Mandarin, see the bibliography in the present volume). Of note is that the XVIIth Congress of the ICLA: International Comparative Literature Association will be held in Hong Kong in 2003, organized by Indiana at Bloomington and Lingnan University's Eugene Eoyang. Further, in Australia there is the new University of Sydney World Literature Series with volume one by Mabel Lee and Meng Hua, eds., *Cultural Dialogue and Misreading* (1997) and volume two by Mabel Lee and A.D. Syrokomla-Stefanowska, eds., *Literary Intercrossings: East Asia and the West* (1998). Further volumes in the series are planned.

In addition to the volumes published in the traditional centers of the discipline I refer to above, I should mention Yves Chevrel's *L'Etudiant chercheur en littérature* (1992), a good manual because despite its general title, as the volume is clearly comparatist. Further, Chevrel's translated volume—by Farida

Elizabeth Dahab—*Comparative Literature Today: Methods and Perspectives* (1994) should also be noted as it can serve as a textbook for students of comparative literature in English-speaking countries. As to manuals in the context of pedagogical tools in and of comparative literature, the single English-language volume of recent years of such, we have John T. Kirby's *The Comparative Reader: A Handlist of Basic Reading in Comparative Literature* (1998). The volume is divided into selected bibliographies of national literatures (further divided into periods), literary and critical theory, various methodologies such as psychological, semiotic, etc., approaches, media and literature including film, postcolonial literatures, and an interesting chapter on the professional and institutional aspects of the discipline of comparative literature. In addition to volumes I already mentioned above, in the USA we also have the 1995 special issue on comparative literature of the journal *World Literature Today* (1995). In Canada—a cultural space that may be considered peripheral or as a center, depending—we have the special issue of the *Canadian Review of Comparative Literature / Revue Canadienne de Littérature Comparée* (1996) and my own volume, *Comparative Literature: Theory, Method, Application* (1998, although published in Holland). Last but not least, there is the US where comparative literature has acquired and still has the strongest presence institutionally: for recent work in comparative literature there, see Manuela Mourão's "Comparative Literature in the United States" in the present volume.

In international comparative literature, we have the collected volume of selected and extended versions of papers from the XIVth Congress of the ICLA: International Comparative Literature Association at Alberta in 1994, *Comparative Literature Now: Theories and Practice / La Littérature comparée à l'heure actuelle. Théories et réalisations* (Ed. Tötösy, Dimić, and Sywenky; see its table of contents at <http://clcwebjournal.lib.purdue.edu/library/champion.html>). The eight volumes of selected papers from the XVth congress of the ICLA in 1997 at Leiden is (more or less) a continuation of the format initiated with the publication of selected papers from the XIVth congress at Alberta, that is, instead of the ICLA tradition to publish *Proceedings* with brief papers, mostly full-length and revised papers are published (see D'haen, General Ed.). A volume of limited rigor with brief papers are the proceedings of the 15th Congress of the World Federation of Humanists, entitled *Humanism and the Good Life*, published in 1998 (Ed. Horwath, Hendrickson, Valdivieso, and Thor).

Last, I elaborate briefly on my fifth observation of the current situation of comparative literature, namely the potential of new media technology and scholarship, that is, specifically the internet and the world wide web and their impact on scholarship in the humanities including comparative literature (see also Grabovszki in the present volume; see also Tötösy 2001c). Here is a quote from a recent article by Robert Lepage, the internationally renown Québéçois-Canadian playwright who recognizes the advantages and positive meaning of a global view for his own plays as well as contemporary Québéçois-Canadian literature as a whole. What he is saying is relevant to my discussion by analogy: the peripheral situation of Québéçois-Canadian literature is similar in concept to the marginalized situation of the humanities and comparative literature in turn within the humanities today. Lepage argues that the world wide web and "its spread is part of the reason why Quebeckers are so abruptly questioning their identity and coming to such new conclusions. New technology leaves no room for xenophobia. How can Quebec sell its Internet products if it continues to have an isolationist image? And if you send me an e-mail, and you don't have all the accents and the c and the little hat [circumflex]—what is so French about it? So a lot of people decided to write in English. These things may seem trivial, but they are hints of a much bigger shift" (69). There is no doubt in my mind that the world wide web and the internet provide possibilities for the study of culture, including comparative literature and the proposed comparative cultural studies and that, in my opinion, scholars in the humanities must exploit. Unfortunately, there is much Ludditism among scholars in the humanities including comparatists while scholars in cultural studies tend to be more interested and competent (for an example of the discussion of this resistance in the humanities—and that is not much discussed in the otherwise numerous books on new media and the humanities in English—see Norbert Gabriel's 1997 *Kulturwissenschaften und Neue Medien. Wissensvermittlung im digitalen Zeitalter*; for another and more recent volume of new media technology and the humanities, see Domenico Fiormonte and Jonathan Usher, eds.'s *New Media and The Humanities: Research and Applications* (2001). With regard to the world wide web, the use of new media technology, and the discipline of comparative literature as in full-text and free-access online journals, there are only few of such in existence: there is the *Bryn Mawr Review of Comparative Literature* at <http://www.brynmawr.edu/bmrcl/> (publishes book reviews only), *Surfaces: Electronic Journal / Revue électronique* <http://pum12.pum.umontreal.ca/revues/surfaces/home.html> (in 2001 the last issue published is in 1998), and *Literary Research / Recherche littéraire: An ICLA/AILC Bulletin of Book Reviews* <http://www.uwo.ca/modlang/ailc/index.html> (it is accessible by password only).

In comparative literature and culture there is one such journal in existence to date, print or online, in free access or subscription based, and this is *CLCWeb: Comparative Literature and Culture: A WWWeb Journal* I founded at the University of Alberta in 1998 and now published by Purdue University Press at <http://clcwebjournal.lib.purdue.edu/> (for a list of comparative literature and comparative literature oriented journals, see <http://clcwebjournal.lib.purdue.edu/library/journals.html>).

There is one more point to make here: while I agree with scholars who argue that the reading of literature hypertextually on the web or as in e-books versus in hard copy is as of yet not only limited but that it may also represent a regression in the quality and cognitive processes of reading, what I miss is the a differentiation between the reading of fiction / creative texts in hypertext and the reading of scholarship in hypertext, that is, on the web. In my mind and in my own practice, there is a clear and obvious distinction between the reading of the two types of text and I believe, as I argue in my paper "The New Knowledge Management: Online Research and Publishing in the Humanities" ([2001c]: <http://clcwebjournal.lib.purdue.edu/clcweb01-1/totosy01.html>; for a recent and much needed empirical analysis of literary reading in hypertext, see David S. Miall and Teresa Dobson's "Reading Hypertext and the Experience of Literature" (2001) at <http://jodi.ecs.soton.ac.uk/Articles/v02/i01/Miall/>).

Granted, there are some infrastructural problems which affect the situation of the web and the internet in general and there are two such problems of major impact: one is the obvious problem of different technological development and availabilities among regions of the world and the second one is the infrastructure of telephone line providers and its economics. Countries in Europe are as of yet still handicapped in the development of the internet in comparison with the US and Canada, for example, for the simple reason that local calls are expensive in Europe while they are much less to minimal in the US and Canada. Clearly, in Europe the monopoly of the state telephone companies will have to be modified and this has started to begin: whether it will evolve to similarly easy access to telephone lines or other ways of web access—such as cable TV—remains to be seen. And there is also the perception of scholars in the humanities of the emergence and significance of web journals. It is true that some web journals do not have a comparable scholarly content traditional hard-copy journals offer. But this can be changed and the time constraints and financial constraints hard-copy journal suffer under will make it ultimately imperative that knowledge transfer and scholarly communication will demand the switch to e-journals and the internet. That an online journal in the free-access mode has much potential is already observable in the case of the said *CLCWeb*. Of interest here is that in the first available period of statistical analysis of the *CLCWeb*'s access and online use, 13–30 April 1999, the journal received 1,950 hits. This means 108 hits per day on the average and for an esoteric subject such as comparative literature and culture this shows high-level and involved use. The statistics also show—among many aspects of the ways, length, precise use of specific sections of the journal, various technical aspects of access, etc.—that *CLCWeb* has been accessed from a large number of countries, including many countries outside of North America and Europe. Interestingly and contrary to my expectations, the relatively large traffic on *CLCWeb* has not subsided and it still draws over 400 per day, this in the journal's third year of publication, in 2001 (for ongoing statistics of web use and traffic, go to the journal's sub-page "web traffic" off the index page).

In closing my observations on new media and comparative literature (and on work in the humanities by extension), I would like to refer briefly to an aspect of institutional policies which have some impact on the situation of not only comparative literature but on scholarship in the humanities in general (see, in more detail, Tötösy 2001c). Briefly put: how is it possible that, for example, the Social Sciences and Humanities Council of Canada (SSHRC) to date refuses to even consider funding of an online journal in the humanities precisely because it is in the free-access mode? After several attempts of explanation, I received the final decision by an SSHRC official that because *CLCWeb* does not have minimum 200 paid subscribers, it is ineligible for funding. My explanations that the *CLCWeb* is in free access and thus does not have paid subscribers was not accepted and the large web traffic with the journal—which clearly shows that the *CLCWeb* is being used by the scholarly community—did not make an impression either. Obviously, this particular government agency is still stuck to a traditional mindset and its policy makers—who include academics—have not followed the developments made possible by the new web culture of scholarship. In my opinion, scholarly communication and knowledge transfer on the world wide web should be facilitated by open and competitive funding by government agencies, just as are other types of scholarly activities. Online journals should be able to compete for such funding because government agencies use taxpayers' money in the first place and this way some of that money is returned to the taxpayers, just like in other areas of scholarly activity. Unfortunately, the present policies of the SSHRC have not followed the emerging situation of scholarship in the humanities where online journals perform the said meaningful service for the scholarly community and where they perform knowledge transfer on an international scale previously unheard of as well as impossible to enact. The said policies are short sighted and counter productive and I hope that the SSHRC will rather sooner than later consider changing its policies of funding online journals in the free-access mode.

Last but not least I would like to touch briefly on a most contentious issue, namely on the comparative study of "Other" literatures and cultures, here with specific reference to East/West comparative literature. The still dominant aspect of the national paradigm and its position with regard to comparative literature and its claim of inclusion is a most important issue in the politics of comparative literature. As I have argued in a previous paper, "A Report on Comparative Literature in Beijing, October 1995 / Rapport sur la littérature comparée à Beijing, Octobre 1995" (1995), for a Western comparatist the inclusion of the Other is problematic at best. But here as always, I argue that it is the "how" and not the "what" that determines scholarship. I quote from my paper: "I took issue with [the] . . . notion that Orientalism can be successfully studied only by an Oriental. This notion, as often as it occurs under the generic notion of "appropriation" in North American scholarship in particular, leads in my opinion to the doctrinization of scholarship and counter-acts the very notion of dialogue, scholarly or other. Cultural communication prescribes dialogue about perception and view from whichever locus one speaks from. If the notion . . . is correct then its logical conclusion is that Orientals should not study the Occident either. Surely, this is an untenable position of either side. Of course, if an Occidental scholar studies Oriental works, any correction of his/her analysis by an Oriental scholar should be welcome and seriously considered. The argument that the post-colonial base of power disqualifies an Occidental to study the Oriental becomes a tool of harm if implemented" (11–12). More recently, Takayuki Yokota-Murakami, in her book *Don Juan East/West: On the Problematics of Comparative Literature* (1999), argues that comparative literature and its claim of and for inclusion is a priori marginalization and exclusion. Yokota-Murakami argues that comparative literature is in principle and throughout its history Eurocentric and its claim of inclusion is an unsuccessfully disguised attempt to "universalize" humanity as expressed in literature but from the said Eurocentric point of view and power. I fully agree with the author that Western humanities and comparative literature in particular "included" the Other from its own Eurocentric locus. But as forceful and insightful Yokota-Murakami's description and arguments are, she does not offer a solution and implicitly we would end up with the untenable situation as I describe in my quote above.

TOWARD COMPARATIVE CULTURAL STUDIES

In recent debates in comparative literature, too, and in the humanities in general, innovation is, as it should always be, a matter of great interest (and, of course, a real necessity). Taking my point of departure from the current interest and large amount of work produced in cultural studies everywhere and applying my approach to comparative literature from within the framework and methodology of the systemic and empirical approach to literature and culture (for my publications in the area, see <http://clcwebjournal.lib.purdue.edu/totosycv.html>; for a selected bibliographies of work in the approach, see Tötösy 1999 at <http://clcwebjournal.lib.purdue.edu/library.html>), I first developed a set of principles for comparative literature and culture, as presented in my book, *Comparative Literature: Theory, Method, Application* (1998, 15–18). Here is a brief dictionary definition of the systemic and empirical approach:

The systemic and empirical approach is a contextual theoretical and methodological framework for the study of culture including several fields such as comparative cultural studies, cultural studies, comparative literature, literary and cultural theory, cultural anthropology, ethnography, audience studies (see Tötösy 2001, "Toward a Framework of Audience Studies" <http://clcwebjournal.lib.purdue.edu/library/audiencestudies.html>), and cognitive sciences. The main question in this framework of study is what happens to products of culture and how: it is produced, published, distributed, read/listened to/seen (etc.), imitated, assessed, discussed, studied, censored, etc. The systemic and empirical study of culture originates as a reaction to, and an attempt at, solving the problematics of hermeneutics. The approach and methodology(ies) of the framework are built on the theory of constructivism (radical, cognitive, etc.), in turn based on the thesis that the subject largely construes its empirical world itself. The consequence of this line of thought— as seen in the work of scholars in Germany, Holland, Belgium, Hungary, Italy, Canada, the USA and elsewhere in several fields and areas of study—is the replacement of (metaphorical) interpretation with the study of culture products and the processes of the products as based on (radical) constructivism,

systems theories, and the empirical (observation and knowledge-based argumentation). The system of culture and actions within are observed from the
outside—not experienced—and roughly characterized as depending on two
conventions (hypotheses) that are tested continually. These conventions are
the aesthetic convention (as opposed to the convention of facts in the daily
language of reference) and the polyvalence convention (as opposed to the
monovalency in the daily empirical world). Thus, the object of study of the
systemic and empirical study of culture is not only the text in itself, but roles
of action and processes within the system(s) of culture, namely, the production, distribution, reception, and the post-processing of culture products. The
methods used are primarily taken from the social sciences, systems theories,
reception theory, cognitive science, psychology, etc. In general, the steps to be
taken in systemic and empirical research are the formation of a hypothesis,
putting it into practice, testing, and evaluation.

Next, I propose an adjusted set of principles for the proposed new approach
of comparative cultural studies. I should like to mention that many of the principles I am suggesting here are obviously part and parcel of various approaches,
theoretical or methodological and/or national and homogeneous literatures. My
point is that it is the cumulative perspective of the approach that may make a
difference and that may be innovative. My notions toward a comparative cultural studies is at this point is obviously not a full-fledged framework. Rather,
the principles represent an approach which will be developed in detail in my
forthcoming work. I should also like to mention that to date, curiously, the comparative aspect in cultural studies is relatively unexplored and there are relatively few universities where there are degree programs in a combination of
comparative literature and cultural studies or an outright program in "comparative cultural studies." Here is a selected list of institutions where such programs exist: the graduate program in Comparative Culture at Sophia University
(Tokyo), the program of Cultural Studies and Comparative Literature at the
University of Minnesota, the Centre for British and Comparative Cultural Studies at the University of Warwick (<http:www.warwick.ac.uk/fac/arts/BCCS/>),
the Centre for Comparative Literature and Cultural Studies at Monash University (<http://www.arts.monash.edu.au/cclcs/>), the Comparative Cultural
Studies program at Trinity College of Vermont (<http://www.trinityvt.edu/
ahum/>), the Center for Comparative Cultural Studies at the Palacky University (<http://compare.upol.cz/aboutthe.htm>) (Czechia), the Comparative
Literary and Cultural Studies program at the University of Connecticut

(<http://www.sp.uconn.edu/~wwwmcl/Programs/Graduate/gCO/gCO.htm>), or
the University of Virginia program in Comparative Cultural Studies (<http://
www.virginia.edu/~cch-surv/>). The situation is much more limited with regard
to theoretical and methodological frameworks for a "comparative cultural
studies" on the landscape of published studies: I am aware of Christian Gerel's
"Urbane Leitkulturen: Eine Perspektive für vergleichende kulturwissenschaftliche
Studien" at <http://www.ifk.or.at/ifk/pages/workshop/ws980004.htm> in German, for example. However, Gerel's work is with regard to cultural studies in
a context of urban studies and not in the context of literature or similar domains
of artistic expression. Perhaps the nearest work to a theoretical framework—
with not much methodology, however—of comparative cultural studies is Itamar Even-Zohar's more recent work such as "Polysystem Theory and Culture
Research" and "Culture Repertoire and the Wealth of Collective Entities" at
<http://www.tau.ac.il/~itamarez/papers/>. An "early" proposal, that is a survey
of theoretical material in understood by the author in the context of comparative cultural studies is David G. Horn's "Reading Theory: Toward a Comparative Cultural Studies. A Review Article" in the journal *Comparative Studies
in Society and History* (1997). Of note is also, despite its brevity (two pages in
total), of Theo D'haen's opinion piece, "From Comparative Literature to Comparative Cultural Studies" (1999).

The above discussed ("peripheral") interest in the discipline of comparative literature outside the established mainstream French-German-American
core may be a result of the often-occurring time shift—delayed reaction time—
within knowledge transfer or it may be a result of the general globalization
here emanating from and taking place in the "peripheries." But there may be
another reason, that of a sophisticated approach to the study of culture by
scholars in many ways located outside or parallel to the French-German-
American mainstream that dominates the study of literature world wide today,
in particular the US schools including the situation where the French Derrida
or the Italian Eco or the German Habermas are translated into English, published in the USA, and there from impact on thinking in cultures where the
first language is not a mainstream European language. What I mean is this: In
Anglo-American, French, and German literary study—general or comparative—the aspect of theory saturation is a well-known situation and the fact
that in recent years the focus in literary study switched from the study of literature proper to all sorts of inquiries of culture in general brought about a
preoccupation of literary scholars with other matter than literature. For com-

paratists in the mainstream German-French-American core this created serious problems because their areas of theory, interdisciplinarity, etc., have been successfully appropriated and today everyone may be a "comparatist." While this may be an interesting development, it appears to me that scholars working in non-mainstream cultures and within that in comparative literature, seem to be interested in maintaining a focus on literature while at the same time they want to study it in an international context writing for a regional scholarly readership. Concurrent to the interest in comparative literature as I perceive it and discussed above, there is of course the impact of cultural studies—mainly although not exclusively from North America—in the humanities everywhere, including in the countries where comparative literature itself is experiencing a renaissance or emerging interest. It this situation that I think we can capitalize on. What I mean is that the interest and new work in comparative literature occurring outside the traditional centres of the discipline can be related and connected to the impact of cultural studies on the one hand and taking the history and intellectual achievements of comparative literature—in particular its aspect of cross-culturality based upon in-depth knowledge and familiarity with other languages and cultures—toward the construction of a framework and practice of comparative cultural studies on the other hand.

I would like to insert here a brief comment about the problematics of globalization versus localization and regionalism. In my opinion, while regionalism is obviously a viable alternative to and meaningful replacement of nationalism and aspirations to cultural homogeneity, globalization can be understood and perceived as a positive force that does not necessarily embody American cultural imperialism. I concur with the view that "global culture doesn't mean just more TV sets and Nike shoes. Linking is humanity's natural impulse, its common destiny. . . . cultures don't become more uniform; instead, both old and new tend to transform each other. The late philosopher Isaiah Berlin believed that, rather than aspire to some utopian ideal, a society should strive for something else: 'not that we agree with each other . . . but that we can understand each other'" (Zwingle 33; see also <http://www.nationalgeographic.com/2000/culture/global>). Among other perspectives, comparative literature and comparative cultural studies aspire to be scholarship precisely in this sense.

As suggested above, it is the US version of cultural studies—although often based in and developed from British cultural studies—that has acquired the most incisive impact in scholarship in the humanities everywhere (for material in cultural studies, see also Tötösy, Aoun, and Nielsen's bibliography in the present volume). Overall, however, my observation is that similar to literary studies, work in cultural studies has produced limited results based on an empirical, that is, evidence- and observation-based perspective in theory and in application. In other words, while cultural studies in the US, in the United Kingdom (see Grossberg 1993), in Germany (see Burns), in France (see Forbes and Kelly), in Spain (see Graham and Labanyi), or in Italy (see Forgacs and Lumley) produce relevant and incisive work, they more often than not lack the type of evidence-based theoretical and methodological approach I propose for both comparative literature and comparative cultural studies I develop from the systemic and empirical approach to literature and culture (in turn based in radical constructivism; for an extensive web site of material, see Riegler at <http://www.univie.ac.at/constructivism/>; see also Tötösy "Constructivism" at <http://clcwebjournal.lib.purdue.edu/library/totosy(constructivism).html>). I am aware, however, that in sociology, ethnology, history, cultural anthropology, ethnography, cognitive science, etc.,—including work related to or about literature—there is a large corpus that is "empirical," contextual, evidence-based, and argued in both theory and application. With regard to cultural studies, while in isolated cases it is briefly mentioned that the historical and conceptual background of cultural studies is based, in many ways, on work (theory and application) in comparative literature, the comparative approach in and for cultural studies is not explored apart from a few rudimentary beginnings such as Aleida Assman's "Cultural Studies and Historical Memories" (1999). Consequently, while there is empirical work with explicit methodology undertaken in cultural anthropology and similar fields which have some impact on cultural studies (see, in particular, Norman Denzin's *Symbolic Interactionism and Cultural Studies*), cultural studies when in literary studies—or the other way around—is almost exclusively hermeneutic, discursive in the essayistic mode, and metaphorical, at best ideological or political. In other words, contextual and evidence-based and argued work in cultural studies appears to be produced in fields and with approaches from sociology, ethnology, cultural anthropology, history, etc., while in the fields of traditional humanities such as English-language literature, such approaches are neglected or even rejected in favor of the said metaphorical and essayistic mode of scholarship and there are scholars few and far between who would agree with the notion that "cultural studies has to be disciplined . . . to get better and useful knowledge takes rigorous *theoretical and empirical work*" (Grossberg 1999, 29; my emphasis; for various sources in cultural studies, see <http://clcwebjournal.lib.purdue.edu/library.html>).

TEN PRINCIPLES TOWARD A FRAMEWORK OF COMPARATIVE CULTURAL STUDIES

The first principle of comparative cultural studies is the postulate that in and of the study, pedagogy, and research of culture—culture is defined as all human activity resulting in artistic production—it is not the "what" but rather the "how" that is of importance. This principle follows the (radical) constructivist tenet of attention to the "how" and process. To "compare" does not—and must not—imply a hierarchy: in the comparative mode of investigation and analysis a matter studied is not "better" than another. This means—among other things as listed below—that it is method that is of crucial importance in comparative cultural studies in particular and, consequently, in the study of literature and culture as a whole.

The second principle of comparative cultural studies is the theoretical as well as methodological postulate to move and to dialogue between cultures, languages, literatures, and disciplines. This is a crucial aspect of the framework, the approach as a whole, and its methodology. In other words, attention to other cultures—that is, the comparative perspective—is a basic and founding element and factor of the framework. The claim of emotional and intellectual primacy and subsequent institutional power of national cultures is untenable in this perspective. In turn, the built-in notions of exclusion and self-referentiality of single culture study and their result of rigidly defined disciplinary boundaries are notions against which comparative cultural studies offers an alternative as well as a parallel field of study. This inclusion extends to all Other, all marginal, minority, border, and peripheral and it encompasses both form and substance. However, attention must be paid of the "how" of any inclusionary approach, attestation, methodology, and ideology so as not to repeat the mistakes of Eurocentrism and "universalization" from a "superior" Eurocentric point of view. Dialogue is the only solution.

The third principle of comparative cultural studies is the necessity for the scholar working in this field to acquire in-depth grounding in more than one language and culture as well as other disciplines before further in-depth study of theory and methodology. However, this principle creates structural and administrative problems on the institutional and pedagogical levels. For instance, how does one allow for development—intellectually as well as institutionally—from a focus on one national culture (exclusionary) towards the inclusive and interdisciplinary principles of comparative cultural studies? The solution of designating comparative cultural studies as a postgraduate discipline only is problematic and counter-productive. Instead, the solution is the allowance for a parallelism in intellectual approach, institutional structure, and administrative practice.

The fourth principle of comparative cultural studies is its given focus to study culture in its parts (literature, arts, film, popular culture, theatre, the publishing industry, the history of the book as a cultural product, etc.) and as a whole in relation to other forms of human expression and activity and in relation to other disciplines in the humanities and social sciences (history, sociology, psychology, etc.). The obstacle here is that the attention to other fields of expression and other disciplines of study results in the lack of a clearly definable, recognizable, single-focused, and major theoretical and methodological framework of comparative cultural studies. There is a problem of naming and designation exactly because of the multiple approach and parallelism. In turn, this lack of recognized and recognizable products results in the discipline's difficulties of marketing itself within the inter-mechanisms of intellectual recognition and institutional power.

The fifth principle of comparative cultural studies is its built-in special focus on English, based on its impact emanating from English-language US cultural studies which is, in turn, rooted in British cultural studies along with influences from French and German thought. This is a composite principle of approach and methodology. The focus on English as a means of communication and access to information should not be taken as Euro-American-centricity. In the Western hemisphere and in Europe but also in many other cultural (hemi)spheres, English has become the lingua franca of communication, scholarship, technology, business, industry, etc. This new global situation prescribes and inscribes that English gain increasing importance in scholarship and pedagogy, including the study of literature. The composite and parallel method here is that because comparative cultural studies is not self-referential and exclusionary; rather, the parallel use of English is effectively converted into a tool for and of communication in the study, pedagogy, and scholarship of literature. Thus, in comparative cultural studies the use of English should not represent any form of colonialism—and if it does, one disregards it or fights it with English rather than by opposing English—as follows from principles one to three. And it should also be obvious that is the English-language speaker who is, in particular, in need of other languages.

The sixth principle of comparative cultural studies is its theoretical and methodological focus on evidence-based research and analysis. This principle is with reference to methodological requirements in the description of theoretical framework building and the selection of methodological approaches. From among the several evidence-based theoretical and methodological approaches available in the study of culture, literary and culture theory, cultural anthropology, sociology of culture and knowledge, etc., the systemic and empirical approach is perhaps the most advantageous and precise methodology for use in comparative cultural studies. This does not mean that comparative cultural studies and/or its methodology comprise a meta theory; rather, comparative cultural studies and its methodologies are implicitly and explicitly pluralistic.

The seventh principle of comparative cultural studies is its attention and insistence on methodology in interdisciplinary study (an umbrella concept), with three main types of methodological precision: Intra-disciplinarity (analysis and research within the disciplines of the humanities), multi-disciplinarity (analysis and research by one scholar employing any other discipline), and pluri-disciplinarity (analysis and research by team-work with participants from several disciplines). In the latter case, an obstacle is the general reluctance of humanities scholars to employ team-work in the study of culture including literature. It should be noted that this principle is built-in in the framework and methodology of the systemic and empirical approach to culture (for an outline of interdisciplinary work in the humanities, see Tötösy, *Comparative Literature* 79–82).

The eighth principle of comparative cultural studies is its content against the contemporary paradox of globalization versus localization. There is a paradoxical development in place with regard to both global movements and intellectual approaches and their institutional representation. On the one hand, the globalization of technology, industry, and communication is actively pursued and implemented. But on the other hand the forces of exclusion as represented by local, racial, national, gender, disciplinary, etc., interests prevail in (too) many aspects. For a change toward comparative cultural studies as proposed here a paradigm shift in the humanities and social sciences will be necessary. Thus, the eighth principle represents the notion of working against the stream by promoting comparative cultural studies as a global, inclusive, and multi-disciplinary framework in an inter- and supra-national humanities.

The ninth principle of comparative cultural studies is its claim on the vocational commitment of its practitioners. In other words, why study and work in comparative cultural studies? The reasons are the intellectual as well as pedagogical values this approach and discipline offers in order to implement the recognition and inclusion of the Other with and by commitment to the in-depth knowledge of several cultures (i.e., languages, literatures, etc.) as basic parameters. In consequence, the discipline of comparative cultural studies as proposed advances our knowledge by a multi-facetted approach based on scholarly rigor and multi-layered knowledge with precise methodology.

The tenth principle of comparative cultural studies is with regard to the troubled intellectual and institutional situation of the humanities in general. That is, the tenth principle is with reference to the politics of scholarship and the academe. We know that the humanities in general experience serious and debilitating institutional—and, depending on one's stand, also intellectual—difficulties and because of this the humanities in the general social and public discourse are becoming more and more marginalized (not the least by their own doing). It is in this context that the principles of a comparative cultural studies is proposed to at least to attempt to adjust the further marginalization and social irrelevance of the humanities.

A definition of comparative cultural studies is as follows. Comparative cultural studies is a field of study where selected tenets of the discipline of comparative literature are merged with selected tenets of the field of cultural studies meaning that the study of culture and culture products—including but not restricted to literature, communication, media, art, etc.—is performed in a contextual and relational construction and with a plurality of methods and approaches, inter-disciplinarity, and, if and when required, including team work. In comparative cultural studies it is the processes of communicative action(s) in culture and the how of these processes that constitute the main objectives of research and study. However, comparative cultural studies does not exclude textual analysis proper or other established fields of study. In comparative cultural studies, ideally, the framework of and methodologies available in the contextual (e.g., systemic and empirical study of culture) are favored. It remains to further research to elaborate and to exemplify the points introduced above.

WORKS CITED

Assmann, Aleida. "Cultural Studies and Historical Memories." *The Contemporary Study of Culture*. Ed. Bundesministerium für Wissenschaft und Verkehr and Internationales Forschungszentrum Kulturwissenschaften.Wien: Turia and Kant, 1999. 85–99.
Bachleitner, Norbert, Alfred Noe, and Hans-Gert Roloff, eds. *Beträge zu Komparatistik und Sozialgeschichte der Literatur*. Amsterdam: Rodopi, 1997.

Bassnett, Susan. *Comparative Literature: A Critical Introduction.* Oxford: Blackwell, 1993.

Bernheimer, Charles, ed. *Comparative Literature in the Age of Multiculturalism.* Baltimore: Johns Hopkins UP, 1995.

Burns, Rob, ed. *German Cultural Studies: An Introduction.* Oxford: Oxford UP, 1995.

Carvalhal, Tania Franco, ed. *Comparative Literature World Wide: Issues and Methods.* Porto Alegre: L&PM Editores, 1997.

Chevrel, Yves. *L'Etudiant chercheur en littérature.* Paris: Hachette, 1992

Chevrel, Yves. *Comparative Literature Today: Methods and Perspectives.* Trans. Farida Elizabeth Dahab. Kirksville: The Thomas Jefferson UP, 1994.

Corbineau-Hoffmann, Angelika. *Einführung in die Komparatistik.* Berlin: Erich Schmidt, 2000.

Daniel, Valentine E., and Jeffrey M. Peck. "Culture/Contexture: An Introduction." *Culture / Contexture: Explorations in Anthropology and Literary Studies.* By Valentine E. Daniel and Jeffrey M. Peck. Berkeley: U of California P, 1996. 1–33.

Denzin, Norman K. *Symbolic Interactionism and Cultural Studies.* Oxford: Blackwell, 1992.

D'haen, Theo. "From Comparative Literature to Comparative Cultural Studies." *Arcadia: Zeitschrift für Allgemeine und Vergleichende Literaturwissenschaft* 34.2 (1999): 374–76.

D'haen, Theo, ed. *Proceedings of the XVth Congress of the International Comparative Literature Association "Literature as Cultural Memory."* Amsterdam-Atlanta, GA: Rodopi, 2000. 8 Vols.

Didier, Bétarice, ed. *Précis de Littérature Européenne.* Paris: PU de Paris, 1998.

Dyserinck, Hugo, and Manfred S. Fischer. *Internationale Bibliographie zu Geschichte und Theorie der Komparatistik.* Stuttgart: Hiersemann, 1985.

Even-Zohar, Itamar. "Polysystem Theory and Culture Research." (1999–): <http://www.tau.ac.il/~itamarez/papers/>.

Even-Zohar, Itamar. "Culture Repertoire and the Wealth of Collective Entities." (1999–): <http://www.tau.ac.il/~itamarez/papers/>.

Fiormonte, Domenico, and Jonathan Usher, eds. *New Media and The Humanities: Research and Applications.* Oxford: Humanities Computing Unit, U of Oxford, 2001.

Forbes, Jill, and Michael Kelly, eds. *French Cultural Studies: An Introduction.* Oxford: Oxford UP, 1995.

Forgacs, David, and Robert Lumley, eds. *Italian Cultural Studies: An Introduction.* Oxford: Oxford UP, 1997.

Francoeur, Marie. *Confrontations. Jalons pour une sémiosis comparative des texts littéraires.* Sherbrooke: Naaman, 1985.

Fredrickson, George M. *The Comparative Imagination: On the History of Racism, Nationalism, and Social Movements.* Berkeley: U of California P, 1997.

Garber, Marjorie, Rebecca L. Walkowitz, and Paul B. Franklin, eds. *Fieldwork: Sites in Literary and Cultural Studies*. New York: Routledge, 1996.

Gerel, Christian. "Urbane Leitkulturen: Eine Perspektive für vergleichende kulturwissenschaftliche Studien" *IFK: Internationales Forschungszentrum Kulturwissenschaften*. Wien: Internationales Forschungszentrum Kulturwissenschaften / International Research Center for Cultural Studies, 1998. <http://www.ifk.or.at/ifk/pages/workshop/ws980004.htm>.

Gnisci, Armando, and Francesca Sinopoli, eds. *Manuale storico di letteratura comparata*. Roma: Meltemi, 1997.

Gnisci, Armando, and Franca Sinopoli, eds. *Comparare i comparatismi*. Roma: Lithos, 1995.

Görling, Reinhold. Heterotopia. *Lektüren einer interkulturellen Literaturwissenschaft*. München: Fink, 1997.

Gossmann, Lionel, and Mihail I. Spariosu, eds., *Building a Profession: Autobiographical Perspectives on the Beginnings of Comparative Literature in the United States*. Albany: State U of New York P, 1994.

Grabovszki, Ernst. "The Impact of Globalization and the New Media on the Notion of World Literature." *Comparative Literature and Comparative Cultural Studies*. Ed. Steven Tötösy de Zepetnek. West Lafayette: Purdue UP, 2002. PAGES?

Graham, Helen, and Jo Labanyi, eds. *Spanish Cultural Studies: An Introduction*. Oxford: Oxford UP, 1995.

Gabriel, Norbert. *Kulturwissenschaften und Neue Medien. Wissensvermittlung im digitalen Zeitalter*. Darmstadt: Primus, 1997.

Grossberg, Lawrence. "The Formation of Cultural Studies: An American in Birmingham." *Relocating Cultural Studies: Developments in Theory and Research*. Ed. Valda Blundell, John Sheppard, and Ian Taylor. London: Routledge, 1993. 21–66.

Grossberg, Lawrence. "Globalization and the 'Economization' of Cultural Studies." *The Contemporary Study of Culture*. Ed. Bundesministerium für Wissenschaft und Verkehr and Internationales Forschungszentrum Kulturwissenschaften. Wien: Turia and Kant, 1999. 23–46.

Guillén, Claudio. *The Challenge of Comparative Literature*. Trans. Cola Franzen. Cambridge: Harvard UP, 1993.

Guillén, Claudio. *Múltiples moradas. Ensayo de literatura comparada*. Barcelona: Tusquets, 1998.

Hendrix, Harald, Joost Kloek, Sophie Levie, and Will van Peer, eds. *The Search for a New Alphabet: Literary Studies in a Changing World*. Amsterdam: John Benjamins, 1996.

Higonnet, Margaret R., ed., *Borderwork: Feminist Engagements with Comparative Literature*. Ithaca: Cornell UP, 1994.

Horn, David G. "Reading Theory: Toward a Comparative Cultural Studies. A Review Article." *Comparative Studies in Society and History* 39.4 (1997): 734–41.

Horwath, Peter, William L. Hendrickson, L. Teresa Valdivieso, and Eric P. Thor, eds. *Humanism and the Good Life: Proceedings of the Fifteenth Congress of the World Federation of Humanists*. New York: Peter Lang, 1998.

Juvan, Marko. "Thematics and Intellectual Content: The XVth Triennial Congress of the International Comparative Literature Association in Leiden." *CLCWeb: Comparative Literature and Culture: A WWWeb Journal* 1.1 (1999): <http://clcwebjournal.lib.purdue.edu/clcweb99-1/juvan99.html>

Kappler, Arno. *Der literarische Vergleich. Beiträge zu einer Vorgeschichte der Komparatistik*. Bern: Peter Lang, 1976.

Kirby, John T. *The Comparative Reader: A Handlist of Basic Reading in Comparative Literature*. New Haven: Chancery P, 1998.

Konstantinović, Zoran. *Grundlagentexte der Vergleichenden Literaturwissenschaft aus drei Jahrzehnten*. Selected and Ed. Beate Burtscher-Bechter, Beate Eder-Jordan, Fridrun Rinner, Martin Sexl, and Klaus Zerinschek. Innsbruck: Studien, 2000.

Lee, Mabel, and Meng Hua, eds. *Cultural Dialogue and Misreading*. Sydney: Wild Peony, 1997.

Leersen, Joep. "Imagology" (1999–): <http://www.hum.uva.nl/images>

Lefevere, André. *Translating Literature: Practice and Theory in a Comparative Literature Context*. New York: Modern Language Association of America, 1992.

Leithmann, Peter Theodor. *Moriz Carriere and the Development of Comparative Literature*. Ann Arbor: Xerox University Microfilms, 1977.

Lepage, Robert. "Guess Who's Here: A Cultural Shift is under Way in Quebec That Puts French and English in a New Perspective." *Time: The Weekly Newsmagazine* Special Report *Canada 2005: CanCult Boom* (9 August 1999): 68–69.

López, Dolores Romero. *Una relectura del "fin de siglo" en el marco de la litteratura comparade. Teoría y praxis*. Bern: Peter Lang, 1998.

López, Dolores Romero, ed. *Orientaciones em literatura comparada*. Madrid: Arco/Libros, 1997.

Losa, Margarida L., Isménia de Sousa, and Gonçalo Vilas-Boas, eds. *Literatura Comparada: Os Novos Paradigmas*. Porto: Afrontamento, 1996.

Miall, David S., and Teresa Dobson. "Reading Hypertext and the Experience of Literature." *Journal of Digital Information* 2.1 (2001): <http://jodi.ecs.soton.ac.uk/Articles/v02/i01/Miall/>.

Mitchell, W.J.T. "Why Comparisons Are Odious." *World Literature Today* 70.2 (1996): 321–24.

Mourão, Manuela. "Comparative Literature in the United States." *Comparative Literature and Comparative Cultural Studies*. Ed. Steven Tötösy de Zepetnek. West Lafayette: Purdue UP, 2002. PAGES?

Riegler, Alexander. *Radical Constructivism* (1998–): <http://www.univie.ac.at/constructivism/>

Nemesio, Aldo, ed. *L'esperienza del testo*. Roma: Meltemi, 1999.

Santos, Montserrat Iglesias, ed. *Teoría de los Polisistemas*. Madrid: Arco / Libros, 1999.

Souiller, Didier, and Wladimir Troubetzkoy, eds. *Littérature comparée*. Paris: PU de Paris, 1997.

Steiner, George. *What is Comparative Literature?* Oxford: Clarendon, 1995.

Strutz, Johann, and Peter V. Zima, eds. *Komparatistik als Dialog. Literatur und interkulturelle Beziehungen in der Alpen-Adria-Region und in der Schweiz*. Bern: Peter Lang, 1991.

Thompson, Leonard. "Comparatively Speaking." *The New York Review of Books* (14 May 1998): 48–51.

Tötösy de Zepetnek, Steven. "Comparative Literature and Applied Cultural Studies, Or, a Report About the XIVth Triennial Congress of the ICLA/AILC (University of Alberta, August 1994)." *Canadian Review of Comparative Literature / Revue Canadienne de Littérature Comparée* 21.3 (1994): 469–90.

Tötösy de Zepetnek, Steven. "A Report on Comparative Literature in Beijing, October 1995 / Rapport sur la littérature comparée à Beijing, Octobre 1995." *Bulletin: Comparative Literature in Canada / La Littérature Comparée au Canada* 26.2 (1995): 10–16.

Tötösy de Zepetnek, Steven. "The Study of Literature in China and Taiwan Today: Impressions of a Visitor." *East Asian Cultural and Historical Perspectives: Histories and Society / Culture and Literatures*. Ed. Steven Tötösy de Zepetnek and Jennifer W. Jay. Edmonton: Research Institute for Comparative Literature, U of Alberta, 1997. 341–50.

Tötösy de Zepetnek, Steven. *Comparative Literature: Theory, Method, Application*. Amsterdam-Atlanta, GA.: Rodopi, 1998.

Tötösy de Zepetnek, Steven. "A Selected Shortlist of Comparative Literature (Text)Books in English, French, and German (1965–1999)." *CLCWeb: Comparative Literature and Culture: A WWWeb Journal (Library)* (1999a–): <http://clcwebjournal.lib.purdue.edu/library/booklist.html>.

Tötösy de Zepetnek, Steven. "Selected Bibliography of Studies on the Theories, Methods, and History of Comparative Literature." *CLCWeb: Comparative Literature and Culture: A WWWeb Journal (Library)* (1999b–): <http://clcwebjournal.lib.purdue.edu/library/clitbib1-99.html>.

Tötösy de Zepetnek, Steven. "A Selected Bibliography of Work in Comparative Literature and Literary Theory." *CLCWeb: Comparative Literature and Culture: A WWWeb Journal (Library)* (1999c–): <http://clcwebjournal.lib.purdue.edu/library/clitbib2-99.html>.

Tötösy de Zepetnek, Steven. "A Selected Bibliography of Work in the Systemic and Empirical, Institution, and Field Approaches to Literature and Culture." *CLCWeb: Comparative Literature and Culture: A WWWeb Journal (Library)* (1999d–): <http://clcwebjournal.lib.purdue.edu/library/sysbib97.html>.

Tötösy de Zepetnek, Steven. "Constructivism and Comparative Cultural Studies." *CLCWeb: Comparative Literature and Culture: A WWWeb Jour-*

nal   (*Library*)   (2001–):   <http://clcwebjournal.lib.purdue.edu/library/totosy(constructivism).html>.

Tötösy de Zepetnek, Steven. "Toward a Framework of Audience Studies." *CLCWeb: Comparative Literature and Culture: A WWWeb Journal* (*Library*) (2001b–): <http://clcwebjournal.lib.purdue.edu/library/audiencestudies.html>.

Tötösy de Zepetnek, Steven. "The New Knowledge Management: Online Research and Publishing in the Humanities." *CLCWeb: Comparative Literature and Culture: A WWWeb Journal* 3.1 (2001c): <http://clcwebjournal.lib.purdue.edu/clcweb01-1/totosy01.html>.

Tötösy de Zepetnek, Steven, Milan V. Dimić, and Irene Sywenky, eds. *Comparative Literature Now: Theories and Practice / La Littérature comparée à l'heure actuelle. Théories et réalisations*. Paris: Honoré Champion, 1999.

Tötösy de Zepetnek, Steven, Steven Aoun, and Wendy C. Nielsen, comp. "Toward Comparative Cultural Studies: A Selected Bibliography of Comparative Literature and Cultural Studies (Theories, Methods, Histories, 1835 to 2002)." *Comparative Literature and Comparative Cultural Studies*. Ed. Steven Tötösy de Zepetnek. West Lafayette: Purdue UP, 2002. 285–342.

Vega, María José, and Neus Carbonell, eds. *Literatura comparada. Principios y métodos*. Madrid: Gredos, 1998.

Villanueva, Darío, ed. *Avances en... teoría de la literatura*. Santiago de Compostela: U de Santiago de Compostela, 1994.

Weisstein, Ulrich. *Einführung in die Vergleichende Literaturwissenschaft*. Stuttgart: Kohlhammer, 1968.

Yokota-Murakami, Takayuki. *Don Juan East/West: On the Problematics of Comparative Literature*. New York: State U of New York P, 1999.

Yue, Daiyun, and Alain Le Pichon, eds. *La Licorne et le dragon. Les Malentendus dans la recherche de l'universel*. Peking: Peking UP, 1995.

Zelle, Carsten. *Kurze Bücherkunde für Literaturwissenschaftler*. Tübingen: Francke, 1998.

Zelle, Carsten, ed.. *Allgemeine Literaturwissenschaft. Konturen und Profile im Pluralismus*. Opladen: Westdeutscher, 1999.

Zima, Peter V. "Zu Wissenschaftsgeschichte der Komparatistik." *Komparatistik. Einführung in die Vergleichende Literaturwissenschaft*. By Peter V. Zima and Johann Strutz. Tübingen: Francke, 1992. 15–59.

Zima, Peter V., and Johann Strutz. *Komparatistik. Einführung in die Vergleichende Literaturwissenschaft*. Tübingen: Francke, 1992.

Zwingle, Erla. "Goods Move. People Move. Ideas Move. And Cultures Change." *Millennium Supplement: Global Culture* Special issue of the *National Geographic* 196.2 (August 1999): 12–33. <http://www.nationalgeographic.com/2000/culture/global>

Comparative Literature in China

Xiaoyi Zhou and Q.S. Tong

On the landscape of modern Chinese literary scholarship, comparative literature is perhaps one of the most versatile and active fields of study. As an academic discipline and a mode of intellectual inquiry and scholarly production, comparative literature was imported to China from the West, via Japan, in the early twentieth century. At a time of major intellectual and social shifts of the country and when many Chinese writers, artists, as well as scholars took upon themselves to reform traditional values and practices, radical intellectuals such as Hu Shi, Chen Duxiu, Lu Xun, and Zhou Zuoren, among others, advocated the importation and acceptance of Western thought. Parallel to this and as a natural result of the said interest, the translation of Western works became a national enterprise and the domains of literature experienced an unprecedented influx of new concepts, formulations, approaches, and practices. In the scholarship of literature new areas of study were established and comparative literature was one of them.

The term comparative literature (*bijiao wenxue*) was first used by the poet and critic Huang Ren (1869–1913), a professor of literature at Suzhou University, in his lecture notes where he refers to Posnett's 1886 *Comparative Literature* (see Xu 109). Next, Lu Xun (1881–1936), the father of modern Chinese literature, encountered Western writings on comparative literature while he was a student in Japan: in a letter he wrote in 1911 to Xu Shoushang, Lu mentions the Japanese translation of Frédéric Loliée's 1906 *Histoire des littératures comparées des origines au XXe siècle* (see Lu Vol. 11, 331) and he has used the comparative method in his work as early as 1907 (see Lu Vol. 1, 63–115). In the early twentieth century, when in China Western culture and thought gained much currency, in literary scholarship a discipline that explores Chinese and Western literatures would have its natural appeal. Thus, the general interest in the subject and approach resulted in a series of translations of Western works. For example, Fu Donghua, a translator of considerable repute, translated and published in 1930 Loliée's *Histoire des littératures comparées* and Paul Van Tieghem's *La Littérature comparée* was brought out in Chinese in 1937 by the poet Dai Wangshu (1905–1950), only six years after its publication in Paris in 1931. Further, poets Zhang Xishen and Wang Fuquan, respectively, translated from Japanese and French works on comparative literature: Zhang's translations appeared in the journal *New China* in the 1920s, later reprinted by the Commercial Press and Wang's translations were published as a series in *Awakening: The Supplement of Republican Daily* (1924). These texts not only popularized comparative literature but also made it possible to institute it formally as an academic subject in university education.

The establishing of comparative literature as a field of study at National Tsinghua University (Beijing) in the 1920s is probably one of the most important events in the early history of comparative literature in China. At Tsinghua, courses on or closely related to comparative literature included Wu Mi's "Zhongxishi zhi bjiao" ("Comparative Studies of Chinese and Western Poetics") in 1926 and Chen Yinke's "Xiren zhi dongfangxue muluxue" ("Bibliography of Sinology") in 1927. And I.A. Richards, who was a visiting professor at Tsinghua University from 1929 to 1931, also taught comparative literature while at Tsinghua (see Xu 111). By the mid-1930s, comparative literature as an academic subject and a mode of cross-cultural inquiry was firmly established and was to further develop into a prominent discipline in the history of modern Chinese literary scholarship. The period from the 1930s to the1950s is the most formative time for the discipline in China. Then, after a period of twenty years of silence, came another active period, from the late 1970s to the early 1990s. In these two main periods, series of books in the field appeared, either authored by Chinese scholars or translated into Chinese from various Western languages. In our brief survey it is not possible to record in detail all the major developments of comparative literature in China; however, here we sketch some significant moments. Our purpose is to consider the intellectual and historical conditions under which comparative literature has obtained such remarkable popularity and prominence in Chinese scholarship and to show that the development and currency of comparative literature is closely related to the formation of China's literary modernity.

COMPARATIVE LITERATURE IN CHINA, 1920s TO THE 1950s

In the early decades of the twentieth century, comparative literature in China was preoccupied with literary and cultural encounters between China and three major cultural sites: India, Russia, and Europe. As is well known, Indian religious culture has had enormous influence on Chinese culture and literature since Buddhism entered China. For instance, Buddhist fables were quickly appropriated and transformed into some of the most famous Chinese narratives in fiction. Later, Buddhist thought constituted an important source of inspiration for Tang poetry, manifested often in the poet's epiphanic understanding of the essence of nature and life in seemingly detached descriptions of landscapes or natural objects. Wang Wei, for example, typically in some of his best-known poems, fuses Zen Buddhist understanding with natural surroundings in an empathetic mode that the poetic self and the natural other become a totality. Although Buddhism has been a very significant source of inspiration for Chinese literary production, it is not until the first half of the twentieth century that Chinese scholars, by then equipped with Western concepts and methodologies from of comparative literary studies, begin to examine the influence of Buddhism on Chinese literature and for that matter on Chinese culture as a whole. In literary studies, work by Hu Shi, Chen Yinke, and Ji Xianlin represent outstanding achievements in the field.

Hu Shi (1819–1962) studied with John Dewey and after his return to China became, together with Chen Duxiu and Lu Xun, a prominent leader of the new cultural movement. He advocated the importance of textual exegesis and achieved a great deal himself in his own practice of textual criticism. In his seminal article, "Xi you ji kaozheng" ("Studies of *Journey to the West*", Hu, 886–925), he identifies Indian sources in this classic Chinese novel. As a leader of the new cultural movement and an admirer of Western scholarship and knowledge, Hu Shi, in directing his readers' attention to the influence of Asian countries' arts on Chinese culture, suggests an underlying political agenda. For him, it is of vital importance for China to look beyond its boundaries and to adopt modern Western knowledge in order to reinvigorate Chinese literature and Chinese culture as a whole (Hu, 670). Similar to Hu Shi, Ji Xianlin (1911–), who spent about ten years in Germany between 1925 and 1945, has an abiding interest in Indian culture and has devoted almost all his life to the study of its influences on Chinese tradition. Although he has been much less involved politically, his research methodology manifests an understanding of modern scholarship that is not totally ideologically innocent. Modern Chinese literature is to a great extent influenced by Russian and Soviet literature, respectively. Since the publication of Lu Xun's "Kuangren riji" ("The Diary of a Madman"), the first text of Chinese modernity, Russian and Soviet literature have been instrumental in the development of modern Chinese literature. A whole generation of Chinese writers such as Mao Dun, Jiang Guangci, Guo Moruo, Shen Congwen, Ai Wu, Xia Yan, Ba Jin, and Sha Ting at some stage showed great interest in Russian and Soviet literature and all were influenced by them to various degrees. Thus, given this importance of Russian and Soviet literature in modern Chinese literature, the study of their reception in China has been a prominent theme of Chinese comparative literary studies. An early example is Zhou Zuoren's "Wenxue shang de erguo yu zhongguo" ("Russia and China in Literature") (1920), in which Zhou, although offering no case studies comparing Russian and Chinese writers, suggests that the two literary traditions share some similarities in terms of their analyses of analogous social and political conditions (see Zhou 5–8). Zhou's analysis in fact suggests the immediate relevance of Russian literature to Chinese literary production and anticipates the centrality of Russian-Soviet literary influence in modern Chinese literature.

Admittedly, the discourse of Chinese revolutionary literature after the 1930s is tinctured pervasively with a Russo-Soviet literary ethos. In responding to this unique aspect of modern Chinese literature, critical studies of Chinese reception of Russian-Soviet literature have become a major strand of comparative literary studies in China between the 1940s and 1950s. For example, Ge Baoquan has published between 1956 and 1962 a series of essays on Russian writers and their influence on Chinese authors and their texts, Han Changjing and Feng Xuefeng published on Lu Xun and Russian literature, and others such as Ye Shuifu, Feng Zhi, and Ge Yihong wrote on Russian-Soviet literature in China. Of course, that Russian-Soviet literature acquired such high visibility in modern Chinese literature and, consequently, received a large an amount of critical attention is by no means extraordinary considering the close political ties between China and the Soviet Union in the 1950s (see, e.g., Xu 241–48).

In Chinese comparative literature concerning Indian and Chinese literature and Russian and Chinese literature, it is noticeable that much of the scholarly attention is focused on how Chinese literature and Chinese culture have been influenced by inspirations drawn from India and Russia, respectively, and comparatively. In contrast, critical inquires into the encounters between Chinese literature and European literature have been largely centered on China's influence on Europe, in particular on English-language literature. In the case of the latter, scholars such as Chen Shouyi, Fang Zhong, and Fan Cunzhong contributed significantly to our historical knowledge of early cultural encounters between England and China in the seventeenth and eighteenth centuries. Chen Shouyi was probably the first one who systematically studied the reception of Chinese literature in Europe. As early as in the 1920s he published a number of studies on the circulation of Chinese literary works in Europe. Among his other studies, Chen studied the process in which the Chinese play *Zhaoshi Guer* (*The Orphan of the Zhaos*) was translated into English, French, German, and Russian, and examined how it was received and parodied in the West. This play is arguably the single most influential Chinese literary work before the nineteenth century in Europe, and a whole group of European authors including Voltaire and Goethe on the continent and Richard Hurd, William Hatchett, and Arthur Murphy in England showed intensive interest in this "exotic" story. Fang Zhong (1902–1991), who studied in Britain and the United States, continued to research in this extraordinarily rich field: in his essay "Shiba shiji yingguo wenxue yu zhong guo" ("Eighteenth-Century English Literature and China") (1931), he discusses English imagination and exoticism as revealed in its discursive formulations about the remote and mysterious "Cathay." Fang divides the English reception of China in the eighteenth century into three stages: from the early eighteenth century to 1740, from 1740 to 1770, and the remaining decades after 1770. According to Fang, in the first stage, China begins to increase its visibility in British consciousness as seen in Addison and Steele's writings. In the second stage, a number of writers such as Oliver Goldsmith and Horace Walpole use cultural material from China extensively. In the last phase, interest in China generally wanes in England, although John Scott, for example, employs Chinese materials in his poetry. Fang argues that in the eighteenth century China is considered a fascinating culture in a positive context while it is only in the nineteenth century that this image of China changes. Like many Chinese scholars of comparative literature, Fang Zhong attempts to present a narrative of the formation of English literary knowledge about China and explains the formations of rationalized historical processes in which changes in the English idea or image of China maybe fully explained.

However, history is far richer than our theoretical imagination. While China is viewed as a model of human civilization in the eighteenth century,

China is at the same time regarded as an example of corruption and degener-ation. For instance Robinson Crusoe's account of China from a negative point of view or James Beattie's views on the Chinese language are other represen-tations of matters Chinese in the late eighteenth century. Fan Cunzhong's stud-ies of Chinese literature in England are built on a massive amount of primary sources and the scope of the topics covered in these articles shows that Fan, in a systematic way, attempts to examine the formation of the English idea of China by offering detailed case studies. Fan Cunzhong's and Fang Zhong's stud-ies represent major steps in the study of English literary knowledge of China in the eighteenth century. At the same time, we note that so far no major stud-ies exist of Chinese literature in nineteenth-century England although we know that English knowledge of China in the nineteenth century continued to expand. Even after the Opium War (1840–42), for instance, there were sev-eral exhibitions of Chinese culture organized in England and some nineteenth-century English authors including Thomas de Quincey produced a substantial amount of writing on China.

This gap in comparative literary scholarship is significant. For one, schol-ars in Chinese comparative literature appear to be curiously selective in the choice of their topics. In the eighteenth century when China as a country and a cultural phenomenon was generally held or imagined as an alternative model of civilization for the West, the European reception of the Chinese political system, the Chinese way of life, and Chinese attitudes and ideas would seem to be more gratifying topics for Chinese scholars. Although Western discur-sive formations of the idea and image of China are mostly manifestations of the Western fancy for the exotic Other, China, presented as such, would help build a sense of national pride.

In the 1950s, although scholars in comparative literature such as Ji Xian-lin and Fan Cunzhong continue to be productive in their areas, it is generally agreed that their research was largely a continuation of their earlier work with-out being able to offer new insights or present new materials. From the 1960s to the 1970s, comparative literature is silent: One obvious explanation for this is that the political situation in China during the time permitted no studies of Western literature, and comparative literature, by definition, is concerned with foreign literature, and thus the interregnum. Obviously, the political exclusion of comparative literature was a consequence of Mao's cultural policy and an extension of the establishment of political uniformity in the domain of liter-ary studies.

COMPARATIVE LITERATURE IN CHINA, 1970s TO THE 1990s

In the West, with the adoption of literary and culture theory beginning with the late 1960s by English and other single-language studies, comparative literature—the discipline where literary and culture theory occupied a prominent position since its inception—has been attracting increasingly less interest and more and more students of literature have turned away from it for a number of reasons. As an academic discipline, comparative literature has lost its vigor and radicalism seen in the 1950s and the1960s and now it appears a discipline waiting to be replaced by cultural studies or translation studies not necessarily taught and worked on in departments of comparative literature. Intellectually, the options to redirect comparative literature into cultural studies and/or translation studies has been suggested, for example by Susan Bassnett who in her *Comparative Literature: A Critical Introduction* (1993) suggests that comparative literature as a discipline is "dead" (47) or, as a more workable alternative we have Steven Tötösy's notion of comparative cultural studies (see in this volume; see also, in Mandarin, Tötösy 1997). While all this may indeed be the situation of the discipline, to various degrees, in the West, in the non-Western world including China, comparative literature has enjoyed an amazing and sustained popularity (on this, see Tötösy in this volume).

Specifically in China, since the late 1970s comparative literature has been one of the most prominent areas of research, attracting a large number of scholars and students. This extraordinary popularity of comparative literature after the 1970s has been construed as a continuity of its establishment in the 1930s and 1940s and Chinese scholars in comparative literature tend to disagree with Bassnett's pronouncements. Instead, they prefer, in general, to turn to the classics of Western comparative literature such as Wellek and Warren's *Theory of Literature* for a theoretical defense and legitimization of the practice of comparative literature, one that is built on the assumption of the existence of commonalities of cultures.

Indeed, one of the main concerns of Chinese comparative literature in the new period is to legitimize itself as a discipline and to reestablish its centrality in the Chinese system of literary scholarship. Again, one useful way to reinforce the discipline's its importance is to make available Western works on comparative literature in Chinese. Thus, in the period in question most seminal texts in English, French, and German have been translated into Chinese.

In addition, a number of anthologies of critical essays on comparative literature have been published. Following this intellectual revival, the Chinese renaissance of comparative literature is now solidified in its institutionalization as well to the point that after 1987 even public interest in comparative literature is manifest in the media. A spate of articles, essays, reviews, etc., appeared in Chinese newspapers thus forming a public forum on comparative literature. Scholars from the older generation such as Ji Xianlin, Ge Baoquan, Fang Zhong, Yang Zhouhan, Li Funing, Fan Cunzhong, Qian Zhongshu, and Jia Zhifang all participated in this extraordinary public discussion of the uses of comparative literature in China. Soon comparative literature found its way into the university classroom on a massive scale. Since Shi Zhecun offered in 1987 his course of comparative literature, the first of its kind after 1949, more than sixty institutions in China have established comparative literature as an academic subject before the end of the 1990s (see Liu and Wang 107–10).

In retrospect, admittedly, translations of Western works on literary theory revitalized and perhaps reinvented comparative literature as one of the most liberal areas of study and research in China. During the period to the 1990s, the remarkable nation-wide enthusiasm for comparative literature brought out a large number of publications in the field, most of which are visibly concerned with either new methodologies in the discipline or the historiography of comparative literature. Arguably, Chinese scholars of comparative literature are generally well informed of the latest critical developments in the West and have an unfailing interest in turning quickly more influential theoretical publications into Chinese. Translation in China has been a national enterprise and has played an instrumental part in the making of China's literary modernity. However, the choice of Western texts for translation often reveals the needs of China's self-fashioning rather than recognition of their inherent values. In the field of comparative literature, René Wellek and Austin Warren and Henry H.H. Remak (e.g., 1961) are the most translated Western scholars because some of their formulations can be readily appropriated for legitimating and strengthening comparative literature, not just as an academic discipline but as an agency enabling a dialogical relationship between Chinese and Western literary traditions and thereby allowing Chinese literature to be integrated into a world system of literature and the study of literature. Embedded in this desire to have a direct and equal dialogue with other literary traditions is the conviction of the existence of a common system of valuation in culture akin to Goethe's much debated notion of *Weltliteratur*.

In the 1980s, a central theme of comparative literature in China has been constructed on the belief in an innate aesthetic value of literary production that was not determined by time and space but is universally shared. The notion of literariness in American New Criticism was understood as a textual quality that defines what literature is and this was rapidly transformed into a principle of critical practice. This focus on literariness in the 1980s represents a major shift from the practice of comparative literature in the 1930s, which, as suggested above, was primarily concerned with archeological discoveries of major foreign cultural sources that found their way into Chinese literature.

THE FUNCTION OF COMPARATIVE LITERATURE IN CHINA

The situation and location of comparative literature in China in the period up to the 1990s are both a result and a source of energy for China's literary modernity. As a discursive literary and critical practice, as a mode and a subject of literary studies, its development mirrors China's social developments in the twentieth century. Although imported and adapted from the West, Chinese comparative literature has gone through a different passage of evolution. In the 1930s and 1940s what attracted most scholarly attention in the field was the intellectual excitement derived from discoveries of early histories of China's encounters with the West and India, for example, similar to the French school of comparative literature. However, in the 1980s Chinese comparative literature, inspired by formulations of American New Criticism, found its own path of progress and process. The large number of Western critical works translated into Chinese during this period were either works by the New Critics or by those associated with them. The resurrection of New Criticism in Chinese comparative literature, both methodological and theoretical, and its notion of literariness have been appropriated into a critical dogma that refuses to consider literature as a social, historical, and political discourse. This approach in Chinese comparative literature in practice refuses the discipline to be incorporated into cultural studies. Thus, generally speaking, Chinese comparative literature in the 1980s has been interested largely in its own self-fashioning and showed a visible indifference to the rise of critical discourse with regard to postmodernism in the Euro-American world, a discourse and critical practice that challenges forms of essentialism including the essentialist notion of literariness.

Ganesh Devy argues that the rise of comparative literature in India is closely tied to the rise of Indian nationalism and that as such has much to do with the politics of identity. In turn, Bassnett considers Devy's view applicable to the rise of comparative literature in the West: the term comparative literature in "Europe . . . first appeared in an age of national struggles, when new boundaries were being erected and the whole question of national culture and national identity was under discussion throughout Europe and the expanding United States of America" (Bassnett 8–9). To consider the historical origin of comparative literature as a discipline is at the same time to specify its political and ideological provenance. Not just in India and the Euro-American world, but also in China, the advent of comparative literature is, historically speaking, interwoven with the narration of nation as a strategy of forming national identity.

In the 1930s and 1940s, a large amount of comparative literary studies were primarily concerned with the possibilities of comparison between Chinese literary productions and those elsewhere, interested in searching for common themes and motifs among them or similarities among writers. Arbitrary comparisons were widely practiced and imposed upon authors or texts that have no relationships whatsoever. For example, Zhao Jingshen, in his study of Chinese Yuan drama, compares Shakespeare with Tang Xianzhu, simply on the basis of the closeness of the dates of birth of the two. And his comparison of Li Yu and Molière is triggered by his observation that "they both wrote comedies" (Zhao 278–83). Zhao Jingshen was a playwright and might be excused for the crudeness of his studies, but comparisons of this kind have been a very popular approach among prominent scholars in Chinese comparative literature. Comparative studies of Li Po and Goethe by Liang Zongdai, Chinese and Western dramaturgy by Bin Xin, and Chinese and Western poetics by Zhu Guangqian tend to be conducted on the basis of observed similarities and are generally devoid of genuine insights and interesting observations (see *Zhongguo bijiao wenxue yanjiu ziliao* [*Research Materials on Chinese Comparative Literature*] 1989, 226–31, 244–65, 240–43, 208–19).

The lack of intellectual rigor of comparative studies of this kind is attributable to a misinformed notion of comparative literature as nothing but "comparison" that, in practice, encourages comparative studies for the sake of comparison. However, the great amount of enthusiasm for this approach among scholars of comparative literature is indicative of a hidden agenda of Chinese comparative literature. In Zhu Guangqian's study, for example,

Western and Chinese views on love and nature are compared. And some of the differences between them, according to Zhu, can be only fully appreciated with recognition of the differences between Chinese national characteristics and their Western counterparts. National characteristics are indeed often understood as the causes of differences or similarities between cultural traditions. What is manifest in this type of comparative studies is, then, an attempt to foreground, by comparing China and the West in terms of their generalized national traits, the uniqueness of Chinese national temperament as if it were a real category that could be grasped and comprehended.

Chinese comparative literature is, therefore, heavily self-referential, and other literary traditions brought in for comparison serve as a Lacanian mirror image in which the self might be understood and constructed, as it were. It is precisely through such comparisons that Fan Cunzhong, for example, has experienced the feeling of national pride in Goldsmith's or Johnson's encomia of China, and it is also through comparisons of this kind that the value and worth of Chinese culture are reconfirmed. It is, then, obvious that the advocacy of the importance of "literariness" as a theme of comparative literary studies in China has an underlying ideological agenda, for the very notion of "literariness" legitimates comparisons between authors, texts, and literary practices regardless of their historical and social specificities and encompasses them in a world system of literature. It is then no surprise that the American New Criticism and Russian Formalism constituted the most important sources of theoretical authority for the practice of comparative literature in China, and some of the most distinguished practitioners of comparative literature in China have either translated works by the New Critics and Formalists or written about them. The influence of New Criticism is still visible today, as manifested in the scholarly tenacity of holding the text as the only legitimate object of study and regarding culture as only providing a context in which "literariness" of the text can be grasped.

In relation to this notion of comparative literature is the desire to build a Chinese school of comparative literature. John Deeney argues, for example, that it is necessary to look seriously into the possibility of a "Third World" comparative literature by employing the mode of Chinese thinking in comparative studies. The Chinese school of comparative literature, according to him, must start with the firm establishment of the sense of China's cultural identity, which will evolve gradually into the stage of self-consciousness (see Deeney 266).

The call for a Chinese school of comparative literature met with enthusiastic responses on the Mainland. In our opinion, however, a careful examination of this proposal for a Chinese school of comparative literature shows a lack of substance as well as impracticality. What underscores this proposal is a politics of recognition that aims to establish Chinese comparative literature as an equal partner on the international stage of comparative literature. In this sense, this movement toward a Chinese school of comparative literature is a strategic one than one that is motivated by serious theoretical as well as ideological and political considerations. The rise and development of Chinese comparative literature in the twentieth century are closely bound up with China's national project of modernization, inspired and supported by Western Enlightenment values. Its renaissance in the late 1970s after the Cultural Revolution further testifies to its close intellectual relation to Enlightenment values and humanism. Since the mid-nineteenth century, the idea or ideal of modernity has been haunting Chinese consciousness. Faced with the real danger of China being dismembered by Western powers and Japan in the early twentieth century, Chinese intellectuals embraced Enlightenment values and practices and were convinced that rationalism, equality, and technological improvement were solutions to what Bertrand Russell once called "the problem of China." But this total acceptance of Enlightenment values and practices has been very costly, as it inevitably means a total acceptance, as a starting point, of such binaries as the traditional and the modern and China and the West as reality. It is known that binarism of this kind has been used as a familiar strategy to configure global economy, centralizing and marginalizing at the same time cultures in an imagined map of world civilizations. Those cultures placed marginally in this global configuration are thus caught in the crisis generated from their own uncertainty about their sense of identity. This is, for example, why Hu Shi, in his comparative studies of Chinese and other eastern countries' arts, came to the conclusion that China should learn from the West (Hu 670). Thus, the desire to dislocate China from its marginal position and to reposition it in relation to the centrality of Western culture has been a cause of the developments of comparative literature in China. Some of the most frequently asked questions include: why is there no epic in Chinese literature (Zhu 1989, 220–25) and why is there no tragedy in China? (Zhu 1983, 215). But why should there be such genres in Chinese literature?

Looking back at some of the concerns of Chinese scholars of comparative literature, one is struck by the lack of sophistication and naivete with which their critical inquiries have been conducted. But those imagined issues, those perceived differences between Chinese and Western literature have unfortunately trapped some of the most distinguished Chinese scholars owing to the said binary mode of thinking. To identify gaps, incongruities, and differences between Chinese and Western literary traditions and practices, in the ultimate analysis, is to reconfirm the existence of the universality of certain literary qualities, values and practices, by which those very gaps, incongruities and differences might be examined. This belief of the universal applicability of literary values is nowhere more manifest than in the pursuit of textual "literariness" and in the call for the establishing of a Chinese school of comparative literature. The former is to extend the New Critics' critical practice into the study of Chinese literary production and the latter is largely for the purpose of popularizing indigenous literary practices and presenting them as indispensable not only for the Chinese but for all cultures.

Chinese comparative literature as a critical practice may thus be considered a product of China's pursuit of modernity in the twentieth century. The crisis of comparative literature that has been a cause of concern for scholars in China in recent years registers, in fact, a deeper level of crisis that is also the crisis of the ideological and political foundation of comparative literature—its conviction in the existence of the universality of literary values. In recent years, the Enlightenment project with all its paradoxes has been brought under close critical scrutiny in the West; and the deconstruction of Eurocentrism has resulted in serious ramifications. Under this new intellectual condition, the ideology of comparative literature has been questioned accordingly, and it is no longer possible, intellectually at least, to conduct comparative studies on the basis of binarism without serious and careful modifications. The crisis of comparative literature is the crises of the ideological understanding of the function of comparative literature, but it may constitute an opportunity to reinvent comparative studies in response to the challenges of recent critical developments.

There is now increasing awareness in China of the invalidity of structuring comparative studies on the principle of binarism. For example, Lydia Liu's *Translingual Practice: Literature, National Culture, and Translated Modernity—China, 1900–1937* (1995) represents much needed new development in cross-cultural studies and thus in comparative literature as well as comparative cultural studies. What is particularly relevant in terms of Liu's work in its critical methodology is her careful discussion of how power relationships are embodied in some of the concepts and keywords that have traveled to China and how these power relationships generate(d) social realities through translingual practice. Liu's study reaches far beyond the scope of orthodox comparative literary studies concerned only with cross-cultural influence and reception or with questions like why and how cross-cultural influence is exercised and what determines cross-cultural reception. If comparative literature wishes to overcome its own perpetual crises, it has to get rid of the rigidity of its self-definition, it has to reach beyond the level of literature and must direct its attention to other forms of cultural production, including literature. And in this sense, it perhaps matters very little how it should be called: comparative literature or (cross-)cultural studies or comparative cultural studies. And we propose that this notion of questioning and re-direction of the discipline is applicable to both Chinese comparative literature and comparative literature in the West and elsewhere.

WORKS CITED

Bassnett, Susan. *Comparative Literature: A Critical Introduction*. Oxford: Blackwell, 1993.

Brunel, Pierre, Claude Pichois, and André Rousseau. *Shenmo shi bijiao wenxue?* (*What is Comparative Literature?*). Trans. Ge Lei. Beijing: Peking UP, 1989.

Chen Shouyi. "Shiba shiji ouzhou wenxue li de Zhaoshi guer" ("The Orphan of the Zhaos in Eighteenth-Century European Literature"). *Lingnan xuebao* (*The Journal of Lingnan College*) 1.1 (1929): 114–46.

Deeney, John. "Bijiao wenxue zhongguo xuepai" ("The Chinese School of Comparative Literature"). *Bijiao wenxue yanjiu zhi xinfangxiang* (*New Orientations for Comparative Literature*). By John Deeney. Taipei: Lianjing, 1986. 265–70.

Devy, Ganesh N. "The Commonwealth 'Period' and Comparative Literature." *Aspects of Comparative Literature: Current Approaches*. Ed. Chandra Mohan. New Delhi: India Publishers and Distributors, 1989. 144–53.

Fan Cunzhong. "Shiqiba shiji yingguo liuxing de zhongguo xi" ("Popular Chinese Dramatic Works in England in the Seventeenth and Eighteenth Centuries"). *Qingnian zhongguo* (*Youthful China*) 2.2 (1940): 172–86.

Fan Cunzhong. "Shiqiba shiji yingguo liuxing de zhongguo sixiang" ("Popular Chinese Thoughts in England in the Seventeenth and Eighteenth Centuries"). *Wenshizhe jikan* (*Literature, History and Philosophy Quarterly*) 1.2-3 (1943).

Fan Cunzhong. "Qiongsi jueshi yu zhongguo wenhua." 1947. ("Sir William Jones and Chinese Culture"). *Zhongguo bijiao wenxue yanjiu ziliao* (*Research Materials on Chinese Comparative Literature*). Beijing: Research Institute for Comparative Literature, Peking UP, 1989. 168–84.

Fan Cunzhong. "Zhaoshi guer zaju zai qimeng shiqi de yingguo" ("The Chinese Orphan in the England of the Age of Enlightenment." 1957. *Bijiao wenxue lunwenji (Comparative Literature Studies: A Collection)*. Ed. Zhang Longxi and Wen Rumin. Beijing: Peking UP, 1984. 83–120.

Fan Cunzhong. *Chinese Culture in the England of the Age of Enlightenment*. Shanghai: Shanghai Foreign Languages Education Press, 1991.

Fang Zhong. "Shiba shiji yingguo wenxue yu zhongguo." 1931. ("Eighteenth-Century English Literature and China"). *Zhongguo bijiao wenxue yanjiu ziliao (Research Materials on Chinese Comparative Literature)*. Beijing: Research Institute for Comparative Literature, Peking UP, 1989. 137–67.

Guyard, Marius-François. *Bijiao wenxue (La Littérature Comparée)*. Trans. Yan Bao. Beijing: Peking UP, 1983.

Hu Shi. *Hu Shi gudian wenxue yanjiu lunji (Studies in Classical Literature)*. Shanghai: Shanghai guji chubanshe, 1988.

Jost, François. *Bijiao wenxue daolun (Introduction to Comparative Literature)*. Trans. Liao Hongjun et al. Changsha: Hunan wenyi chubanshe, 1988.

Liu, Lydia. *Translingual Practice: Literature, National Culture, and Translated Modernity—China, 1900–1937*. Stanford: Stanford UP, 1995.

Liu Xianbiao and Wang Zhenmin. *Bijiao wenxue yu xiandaiwenxue (Comparative Literature and Modern Literature)*. Hangzhou: Zhongguo meishu xueyuan chubanshe, 1994.

Loliée, Frédéric A. *Bijiao wenxueshi (Histoire des littératures comparées des origines au XXe siècle)*. Trans. Fu Donghua. Shanghai: The Commercial Press, 1930.

Lu Xun. *Lun Xun quanji (Collected Works of Lu Xun)*. Beijing: Renmin wenxue chubanshe, 1981. 16 Vols.

Miner, Earl. *Bijiao shixue (Comparative Poetics)*. Trans. Wang Yugen and Song Weijie. Beijing: Zhongyang bianyi chubanshe, 1998.

Posnett, Hutcheson Macaulay. *Comparative Literature*. 1886. New York: Johnson, 1970.

Remak, H.H. Henry. "Bijiao wenxue de dingyi yu gongyong" ("Comparative Literature: Its Definition and Function"). 1961. *Bijiao wenxue yanjiu ziliao (Materials in Comparative Literature Studies)*. Ed. Research Group in Comparative Literature, Department of Chinese, Beijing Normal University. Beijing: Beijing Normal UP, 1986, 1–14.

Tötösy de Zepetnek, Steven. *Wen hsüe yen chiu ti ho fa hua—Chen t'i hua ho ching yen chu i wen hsüe yü wen hua yen chiu fang fa (Legitimizing the Study of Literature. A New Pragmatism: The Systemic Approach to Literature and Culture.)* Trans. Ma Jui-ch'i. Beijing: Peking UP, 1997.

Tötösy de Zepetnek, Steven. "From Comparative Literature Today Toward Comparative Cultural Studies." *Comparative Literature and Comparative Cultural Studies*. Ed. Steven Tötösy de Zepetnek. West Lafayette: Purdue UP, 2002. 235–67.

Van Tieghem, Paul. *Bijiao wenxue lun* (*La Littérature comparée*). Trans. Dai Wangshu. 1937. Taipei: The Commercial Press, 1995.

Wellek, René, and Warren, Austin. *Wenxue lilun* (*Theory of Literature*). 1942. Trans. Liu Xiangyu, Xing Peiming, Chen shengsheng and Li Zheming. Beijing: Sanlian shudian, 1984.

Xu Yangshang. *Zhongguo bijiao wenxue yuanliu* (*Origins and Developments of Comparative Literature in China*). Zhengzhou: Zhongzhou guji chubanshe, 1998.

Zhao Jingshen. "Tang xianzu yu shashibiya" ("Tang Xianzu and Shakespeare"). *Zhongguo bijiao wenxue yanjiu ziliao* (*Research Materials on Chinese Comparative Literature*). Beijing: Research Institute for Comparative Literature, Peking UP, 1989. 278–83.

Zhongguo bijiao wenxue yanjiu ziliao (*Research Materials on Chinese Comparative Literature*). Beijing: Research Institute for Comparative Literature, Peking UP, 1989.

Zhou Zuoren. "Wenxue shang de eguo yu zhongguo" ("Russia and China in Literature." 1920. *Zhongguo bijiao wenxue yanjiu ziliao* (*Research Materials on Chinese Comparative Literature*). Beijing: Research Institute for Comparative Literature, Peking UP, 1989. 5–12.

Zhu Guangqian. *Beiju xilixue* (*The Psychology of Tragedy: A Critical Study of Various Theories of Tragic Pleasure*). Trans. Zhang Longxi, Beijing: Renmin wenxue chubanshe, 1983.

Zhu Guangqian. "Changpianshi zai zhongguo heyi bufada" ("Why There is No Epic in Chinese Literature"). *Zhongguo bijiao wenxue yanjiu ziliao* (*Research Materials on Chinese Comparative Literature*). Beijing: Research Institute for Comparative Literature, Peking UP, 1989. 220–25.

Toward Comparative Cultural Studies

A Selected Bibliography of Comparative Literature and Cultural Studies
(Theories, Methods, Histories, 1835 to 2002)

Steven Tötösy de Zepetnek, Steven Aoun, and Wendy C. Nielsen, comp.

1) Selected Bibliography of Bibliographies of Studies in Comparative Literature and Culture

Baldensperger, Fernand, and Werner P. Friedrich. *Bibliography of Comparative Literature.* 1950. Rpt. New York: Russell and Russell, 1960.

Dyserinck, Hugo, and Manfred S. Fischer. *Internationale Bibliographie zur Geschichte und Theorie der Komparatistik.* Stuttgart: Anton Hiersemann, 1985.

International Bibliography of the Modern Language Association of America. New York: Modern Language Association of America, 1968–. Hard-Copy, CD-ROM, and *World Wide Web* (subscription is necessary): <http://www.mla.org/>.

Liu, Jiemin, and John J. Deeney. *Twentieth-Century Comparative Literature Bibliography from Chinese Perspectives.* Hong Kong: The Chinese U of Hong Kong, Comparative Literature Research Program, 1994.

Thompson, G.A. *Key Sources in Comparative and World Literature: An Annotated Guide to Reference Materials.* New York: Ungar, 1982.

Tötösy de Zepetnek, Steven. "Web Sites for Research and Information in Comparative Literature and Culture." *CLCWeb: Comparative Literature and Culture: A WWWeb Journal (Library)* (2000–): <http://clcwebjournal.lib.purdue.edu/library.html>.

Note: A list of comparative literature and comparative literature oriented journals, with addresses, is available online at <http://clcwebjournal.lib.purdue.edu/library/journals.html>.

2) Selected Bibliography of Theories, Methods, and Histories of Comparative Literature and Culture

Abe, Jiro. *Hikaku bungaku (Comparative Literature).* Tokyo: Iwanami shoten, 1932. 2 vols.

Abousenna, Mona. "Nationalism versus Universalism in Comparative Literature." *Differential Multilogue: Comparative Literrature and National Literatures*. Ed. Gurbhagat Singh. Delhi: Ajanta, 1991. 115–25.

Adam, Barbara, and Stuart Allan, eds. *Theorizing Culture: An Interdisciplinary Critique after Postmodernism*. New York: New York UP, 1995.

Ahearne, Ed, and Arnold Weinstein. "The Function of Criticism at the Present Time; The Promise of Comparative Literature." *Comparative Literature in the Age of Multiculturalism*. Ed. Charles Bernheimer. Baltimore: Johns Hopkins UP, 1995. 77–85.

Aldridge, A. Owen. "The Comparative Literature Syndrome." *Modern Language Journal* 53.2 (1969): 110–16.

Aldridge, A. Owen. *The Reemergence of World Literature: A Study of Asia and the West*. Newark: U of Delaware P, 1986.

Aldridge, A. Owen, ed. *Comparative Literature: Matter and Method*. Urbana: U of Illinois P, 1969.

Alewyn, Richard. "Comparative Literature in Germany." *Comparative Literature NewsLetter* 1.4 (1942–43): 1–2.

Al-Khateeb, Hussam. "Comparative Literature in Arabic: History and Major Tendencies to the 1980s." *Yearbook of Comparative and General Literature* 41 (1994): 12–20.

Alphonso-Karkal, John B. *Comparative World Literature: Essays*. Bombay: Popular Books, 1974.

Anonymous. "Twenty-five Years of Comparative Literature in India, 1956–1981." *Jadavpur Journal of Comparative Literature* 16–17 (1978–79): 110–15.

Anonymous. "Not So Odious: English Neglect of Comparative Literature." *The Times: Literary Supplement* 12.03 (1964): 215.

Anonymous. "Société algérienne de littérature comparée." *Revue de Littérature Comparée* 39 (1965): 493–95.

Apter, Emily. "Comparative Exile: Competing Margins in the History of Comparative Literature." *Comparative Literature in the Age of Multiculturalism*. Ed. Charles Bernheimer. Baltimore: Johns Hopkins UP, 1995. 86–96.

Arnold, James, ed. *A History of Literature in the Caribbean*. Amsterdam: John Benjamins, 1997.

Arnold, Stephen H. "Comparative African Literary Studies: A New Discipline." *Aspects of Comparative Literature: Current Approaches*. Ed. Chandra Mohan. New Delhi: India Publishers & Distributors, 1989. 82–94.

Asante-Darko, Kwaku. "Language and Culture in African Postcolonial Literature." *Comparative Literature and Comparative Cultural Studies*. Ed. Steven Tötösy de Zepetnek. West Lafayette: Purdue UP, 2002. 1–10.

Auerbach, Erich. "Philologie der Weltliteratur." *Weltliteratur*. By Erich Auerbach. Bern: Francke, 1952. 39–50.

Bacchilega, Cristina, ed. *Constructions and Confrontations: Changing Representations of Women and Feminisms, East and West: Selected Essays.* Honolulu: U of Hawaii P, 1997.

Backer, F. de. "Littérature comparée: questions de méthode." *Bulletin de l'Academie Royale de Belgique. Classe des lettres et des sciences morales et politiques* 45 (1959): 208–11.

Badallic, Josip. "Wege und Perspektiven der Methode der Vergleichenden Literaturwissenschaft." *Festschrift für Alfred Rammelmeyer.* Ed. Hans-Bernd Harder. München: de Gruyter, 1975. 11–19.

Baker, Houston Jr., Manthia Diawara, and Ruth Lindeborg, eds. *Black British Cultural Studies: A Reader.* Chicago: U of Chicago P, 1996.

Baker, Stephen. *The Fiction of Postmodernity.* New York: Rowman and Littlefield, 2000.

Balakian, Anna. "Literary Theory and Comparative Literature." *Toward a Theory of Comparative Literature.* Ed. Mario J. Valdés. New York: Peter Lang, 1990. 17–24.

Balakian, Anna. "How and Why I Became a Comparatist." *Building a Profession: Autobiographical Perspectives on the Beginnings of Comparative Literature in the United States.* Ed. Lionel Gossman and Mihai I. Spariosu. Albany: State U of New York P, 1994. 75–87.

Balakian, Anna. *The Snowflake on the Belfry: Dogma and Disquietude in the Critical Arena.* Bloomington: Indiana UP, 1994.

Balakian, Anna. "Theorizing Comparison: The Pyramid of Similitude and Difference." *World Literature Today* 69.2 (1995): 263–67.

Baldensperger, Fernand. "Où nous en somme: examen de conscience d'un 'comparatiste'." *Revue universitaire* 28 (1919): 260–73.

Baldensperger, Fernand. "Littérature comparée. Le Mot et la chose." *Revue de littérature comparée* 1 (1921): 5–29.

Baldensperger, Fernand. "Solidarité internationale de littérature comparée." *Comparative Literature Studies* 5.16 (1945): 2–4.

Barr, Marleen. *Genre Fission: A New Discourse Practice for Cultural Studies.* Iowa: U of Iowa P, 2000.

Barricelli, Jean-Pierre. "A View from My Balcony: Perspectives on Comparative Literature in 1995." *The Comparatist: Journal of the Southern Comparative Literature Association* 20 (1996): 6–20.

Barricelli, Jean-Pierre, and Joseph Gibaldi, eds. *Interrelations of Literature.* New York: Modern Language Association of America, 1982.

Barry, Peter. *Beginning Theory: An Introduction to Literary and Cultural Theory.* Manchester: Manchester UP, 1995.

Bassel, Naftali. *Rahvuskirjandus ja mmailmakirjandus (National Literature and World Literature).* Tallin: Eesti Raamat, 1972.

Bassnett, Susan. *Comparative Literature: A Critical Introduction*. Oxford: Blackwell, 1993.

Bauer, Gerhard. "Theorie der Literatur in der Allgemeinen und Vergleichenden Literaturwissenschaft." *Zur Theorie der Vergleichenden Literaturwissenschaft*. Ed. Horst Rüdiger, G. Bauer, E. Koppen, and M. Gsteiger. Berlin: de Gruyter, 1971. 15–40.

Baur, Frank. "De Philologie van het letterkundige comparatisme." *Handlingen van het XXIIe vlaams filologen congres*. Leuven: U of Leuven, 1957. 31–64.

Bauer, Roger. "Der Fall der Vergleichenden Literaturwissenschaft." *Kontinuität / Diskontinuität in den Geisteswissenschaften*. Ed. Hans Trümpy. Darmstadt: Wissenschaftliche Buchgesellschaft, 1973. 167–88.

Beall, Chandler, and Henry H.H. Remak. "Comparative Literature." *Yearbook of Comparative and General Literature* 38 (1989): 9–15.

Beil, Else. *Zur Entwicklung des Begriffs Weltliteratur*. PhD Diss. Leipzig: U of Leipzig, 1915.

Behar, Lisa Block de. "Uruguayan Comparative Literature: The Need for a Double Bet." *Comparative Literature World Wide: Issues and Methods / La Littérature comparée dans le monde: Questions et méthodes*. Ed. Tânia Franco Carvalhal. Porto Alegre: L&PM Editores, 1997. 149–72.

Beker, Miroslav. *Uvod u komparativnu knjievnost (Introduction to Comparative Literature)*. Zagreb: Skolska knjiga, 1995.

Belic, Oldrich. *Verso español y verso europeo. Introducción a la teoría del verso español en el contexto europeo*. Santafé de Bogotá: Instituto Caro y Cuervo, 2000.

Benloew, L. *Introduction à l'histoire comparée des littératures*. Dijon: Loireau-Feuchot, 1849.

Berczik, Árpád. "Les Débuts hongrois de l'histoire littéraire comparée." *Acta litteraria* 2 (1959): 215–49.

Berczik, Árpád. "Eine ungarische Konzeption der Weltliteratur." *La Littérature comparée en Europe orientale*. Ed. István Sőtér, K. Bor, T. Klaniczay, and Gy.M. Vajda. Budapest: Akadémiai, 1963. 287–94.

Berczik, Árpád. "Hundert Jahre der ungarischen Komparatistik." *Acta Litteraria Academia Scientiarum Hungaricae* 18.3–4 (1976): 416–23.

Berger, Arthur Asa. *Cultural Criticism: A Primer of Key Concepts*. Thousand Oaks: SAGE, 1995.

Bernheimer, Charles. "Introduction: The Anxieties of Comparison." *Comparative Literature in the Age of Multiculturalism*. Ed. Charles Bernheimer. Baltimore: Johns Hopkins UP, 1995. 1–17.

Bertens, Hans. "From Over-Confidence to Clear and Present Danger: Comparative Literature and Intellectual Fashion." *The Search for a New Alphabet: Literary Studies in a Changing World*. Ed. Harald Hendrix, Joost Kloek, Sophie Levie, and Will van Peer. Amsterdam: John Benjamins, 1966. 7–12.

Bertens, Hans, and Douwe Fokkema, eds. *International Postmodernism: Theory and Literary Practice*. Amsterdam: John Benjamins, 1997.

Bery, Ashok, and Patricia Murray, eds. *Comparing Postcolonial Literatures: Dislocations*. New York: St. Martin's P, 2000.

Bessière, Jean. "Literature, Cultural Relativism and the Efficacy of Cognitive Minimalism." *The Search for a New Alphabet: Literary Studies in a Changing World*. Ed. Harald Hendrix, Joost Kloek, Sophie Levie, and Will van Peer. Amsterdam: John Benjamins, 1966. 13–18.

Bessière, Jean. "Littérature comparée et littérature générale." *La Recherche en littérature générale et comparée en France*. Paris: Société Française de Littérature Générale et Comparée, 1983. 281–92.

Bessière, Jean, ed. *Littérature et théorie. Intentionnalité, décontextualisation, communication*. Paris: Honoré Champion, 1998.

Betz, Louis-Paul. "Critical Observations on the Nature, Function and Meaning of Comparative Literary History." 1896. *Comparative Literature: The Early Years*. Ed. Hans-Joachim Schulz and Phillip H. Rhein. Chapel Hill: U of North Carolina P, 1973. 133–51.

Betz, Louis-Paul. *Studien zur vergleichenden Literaturgeschichte der neueren Zeit*. Frankfurt, 1902.

Beverely, John. *Subalternity and Representation: Arguments in Cultural Theory*. Durham: Duke UP, 1999.

Bierwirch, Gerhard. "The First Congress of the German Society for General and Comparative Literature." *Jadavpur Journal of Comparative Literature* 10 (1972): 77–83.

Bierwirch, Gerhard. "Departments of Comparative Literature at West German Universities." *Jadavpur Journal of Comparative Literature* 10 (1972): 72–76.

Birus, Hendrik. "The Goethean Concept of World Literature and Comparative Literature." *Comparative Literature and Comparative Cultural Studies*. Ed. Steven Tötösy de Zepetnek. West Lafayette: Purdue UP, 2002. 11–22.

Bisztray, George. "The Theory of Interaction in Sociology and Comparative Literature." *Sensus Communis: Contemporary Trends in Comparative Literature / Panorama de la situation actuelle en Littérature Comparée*. Ed. János Riesz, Peter Boerner, and Bernhard Scholz. Tübingen: Gunter Narr, 1986. 213–19.

Bisztray, George. "A Theoretical Model of Comparative Literature." *arcadia: Zeitschrift für Vergleichende Literaturwissenschaft* 21.3 (1986): 226–32.

Bjornson, Richard. "Comparativism is a Humanism: A Personal View." *Neohelicon: Acta Comparationis Litterarum Universarum* 13.1 (1986): 365–81.

Bleicher, Thomas. "Einführung in die Komparatistik. Ein Mainzer Versuch." *Mainzer Komparatistische Hefte* 2 (1978): 39–56.

Bleicher, Thomas. "Allgemeine und Vergleichende Literaturwissenschaft: Grundlegung und Modell." *Neohelicon: Acta Comparationis Litterarum Universarum* 6 (1979): 83–126.

Bleicher, Thomas. "Literaturkomplexe in komparatistischer Perspektive." *Neohelicon: Acta Comparationis Litterarum Universarum* 8 (1981): 9–42.

Bloch, Peter A. *Vergleichende Literaturwissenschaft. Eine Einführung in die Geschichte, die Methoden und Probleme der Komparatistik.* Düsseldorf: Wissenschaftliche Buchgesellschaft, 1971.

Block, Haskell M. "The Concept of Influence in Comparative Literature." *Yearbook of Comparative and General Literature* 7 (1957): 30–37.

Block, Haskell M. *Nouvelles tendances en littérature comparée.* Paris: Nizet, 1974.

Blodgett, E.D. "What is Comparative Canadian Literature?" *Aspects of Comparative Literature: Current Approaches.* Ed. Chandra Mohan. New Delhi: India Publishers & Distributors, 1989. 46–64.

Blundell, Valda, John Shepherd, and Ian Taylor, eds. *Relocating Cultural Studies: Developments in Theory and Research.* New York: Routledge, 1993.

Body, Jacques. "Les Comparatismes vus de France." *Neohelicon: Acta Comparationis Litterarum Universarum* 1.1-2 (1973): 354–59.

Body, Jacques. "Enseigner l'histoire comparée du théâtre?" *Neohelicon: Acta Comparationis Litterarum Universarum* 12.1 (1985): 9–15.

Boening, John. "Comparative Literature, Incommensurability, and Cultural Misreading." *Cultural Dialogue and Misreading.* Ed. Mabel Lee and Meng Hua. Sydney: Wild Peony, 1997. 153–62.

Bohn, Willard. "Comparative Literature and the Avant-Garde." *ACLA: American Comparative Literature Association Bulletin* 14.2 (1993): 139–55.

Bonnell, Victoria, and Linda Hunt, eds. *Beyond the Cultural Turn: New Directions in the Study of Society and Culture.* California: U California P, 1999.

Borenman, John. *Subversions of International Order: Studies in the Political Anthropology of Culture.* New York: State U of New York P, 1998.

Borghi, L., D. Carpi Sertori, M.P. De Angelis, and V. Fortunati, eds. *La letteratura comparata. Metodi e prospettive.* Ravenna: Longo, 1992.

Bose, Buddhadeva. "Comparative Literature in India." *Yearbook of Comparative and General Literature* 8 (1959): 1–10.

Böhme, Hartmut. "Neue Perspektiven: Vergleichende Interkulturelle Literaturwissenschaft?" *Wie international ist die Literaturwissenschaft?* Ed. Lutz Danneberg, Friedrich Vollhardt, Hartmut Böhme, and Jörg Schönert. Stuttgart: Metzler, 1996. 493–98.

Brandt Corstius, Jan. "The Impact of Cosmopolitanism and Nationalism on Comparative Literature from the Beginnings to 1880." *Actes du IVe Congrès de l'Association Internationale de Littérature Comparée.* Ed. W.A.P. Smit. The Hague: Mouton, 1966. 380–89.

Brandt Corstius, Jan. *Introduction to the Comparative Study of Literature.* New York: Random House, 1968.

Brooker, Peter. *A Concise Glossary of Cultural Theory.* London: Arnold, 1999.

Brooks, Peter. "Must We Apologize?" *Comparative Literature in the Age of Multiculturalism.* Ed. Charles Bernheimer. Baltimore: Johns Hopkins UP, 1995. 97–106.

Brooks, Peter. "Literature *And.*" *Comparative Literature: History and Contemporaneity / Littérature Comparée: Histoire et contemporanéité.* Ed. Milan V. Dimić and Steven Tötösy de Zepetnek. *Canadian Review of Comparative Literature / Revue Canadienne de Littérature Comparée* 23.1 (1996): 15–26.

Brown, Calvin S. "Comparative Literature." *The Georgia Review* 13 (1959): 167–89.

Brunel, Pierre. "L'Etude des mythes en littérature comparée." *Sensus Communis: Contemporary Trends in Comparative Literature / Panorama de la situation actuelle en Littérature Comparée.* Ed. János Riesz, Peter Boerner, and Bernhard Scholz. Tübingen: Gunter Narr, 1986. 117–23.

Brunel, Pierre. "L'Usage de la comparaison en littérature comparée." *Europa Provincia Mundi: Essays in Comparative Literature and European Studies.* Ed. Joep Leerssen and Karl Ulrich Syndram. Amsterdam: Rodopi, 1992. 3–11.

Brunel, Pierre, ed. *Companion to Literary Myths, Heroes and Archetypes.* London: Routledge, 1992.

Brunel, Pierre, and Yves Chevrel, eds. *Précis de littérature comparée.* Paris: PU de France, 1989.

Brunel, Pierre, Claude Pichois, and André Michel Rousseau. *Qu'est-ce la littérature comparée?* 1983. Paris: Colin, 1996.

Brunetière, Ferdinand. "European Literature." 1900. *Comparative Literature: The Early Years.* Ed. Hans Joachim Schulz and Phillip H. Rhein. Chapel Hill: U of North Carolina P, 1973. 153–82.

Bryden, Diana, ed. *Postcolonialism: Critical Concepts in Literary and Cultural Studies.* New York: Routledge, 2000.

Buescu, Helena Carvalhao. "La Littérature comparée au Portugal: Tendences théoriques et institutionnelles." *Comparative Literature World Wide: Issues and Methods / La Littérature comparée dans le monde: Questions et méthodes.* Ed. Tânia Franco Carvalhal. Porto Alegre: L&PM Editores, 1997. 139–47.

Burke, Lucy, ed. *Routledge Language and Cultural Theory Reader.* New York: Routledge, 2000.

Burns, Rob, ed. *German Cultural Studies: An Introduction.* New York: Clarendon, 1996.

Cambon, Glauco. "The Future of that Unlikely Thing, Comparative Literature." *Michigan Germanic Studies* 5 (1979): 159–69.

Cammarota, Antonio. "Entwicklungen der Komparatistik in Italien im 20. Jahrhundert." *Europa Provincia Mundi: Essays in Comparative Literature and European Studies.* Ed. Joep Leerssen and Karl Ulrich Syndram. Amsterdam: Rodopi, 1992. 13–21.

Campbell, Neil, and Alasdair Kean, eds. *American Cultural Studies: An Introduction to American Culture.* New York: Routledge, 1998.

Campbell, Oscar J. "What is Comparative Literature?" *Essays in Memory of Barrett Wendell.* Ed. W.R. Castle Jr. and P. Kaufman. Cambridge: Harvard UP, 1926. 23–40.

Cao, Shunqing, ed. *Bijiao wenxüe shi (A History of Comparative Literature)*. Chengdu: Sichuan People's P, 1991.

Caramaschi, Enzo. "Pour une convergence de méthodes." *Sensus Communis: Contemporary Trends in Comparative Literature / Panorama de la situation actuelle en Littérature Comparée*. Ed. János Riesz, Peter Boerner, and Bernhard Scholz. Tübingen: Gunter Narr, 1986. 3–9.

Carré, Jean-Marie. "La Littérature comparée depuis un demisiècle." *Annales du Centre Universitaire Méditerranéen* 3 (1949–50): 69–77.

Carriere, Moritz. *Die Poesie. Ihr Wesen und ihre Formen mit Grundzügen der vergleichenden Literaturgeschichte*. 1854. Leipzig, 1884.

Carter, Erica, James Donald, and Judith Squires, eds. *Cultural Remix: Theories of Politics and the Popular*. London: Lawrence and Wishart, 1995.

Carvalhal, Tânia Franco. *Literatura comparada*. São Paolo: Editora Atica, 1986.

Carvalhal, Tânia Franco. "Comparare i comparatismi. La letteratura comparata in Americo Latina." Trans. Anna Trocchi. *Comparare i comparatismi. La comparatistica letteraria oggi in Europa e nel mondo*. Ed. Armando Gnisci and Franca Sinopoli. Roma: Lithos, 1995. 14–26.

Carvalhal, Tânia Franco. "Literatura comparada na América-Latina: contribuição para novos paradigmas." *Literature Comparada: Os novos paradigmas*. Ed. Margarida L. Losa, Isménia de Sousa, and Gonçalo Vilas-Boas. Porto: Afrontamento, 1996. 465–72.

Cassirer, Ernst. *The Logic of the Cultural Sciences: 5 Studies*. New Haven: Yale UP, 2000.

Cavell, Richard. "Same Difference: On the Hegemony of 'Language' and 'Literature' in Comparative Studies." *Comparative Literature: History and Contemporaneity / Littérature Comparée: Histoire et contemporanéité*. Ed. Milan V. Dimić and Steven Tötösy de Zepetnek. *Canadian Review of Comparative Literature / Revue Canadienne de Littérature Comparée* 23.1 (1996): 27–34.

Caws, Mary Ann. "What Are We About? For a Personal Criticism." *Comparative Literary History as Discourse*. Ed. Mario J. Valdés, Daniel Javitch, and A. Owen Aldridge. Bern: Peter Lang, 1992. 101–14.

Ceserani, Remo. "Gli studi di comparatistica: esperienze a confronto, difficoltà e prospettive." *Teoria e critica letteraria oggi*. Ed. R. Luperini. Milano: Angeli, 1991. 44–68.

Chambers, Leland H. "Comparative Literature Programs in the United States and Canada." *Yearbook of Comparative and General Literature* 31 (1982): 96–119.

Chandler, Frank W. "Comparative Literature: Is it Dead?" *Books Abroad: An International Library Quarterly* 10 (1936): 136–38.

Chandler, Frank W. "The Comparative Study of Literature." 1910. *Yearbook of Comparative and General Literature* 15 (1966): 50–62.

Chang, Han-liang, ed. *Concepts of Literary Theory East and West*. Taipei: Comparative Literature Association of the Republic of China / Bookman Books, 1993.

Chang, Lung-hsi. "Chien Chung-shu on Comparative Literature and Comparison of Literatures." *Peking University Comparative Literature Association Newsletter* 1.2 (1981): 4-11.

Charbonnel, Roger J. "Le Comparatisme et l'extension universitaire." *Revue internationale de l'enseignement* 74 (1920): 135–48.

Chasles, Philarète. "Foreign Literature Compared." 1835. *Comparative Literature: The Early Years.* Ed. Hans-Joachim Schulz and Phillip H. Rhein. Chapel Hill: U of North Carolina P, 1973. 13–37.

Chauvin, Danièle, and Yves Chevrel. *Introduction à la littérature comparée. Du commentaire à la dissertation.* Paris: Dunod, 1996.

Chellappan, K. "Comparative Literary Theory: An Indian Perspective." *Comparative Literature: Theory and Practice.* Ed. Amiya Dev and Sisir Kumar Das. Shimla: Indian Institute of Advanced Study, 1989. 295–306.

Chellappan, K. "Thematology of Comparative Indian Literature." *Aspects of Comparative Literature: Current Approaches.* Ed. Chandra Mohan. New Delhi: India Publishers and Distributors, 1989. 109–16.

Chen, Dun, Sun Jingyao, and Xie Tianzhen, eds. *Bijiao wenxüe (Comparative Literature).* Beijing: Higher Education P, 1997.

Chen, Peng-hsiang. *From Thematics to the "Chinese School" of Comparative Literature.* Taipei: Bookman Books, 1992.

Chen, Yuehong. "Cultural Barriers, Cultural Tradition and Cultural Interpretation: Misreading in Crosscultural Communication and Its Solution." *La Licorne et le dragon. Les malentendus dans la recherche de l'universel.* Ed. Yue Daiyun and Alain Le Pichon. Beijing: Peking UP and Transcultura, 1995. 145–58.

Chevigny, Bell Gale. "Teaching Comparative Literature of the United States and Spanish America." *American Literature: A Journal of Literary History, Criticism, and Bibliography* 65.2 (1993): 354–58.

Chevrel, Yves. "Littérature générale et comparée et rénovation des études de lettres." *L'Information Littéraire* 27.5 (1976): 231–40.

Chevrel, Yves. "Littérature générale et comparée en Europe: perspectives pour la formation des maîtres." *Documents pour le renseignement* 22.2 (1977): 13–20.

Chevrel, Yves. "Le Discours de la critique sur les oeuvres étrangères: Littérature comparée, esthétique de la réception et histoire littéraire nationale." *Romanistische Zeitschrift für Literaturgeschichte* 1 (1977): 336–52.

Chevrel, Yves. "The Teaching of Comparative Literature: Lessons of an ICLA Workshop." *Yearbook of Comparative and General Literature* 30 (1981): 77–83.

Chevrel, Yves. "Champs des études comparatistes de réception. Etat des recherches." *Oeuvres et critique: Revue internationale d'étude de la réception critiques des oeuvres littéraires de langue française* 11.2 (1986): 147–60.

Chevrel, Yves. *La littérature comparée.* Paris: PU de France, 1989.

Chevrel, Yves. "Multiple Points of View: A Study of French Comparative Literature Syllabi." *The Hospitable Canon: Essays on Literary Play, Scholarly*

Choice, and Popular Pressures. Ed. Virgil Nemoianu and Robert Royal. Philadelphia: Benjamins, 1991. 137–52.

Chevrel, Yves. "Une decennie (1981–1990) de travaux comparatistes d'expression française: Interrogations sur un bilan." *Europa Provincia Mundi: Essays in Comparative Literature and European Studies.* Ed. Joep Leerssen and Karl Ulrich Syndram. Amsterdam: Rodopi, 1992. 23–31.

Chevrel, Yves. *Comparative Literature Today: Methods and Perspectives.* Trans. Farida Elizabeth Dahab. Kirksville: The Thomas Jefferson UP, 1995.

Chevrel, Yves. "On the Need for New Comparative Literature Handbooks." *The Search for a New Alphabet: Literary Studies in a Changing World.* Ed. Harald Hendrix, Joost Kloek, Sophie Levie, and Will van Peer. Amsterdam: John Benjamins, 1996. 53–56.

Chevrel, Yves. "Littérature (générale et) comparée: La Situation de la France." *Comparative Literature World Wide: Issues and Methods / La Littérature comparée dans le monde: Questions et méthodes.* Ed. Tânia Franco Carvalhal. Porto Alegre: L&PM Editores, 1997. 53–79.

Chevrel, Yves. "Littérature comparée et histoire des mentalités. Concurrence ou collaboration?" *Comparative Literature Now: Theories and Practice / La Littérature comparée à l'heure actuelle. Théories et réalisations.* Ed. Steven Tötösy de Zepetnek, Milan V. Dimić, and Irene Sywenky. Paris: Honoré Champion, 1999. 51–63.

Chi, Ch'iu-lang. "The Concept of Sincerity and Impersonality: An Essay in Comparative Poetics." *Tamkang Review* 21.1 (1990): 75–91.

Chiimia, I.C., ed. *Studii de literatur universal i comparate (The Study of World Literature and Comparative Literature).* Bucuresti: Academia Republicii Socialiste Românâ, Institutul de istorie i teorie literar, 1970.

Cizevskij, Dmitrij. *Comparative History of Slavic Literatures.* Nashville: Vanderbilt UP, 2000.

Chow, Rey. "In the Name of Comparative Literature." *Comparative Literature in the Age of Multiculturalism.* Ed. Charles Bernheimer. Baltimore: Johns Hopkins UP, 1995. 107–16.

Chow, Rey. *Writing Diaspora: Tactics of Intervention in Contemporary Cultural Studies.* Indiana: Indiana UP, 1995.

Chrapcenko, M.B. "Typologische Literaturforschung und ihre Prinzipien." *Aktuelle Probleme der vergleichenden Literaturforschung.* Ed. Gerhard Ziegengeist. Berlin: Akademie, 1968. 17–46.

Christy, Arthur E. "A Guide to Comparative Literature." *Comparative Literature News-Letter* 2.2 (1943–44): 2–4.

Cioranescu, Alejandro. *Principios de literatura comparada.* Teneriffa: Universidad de La Laguna, 1964.

Clarke, Bruce, and Wendell Aycock. *The Body and the Text: Comparative Essays in Literature and Medicine.* Lubbock: Texas Tech UP, 1990.

Claudon, Francis. "La Littérature comparée et les arts." *Neohelicon: Acta Comparationis Litterarum Universarum* 16.1 (1989): 259–84.

Claudon, Francis. "Opera et littérature comparée." *Bologna, la cultura italiana e le letterature straniere moderne.* Ed. Vita Fortunati. Ravenna: Longo, 1992. Vol. 2, 397–402.

Claudon, Francis, and Karen Haddad-Wotling. *Précis de littérature comparée. Théories et méthodes de l'approche comparatiste.* Paris: Nathan, 1992.

Clements, Robert J. *Comparative Literature as Academic Discipline: A Statement of Principles, Praxis, Standards.* New York: Modern Language Association of America, 1978.

Clüver, Claus. "The Difference of Eight Decades: World Literature and the Demise of National Literatures." *Yearbook of Comparative and General Literature* 35 (1986): 14–24.

Cohen, Tom. *Ideology and Inscription: "Cultural Studies" after Benjamin, De Man, and Bakhtin.* Cambridge: Cambridge UP, 1998.

Cohen, Walter. "The Concept of World Literature." *Comparative Literature East and West: Traditions and Trends.* Ed. Cornelia Moore and Raymond A. Moody. Honolulu: U of Hawaii P, 1989. 3–10.

Coutinho, Eduardo F. "Literatura comparada na América Latina: do ethnocentrismo ao diálogo de culturas." *Literature Comparada: Os novos paradigmas.* Ed. Margarida L. Losa, Isménia de Sousa, and Gonçalo Vilas-Boas. Porto: Afrontamento, 1996. 133–38.

Coutinho, Eduardo, and Tânia Franco Carvalhal, eds. *Literatura comparada. Textos fundadores.* Rio de Janeiro: Rocco, 1994.

Corbineau-Hoffmann, Angelika. *Einführung in die Komparatistik.* Berlin: Erich Schmidt, 2000.

Cornea, Paul. *Introduzione alla teoria della lettura.* Ed. Gheorghe Carageani. Firenze: Sansoni, 1993.

Cornea, Paul. "La Littérature comparée en Roumanie." *Comparative Literature World Wide: Issues and Methods / La Littérature comparée dans le monde: Questions et méthodes.* Ed. Tânia Franco Carvalhal. Porto Alegre: L&PM Editores, 1997. 99–137.

Cornea, Paul. "Genres traditionnels de l'histoire littéraire à la recherche d'une nouvelle identité: Statut actuel de l'histoire de la littérature et de l'anthologie." *Comparative Literature Now: Theories and Practice / La Littérature comparée à l'heure actuelle. Théories et réalisations.* Ed. Steven Tötösy de Zepetnek, Milan V. Dimic, and Irene Sywenky. Paris: Honoré Champion, 1999. 307–17.

Corngold, Stanley. "Remembering Paul de Man: An Epoch in the History of Comparative Literature." *Building a Profession: Autobiographical Perspectives on the Beginnings of Comparative Literature in the United States.* Ed. Lionel Gossman and Mihai I. Spariosu. Albany: State U of New York P, 1994. 177–92.

Crabbe, P., ed. *Theory and Practice in Comparative Studies*. Sydney: Anzacs, 1983.

Croce, Benedetto. "Comparative Literature." 1903. *Comparative Literature: The Early Years*. Ed. Hans-Joachim Schulz and Phillip H. Rhein. Chapel Hill: U of North Carolina P, 1973. 215–23.

Crnkovic, Gordana. *Imagined Dialogues: Eastern European Literature in Conversation with American and English Literature*. Evanston: Northwestern UP, 2000.

Cubelic, Tvrtko. "Komparatizam, komparatisticki aspekt i komparatisticke koncepcije u proucavanju usmene narodne knjievnosti" ("Comparativism and Aspects and Concepts of Comparativism for the Study of Oral Folk Literature"). *Midwest Folklore* 2.3-4 (1969): 17–39.

Culler, Jonathan. "Comparative Literature and Literary Theory." *Michigan Germanic Studies* 5 (1979): 170–84.

Culler, Jonathan. "Comparative Literature and the Pieties." *Profession 1986: The Modern Language Association of America* (1986): 30–32.

Culler, Jonathan. "Comparative Literature, At Last!" *Comparative Literature in the Age of Multiculturalism*. Ed. Charles Bernheimer. Baltimore: Johns Hopkins UP, 1995. 117–21.

Culler, Jonathan. "Comparability." *World Literature Today* 69.2 (1995): 268–70.

Culler, Jonathan. "The Fortunes of the Performative in Literary and Cultural Theory." *Literature & Psychology*. 45 1-2. (1999):7–28.

Curtius, Ernst Robert. "Antike Rhetorik und Vergleichende Literaturwissenschaft." *Comparative Literature* 1 (1949): 24–43.

Cvetkovich, Ann, and David Kellner, eds. *Articulating the Global and the Local: Globalization and Cultural Studies*. Colorado: Westview P, 1997.

Daalder, Joost. "National, International, and Comparative Literary Approaches: What We Are About?" *Council of National Literatures: Quarterly World Report* 2.4 (1979): 4–6.

Dallmayr, Fred. *Beyond Orientalism: Essays on Cross-Cultural Encounter*. New York: State U of New York P, 1996.

Damblemont, Gerhard. "Komparatistik in Rumänien." *arcadia: Zeitschrift für Vergleichende Literaturwissenschaft* 25.1 (1990): 80–97.

Damrosch, David. "Literary Study in an Elliptical Age." *Comparative Literature in the Age of Multiculturalism*. Ed. Charles Bernheimer. Baltimore: Johns Hopkins UP, 1995. 122–33.

Danneberg, Lutz, and Jörg Schönert. "Zur Transnationalität und Internationalisierung von Wissenschaft." *Wie international ist die Literaturwissenschaft?* Ed. Lutz Danneberg, Friedrich Vollhardt, Hartmut Böhme, and Jörg Schönert. Stuttgart: Metzler, 1996. 7–85.

Das, Sisir Kumar. "Comparative Literature in India: A Historical Perspective." *Aspects of Comparative Literature: Current Approaches*. Ed. Chandra Mohan. New Delhi: India Publishers & Distributors, 1989. 1–14.

Das, Sisir Kumar. "Why Comparative Indian Literature?" *Comparative Literature: Theory and Practice*. Ed. Amiya Dev and Sisir Kumar Das. Shimla: Indian Institute of Advanced Study, 1989. 94–103.

Dasgupta, Subha. "The French School of Comparative Literature." *Comparative Literature: Theory and Practice*. Ed. Amiya Dev and Sisir Kumar Das. Shimla: Indian Institute of Advanced Study, 1989. 19–26.

Davidson, Olga. *Comparative Literature and Classical Persian Poetics: Seven Essays*. California. Mazda Publishing, 1999.

Davies, Ioan. *Cultural Studies and Beyond: Fragments of an Empire*. London: Routledge, 1995.

Deanovic, Mirko. "La Littérature comparée et les pays slaves." *Comparative Literature: Proceedings of the IInd Congress of the International Comparative Literature Association*. Ed. Werner P. Friederich. Chapel Hill: U of North Carolina P, 1959. Vol. 1, 70–79.

Dédéyan, Charles. *Le Critique en voyage ou esquisse d'une histoire littéraire comparée*. Paris: Éditions Techniques, 1985.

Deeney, John J. "Comparative Literature Studies in Taiwan." *Tamkang Review* 1.1. (1970): 119–45.

Deeney, John J. "Comparative Literature Activities in Taiwan." *Tamkang Review* 4.1 (1975): 189–202.

Deeney, John J. "Some Reflections on the History of Comparative Literature in China." *Tamkang Review* 6.2 (1975–76): 219–28.

Deeney, John J. "Modern Developments in Chinese-Western Comparative Literature Studies: A Golden Decade (1977–87) for the 'Chinese School'." *Tamkang Review* 18.1-4 (1987–88): 39–64.

Deeney, John J. "Poetics Chinese Style." *Comparative Literary Theory: New Perspectives*. Ed. Anne Paolucci. *Review of National Literatures* 15. New York: Griffon House Publications, 1989. 78–109.

Deeney, John J. "The Chinese Comparative Literature Scene: Implications for Regional and International Developments." *Inter-Asian Comparative Literature*. Ed. Kawamoto Koji, Heh-Hsiang Yuan, and Ohsawa Yoshihiro. Tokyo: U of Tokyo P, 1995. 213–21.

Deeney, John J., ed. *Chinese-Western Comparative Literature Theory and Strategy*. Hong-Kong: The Chinese UP, 1980.

Desonay, Fernand. "Littérature comparée." *Revue Belge de Philologie et d'Histoire* 9 (1930): 307–36.

Desvignes, Lucette. "En guise d'éditorial: Défense du comparatisme." *Travaux comparatistes*. Ed. Lucette Desvignes. Saint-Etienne: Centre d'Etudes Comparatistes et de Recherche sur l'Expression Dramatique, U de Saint-Etienne, 1978. 5–20.

Deugd, Corn de. *De Eenheid van het comparatisme*. Utrecht: Instituut voor Vergelijkend Literatuuronderzoek, Utrecht U, 1962.

Dev, Amiya. "Literary History and Comparative Literature: A Methodological Question." *Jadavpur Journal of Comparative literature* 15 (1977): 76–84.

Dev, Amiya. *The Idea of Comparative Literature in India.* Calcutta: Papyrus, 1984.

Dev, Amiya. "The Concept of 'Influence' in the Indian Context." *Sensus Communis: Contemporary Trends in Comparative Literature / Panorama de la situation actuelle en Littérature Comparée.* Ed. János Riesz, Peter Boerner, and Bernhard Scholz. Tübingen: Gunter Narr, 1986. 227–35.

Dev, Amiya. "Towards Comparative Indian Literature." *Aspects of Comparative Literature: Current Approaches.* Ed. Chandra Mohan. New Delhi: India Publishers & Distributors, 1989. 35–45.

Dev, Amiya. "Literary History from Below." *Comparative Literature: Theory and Practice.* Ed. Amiya Dev and Sisir Kumar Das. Shimla: Indian Institute of Advanced Study, 1989. 319–28.

Dev, Amiya. "Literary History, Literary Theory and Comparative Literature." *Neohelicon: Acta Comparationis Litterarum Universarum* 20.2 (1993): 23–29.

Dev, Amiya. "Globalization and Literary Value." *The Search for a New Alphabet: Literary Studies in a Changing World.* Ed. Harald Hendrix, Joost Kloek, Sophie Levie, and Will van Peer. Amsterdam: John Benjamins, 1996. 62–66.

Dev, Amiya. "Comparative Literature in India." *Comparative Literature and Comparative Cultural Studies.* Ed. Steven Tötösy de Zepetnek. West Lafayette: Purdue UP, 2002. 23–33.

Devy, G.N. "The Commonwealth 'Period' and Comparative Literature." *Aspects of Comparative Literature: Current Approaches.* Ed. Chandra Mohan. New Delhi: India Publishers and Distributors, 1989. 144–53.

Dima, Alexandru. *Principii de literatur comparate (Principles of Comparative Literature).* Bucuresti: Pentru Literaturá, 1969.

Dima, Alexandru. *Principy sravnitel'nogo literaturovedenija (Principles of Comparative Literature).* Trans. M.W. Fridman. Moskva: Progress, 1977.

Dima, Alexandru. "Propositions en vue d'une systématization des domaines de la littérature comparée." *Actes du VIIIe Congres de l'Association Internationale de Littérature Comparée / Proceedings of the VIIIth Congress of the International Comparative Literature Association.* Ed. Béla Köpeczi and György M. Vajda. Stuttgart: Bieber, 1980. Vol. 2, 523–26.

Dimić, Milan V. "La Littérature comparée d'après les nouvelles introductions à cette discipline." *Filoloski pregled / Revue de Philologie* 8.1-4 (1970): 169–86.

Dimić, Milan V. "Valeurs esthétiques et histoire comparée des littératures." *Neohelicon: Acta Comparationis Litterarum Universarum* 1.1-2 (1973): 86–93.

Dimić, Milan V. "Comparative Literature in Canada." *Neohelicon: Acta Comparationis Litterarum Universarum* 12.1 (1985): 59–74.

Dimić, Milan. V. "Comparative Literature." *The Canadian Encyclopedia.* Ed. James H. Marsch. 4 vols. Edmonton: Hurtig, 1988. Vol 1, 477–78.

Dimić, Milan V. "Littératures canadiennes comparées: modèles d'étude proposés." *Histoire littéraire. Théories, méthodes, pratiques.* Ed. Clément Moisan. Québec: PU Laval, 1989. 179–94.

Dornheim, Nicolás Jorge. "La literatura comparada en la Argentina." *Boletin de literatura comparada* 3.1-2 (1978): 17–47.

Dornheim, Nicolás Jorge. "Germanistik und Komparatistik in Lateinamerika: Aspekte einer fruchtbaren Kontroverse." *Kontroversen, alte und neue*. Ed. János Riesz. Tübingen: Niemeyer, 1986. 95–102.

Dorsey, John T. "National and Comparative Literature in Japan." *Comparative Literature East and West: Traditions and Trends*. Ed. Cornelia Moore and Raymond A. Moody. Honolulu: U of Hawaii P, 1989. 184–89.

Douglass, William, Carmelo Urza, and Linda White, eds. *Basque Cultural Studies*. Nevada: U of Nevada P, 2000.

Dufour, Pierre. "La Relation peinture/littérature: Notes pour un comparatisme interdisciplinaire." *Neohelicon: Acta Comparationis Litterarum Universarum* 5.1 (1977): 141–90.

Dugast, Jacques. "La Notion de littérature européenne." *Comparative Literature Now: Theories and Practice / La Littérature comparée à l'heure actuelle. Théories et réalisations*. Ed. Steven Tötösy de Zepetnek, Milan V. Dimić, and Irene Sywenky. Paris: Honoré Champion, 1999. 75–83.

Ďurišin, Dionýz. *Problémy literárnej komparatistiky (Problems in Comparative Literature)*. Bratislava: Slovenská akademia vied, 1967.

Ďurišin, Dionýz. *Sources and Systematics of Comparative Literature*. Trans. Peter Tkác. Bratislava: Univerzita Komenského, 1974.

Ďurišin, Dionýz. "Zu aktuellen Problemen der marxistisch-leninistischen Theorie der Vergleichenden Literaturwissenschaft." *Weimarer Beiträge* 21.2 (1975): 5–22.

Ďurišin, Dionýz. *Vergleichende Literaturforschung. Versuch eines methodisch-theoretischen Grundrisses*. 1972. Trans. Ludwig Richter. Berlin: Akademie, 1976.

Ďurišin, Dionýz. "Comparative Investigation in Literature and in Art." *Neohelicon: Acta Comparationis Litterarum Universarum* 5.1 (1977): 125–40.

Ďurišin, Dionýz. *Theory of Literary Comparatistics*. Trans. Jessie Kocmanová. Bratislava: Slovak Academy of Sciences, 1984.

Ďurišin, Dionýz. *Teória literárnej komparatistiký (Theory of Comparative Literature)*. 1975. Bratislava: Slovenský spisovatel', 1985.

Ďurišin, Dionýz. "The Limits and Possibilities of the Term 'Literary Comparatistics'." *Sensus Communis: Contemporary Trends in Comparative Literature / Panorama de la situation actuelle en Littérature Comparée*. Ed. János Riesz, Peter Boerner, and Bernhard Scholz. Tübingen: Gunter Narr, 1986. 237–44.

Ďurišin, Dionýz. *Theory of Interliterary Process*. Trans. Jessie Kocmanová and Zdenek Pistek. Bratislava: Slovak Academy of Sciences, 1989.

Duţu, Alexandru. "Niveaux temporels, niveaux culturels et comparaison littéraire." *Revue de Littérature Comparée* 56 (1982): 5–20.

Duţu, Alexandru. *Literatura comparat i istoria mentalitilor (Comparative Literature and History of Ideas)*. Bucuresti: Univers, 1982.

Dyserinck, Hugo. *Komparatistik. Eine Einführung*. Bonn: Bouvier, 1977.

Dyserinck, Hugo. "Über Möglichkeiten und Grenzen der Komparatistik." *Mainzer Komparatistische Hefte* 2 (1978): 15–25.

Dyserinck, Hugo. "Komparatistische Imagologie jenseits von 'Werkimmanenz' und 'Werktranszendenz'." *Synthesis: Bulletin du Comité National de Littérature Comparée de la Republique Socialiste de Roumanie* 9 (1982): 27–40.

Dyserinck, Hugo. "Komparatistische Imagologie. Zur politischen Tragweite einer europäischen Wissenschaft von der Literatur." *Europa und das nationale Selbstverständnis. Imagologische Probleme in Literatur, Kunst und Kultur des 19. und 20. Jahrhunderts*. Ed. Karl Ulrich Syndram and Hugo Dyserinck. Bonn: Bouvier, 1988. 13–37.

Dyserinck, Hugo. "Komparatistik als Europaforschung." *Komparatistik und Europaforschung. Perspektiven vergleichender Literatur- und Kulturwissenschaft*. Ed. Hugo Dyserinck and Karl Ulrich Syndram. Bonn: Aachener Beiträge zur Komparatistik, 1992.

Dyserinck, Hugo. "Betrachtungen zur Sonderstellung der innereuropäischen Grenz- und Überscheidungsregionen in ihrer Bedeutung für Komparatistik." *Celebrating Comparativism*. Ed. Katalin Kürtösi and József Pál. Szeged: József Attila U, 1994. 113–30.

Dyserinck, Hugo. "Il Punto di vista sovranazionale dello studio litterario comparato e la sua applicazione all'imagologia." Trans. Nora Moll. *Comparare i comparatismi. La comparatistica letteraria oggi in Europa e nel mondo*. Ed. Armando Gnisci and Franca Sinopoli. Roma: Lithos, 1995. 52–66.

Easthope, Anthony. *Literary into Cultural Studies*. London: Routledge, 1991.

Easthope, Anthony, and Kate McGowan, eds. *A Critical and Cultural Theory Reader*. Toronto: U of Toronto P, 1992.

Edebiri, U. "The African Dimension in Comparative Literature Studies." *Proceedings of the XIth Congress of the International Comparative Literature Association*. Ed. Gerald Gillespie. New York: Peter Lang, 1991. Vol. 5, 138–43.

Edgar, Andrew, ed. *Key Concepts in Cultural Theory*. New York: Routledge, 2000.

Egri, Peter. *Literature, Painting, and Music: An Interdisciplinary Approach to Comparative Literature*. New York: State Mutual Book and Periodical Service, 1988.

Elster, Ernst. "World Literature and Comparative Literature." 1901. *Yearbook of Comparative and General Literature* 35 (1986): 7–13.

Eoyang, Eugene Chen. *The Transparent Eye: Reflections on Translation, Chinese Literature, and Comparative Poetics*. Honolulu: U of Hawaii P, 1993.

Escarpit, Robert. "La Littérature comparée dans les universitiés françaises de provence." *Yearbook of Comparative and General Literature* 5 (1956): 8–12.

Escarpit, Robert. "De la Littérature comparée aux problèmes de la littérature de masse." *Etudes françaises* 2 (1966): 349–58.

Etiemble, René. *Comparaison n'est pas raison. La Crise de la littérature comparée*. Paris: Gallimard, 1963.

Etiemble, René. "Histoire des genres et littérature comparée." *La Littérature Comparée en Europe orientale*. Ed. István Sőtér, K. Bor, T. Klaniczay, and Gy.M. Vajda. Budapest: Akadémiai, 1963. 293–97.

Etiemble, René. *The Crisis in Comparative Literature*. Trans. Georges Joyaux and Herbert Weisinger. East Lansing: Michigan State UP, 1966.

Etiemble, René. "Faut-il réviser la notion de Weltliteratur?" *Actes du IVe Congrès de l'AILC / Proceedings of the IVth Congress of the ICLA*. Ed. François Jost. La Haye: Mouton, 1966. 5–16.

Etiemble, René. *Essais de littérature (vraiment) générale*. Paris: Gallimard, 1974.

Etiemble, René. *Quelques essais de littérature universelle*. Paris: Gallimard, 1982.

Etiemble, René. "Pour une littérature générale et comparée du monde fini." *La Recherche en littérature générale et comparée* (1983): 409–16.

Etiemble, René. *Ouverture(s) sur un comparatisme planétaire*. Paris: Christian Bourgois, 1988.

Etzioni, Amitai, and Fredric Dubow, eds. *Comparative Perspectives: Theories and Methods*. Boston: Little Brown, 1970.

Eupen, A.M.M.P. van. "The Growth of Comparative Literature in the Netherlands." *Yearbook of Comparative and General Literature* 4 (1955): 21–25.

Fáj, Attila. "Considerazioni sulla letteratura comparata." *Forum Italicum* 3 (1969): 337–54.

Farinelli, Arturo. "Gli influssi letterari e l'insuperbire delle nazioni." *Mélanges d'histoire littéraire générale et comparée offerts à Fernand Baldensperger*. Ed. Carlo Pellegrini. Paris: Champion, 1930. 271–90.

Ferraz, Maria de Lourdes. "Literatura comparada e teoria da literature: alguns motivos para discussão." *Dedalus: Revista Portuguesa de Literatura Comparada* 1 (1989): 47–53.

Fiedler, Leonhard M. "Zur gegenwärtigen Situation der Komparatistik. 7. Kongreß der Association Internationale de Littérature Comparée in Montréal und Ottawa." *Schweizer Monatshefte: Zeitschrift für Politik, Wirtschaft, Kultur* 53.2 (1973): 523–30.

Figueiredo, Fidelino de. "Comparative Literature and Source Criticism." *Yearbook of Comparative and General Literature* 34 (1984): 9–11.

Fiormonte, Domenico, and Jonathan Usher, eds. *New Media and The Humanities: Research and Applications*. Oxford: Humanities Computing Unit, U of Oxford, 2001.

Fischer, Manfred S. "The Single vs. the Comparative: A German Conflict." *Neohelicon: Acta Comparationis Litterarum Universarum* 15.1 (1988): 209–26.

Fiser, Ernest, and Franjo Grcevic, eds. *Komparativno proucavanje jugoslavenskih knjievnosti (Comparative Research on Yugoslav Literatures)*. Varasdin: "Gesta," 1987.

Flaker, Aleksandr. *Knjievne poredbe (Literary Comparisons)*. Zagreb: Naprijed, 1968.

Fleischmann, Wolfgang Bernhard. "Das Arbeitsgebiet der Vergleichenden Literaturwissenschaft." *arcadia: Zeitschrift für Vergleichende Literaturwissenschaft* 1 (1966): 221–30.

Flemming, Willi. "Weltliteratur; Encyclopädische Literaturvergleichung; Vergleichende Literaturbetrachtung; Weltliteratur. *Bausteine zur systematischen Literaturwissenschaft.* By Willi Flemming. Meiseheim: Hain, 1965. 18–26.

Fletcher, John. "The Criticism of Comparison: The Approach through Comparative Literature and Intellectual History." *Contemporary Criticism.* Ed. Malcolm Bradbury and David Palmer. London: Edward Arnold, 1970. 106–29.

Fletcher, John. "Comparative Literature and the Sociology of Art." *Cahiers Roumains d'Etudes Littéraires* 2 (1980): 55–66.

Fokkema, Douwe W. "Cultural Relativism and Comparative Literature." *Tamkang Review* 3.2 (1972): 59–63.

Fokkema, Douwe W. "Method and Programme of Comparative Literature." *Synthesis: Bulletin du Comité National de Littérature Comparée de la République Socialiste de Roumanie* 1 (1974): 51–63.

Fokkema, Douwe W. "Comparative Literature and the New Paradigm." *Canadian Review of Comparative Literature / Revue Canadienne de Littérature Comparée* 9 (1982): 1–18.

Fokkema, Douwe W. "Cultural Relativism Reconsidered: Comparative Literature and Intercultural Relations." *Douze cas d'interaction culturelle dans l'Europe ancienne et l'Orient proche ou lointain.* Paris: UNESCO, 1984. 239–55.

Fokkema, Douwe. *Issues in General and Comparative Literature.* Calcutta: Papyrus, 1987.

Fokkema, Douwe. "Towards a Methodology in Intercultural Studies." *Aspects of Comparative Literature: Current Approaches.* Ed. Chandra Mohan. New Delhi: India Publishers & Distributors, 1989. 117–130.

Fokkema, Douwe. "Can Cultural Knowledge and Cultural Conventions Be Taught and Learned? A Note on Cultural Identity." *Differential Multilogue: Comparative Lierrature and National Literatures.* Ed. Gurbhagat Singh. Delhi: Ajanta, 1991. 33–45.

Fokkema, Douwe. "Comparative Literature and the Problem of Canon Formation." *Comparative Literature: History and Contemporaneity / Littérature Comparée: Histoire et contemporanéité.* Ed. Milan V. Dimić and Steven Tötösy de Zepetnek. *Canadian Review of Comparative Literature / Revue Canadienne de Littérature Comparée* 23.1 (1996): 51–66.

Fokkema, Douwe. "Cultural Relativism and Cultural Identity: Contradictory Tendencies." *Comparative Literature Now: Theories and Practice / La Littérature comparée à l'heure actuelle. Théories et réalisations.* Ed. Steven Tötösy de Zepetnek, Milan V. Dimić, and Irene Sywenky. Paris: Honoré Champion, 1999. 85–93.

Folkierski, W. "Littérature comparée ou histoire littéraire nationale?" *Bulletin of the International Committee of Historical Sciences* 4 (1932): 126–32.

Forbes, Jill, and Michael Kelly, eds. *French Cultural Studies: An Introduction.* Oxford: Oxford UP, 1995.

Forgacs, David, and Robert Lumley, eds. *Italian Cultural Studies: An Introduction.* Oxford: Oxford UP, 1996.

Fornäs, Johan. *Cultural Theory & Late Modernity.* London: SAGE, 1995.

Foster, Gwendolyn. *Captive Bodies: Postcolonial Subjectivity in Cinema.* New York: State U of New York P, 1999.

Fox-Genovese, Elizabeth. "Between Elitism and Populism: Whither Comparative Literature?" *Comparative Literature in the Age of Multiculturalism.* Ed. Charles Bernheimer. Baltimore: Johns Hopkins UP, 1995. 134–42.

Franci, Giovanna, ed. *Remapping the Boundaries: A New Perspective in Comparative Studies.* Bologna: CLUEB, 1997.

Francoeur, Marie. *Confrontations. Jalons pour une sémiosis comparative des texts littéraires.* Sherbrooke: Naaman, 1985.

Fransen, J. *Iets over vergelijkende literatuurstudie, "perioden" en "invloeden."* Groningen: Wolters, 1936.

Frenz, Horst, and Newton Stallknecht, eds. *Comparative Literature: Method and Perspective.* Illinois: Southern Illinois UP, 1961.

Friederich, Werner P. "The Case of Comparative Literature." *AAUP Bulletin* 31 (1945): 208–219.

Friederich, Werner P. "Comparative Literature in Japan." *Yearbook of Comparative and General Literature* 4 (1955): 73–74.

Friederich, Werner P. "Zur Vergleichenden Literaturgeschichte in den Vereinigten Staaten." *Forschungsprobleme der Vergleichenden Literaturgeschichte.* Ed. Fritz Ernst and Kurt Wais. Tübingen: Niemeyer, 1958. 179–91.

Friederich, Werner P. *The Challenge of Comparative Literature from the Earliest Times to the Present Days.* Port Washington: Kennikat, 1970.

Friederich, Werner P., and David H. Malone. *Outline of Comparative Literature: From Dante to O'Neill.* Chapel Hill: U of North Carolina P, 1954.

Friggieri, Oliver. "Aspects of Comparative Literature." *Neohelicon: Acta Comparationis Litterarum Universarum* 24.2 (1997): 19–25.

Frow, John, and Meaghan Morris, eds. *Australian Cultural Studies: A Reader.* Urbana: U of Illinois P, 1993.

Frybes, Stanislaw. "Le Littératures slaves et la littérature comparée." *Littératures sans frontières.* Ed. Jacques Gaucheron and Philippe Ozouf. Clermont-Ferrand: Adosa, 1991. 75–80.

Fügen, Hans-Norbert, ed. *Vergleichende Literaturwissenschaft.* Düsseldorf: Econ, 1973.

Fürst, Lilian R. "Born to Compare." *Building a Profession: Autobiographical Perspectives on the Beginnings of Comparative Literature in the United States.* Ed. Lionel Gossman and Mihai I. Spariosu. Albany: State U of New York P, 1994. 107–24.

Gálik, Marián. "Comparative Literature in Soviet Oriental Studies." *Neohelicon: Acta Comparationis Litterarum Universarum* 3 (1975): 3–4.

Gálik, Marián. *Milestones in Sino-Western Literary Confrontation (1898–1979)*. Wiesbaden: O. Harrassowitz, 1986.

Gálik, Marián. "East-West Interliterariness: A Theoretical Sketch and a Historical Overview." *Comparative Literature: Theory and Practice*. Ed. Amiya Dev and Sisir Kumar Das. Shimla: Indian Institute of Advanced Study, 1989. 116–28.

Gálik, Marián. "Comparative Literature in Slovakia." *Comparative Literature: History and Contemporaneity / Littérature Comparée: Histoire et contemporanéité*. Ed. Milan V. Dimić and Steven Tötösy de Zepetnek. *Canadian Review of Comparative Literature / Revue Canadienne de Littérature Comparée* 23.1 (1996): 101–11.

Gálik, Marián. "Comparative Literature as Concept of Interliterariness and Interliterary Process." *Comparative Literature and Comparative Cultural Studies*. Ed. Steven Tötösy de Zepetnek. West Lafayette: Purdue UP, 2002. 34–44.

Garber, Marjorie, and Paul Franklin, eds. *Field Work: Sites in Literary and Cultural Studies*. New York: Routledge, 1996.

Gayley, Charles Mills. "What is Comparative Literature?" 1903. *Comparative Literature: The Early Years*. Ed. Hans-Joachim Schulz and Phillip H. Rhein. Chapel Hill: U of North Carolina P, 1973. 84–103.

Gayley, Charles Mills, and Fred Newton Scott. "Comparative Literature." *An Introduction to the Methods and Materials of Literary Criticism: The Basis in Aesthetics and Poetics*. By Charles Mills Gayley and Fred Newton Scott. Boston: Ginn and Co., 1899. 248–78.

Genot, Gerara. "Niveaux de la comparaison." *Actes du VIIIe Congres de l'Association Internationale de Littérature Comparée / Proceedings of the VIIIth Congress of the International Comparative Literature Association*. Ed. Béla Köpeczi and György M. Vajda. Stuttgart: Bieber, 1980. Vol. 2, 743–50.

Gérard, Albert S. "Sur la crise de croissance de la littérature comparée." *Revue des Langues Vivantes* 30 (1964): 533–43.

Gérard, Albert S. "New Frontier for Comparative Literature: Africa." *Komparatistische Hefte* 1 (1980): 8–13.

Gicovate, Bernardo. *Conceptos fundamentales de literatura comparada. Iniciación de la poesía modernista*. San Juan: Ediciones Asomante con la Universidade de Tulane, 1962.

Gifford, Henry. *Comparative Literature*. London: Routledge and Kegan Paul, 1969.

Gillespie, Gerald. "Elitist Dilemmas: Cultural Cross-Currents and Prospects of Comparative Studies on the National and Global Level." *Journal of Intercultural Studies* (Kansai U) 14 (1987): 116–23.

Gillespie, Gerald. "Newer Trends of Comparative Studies in the West." *Aspects of Comparative Literature: Current Approaches.* Ed. Chandra Mohan. New Delhi: India Publishers & Distributors, 1989. 17–34.

Gillespie, Gerald. "The 'Impossiblity' of Comparative Literature, or Coping with Cultural Diversity." *Differential Multilogue: Comparative Literrature and National Literatures.* Ed. Gurbhagat Singh. Delhi: Ajanta, 1991. 20–32.

Gillespie, Gerald. "Home Truths and Institutional Falsehoods." *Building a Profession: Autobiographical Perspectives on the Beginnings of Comparative Literature in the United States.* Ed. Lionel Gossman and Mihai I. Spariosu. Albany: State U of New York P, 1994. 159–75.

Gillespie, Gerald. "Comparative Literature of the 1990s in the USA." *Comparative Literature World Wide: Issues and Methods / La Littérature comparée dans le monde: Questions et méthodes.* Ed. Tânia Franco Carvalhal. Porto Alegre: L&PM Editores, 1997. 15–37.

Gillies, Alexander. "Some Thoughts on Comparative Literature." *Yearbook of Comparative and General Literature* 1 (1952): 15–25.

Giroux, Henry A. *Impure Acts: The Practical Politics of Cultural Studies.* New York: Routledge, 2000.

Gnisci, Armando. "Letteratura comparata: curricolo? Disciplina? Pratica didattica?" *Fare e sapere letterario. Il teatro della didattica.* Ed. C. Bartoccioni, M. Cambioni, S. Del Lungo Luzzi, A. Gnisci, A. Goldoni, and R. Mordenti. Roma: Carucci, 1986. 232–301.

Gnisci, Armando. *Appuntamenti. Saggi di letteratura comparata II.* Roma: Carucci, 1990.

Gnisci, Armando. *Appunti per un avviamento allo studio generale e comparato della letteratura.* Roma: Carucci, 1991.

Gnisci, Armando. "La littérature comparée comme discipline de la réciprocité." *Celebrating Comparativism.* Ed. Katalin Kürtösi and József Pál. Szeged: József Attila U, 1994. 69–76.

Gnisci, Armando. "La letteratura comparata in Italia." *Slumgullion. Saggi di letteratura comparata.* By Armando Gnisci. Roma: Sovera, 1994. 13–28.

Gnisci, Armando. "Comparare i comparatismi. Alcune considerazioni preliminari ai lavori del nostro seminario." *Comparare i comparatismi. La comparatistica letteraria oggi in Europa e nel mondo.* Ed. Armando Gnisci and Franca Sinopoli. Roma: Lithos, 1995. 9–13.

Gnisci, Armando. "Bisogna de-colonizzare noialtri europei da noi stessi, ma non da soli, ovvero la letteratura comparata come disciplina della reciprocità." *Letteratura comparata. Storia e testi.* Ed. Armando Gnisci and Franca Sinopoli. Roma: Sovera Multimedia, 1995. 205–18.

Gnisci, Armando. "La Littérature comparée comme discipline de décolonisation." *Comparative Literature: History and Contemporaneity / Littérature Comparée: Histore et contemporanéité.* Ed. Milan V. Dimić and Steven Tötösy de

Zepetnek. *Canadian Review of Comparative Literature / Revue Canadienne de Littérature Comparée* 23.1 (1996): 67–73.

Gnisci, Armando, ed. *Introduzione alla letteratura comparata*. Milano: Bruno Mondadori, 1999.

Gnisci, Armando, and Franca Sinopoli, eds. *Letteratura comparata. Storia e testi*. Roma: Sovera Multimedia, 1995.

Gnisci, Armando, and Franca Sinopoli, eds. *Manuale storico di letterature comparata*. Roma: Meltemi, 1997.

Gobbers, Walter. "Hoever staan we met het komparatisme? *Wetenschappelijke Tijdingen* 16 (1956): 11–20.

Godzich, Wlad. "Emergent Literature and the Field of Comparative Literature." *The Culture of Literacy*. By Wlad Godzich. Cambridge: Harvard UP, 1994. 274–92.

González Echevarría, Roberto. "Latin American and Comparative Literatures." *Language and Literature Today*. Ed. Neide de Faria. Brasília: U of Brasília, 1996. 1017–29.

Goodwin, Sarah Webster. "Cross Fire and Collaboration among Comparative Literature, Feminism, and the New Historicism." *Borderwork: Feminist Engagements with Comparative Literature*. Ed. Margaret R. Higonnet. Ithaca: Cornell UP, 1994. 247–66.

Gordon, Paul. "Romanticism, Figuration and Comparative Literature." *Neohelicon: Acta Comparationis Litterarum Universarum* 15.2 (1988): 239–59.

Gorp, Hendrik van, and John Neubauer. "Comparative Literature in the Low Countries: Issues and Methods." *Comparative Literature World Wide: Issues and Methods / La Littérature comparée dans le monde: Questions et méthodes*. Ed. Tânia Franco Carvalhal. Porto Alegre: L&PM Editores, 1997. 233–49.

Gossman, Lionel. "Out of a Gothic North." *Building a Profession: Autobiographical Perspectives on the Beginnings of Comparative Literature in the United States*. Ed. Lionel Gossman and Mihai I. Spariosu. Albany: State U of New York P, 1994. 193–204.

Görling, Reinhold. "Diskurs (I)." *Heterotopia. Lektüren einer interkulturellen Literaturwissenschaft*. By Reinhold Görling. München: Fink, 1997. 49–66.

Grabovszki, Ernst. "The Impact of Globalization and the New Media on the Notion of World Literature." *Comparative Literature and Comparative Cultural Studies*. Ed. Steven Tötösy de Zepetnek. West Lafayette: Purdue UP, 2002. 45–57.

Graf, A. *Storia letteraria e comparazione. Prolusione al corso di storia comparata delle letterature neolatine*. Torino: U di Torino, 1876.

Graham, Helen, and Jo Labanyi, eds. *Spanish Cultural Studies: An Introduction*. Oxford: Oxford UP, 1996.

Grant, Colin B. *Functions and Fictions of Communication*. Bern: Peter Lang, 2000.

Gray, Ann, and Jim McGuigan. *Studying Culture: An Introductory Reader*. London: Arnold, 1993.

Grcevic, Franjo. "Début de l'étude comparée des littératures yougoslaves." *Osobitné medziliterárne spolocenstvá 3 / Communautés interlittéraires spécifiques 3*. Bratislava: Slovenská Akadémia Vied, 1991. 60–65.

Greene, Roland. "Their Generation." *Comparative Literature in the Age of Multiculturalism*. Ed. Charles Bernheimer. Baltimore: Johns Hopkins UP, 1995. 143–54.

Greene, Roland. "American Comparative Literature: Reticence and Articulation." *World Literature Today* 69.2 (1995): 293–98.

Greene, Thomas M. "Language and the Scattered Word." *Comparative Literary History as Discourse*. Ed. Mario J. Valdés, Daniel Javitch, and A. Owen Aldridge. Bern: Peter Lang, 1992. 81–100.

Greene, Thomas M. "Versions of a Discipline." *Building a Profession: Autobiographical Perspectives on the Beginnings of Comparative Literature in the United States*. Ed. Lionel Gossman and Mihai I. Spariosu. Albany: State U of New York P, 1994. 37–48.

Groden, Michael, and Martin Kreiswirth, eds. *The Johns Hopkins Guide to Literary Theory and Criticism*. Baltimore: The Johns Hopkins UP, 1994.

Grossberg, Lawrence, Cary Nelson, and Paula Treichler, eds. *Cultural Studies*. New York: Routlefdge, 1992.

Gsteiger, Manfred. "Theorie und Praxis der vergleichenden Literaturwissenschaft." *Schweizer Monatshefte* 48 (1968–69): 1127–33.

Gsteiger, Manfred. "Zum Begriff und über das Studium der Literatur in vergleichender Sicht." *Zur Theorie der Vergleichenden Literaturwissenschaft*. Ed. Horst Rüdiger, G. Bauer, E. Koppen, and M. Gsteiger. Berlin: de Gruyter, 1971. 65–85.

Gsteiger, Manfred. "Pourquoi la littérature comparée?" *Etudes des Lettres* 3.7 (1974): 1–14.

Gual, Carlos García. "Sur les études de littérature comparée en Espagne et leur perspectives actuelles (quelques remarques générales)." *Comparative Literature World Wide: Issues and Methods / La Littérature comparée dans le monde: Questions et méthodes*. Ed. Tânia Franco Carvalhal. Porto Alegre: L&PM Editores, 1997. 273–81.

Guérard, Albert J. "Comparative Literature?" *Yearbook of Comparative and General Literature* 7 (1958): 1–6.

Guérard, Albert J. "Comparative Literature, Modern Thought and Literature." *Building a Profession: Autobiographical Perspectives on the Beginnings of Comparative Literature in the United States*. Ed. Lionel Gossman and Mihai I. Spariosu. Albany: State U of New York P, 1994. 89–97.

Guha, Naresh, ed. *Contribution to Comparative literature: Germany and India*. Calcutta: Jadavpur UP, 1973.

Guillén, Claudio. "Sobra la vocación del comparatista." *Comparative Literary Studies*. Ed. István Fried, Zoltán Kanyó, and József Pál. Szeged: József Attila U, 1983. 47–55.

Guillén, Claudio. *Entre lo uno et lo diverso: Introducción a la literatura comparada.* Barcelona: Editorial Crítica, 1985.

Guillén, Claudio. *The Challenge of Comparative Literature.* Trans. Cola Franzen. Cambridge: Harvard UP, 1993.

Guyard, Marius-François. *La Littérature comparée.* 1951. Paris: PU de France, 1978.

Habermas, Jürgen. *The New Conservatism: Cultural Criticism and the Historians' Debate.* New York: MIT Press, 1990.

Halász, Előd. "Romanmodelle und Vergleichende Literaturwissenschaft." *Acta Litteraria* 5 (1962): 213–23.

Hallam, Elizabeth, and Brian Street, eds. *Cultural Encounters: Representing Otherness.* New York: Routledge, 2000.

Halman, Talat S. "Comparative Literature Prospects for Turkey and the Islamic World." *Council on National Literatures Report* 5 (1976): 3.

Haney, William S., and Nicholas Pagan, eds. *The Changing Face of English Literary and Cultural Studies in a Transnational Environment.* Lewiston: Edwin Mellen, 1999.

Hankiss, Jean. "Littérature universelle?" *Helicon* 1 (1938): 156–71.

Hankiss, Jean. "La Terminologie d'histoire littéraire et les littératures comparées." *Neophilologus* 23 (1937–38): 365–69.

Hankiss, János. "Theorie de la littérature et littérature comparée." *Comparative Literature: Proceedings of the Second Congress of the ICLA.* Ed. W.P. Friederich. 2 vols. Chapel Hill: U of North Carolina P, 1959. 2, 98–112.

Harris, Michael. *Outsiders and Insiders: Perspectives of Third World Culture in British and Post-Colonial Fiction.* New York: Peter Lang, 1992.

Hart, Jonathan. "A Comparative Pluralism: The Heterogeneity of Methods and the Case of Fictional Worlds." *Canadian Review of Comparative Literature / Revue Canadienne de Littérature Comparée* 14.3-4 (1988): 320–45.

Hart, Jonathan. "The Ever-Changing Configurations of Comparative Literature." *Canadian Review of Comparative Literature / Revue Canadienne de littérature comparée* 19.1-2 (1992): 1–20.

Hart, Thomas R. "Comparative Literature, CL, and I." *Building a Profession: Autobiographical Perspectives on the Beginnings of Comparative Literature in the United States.* Ed. Lionel Gossman and Mihai I. Spariosu. Albany: State U of New York P, 1994. 99–106.

Hatzfeld, Helmut. "Comparative Literature as a Necessary Method." *The Disciplines of Criticism: Essays in Literary Theory, Interpretation, and History.* Ed. Peter Demetz, Thomas Greene, and Lowry Nelson Jr. New Haven: Yale UP, 1968. 79–92.

Hays, Edna. "Comparative Literature in American Universities." *Comparative Literature News-Letter* 2.1 (1943): 2–4.

Hazard, Paul. "La littérature comparée." *La Civilisation française* 1 (1919): 346–52.

Herman, Andrew, and Thomas Swiss, eds. *The World Wide Web and Contemporary Cultural Theory: Magic, Metaphor, Power.* New York: Routledge, 2000.

Hernadi, Paul. "What Isn't Comparative Literature?" *Profession 1986: The Modern Language Association of America* (1986): 22–24.

Highet, Gilbert. *The Classical Tradition: Greek and Roman Influences on Western Literature.* New York: Oxford UP, 1985.

Higonnet, Margaret R. "Comparative Literature on the Feminist Edge." *Comparative Literature in the Age of Multiculturalism.* Ed. Charles Bernheimer. Baltimore: Johns Hopkins UP, 1995. 155–64.

Higonnet, Margaret R., ed. *Borderwork: Feminist Engagements with Comparative Literature.* Ithaca: Cornell UP, 1995.

Hill, Muhammad Ghunayami. *Comparative Literature in Contemporary Arabic Literature.* Cairo: n.p., 1962.

Hirth, Friedrich. "Vom Geiste vergleichender Literaturwissenschaft." *Universitas* 2 (1947): 1301–20.

Ho, Koon Ki T. "The Application of the Structuralist Approach in East-West Comparative Literature: Problems and Prospects." *Tamkang Review* 14.1-4 (1983–84): 297–324.

Hogan, Patrick. *Philosophical Approaches to the Study of Literature.* Gainesville: UP of Florida, 2000.

Hokenson, Jan Walsh. "Comparative Literature and the Culture of the Context." *Comparative Literature and Comparative Cultural Studies.* Ed. Steven Tötösy de Zepetnek. West Lafayette: Purdue UP, 2002. 58–75.

Holdheim, Wolfgang W. "Komparatistik und Literaturtheorie." *arcadia: Zeitschrift für Vergleichende Literaturwissenschaft* 7 (1972): 297–303.

Höllerer, Walter. "Methoden und Probleme der vergleichenden Literaturwissenschaft." *Germanisch-Romanische Monatsschrift* (Neue Folge) 2 (1952): 116–31.

Höllerer, Walter. "Die Vergleichende Literaturwissenschaft in Deutschland nach dem Kriege." *Rivista di letterature moderne* 3 (1952): 285–99.

Holloway, Karla. *Moorings & Metaphors: Figures of Culture and Gender in Black Women's Literature.* New Jersey: Rutgers UP, 1992.

Holmes, Urban T. "Comparative Literature, Past and Future." *Studies in Language and Literature.* Ed. G.R. Coffmann. Chapel Hill: U of North Carolina P, 1945. 62–75.

Holquist, Michael. "A New Tower of Babel: Recent Trends Linking Comparative Literature Departments, Foreign Language Departments, and Area Studies Programs." *Profession 1996: The Modern Language Association of America* (1996): 103–14.

Horn, David G. "Reading Theory: Toward a Comparative Cultural Studies. A Review Article." *Comparative Studies in Society and History* 39.4 (1997): 734–41.

Horwath, Peter, William L. Hendrickson, L. Teresa Valdivieso, and Eric P. Thor, eds. *Humanism and the Good Life: Proceedings of the Fifteenth Congress of the World Federation of Humanists*. New York: Peter Lang, 1998.

Hrabák, Josef. *Literárni komparatistika (Comparative Literature)*. Praha: Státní pedagogické nakladatelstvi, 1976.

Hutcheon, Linda. "Comparative Literature's 'Anxiogenic' State." *Comparative Literature: History and Contemporaneity / Littérature Comparée: Histoire et contemporanéité*. Ed. Milan V. Dimić and Steven Tötösy de Zepetnek. *Canadian Review of Comparative Literature / Revue Canadienne de Littérature Comparée* 23.1 (1996): 35–41.

Hyun, Theresa. "Comparative Literature in Korea." *Comparative Literature World Wide: Issues and Methods / La Littérature comparée dans le monde: Questions et méthodes*. Ed. Tânia Franco Carvalhal. Porto Alegre: L&PM Editores, 1997. 197–209.

Idris, Muhammad Jala'. *Al-Adab al-muqaran: qadaya wa-tatbiqat (Comparative Literature: Theories and Practice)*. Cairo: Dar al-Thaqafah al-'Arabiyah, 2000.

Ifekwunigwe, Jayne. *Scattered Belongings: Cultural Paradoxes of Race, Nation and Gender*. New York: Routledge, 1998.

Inglis, Fred. *Cultural Studies*. Oxford: Blackwell, 1993.

Isstaif, Abdul-Nabi. "Beyond the Notion of Influence: Notes Toward an Alternative." *World Literature Today* 69.2 (1995): 281–86.

Jackson, Barry. *Art, Culture, and the Semiotics of Meaning: Culture's Changing Signs of Life in Poetry, Drama, Painting, and Sculpture*. New York: St. Martin's P, 1999.

Jackson, Richard. *Black Writers and Latin America: Cross-Cultural Affinities*. Washington: Howard UP, 1998.

Jain, Nirmala. "Comparative Literature: The Indian Context." *Comparative Literature: Theory and Practice*. Ed. Amiya Dev and Sisir Kumar Das. Shimla: Indian Institute of Advanced Study, 1989. 79–86.

Jan, Eduard von. "Französische Literaturgeschichte und vergleichende Literaturbetrachtung." *Germanisch-Romanische Monatsschrift* 15 (1927): 305–17.

Jantz, Harold S. "The Fathers of Comparative Literature." *Books Abroad: An International Library Quarterly* 10 (1936): 401–03.

Jenks, Chris. *Culture: Key Ideas*. London: Routledge, 1993.

Jenks, Chris, ed. *Cultural Reproduction*. London: Routledge, 1993.

Jeune, Simon. *Littérature générale et littérature comparée. Essai d'orientation*. Paris: Minard, 1968.

Johansen, Jorgen Dines. "Semiotics and Comparative Literature." *Sensus Communis: Contemporary Trends in Comparative Literature / Panorama de la situation actuelle en Littérature Comparée*. Ed. János Riesz, Peter Boerner, and Bernhard Scholz. Tübingen: Gunter Narr, 1986. 23–38.

Johansen, Jorgen Dines. "Literary Theory: Parochial or Universal?" *Differential Multilogue: Comparative Literrature and National Literatures*. Ed. Gurbhagat Singh. Delhi: Ajanta, 1991. 99–111.

Joliat, Eugene. "The Present Situation in National and International Comparative Literature Associations." *Comparative Literature in Canada / Littérature Comparée au Canada* 1.1 (1969): 3–7.

Jon, Kyu-T'ae. *Pigyo Munhakgwa Pigyo Munhwa* (*Comparative Literature and Comparative Culture*). Seoul: Bando Ch'ulp'an Sa, 1984.

Jones, M. "Schiller, Goebbels, and Paul de Man: The Dangers of Comparative Studies." *Mosaic: A Journal for the Interdisciplinary Study of Literature* 32.4 (1999): 53–72.

Jost, François. "La Littérature comparée en Suisse." *Comparative Literature: Proceedings of the IInd Congress of the International Comparative Literature Association.* Ed. Werner P. Friederich. Chapel Hill: U of North Carolina P, 1959. Vol. 1, 62–70.

Jost, François. "La Littérature comparée, une philosophie des lettres." *Essais de littérature comparée.* By François Jost. Fribourg: Editions Universitaires, 1964.

Jost, François. "Littérature comparée et littérature universelle." *Orbis litterarum* 27 (1972): 13–27.

Jost, François. *Introduction to Comparative Literature.* Indianapolis: Pegasus, 1974.

Jost, François. "Le Comparativisme: Chemin faisant." *Bologna, la cultura italiana e le letterature straniere moderne.* Ed. Vita Fortunati. Ravenna: Longo, 1992. Vol. 2, 75–78.

Juvan, Marko. "On Literariness: From Post-structuralism to Systems Theory." *Comparative Literature and Comparative Cultural Studies.* Ed. Steven Tötösy de Zepetnek. West Lafayette: Purdue UP, 2002. 76–96.

Kaiser, Gerhard R. *Einführung in die Vergleichende Literaturwissenschaft. Forschungsstand—Kritik—Aufgaben.* Darmstadt: Wissenschaftliche Buchgesellschaft, 1980.

Kalff, G. "Algemeene en vergelijkende letterkunde." *Vragen des Tijds* 1 (1916): 451–76.

Kamei, Shun'suke. "Hikaku bungaku no tenbou" ("Panorama of Comparative Literature"). *Hikaku bungaku* (*Comparative Literature*). Ed. Haga Toru et al. Tokyo: U of Tokyo P, 1976. Vol. 8, 1–20.

Kao, Karl Y.S. "Comparative Literature and the Ideology of Metaphor, East and West." *Comparative Literature and Comparative Cultural Studies.* Ed. Steven Tötösy de Zepetnek. West Lafayette: Purdue UP, 2002. 97–110.

Kappler, Arno. *Der literarische Vergleich. Beiträge zu einer Vorgeschichte der Komparatistik.* Bern: Peter Lang, 1976.

Kelly, Catriona, and David Shepherd, eds. *Russian Cultural Studies: An Introduction.* London: Oxford UP, 1998.

Kennedy, George. *Comparative Rhetoric: An Historical and Cross-Cultural Introduction.* Oxford: Oxford UP, 1997.

Kim, Hak-Dong. *Pigyo Munhak Non* (*Theory of Comparative Literature*). Seoul: Saemun Sa, 1990.

King, Bruce. "The New Literatures: Some Implications." *Comparative Literary Theory: New Perspectives*. Ed. Anne Paolucci. *Review of National Literatures 15*. New York: Griffon House Publications, 1989. 56–77.

King, Geoff. *Mapping Reality: An Exploration of Cultural Cartographies*. New York: St. Martin's P, 1996.

Kirby, John T. *The Comparative Reader: A Handlist of Basic Reading in Comparative Literature*. New Haven: Chancery P, 1998.

Kleen de Hinojosa, Elisabeth. "Literatura Comparada. Breve exposición de su historia, definición, método y otros aspectos." *Humanitas 8* (1967): 241–55.

Klinghorn, A.M. "Comparative Literature and the 'Universal' Ideal." *Neophilologus 66.1* (1982): 1–15.

Klaniczay, Tibor. "Les possibilités d'une littérature comparée de l'Europe orientale." *Europe orientale* (1963): 115–27.

Klein, Holger. "Areas, Objectives and Alignments in the Study of Literature." *Differential Multilogue: Comparative Literrrature and National Literatures*. Ed. Gurbhagat Singh. Delhi: Ajanta, 1991. 71–78.

Kobayashi, Tadashi. *Hikaku Bungaku nyumon (Introduction to Comparative Literature)*. Tokyo: U of Tokyo P, 1971.

Koch, Max. "Introduction." 1887. *Comparative Literature: The Early Years*. Ed. Hans-Joachim Schulz and Phillip H. Rhein. Chapel Hill: U of North Carolina P, 1973. 63–77.

Kogoj-Kapetanic, Breda. "Komparativna istraivanja u hrvatskoj knjievnosti" ("Comparative Research in Croatian Literature"). *Rad 350: Odjel za suvremenu knjievnost 10 (Volume 350: Department of Contemporary Literature 10)*. Zagreb: Jugoslavenska Akademija Znanosti i Umjetnosti, 1968. 305–404.

Komar, Kathleen L. "The State of Comparative Literature: Theory and Practice 1994." *World Literature Today 69.2* (1995): 287–92.

Komar, Kathleen L. "Feminist/Comparatists and the Art of 'Resisting Teaching'." *New Visions of Creation: Feminist Innovations in Literary Theory*. Ed. María Elena de Valdés and Margaret R. Higonnet. Tokyo: U of Tokyo P, 1995. 180–86.

Konrad, K.I. "Contemporary Comparative Literature: A Soviet View." *Aspects of Comparative Literature: Current Approaches*. Ed. Chandra Mohan. New Delhi: India Publishers & Distributors, 1989. 65–81.

Konstantinović, Zoran. *Grundlagentexte der Vergleichenden Literaturwissenschaft aus drei Jahrzehnten*. Selected and Ed. Beate Burtscher-Bechter, Beate Eder-Jordan, Fridrun Rinner, Martin Sexl, and Klaus Zerinschek. Innsbruck: Studien, 2000.

Köpeczi, Béla. "La Méthode comparatives et les littératures contemporaines des pays socialistes européens." *Europe orientale* (1963): 129–32.

Koppen, Erwin. "Hat die Vergleichende Literaturwissenschaft eine eigene Theorie? Ein Exempel: Der literarische Einfluß." *Zur Theorie der Vergleichenden*

Literaturwissenschaft. Ed. Horst Rüdiger, G. Bauer, E. Koppen, and M. Gsteiger. Berlin: de Gruyter, 1971. 41–64.

Koppen, Erwin. "Die Vergleichende Literaturwissenschaft als akademisches Fach." *Mainzer Komparatistische Hefte* 2 (1978): 26–38.

Koren, E. *Comparative Literature and Literary Scholarship.* Ljubljana: Institute for Slovene Literature and Literary Science, 1990.

Kos, Janko. *The Theory and Practice of Slovene Comparative Literature.* Ljubljana: Institute for Slovene Literature and Literary Science, 1978.

Kos, Janko. "The Theory and Practice of Comparative Literature in Slovenia." *Primerjalna knjievnost* 17.1 (1994): 3–16.

Koshy, K.A., ed. *Towards Comparative Indian Literature.* Aligarh: Department of Modern Indian Languages, Aligarh Muslim University, 1987.

Kozak, Krištof Jacek. "Comparative Literature in Slovakia." *Comparative Literature and Comparative Cultural Studies.* Ed. Steven Tötösy de Zepetnek. West Lafayette: Purdue UP, 2002. 111–29.

Krauss, Werner. *Probleme der vergleichenden Literaturgeschichte.* Berlin: Deutsche Akademie der Wissenschaften, 1965.

Krauss, Werner. "Nationale und Vergleichende Literaturgeschichte." *Grundprobleme der Literaturwissenschaft. Zur Interpretation literarischer Werke.* By Werner Krauss. Hamburg: Rowohlt, 1968. 105–18.

Kreutzer, Leo. "Eigensinn und Geschichte. Überlegungen zu einer Literaturwissenschaft als interkultureller Entwicklungsforschung." *Wie international ist die Literaturwissenschaft?* Ed. Lutz Danneberg, Friedrich Vollhardt, Hartmut Böhme, and Jörg Schönert. Stuttgart: Metzler, 1996. 591–99.

Kröller, Eva-Marie. "Comparative Canadian Literature: Notes on its Definition and Method." *Canadian Review of Comparative Literature / Revue Canadienne de Littérature Comparée* 6.2 (1979): 139–50.

Kröller, Eva-Marie. "The Cultural Contribution of the 'Other' Ethnic Groups: A New Challenge to Comparative Canadian Literature." *Critical Approaches to the New Literatures in English.* Ed. Dieter Riemenschneider. Essen: Blaue Eule, 1989. 83–90.

Kuan-Hsing, Chen, and Ian Ang, eds. *Trajectories: Inter-Asia Cultural Studies.* New York: Routledge, 1998.

Kühnemann, Eugen. "Zur Aufgabe der vergleichenden Literaturgeschichte." *Centralblatt für Bibliothekswesen* 18 (1901): 1–11.

Kushner, Eva. "Comparative Literary History among the Human Sciences." *Comparative Literary History as Discourse.* Ed. Mario J. Valdés, Daniel Javitch, and A. Owen Aldridge. Bern: Peter Lang, 1992. 69–80.

Kushner, Eva. "Comparative Literary History as Dialogue among Nations." *Neohelicon: Acta Comparationis Litterarum Universarum* 20.2 (1993): 37–50.

Kushner, Eva. "Towards a Typology of Comparative Literature Studies?" *Powers of Narration.* Ed. Gerald Gillespie and André Lorant. Tokyo: U of Tokyo P, 1995. 502–10.

Kushner, Eva. "Comparative Literature in Canada: Whence and Whither?" *Comparative Literature World Wide: Issues and Methods / La Littérature comparée dans le monde: Questions et méthodes.* Ed. Tânia Franco Carvalhal. Porto Alegre: L&PM Editores, 1997. 81–97.

Kushner, Eva. "Is Comparative Literature Ready for the Twenty-First Century?" *Comparative Literature Now: Theories and Practice / La Littérature comparée à l'heure actuelle. Théories et réalisations.* Ed. Steven Tötösy de Zepetnek, Milan V. Dimić, and Irene Sywenky. Paris: Honoré Champion, 1999. 129–39.

Kutsukake, Iosihiko. "La letteratura comparata in Giappone." *Comparare i comparatismi. La comparatistica letteraria oggi in Europa e nel mondo.* Ed. Armando Gnisci and Franca Sinopoli. Roma: Lithos, 1995. 27–36.

La Drière, Craig. "The Comparative Method in the Study of Prosody." *Comparative Literature: Proceedings of the Second Congress of the ICLA.* Ed. W.P. Friedrich. Chapel Hill: U of North Carolina P, 1959. Vol. 1, 160–75.

Lacour, Claudia Brodsky. "Grounds of Comparison." *World Literature Today* 69.2 (1995): 271–74.

Laird, Charlton. "Comparative Literature." *Contemporary Literary Scholarship: A Critical Review.* Ed. Lewis Leary. New York: Appleton Century Crofts, 1958. 339–68.

Lambert, José. "Playdoyer pour un programme des études comparatistes. Littérature comparée et théorie du polysystème." *Orientations de recherche et méthodes en Littérature Comparée.* 2 vols. Montpellier: Société Française de Littérature Générale et Comparée et Université Paul-Valéry, 1984. Vol. 1, 59–69.

Lambert, José. "Les Relations littéraires internationales comme problème de réception." *Sensus Communis: Contemporary Trends in Comparative Literature / Panorama de la situation actuelle en Littérature Comparée.* Ed. János Riesz, Peter Boerner, and Bernhard Scholz. Tübingen: Gunter Narr, 1986. 49–63.

Lang, George. "*No hay centro:* Postmodernism and Comparative New World Criticism." *Canadian Review of Comparative Literature / Revue Canadienne de Littérature Comparée* 20.1-2 (1993): 105–24.

Lang, George. *Entwisted Tongues: Comparative Creole Literatures.* Amsterdam: Rodopi, 2000.

Lange, Victor. "Stand und Aufgaben der vergleichenden Literaturgeschichte in den USA." *Forschungsprobleme der Vergleichenden Literaturgeschichte.* Ed. Fritz Ernst and Kurt Wais. Tübingen: Niemeyer, 1951. 141–57.

Lanyi, Gabriel. "Comparative Literature: The Widest Meaning of a Non-Discipline." *Michigan Germanic Studies* 5.2 (1979): 211–16.

Lasater, Alice. *Spain to England: A Comparative Study of Arabic, European, and English Literature of the Middle Ages.* Jackson: UP of Mississippi, 1974.

Laurette, Pierre. "La Littérature comparée et ses fantômes théoriques. Reflexions métathéoriques." *Neohelicon: Acta Comparationis Litterarum Universarum* 13.2 (1986): 15–44.

Laurette, Pierre. "Universalité et comparabilité." *Theorie littéraire*. Ed. Marc Angenot, Jean Bessière, Douwe Fokkema, and Eva Kushner. Paris: PU de France, 1989. 51–60.

Lawall, Sarah. "Comparative Patterns in Literary Texts." *Actes du VIIIe Congres de l'Association Internationale de Littérature Comparée / Proceedings of the VIIIth Congress of the International Comparative Literature Association*. Ed. Béla Köpeczi and György M. Vajda. Stuttgart: Bieber, 1980. Vol. 2, 899–904.

Lawall, Sarah N. "The Canon's Mouth: Comparative Literature and the Western Masterpiece Anthology." *Profession 1986: The Modern Language Association of America* (1986): 25–27.

Lawall, Sarah. "World Literature, Comparative Literature, Teaching Literature." *Proceedings of the XIIth Congress of the International Comparative Literature Association / Actes du XIIe congres de l'Association Internationale de Littérature Comparée*. Ed. Roger Bauer. München: iudicium, 1990. Vol. 5, 219–24.

Lawall, Sarah N. "Shifting Paradigms in World Literature." *ACLA: American Comparative Literature Association Bulletin* 24.2 (1993): 11–28.

Lawall, Sarah, ed. *Reading World Literature: Theory, History, Practice*. Austin: U of Texas P, 1994.

Le Hir, Marie-Pierre, and Dana Strand, eds. *French Cultural Studies: Criticism at the Crossroads*. New York: State U of New York P, 2000.

Lehtonen, Mikko. *The Cultural Analysis of Texts*. Trans. Aija-Leena Ahonen and Kris Clarke. London: SAGE, 2000.

Lee, Alison, and Cate Poynton, eds. *Culture & Text: Discourse and Methodology in Social Research and Cultural Studies*. Oxford: Rowman & Littlefield, 2000.

Lee, A. van der. "Zur Komparatistik im niederländischen Sprachraum." *Forschungsprobleme der Vergleichenden Literaturgeschichte*. Ed. Fritz Ernst and Kurt Wais. Tübingen: Niemeyer, 1958. 173–77.

Lee, Benjamin. "Toward an International and Cultural Multiculturalism." *New Perspectives: A Comparative Literature Yearbook* 1 (1995): 100–31.

Lee, Ch'ang-Yong. *Pigyo Munhakeui Iron (Theory of Comparative Literature)*. Seoul: Ilji Sa, 1990.

Lee, Hae-Soon. *Pigyo Munhak (Comparative Literature)*. Seoul: Gwahak Ch'ongbo Sa, 1986.

Lee, Kyong-Son. *Pigyo Munhak Nongo (Theory of Comparative Literature)*. Seoul: Iljo Kak, 1976.

Lee, Sang-Kyong. *East Asia and America : Encounters in Drama and Theatre*. Honolulu: U of Hawaii P, 2000.

Lefevere, André. *Translating Literature: Practice and Theory in a Comparative Literature Context*. New York: Modern Language Association of America, 1992.

Lempicki, S. "Vergleichende Literaturgeschichte." *Reallexikon der deutschen Literaturgeschichte*. Ed. Paul Merker and Wolfgang Stammler. Berlin: de Gruyter, 1928–29. Vol. 3, 440–42.

Lepke, A.K. "Emphases in the Teaching of Comparative Literature." *The Modern Language Journal* 41 (1957): 157–67.

Levin, Harry. *Grounds for Comparison.* Cambridge: Harvard UP, 1972.

Levin, Harry. "Towards World Literature." *Tamkang Review* 6–7 (1975–76): 21–30.

Levin, Harry. "Preface: What is Literature if not Comparative?" *The Chinese Text.* Ed. Chou Ying-hsiung. Hong Kong: The Chinese UP, 1986. vii–xiii.

Lindenberger, Herbert. "Self-Portrait in the Unembellished Mode." *Building a Profession: Autobiographical Perspectives on the Beginnings of Comparative Literature in the United States.* Ed. Lionel Gossman and Mihai I. Spariosu. Albany: State U of New York P, 1994. 141–58.

Lindfors, Bernth. *Comparative Approaches to African Literatures.* Amsterdam: Rodopi, 1994.

Lionnet, Françoise. "Spaces of Comparison." *Comparative Literature in the Age of Multiculturalism.* Ed. Charles Bernheimer. Baltimore: Johns Hopkins UP, 1995. 165–74.

Liu, Jiemin. *Bijiao wenxüe fangfalun (The Methodology of Comparative Literature).* Tianjin: Tianjin People's P, 1993.

Loliée, Frédéric. *A Short History of Comparative Literature: From the Earliest Times to the Present Day.* 1906. Trans. M. Douglas Power. London: Kennikat P, 1970.

López, Dolores Romero, ed. *Orientaciones em literatura comparada.* Madrid: Arco, 1997.

Lorant, André, and Jean Bessière, eds. *Littérature comparée. Théorie et pratique.* Paris: Honoré Champion, 1999.

Loriggio, Francesco. "Comparative Literature and the Genres of Interdisciplinarity." *World Literature Today* 69.2 (1995): 257–62.

Losada Goya, José Manuel. "L'Alterité en tant que premisse de la littérature comparée." *Bulletin de Littérature Générale et Comparée* 19 (1996): 9–17.

Losada Goya, José Manuel. "Intertextuality and Comparative Literature." *The Intertextual Dimension of Discourse: Pragmalinguistic—Cognitive—Hermeneutic Approaches.* Ed. Beatríz Penas Ibañez. Zaragoza: U de Zaragoza, 1996. 107–30.

Losada Goya, José Manuel. "La Littérature comparée en Espagne." *Bulletin de Littérature Générale et Comparée* 19 (1996): 39–47.

Losada Goya, José Manuel. "Principes méthodologiques pour les bibliographies comparées." *Comparative Literature Now: Theories and Practice / La Littérature comparée à l'heure actuelle. Théories et réalisations.* Ed. Steven Tötösy de Zepetnek, Milan V. Dimić, and Irene Sywenky. Paris: Honoré Champion, 1999. 141–151.

Lukács, Borbála H. "Recent Comparative Research in the Soviet Union." *Neohelicon: Acta Comparationis Litterarum Universarum* 1.1-2 (1973): 367–75.

Lukács, Borbála H. "Die komparative Literaturgeschichte—eine verdächtige Mode?" *Contemporary Studies in Methodology: Current Trends in Literary Theory.* Ed. Z. Konstantinović. Belgrade: Institute for Literature and Art, of Belgrade, 1990. 199–208.

Lull, James. *Media, Communication, Culture: A Global Approach.* New York: Columbia UP, 1995.

McCormick, John. *American & European Literary Imagination, 1919–1932.* New Brunswick: Transaction Publishers, 2000.

Machado, Álvaro Manuel, and Daniel-Henri Pageaux. *Da Literatura comparada à Teoria da Literatura.* Lisboa: Setenta, 1988.

Macmillan, M. "The Study of Comparative Literature in British Universities." *Jadavpur Journal of Comparative Literature* 14–15 (1976–77): 60–75.

Mainkar, T.G. "Comparative Literature for India." *Jadavpur Journal of Comparative Literature* 14–15 (1976–77): 50–59.

Majumdar, Swapan. *Comparative Literature, Indian Dimensions.* Calcutta: Papyrus, 1987.

Makaryk, Irena R., ed. *Encyclopedia of Contemporary Literary Theory: Approaches, Scholars, Terms.* Toronto: U of Toronto P, 1993.

Malone, David H. "The 'Comparative' in Comparative Literature." *Yearbook of Comparative and General Literature* 3 (1954): 13–20.

Malone, David H. "Literature and 'Comparative Literature'." *Medieval Epik to the "Epic Theater" of Brecht.* Ed. Rosario P. Armato and John M. Spalek. Los Angeles: U of Southern California P, 1968. 1–7.

Marcus, George, and Michael Fischer, eds. *Anthropology as Cultural Critique: An Experimental Moment in the Human Sciences.* Chicago: U of Chicago P, 1999.

Margolin, Uri. "Formal, Semantic, and Pragmatic Aspects of Metatextuality: Comparatism Revisited." *Comparative Literature Now: Theories and Practice / La Littérature comparée à l'heure actuelle. Théories et réalisations.* Ed. Steven Tötösy de Zepetnek, Milan V. Dimić, and Irene Sywenky. Paris: Honoré Champion, 1999. 153–63.

Marino, Adrian. *Comparatisme et théorie de la littérature.* Paris: PU de France, 1988.

Marino, Adrian. "'European' and 'World' Literature: A New Comparative View." *Powers of Narration.* Ed. Gerald Gillespie and André Lorant. Tokyo: U of Tokyo P, 1995. 299–308.

Markiewicz, Henryk. "Forschungsbereich und Systematik der vergleichenden Literaturwissenschaft." *Weimarer Beiträge* (1968): 1320–30.

Marsh, Athur Richmond. "The Comparative Study of Literature." 1896. *Comparative Literature: The Early Years.* Ed. Hans-Joachim Schulz and Phillip H. Rhein. Chapel Hill: U of North Carolina P, 1973. 113–31.

Martin, Elaine. "The Framing of Literary Studies, or, is Comparative to Literature as Cultural is to Studies?" *The Comparatist: Journal of the Southern Comparative Literature Association* 20 (1996): 25–40.

Matlaw, Ralph E. "Comparative Literature in Eastern Europe." *Yearbook of Comparative and General Literature* 13 (1964): 49–55.

Matsuda, Minoru, ed. *Hikaku bungaku jiten (Dictionary of Comparative Literature)*. Tokyo: Tokyo-do shuppan, 1978.

Maury, Lucien. "Coopération intellectuelle et littérature comparée." *Revue bleue* (1927): 340–43.

Maury, Paul. *Arts et littératures comparés. État présent de la question*. Paris: Les Belles Lettres, 1934.

Maurya, Abhai. *Confluence: Historico-Comparative and Other Literary Studies*. New Delhi: Sterling Publishers Private Ltd., 1988.

Mayo, Robert S. *Herder and the Beginnings of Comparative Literature*. Chapel Hill: U of North Carolina P, 1969.

Mazzio, Carla, ed. *Historicism, Psychoanalysis, and Early Modern Culture*. New York: Routledge, 2000.

McCormick, John O. *A Syllabus of Comparative Literature*. Metuchen: The Scarecrow P, 1972.

McCutchion, David. "Comparative Literature in Eastern Europe." *Jadavpur Journal of Comparative Literature* 5 (1965): 88–100.

McCutchion, David. "Comparative Literature in England." *Jadavpur Journal of Comparative Literature* 6 (1966): 145–49.

McCutchion, David. "Comparative Literature in France." *Jadavpur Journal of Comparative Literature* 9 (1969): 1–10.

Melas, Natalie. "Versions of Incommensurability." *World Literature Today* 69.2 (1995): 275–80.

Meltzl de Lomnitz, Hugo. "Present Tasks of Comparative Literature." 1877. *Comparative Literature: The Early Years*. Ed. Hans-Joachim Schulz and Phillip H. Rhein. Chapel Hill: U of North Carolina P, 1973. 56–62.

Meltzl de Lomnitz, Hugo. "Das Prinzip des Polyglottismus." *Acta Comparationis Litterarum Universarium* (1877): 179–82 and 307–15.

Meregalli, Franco. "La Littérature comparée en Italie." *Neohelicon: Acta Comparationis Litterarum Universarum* 4.1-2 (1976): 303–14.

Meregalli, Franco. "Sur la délimitation de l'objet de la littérature comparée." *Sensus Communis: Contemporary Trends in Comparative Literature / Panorama de la situation actuelle en Littérature Comparée*. Ed. János Riesz, Peter Boerner, and Bernhard Scholz. Tübingen: Gunter Narr, 1986. 275–79.

Michaud, Stéphane, and Jacqueline Sessa, eds. *Territoires du comparatisme. Pluridisciplinarité et innovation pédagogique*. St. Etienne: Centre Interdisciplinaire d'Etudes et de Recherches sur l'Expression Contemporaine, 1986.

Mignolo, Walter D. "Canon and Corpus: An Alternative View of Comparative Literary Studies in Colonial Situations." *Dedalus: Revista Portuguesa de Literatura Comparada* 1 (1991): 219–43.

Miller, J. Hillis. "Theory and Translation in Comparative Literature." *Bologna, la cultura italiana e le letterature straniere moderne*. Ed. Vita Fortunati. Ravenna: Longo, 1992. Vol. 2, 31–41.

Milner, Andrew. *Contemporary Cultural Theory: An Introduction*. London: U College London P, 1994.

Miner, Earl. "Some Theoretical and Methodological Topics for Comparative Literature." *Poetics Today* 8.1 (1987): 123–40.

Miner, Earl. "Etudes comparées interculturelles." *Théorie littéraire*. Ed. Marc Angenot, Jean Bessière, Douwe Fokkema et Eva Kushner. Paris: PU de France, 1989. 161–79.

Miner, Earl. *Comparative Poetics: An Intercultural Essay on Theories of Literature*. New Jersey : Princeton UP, 1990.

Miner, Earl. "Canons and Comparatists." *The Search for a New Alphabet: Literary Studies in a Changing World*. Ed. Harald Hendrix, Joost Kloek, Sophie Levie, and Will van Peer. Amsterdam: John Benjamins, 1996. 151–55.

Mohan, Chandra. "Comparative Indian Literature: Recent Trends." *Aspects of Comparative Literature: Current Approaches*. Ed. Chandra Mohan. New Delhi: India Publishers & Distributors, 1989. 95–105.

Mohan, Devinder. "Indian Comparative Literature and Its Pedagogical Implication." *Comparative Literature: Theory and Practice*. Ed. Amiya Dev and Sisir Kumar Das. Shimla: Indian Institute of Advanced Study, 1989. 87–93.

Moisan, Clément. *Comparaison et raison. Essai sur l'histoire et l'institution des littératures canadienne et québecoise*. Montréal: Hurtubise HMH, 1987.

Moisan, Clément. *Le Phénomène de la littérature. Essai*. Montréal: l'Hexagone, 1996.

Moore, Cornelia N., and Raymond Moody, eds. *Comparative Literature East and West: Tranditions and Trends*. Honolulu: U of Hawaii P, 1989.

Mortier, Daniel. "Réception n'est pas raison ou les objectifs des études en littérature comparée." *Oeuvres et critique: Revue internationale d'étude de la réception critiques des oeuvres littéraires de langue française* 11.2 (1986): 135–41.

Mortier, R. "Cent ans de littérature comparée, l'acquis, les perspectives." *Proceedings of the IXth Congress of the International Comparative Literature Association*. Ed. Zoran Konstantinović. Innsbruck: Institut für Sprachwissenschaft, U of Innsbruck, 1981. Vol. 1, 11–17.

Moser, Walter. "La Littérature comparée et la crise des études littéraires." *Comparative Literature: History and Contemporaneity / Littérature Comparée: Histoire et contemporanéité*. Ed. Milan V. Dimić and Steven Tötösy de Zepetnek. *Canadian Review of Comparative Literature / Revue Canadienne de Littérature Comparée* 23.1 (1996): 43–50.

Motekat, Helmut. "Vergleichende Literaturwissenschaft." *Germanisch-Romanische Monatsschrift* 2 (1951–52): 324–26.

Moulton, Richard G. "World Literature and Its Place in General Culture." 1911. *Yearbook of Comparative and General Literature* 39 (1990–91): 16–22.

Mourão, Manuela. "Comparative Literature in the United States." *Comparative Literature and Comparative Cultural Studies*. Ed. Steven Tötösy de Zepetnek. West Lafayette: Purdue UP, 2002. 130–41.

Mukerji, Chandra, and Michael Schudson, eds. *Rethinking Popular Culture: Contemporary Perspectives in Cultural Studies*. Berkeley: U of California P, 1991.

Mullaney, Kathleen. "Comparatists as Travellers: Teaching Theory to Undergraduate Comparative Literature Students." *ACLA: American Comparative Literature Association Bulletin* 14.2 (1993): 168–82.

Mühlmann, Wilhelm E. *Pfade in die Weltliteratur*. Königstein: Athenäum, 1984.

Muller, H.C. "L'Etude scientifique de la littérature comparée." *Revue internationale de l'enseignement* 35 (1898): 289–98.

Munns, Jessica, and Gita Rajan, eds. *A Cultural Studies Reader: History, Theory, Practice*. New York: Longman, 1995.

Munteano, Basil. "La Littérature comparée en Roumanie." *Revue de Littérature Comparée* 11 (1931): 111–14.

Munteano, Basil. "Situation de la littérature comparée. Sa portée humaine et sa legitimité." *Constantes dialectiques en littérature et en histoire*. Ed. Basil Munteano. Paris: Didier, 1967. 85–135.

Mwaria, Cheryl, Silvia Federici, and Joseph McLaren, eds. *African Visions: Literary Images, Political Change, and Social Struggle in Contemporary Africa*. Westport: Greenwood, 2000.

Nahke, Evamaria. "IV. Kongress der Internationalen Vereinigung für vergleichende Literatur." *Weimarer Beiträge* (1965): 252–62.

Nakajima, Kenzo, and Nekano Yoshio. *Hikaku Bungaku josetsu (Introduction to Comparative Literature)*. Tokyo: U of Tokyo P, 1951.

Ndong, Norbert. "Aspekte der Beziehung zwischen afrikanischer und europäischer Literaturwissenschaft." *Wie international ist die Literaturwissenschaft?* Ed. Lutz Danneberg, Friedrich Vollhardt, Hartmut Böhme, and Jörg Schönert. Stuttgart: Metzler, 1996. 600–19.

Nelson, Lowry, Jr. "Defining and Defending Comparative Literature." *The Comparative Perspective on Literature*. Ed. Clayton Koelb and Susan Noakes. Ithaca: Cornell UP, 1988. 37–47.

Nemoianu, Virgil, ed. *Multicomparative Theory, Definitions, Realities*. Whitestone: Council of National Literatures World Report, 1996.

Neri, Ferdinando. "La Tavola dei valori del comparatista." *Giornale storico della letteratura italiana* (1937): 270–79.

Neri, Francesca. "La Letteratura comparata e le teorie postcoloniali." *Comparare i comparatismi. La comparatistica letteraria oggi in Europa e nel mondo*. Ed. Armando Gnisci and Franca Sinopoli. Roma: Lithos, 1995. 123–35.

Neubauer, John. "Kipling, Baden-Powell, and Edward Said: Reflections on Comparative Literature in a Post-Colonial Era." *Differential Multilogue: Comparative Literrature and National Literatures*. Ed. Gurbhagat Singh. Delhi: Ajanta, 1991. 46–55.

Neupokoeva, Irina Grigor'evna. "Dialectics of Historical Development of National and World Literature." *Neohelicon: Acta Comparationis Litterarum Universarum* 1.1-2 (1973): 115–30.

Nichev, Boian. *Osnovi na sravnitelnoto literaturoznanie: Sravnitelnoto izucavane na literaturata i problemite na svremennata literaturna nauka (Theoretical Foundations of Comparative Literature: Comparing Literature and Other Issues of Contemporary Literary Scholarship)*. Sofia: Izdatelstvo Nauka i Izkustvo, 1986.

Nichols, Stephen G., Jr., and Richard Vowles, eds. *Comparatists at Work: Studies in Comparative Literature*. Waltham: Blaisdell, 1968.

Nitrini, Sandra. "La Littérature comparée au Brésil. Un fragment de son histoire." *Comparative Literature: History and Contemporaneity / Littérature Comparée: Histoire et contemporanéité*. Ed. Milan V. Dimić and Steven Tötösy de Zepetnek. *Canadian Review of Comparative Literature / Revue Canadienne de Littérature Comparée* 23.1 (1996): 75–90.

Nuñes, Estuardo. "Literatura comparada en Hispanoamérica." *Comparative Literature Studies* 1 (1964): 41–45.

Nwezeh, E.C. "The Comparative Approach to Modern African Literature." *Actes du VIIIe Congres de l'Association Internationale de Littérature Comparée / Proceedings of the VIIIth Congress of the International Comparative Literature Association*. Ed. Béla Köpeczi and György M. Vajda. Stuttgart: Bieber, 1980. Vol. 2, 321–28.

Nyirő, Lajos. "Problèmes de littérature comparée et théorie de littérature." *Littérature hongroise, littérature comparée*. Ed. I. Sötér and O. Süpek. Budapest: Akadémiai, 1964. 505–24.

Nyirő, Lajos. "Les Niveaux logiques des recherches de la littérature comparée." *Neohelicon: Acta Comparationis Litterarum Universarum* 13.2 (1986): 159–75.

Nyirő, Lajos. "L'Aspect empirique et théorique des recherches en littérature comparée." *Toward a Theory of Comparative Literature*. Ed. Mario J. Valdés. New York: Peter Lang, 1990. 67–75.

Ocvirk, Anton. *Teorija primerjalne literarne zgodovine (Theory of Comparative Literary History)*. 1936. Ljubljana: Partizanska knjiga, 1975.

Oliver, Kenneth. "Comparative Literature as General Education." *Yearbook of Comparative and General Literature* 6 (1957): 11–16.

Onís, José de. "Literatura Comparada como disciplina literaria." *Cuadernos* 56 (1962): 63–69.

Orsini, Gian N.G. "Croce as Comparatist." *Yearbook of Comparative and General Literature* 10 (1961): 63–65.

O'Sullivan, Emer. *Kinderliterarische Komparatistik*. Heidelberg: C. Winter, 2000.

Ota, Saburo. "The First Decade of the Japan Society of Comparative Literature." *Yearbook of Comparative and General Literature* 6 (1957): 1–6.

Ota, Saburo. "Comparative Literature in Japan." *Jadavpur Journal of Comparative Literature* 3 (1963): 1–10.

Pageaux, Daniel-Henri. "Dix ans de recherche en littérature générale et comparée." *L'Information Littéraire* 32.4 (1980): 152–54.

Pageaux, Daniel-Henri. "Littérature comparée et sciences humaines. Pour un renouveau des études comparatistes." *Sensus Communis: Contemporary Trends in Comparative Literature / Panorama de la situation actuelle en Littérature Comparée.* Ed. János Riesz, Peter Boerner, and Bernhard Scholz. Tübingen: Gunter Narr, 1986. 65–75.

Pageaux, Daniel Henri. "De l'Imagologie à la théorie en littérature comparée. Elements de reflexion." *Europa Provincia Mundi: Essays in Comparative Literature and European Studies.* Ed. Joep Leerssen and Karl Ulrich Syndram. Amsterdam : Rodopi, 1992. 297–307.

Pageaux, Daniel-Henri. *La Littérature générale et comparée.* Paris: Armand Collin, 1994.

Pál, Joszef [József]. "L'Associazione internazionale di letteratura comparata e i suoi lavori di storiografia letteraria." *Comparare i comparatismi. La comparatistica letteraria oggi in Europa e nel mondo.* Ed. Armando Gnisci and Franca Sinopoli. Roma: Lithos, 1995. 82–88.

Palencia-Roth, Michael. "Comparing Literature, Comparing Civilizations." *Comparative Civilizations Review* 21 (1989): 1–19.

Palencia-Roth, Michael. "Contrastive Literature." *ACLA: American Comparative Literature Association Bulletin* 24.2 (1993): 47–60.

Palermo, Zulma. "Cultural Articulation of the Comparative Literary Studies: The Argentinian Case." *Comparative Literature World Wide: Issues and Methods / La Littérature comparée dans le monde: Questions et méthodes.* Ed. Tânia Franco Carvalhal. Porto Alegre: L&PM Editores, 1997. 211–31.

Palumbo-Liu, David, and Hans Ulrich Gumbrecht, eds. *Streams of Cultural Capital: Transnational Cultural Studies.* Stanford: Stanford UP, 1998.

Paolucci, Anne. "Multinational Literature and Integration into Existing Programs." *Geolinguistic Perspectives.* Ed. Jesse Levitt. Lanham: UP of America, 1987. 195–202.

Paolucci, Anne. "Multi-Comparative Literary Perspectives." *Comparative Literary Theory: New Perspectives.* Ed. Anne Paolucci. *Review of National Literatures* 15. New York: Griffon House Publications, 1989. 1–29.

Paolucci, Anne. "II. Restructuring and Future Plans: a 3-Year Pilot Project to Expand Comparative Literary Studies." *Toward the 21st Century: New Directions. Council on National Literatures: World Report.* Whitestone: Council on National Literatures, 1994. 35–42.

Parsons, Coleman O. "History of Comparative Literature, 1923–1958." *Yearbook of Comparative and General Literature* 8 (1959): 53–56.

Partridge, Eric. "The Comparative Study of Literature." *A Critical Medley: Essays, Studies and Notes in English, French and Comparative Literature.* By Eric Partridge. Paris: Champion, 1926. 159–226.

Payne, Michael, ed. *A Dictionary of Cultural and Critical Theory.* Oxford: Blackwell, 1998.

Peer, Larry, and Diane Hoeveler, eds. *Comparative Romanticisms: Power, Gender, Subjectivity*. New Jersey: Camden House, 1998.

Perloff, Marjorie. "On Wanting to Be a Comparatist." *Building a Profession: Autobiographical Perspectives on the Beginnings of Comparative Literature in the United States*. Ed. Lionel Gossman and Mihai I. Spariosu. Albany: State U of New York P, 1994. 125–40.

Perloff, Marjorie. "'Living in the Same Place': The Old Mononationalism and the New Comparative Literature." *World Literature Today* 69.2 (1995): 249–55.

Perloff, Marjorie. "'Literature' in the Expanded Field." *Comparative Literature in the Age of Multiculturalism*. Ed. Charles Bernheimer. Baltimore: Johns Hopkins UP, 1995. 175–86.

Perron, Paul, and Marcel Danesi, eds. *Analyzing Cultures: An Introduction and Handbook*. Bloomington: Indiana UP, 1999.

Peters, Michael, ed. *After the Disciplines: The Emergence of Cultural Studies*. Westport: Bergin & Garvey, 1999.

Petersen, Julius. "Nationale oder vergleichende Literaturgeschichte?" *Deutsche Vierteljahrsschrift für Literaturwissenschaft und Geistesgeschichte* 6 (1928): 36–61.

Peyre, Henri. "A Glance at Comparative Literature in America." *Yearbook of Comparative and General Literature* 1 (1952): 1–8.

Peyre, Henri. "Seventy-five Years of Comparative Literature. A Backward and a Forward Glance." *Yearbook of Comparative and General Literature* 8 (1959): 18–26.

Pichois, Claude, and André-Marie Rousseau. *La Littérature comparée*. Paris: Colin, 1967.

Pivato, Joseph. "Minority Writing and Comparative Literature." *Echo: Essays on Other Literatures*. By Joseph Pivato. Toronto: Guernica, 1994. 53–75.

Pizer, John. "Friedrich Schlegel's Comparative Approach to Literature." *Selecta: Journal of the Pacific Northwest Council on Foreign Languages* 3 (1982): 31–36.

Podestà, Giuditta. *Letteratura Comparata: Saggi*. Genoa: Di Stefano, 1966.

Pogacnik, J. *Differenzen and Interferenzen. Studien zur literarhistorischen Komparativistik bei den Südslaven*. München: Sagner, 1989.

Poggioli, Renato. "Comparative Literature." *Dictionary of World Literature: Criticism, Forms, Technique*. Ed. Joseph Twadell Shipley. New York: Philosophical Library, 1943. 116–17.

Polet, Jean-Claude. "Histoire littéraire et littérature comparée." *Methodes du texte. Introduction aux études littéraires*. Ed. Maurice Delacroix and Fernand Hallyn. Paris: Duclot, 1987. 45–63.

Politou-Marmarinou, Eleni. *I sigritiki filologia, xoros, skopos kai methodi erevnas, ekdosis kardamitsas (Comparative Literature: Field, Aims, and Research Methods)*. Athens: Kardamitsa, 1981.

Porta, Antonio. *La letteratura comparata nella storia e nella critica*. Milano: C. Marzorati, 1951.

Posner, Richard, et al., eds. *A Handbook on the Sign-Theoretic Foundations of Nature and Culture*. Berlin: de Guytner, 1997.

Posnett, Hutcheson Macaulay. *Comparative Literature*. 1886. New York: Johnson, 1970.

Posnett, Hutcheson Macaulay. "The Science of Comparative Literature." 1901. *Comparative Literature: The Early Years*. Ed. Hans-Joachim Schulz and Phillip H. Rhein. Chapel Hill: U of North Carolina P, 1973. 183–206.

Pratt, Mary Louise. "Comparative Literature as a Cultural Practice." *Profession 1986: The Modern Language Association of America* (1986): 33–35.

Pratt, Mary Louise. "Comparative Literature and Global Citizenship." *Comparative Literature in the Age of Multiculturalism*. Ed. Charles Bernheimer. Baltimore: Johns Hopkins UP, 1995. 58–65.

Prawer, S.S. *Comparative Literary Studies: An Introduction*. London: Duckworth, 1973.

Prawer, S.S. "The State of the Art: Recent Books on Comparative Literature." *Comparative Criticism* 8 (1986): 295–300.

Puhvel, J. *Comparative Literature*. Baltimore: Johns Hopkins UP, 1984.

Puibusque, A. de. *Histoire comparée des littératures espagnole et française*. Paris: Dentu, 1843.

Putnam, Samuel. "Comparative Literature: Can it Come Alive?" *Books Abroad: An International Library Quarterly* 10 (1936): 133–36.

Raab, Harald. "Zu den gegenwärtigen Aufgaben der Vergleichenden Literaturwissenschaft." *Wissenschaftliche Zeitschrift der Wilhelm-Pieck-Universität Rostock* 9.1 (1959–60): 1–4.

Rahimieh, Nasrin. *Oriental Responses to the West: Comparative Essays in Select Writers from the Muslim World*. Leiden: E.J. Brill, 1990.

Ranković, Milan. *Komparativna estetika (Comparative Aesthetics)*. Beograd: Umetnicka akademija, 1973.

Remak, Henry H.H. "Comparative Literature at the Crossroads: Diagnosis, Therapy, and Prognosis." *Yearbook of Comparative and General Literature* 9 (1960): 1–28.

Remak, Henry H.H. "Comparative Literature: Its Definition and Function." *Comparative Literature: Method and Perspective*. 1961. Ed. Newton P. Stallknecht and Horst Frenz. Carbondale: Southern Illinois UP, 1971. 3–57.

Remak, Henry H.H. "Definition und Funktion der Vergleichenden Literaturwissenschaft." *Komparatistik. Aufgaben und Methoden*. Ed. Horst Rüdiger. Stuttgart: Kohlhammer, 1973. 11–54.

Remak, Henry H.H. "A Comparative History of Literatures in European Languages: Progress and Problems." *Synthesis: Bulletin du Comité National de Littérature Comparée de la Republique Socialiste de Roumanie* 3 (1976): 11–23.

Remak, Henry H.H. "The Future of Comparative Literature." *Actes du VIIIe Congres de l'Association Internationale de Littérature Comparée / Proceedings of the VIIIth Congress of the International Comparative Literature Association.* Ed. Béla Köpeczi and György M. Vajda. Stuttgart: Bieber, 1980. Vol. 2, 429–39.

Remak, Henry H.H. "Wie kann man heutzutage komparatistische Literaturgeschichte schreiben?" *Comparative Literary Studies.* Ed. István Fried, Zoltán Kanyó, and József Pál. Szeged: József Attila U, 1983. 37–45.

Remak, Henry H.H. "The Situation of Comparative Literature in the Universities." *Colloquium Helveticum* (1985): 7–14.

Remak, Henry H.H. "Comparative Criticism: Cultural and Historical Roots in the Theoretical Forest." *Neohelicon: Acta Comparitionis Litterarum Universarum* 17.1 (1990): 161–99.

Remak, Henry H.H. "Between Scylla and Charybdis: Quality Judgment in Comparative Literature." *Aesthetics and the Literature of Ideas.* Ed. François Jost. Newark: U of Delaware P, 1990. 21–33.

Remak, Henry H.H. "Traumas and Triumphs: The *Yearbook of Comparative and General Literature,* 1952–1990." *Europa Provincia Mundi: Essays in Comparative Literature and European Studies.* Ed. Joep Leerssen and Karl Ulrich Syndram. Amsterdam: Rodopi, 1992. 71–80.

Remak, Henry H.H. "Literary History and Comparative Literary History. The Odds for and against it in Scholarship." *Neohelicon: Acta Comparationis Litterarum Universarum* 20.2 (1993): 95–118.

Remak, Henry H.H. "Comparative Literature and Literary Theory: Will the Twain Ever Meet?" *Celebrating Comparativism.* Ed. Katalin Kürtösi and József Pál. Szeged: József Attila U, 1994. 13–25.

Reynolds, Sian, and William Kidd, eds. *Contemporary French Cultural Studies.* Oxford: Oxford UP, 2000.

Ribeiro, João. "Comparative Literature." 1902. *Yearbook of Comparative and General Literature* 34 (1985): 15–16.

Ribeiro, Manuel. "Le Discours critique littéraire: Un enjeu nécessaire du comparatisme." *Comparative Literature Now: Theories and Practice / La Littérature comparée à l'heure actuelle. Théories et réalisations.* Ed. Steven Tötösy de Zepetnek, Milan V. Dimić, and Irene Sywenky. Paris: Honoré Champion, 1999. 173–81.

Richards, David. *Masks of Difference: Cultural Representations in Literature, Anthropology and Art.* Cambridge: Cambridge UP, 1995.

Riemenschneider, Dieter. "The 'New' English Literatures in Historical and Political Perspective: Attempts toward a Comparative View of North/South Relationship in 'Commonwealth Literature'." *New Literary History* 18.2 (1987): 425–35.

Riffaterre, Michael. "On the Complementarity of Comparative Literature and Cultural Studies." *Comparative Literature in the Age of Multiculturalism.* Ed. Charles Bernheimer. Baltimore: Johns Hopkins UP, 1995. 66–73.

Rinner, Fridrun. "Y a-t-il une théorie propre à la littérature comparée?" *Toward a Theory of Comparative Literature*. Ed. Mario J. Valdés. New York: Peter Lang, 1990. 173–80.

Rod, Edouard. *De la Littérature comparée. Discours d'inauguration du cours d'histoire générale des littératures modernes à l'Université de Genéve*. Genève: H. Georg, 1886.

Roddier, Henri. "Littérature comparée et histoire des idées." *Revue de Littérature Comparée* 27 (1953): 43–49.

Roddier, Henri. "De l'Emploi de la méthode génétique en littérature comparée." *Comparative Literature: Proceedings of the Second Congress of the ICLA*. Ed. W.P. Friedrich. 2 vols. Chapel Hill: U of North Carolina P, 1959. Vol. 1, 113–24.

Roe, Frederick C. "Comparative Literature in the United Kingdom." *Yearbook of Comparative and General Literature* 3 (1954): 1–12.

Roe, Frederick C. "Deuxième congrès de littérature comparée à Oxford, 10–15 septembre 1954." *Convivium* 1 (1955): 120.

Rosenberg, Rainer. "Some Theoretical and Methodological Problems of the Comparative Study of 19th Century European Literature." *Actes du VIIIe Congres de l'Association Internationale de Littérature Comparée / Proceedings of the VIIIth Congress of the International Comparative Literature Association*. Ed. Béla Köpeczi and György M. Vajda. Stuttgart: Bieber, 1980. Vol. 2, 705–08.

Roth, Michael. *Das Selbstverständnis der Komparatistik. Analytischer Versuch über die Programmatik der Vergleichenden Literaturwissenschaft*. Frankfurt: Peter Lang, 1987.

Rousseau, André Michel. "Vingt ans de littérature comparée en France. Bilan et perspectives." *L'Information Littéraire* 21.5 (1969): 199–204.

Rousseau, André Michel. "Arts et littérature. Un état présent et quelques réflexions." *Synthesis: Bulletin du Comité National de Littérature Comparée de la République Socialiste de Roumanie* 4 (1977): 35–51.

Routh, H.V. "The Future of Comparative Literature." *Modern Language Review* 8 (1913): 1–14.

Rüdiger, Horst. "Nationalliteraturen und europäische Literatur: Methoden und Ziele der vergleichnedem Literaturwissenschaft." *Schweizer Monatshefte* 42 (1962): 195–211.

Rüdiger, Horst. "Introduction to the Study of Comparative Literature in Germany." Trans. David McCutchion. *Jadavpur Journal of Comparative Literature* 10 (1972): 65–71.

Rüdiger, Horst. "Vergleichende Literaturwissenschaft." *Handlexikon zur Literaturwissenschaft*. Ed. Diether Krywalski. München: Ehrenwirth, 1974. 493–99.

Runte, Roseann. "Comparative Literature and a Redefinition of the Canon." *Journal of Intercultural Studies* 19 (1992): 1–5.

Runte, Roseann. "On the Necessity of Comparative Literature." *Neohelicon: Acta Comparationis Litterarum Universarum* 24.2 (1997): 33–37.

Ruprecht, Hans-George. "Comparatisme et connaissance. Hypothèses sémiotiques sur la littérature comparée." *Exigences et perspectives de la sémiotique / Aims and Prospects of Semiotics.* Ed. H. Parret et H.-G. Ruprecht. Amsterdam: John Benjamins, 1985. Vol. 1, 307–24.

Ruprecht, Hans-George. "Littérature comparée et rationalité théorique. *Neohelicon: Acta Comparationis Litterarum Universarum* 13.2 (1986): 193–206.

Ruprecht, Hans-George. "Littérature comparée." *Sémiotique: Supplément au Dictionnaire raisonné de la théorie du langage.* Ed. A.J. Greimas and J. Courtés. Paris: Hachette, 1986. Vol. 2, 45–46.

Ruprecht, Hans-George. "Sémiotique et comparatisme littéraire: Pertinence des universaux?" *Signs of Humanity: Approaches to Semiotics.* Ed. M. Balat and J. Deledalle-Rhodes. Berlin: de Gruyter, 1992. 521–27.

Rusev, Penjo. "Littérature comparée, sémiotique littéraire, ou théorie de la communication culturelle." *Actes du VIIIe Congres de l'Association Internationale de Littérature Comparée / Proceedings of the VIIIth Congress of the International Comparative Literature Association.* Ed. Béla Köpeczi and György M. Vajda. Stuttgart: Bieber, 1980. Vol. 2, 789–94.

Russo, Mary. "Telling Tales out of School: Comparative Literature and Disciplinary Recession." *Comparative Literature in the Age of Multiculturalism.* Ed. Charles Bernheimer. Baltimore: Johns Hopkins UP, 1995. 187–94.

Ruttkowski, Wolfgang, ed. *Nomenclatur litterarius.* München: Francke, 1980.

Ryan, Judith. "Skinside Inside: The National Literature Major versus Comparative Literature." *Profession 1991: The Modern Language Association of America* (1991): 49–52.

Saburo, Ota. *Hikaku Bungaku (Comparative Literature).* Tokyo: Kenkyu-sha, 1955.

Sachithanandan, V. *Oppilakkiyam: Or Arinukam (Comparative Literature: An Introduction).* Madras: Oxford UP, 1985.

Samarin, Roman M. "Vom gegenwärtigen Stand des vergleichenden Literaturstudiums in der ausländischen Wissenschaft." *Kunst und Literatur in der Sowjetunion* 9 (1961): 11–34.

Samarin Roman M. "Über die Krise des modernen westlichen Komparativismus." *Wissenschaft am Scheidewege. Beiträge über Slawistik, Literaturwissenschaft und Ostforschung in Westdeutschland.* Ed. Gerhard Ziegengeist. Berlin: Akademie, 1964. 174–82.

San Juan, E., Jr. *Reading the West/Writing the East: Studies in Comparative Literature and Culture.* New York: Peter Lang, 1992.

San Juan, E., Jr. *Hegemony and Strategies of Transgression: Essays in Cultural Studies and Comparative Literature.* Ithaca: SUNY, 1995.

Santerres-Sarkany, Stéphane. *Théorie de la littérature.* Paris: PU de France, 1990.

Sayce, R.A. "Comparative Literature." *Times Educational Supplement* (26 March 1965): 915.

Sharrock, Alison, and Helen Morales. *Intratextuality: Greek and Roman Textual Relations*. New York: Oxford UP, 2000.

Scaglione, Aldo. "Comparative Literature as Cultural History: The Educational and Social Background of Renaissance Literature." *The Comparative Perspective on Literature: Approaches to Theory and Practice*. Ed. Clayton Koelb and Susan Noakes. Ithaca: Cornell UP, 1988. 147–61.

Schall, Frank L. "Littérature comparée et littérature générale aux Etats-Unis." *Études françaises* 6 (1925): 43–60.

Schiralli, Martin. *Constructive Postmodernism: Toward Renewal in Cultural and Literary Studies*. Westport: Bergin & Garvey, 2000.

Scheunemann, Dietrich. "Komparatistik." *Erkenntnis der Literatur. Theorien, Konzepte, Methoden der Literaturwissenschaft*. Ed. Dietrich Harth and Peter Gebhardt. Stuttgart: Metzler, 1982. 228–42.

Schipper, Mineke. "Towards an Intercultural Comparative Study of Critical Texts." *Toward a Theory of Comparative Literature*. Ed. Mario J. Valdés. New York: Peter Lang, 1990. 195–208.

Schmeling, Manfred. "Vergleichende Literaturwissenschaft. Theorie und Praxis." *Vergleichende Literaturwissenschaft. Theorie und Praxis*. Ed. Manfred Schmeling. Wiesbaden: Athenaion, 1981. 1–24.

Schmeling, Manfred. "Point de vue narratif et alterité culturelle." *Comparative Literature Now: Theories and Practice / La Littérature comparée à l'heure actuelle. Théories et réalisations*. Ed. Steven Tötösy de Zepetnek, Milan V. Dimić, and Irene Sywenky. Paris: Honoré Champion, 1999. 195–207.

Schmeling, Manfred, ed. *Vergleichende Literaturwissenschaft. Theorie und Praxis*. Wiesbaden: Athenaion, 1981.

Schmeling, Manfred, ed. *Weltliteratur heute. Konzepte und Perspektiven*. Würzburg: Königshausen and Neumann, 1995.

Schober, Rita. "Hauptrichtungen der modernen vergleichenden Literaturwissenschaft." *Wissenschaftliche Zeitschrift der Humboldt-Universität zu Berlin* 6.2 (1956–57): 97–101.

Schrimpf, Hans Joachim. *Goethes Begriff der Weltliteratur*. Stuttgart: Metzler, 1968.

Schröder, Susanne. *Komparatistik und Ideengeschichte. "History of Ideas" und Geistesgeschichte in ihrem Einfluß auf die internationale Komparatistik*. Bern: Peter Lang, 1981.

Schulz-Buschhaus, Ulrich. "Die Unvermeidlichkeit der Komparatistik. Zum Verhältnis von einzelnen Literaturen und Vergleichender Literaturwissenschaft." *arcadia: Zeitschrift für Vergleichende Literaturwissenschaft* 14 (1979): 223–36.

Schwarz, Egon. "Fragen und Gedanken zur vergleichenden Literaturwissenschaft vom Standpunkt eines Germanisten." *German Quarterly* 38 (1965): 318–24.

Segesvary, Victor. *Inter-Civilizational Relations and the Destiny of the West: Dialogue or Confrontation*. Boston: UP of America, 2000.

Seidler, Herbert. "Was ist Vergleichende Literaturwissenschaft?" *Sitzungsberichte. Österreichische Akademie der Wissenschaften, Philologisch-historische Klasse.* Wien: Österreichische Akademie der Wissenschaften, 1973. 3–18.

Seidler, Herbert. "Sprachkunstforschung als wichtige Aufgabe der vergleichenden Literaturwissenschaft." *Comparative Literary Studies.* Ed. István Fried, Zoltán Kanyó, and József Pál. Szeged: József Attila U, 1983. 13–23.

Sen, Nabaneeta Dev. "The Concept of an Indian Literature Today: Another Name for Comparative Literature?" *Counterpoints: Essays in Comparative Literature.* Ed. Nabaneeta Dev Sen. Calcutta: Prajna, 1985. 1–13.

Sexl, Martin. "Fragmentarische Bemerkungen zu zwei Herausforderungen an die Vergleichende Literaturwissenschaft." *Neohelicon: Acta Comparationis Litterarum Universarum* 24.2 (1997): 39–49.

Shackford, Charles Chauncey. "Comparative Literature." 1876. *Comparative Literature: The Early Years.* Ed. Hans-Joachim Schulz and Phillip H. Rhein. Chapel Hill: U of North Carolina P, 1973. 39–51.

Shaddy, Virginia M., ed. *International Perspectives in Comparative Literature.* Lewiston: Edwin Mellen, 1991.

Shouldice, Larry. "Wide Latitudes: Comparing New World Literature." *Canadian Review of Comparative Literature / Revue Canadienne de Littérature Comparée* 9.1 (1982): 46–55.

Siaflekis, Zacharias I. *Singritismos kai istoria tis logotexnias (Comparative Literature and Literary History).* 1988. Athens: Epikerotita, 1994.

Siaflekis, Zacharias I. "La Présence de la littérature comparée en Grèce." *Comparative Literature World Wide: Issues and Methods / La Littérature comparée dans le monde: Questions et méthodes.* Ed. Tânia Franco Carvalhal. Porto Alegre: L&PM Editores, 1997. 251–58.

Siciliano, Italo. "Quelques remarques sur la littérature comparée." 1956. *Venezia nelle letterature moderne.* Ed. Carlo Pellegrini. Venezia: Istituto per la collaborazione culturale, 1961. 4–10.

Siebers, Tobin. "Sincerely Yours." *Comparative Literature in the Age of Multiculturalism.* Ed. Charles Bernheimer. Baltimore: Johns Hopkins UP, 1995. 195–203.

Simms, Norman. "Comparative Literature in New Zealand." *Comparative Literary Theory: New Perspectives.* Ed. Anne Paolucci. *Review of National Literatures* 15. New York: Griffon House Publications, 1989. 110–20.

Simone, Franco. "Benedetto Croce et la littérature comparée en Italie." *Revue de littérature comaprée* 27 (1953): 5–16.

Singh, Gurbhagat. "Comparative Literature: Towards a Non-Logocentric Paradigm." *Comparative Literature: Theory and Practice.* Ed. Amiya Dev and Sisir Kumar Das. Shimla: Indian Institute of Advanced Study, 1989. 71–78.

Singh, Gurbhagat. "Towards International Poetics." *Toward a Theory of Comparative Literature.* Ed. Mario J. Valdés. New York: Peter Lang, 1990. 209–17.

Singh, Gurbhagat. "Differential Multilogue: Comparative Literature and National Literatures." *Differential Multilogue: Comparative Literrature and National Literatures*. Ed. Gurbhagat Singh. Delhi: Ajanta, 1991. 11–19.

Singh, Gurbhagat. "Futuristic Directions for Comparative Literature." *Powers of Narration*. Ed. Gerald Gillespie and André Lorant. Tokyo: U of Tokyo P, 1995. 309–17.

Sinopoli, Franca. "La letteratura comparata nel dipartimento di italianistica de La Sapienza' di Roma." *Comparare i comparatismi. La comparatistica letteraria oggi in Europa e nel mondo*. Ed. Armando Gnisci and Franca Sinopoli. Roma: Lithos, 1995. 136–51.

Sinopoli, Franca. *Storiografia e comparazione. Le origini della storia comparata della letteratura tra settecento e ottocento*. Roma: Bulzoni, 1996.

Sinopoli, Franca. "Gli strumenti di lavoro del comparatista." *Introduzione alla letteratura comparata*. Ed. Armando Gnisci. Milano: Bruno Mondadori, 1999. 341–48.

Škulj, Jola. "Comparative Literature and Cultural Identity." *Comparative Literature and Comparative Cultural Studies*. Ed. Steven Tötösy de Zepetnek. West Lafayette: Purdue UP, 2002. 142–51.

Smith, G. Gregory. "The Foible of Comparative Literature." 1901. *Yearbook of Comparative and General Literature* 19 (1970): 58–66.

Smith, G. Gregory. "Some Notes on the Comparative Study of Literature." *Modern Language Review* 1 (1905): 1–8.

Smith, Henry. "Comparative Literature: A Useful Tool in Skillful Hands." *Books Abroad: An International Library Quarterly* 10 (1936): 365–69.

Sollors, Werner. *Neither Black Nor White Yet Both: Thematic Explorations of Interracial Literature*. New York: Oxford UP, 1997.

Sorrento, Luigi. "Per la storia comparata delle lingua e letterature romanze." *Cultura* 10 (1931): 175–78.

Souiller, Didier, and Wladimir Troubetzkoy, eds. *Littérature comparée*. Paris: PU de France, 1997.

Souza, Eneide Maria de, and Wander Melo Miranda. "Perspectives de la littérature comparée au Brésil." *Comparative Literature World Wide: Issues and Methods / La Littérature comparée dans le monde: Questions et méthodes*. Ed. Tânia Franco Carvalhal. Porto Alegre: L&PM Editores, 1997. 39–52.

Sőtér, István. "On the Comparatist Method." *Neohelicon: Acta Comparationis Litterarum Universarum* 2.1-2 (1974): 9–30.

Stabile, Carol, ed. *Turning the Century: Essays in Media and Cultural Studies*. Boulder: Westview P, 2000.

Stark, Susanne. *The Novel in Anglo-German Context: Cultural Cross-currents and Affinities*. Amsterdam: Rodopi, 2000.

Steiner, George. "Die Perspektive als literaturgeschichtliche Kategorie und ihre Bedeutung für die vergleichende Literaturgeschichte." *La Littérature Comparée en Europe orientale.* Ed. István Sőtér, K. Bor, T. Klaniczay, and Gy.M. Vajda. Budapest: Akadémiai, 1963. 194–201.

Steiner, George. "What is Comparative Literature?" *No Passion Spent: Essays 1975–96.* By George Steiner. London: Faber and Faber, 1996. 142–59.

Steinmetz, Horst. "Weltliteratur. Umriss eines literaturgeschichtlichen Konzepts." *arcadia: Zeitschrift für Vergleichende Literaturwissenschaft* 20 (1985): 2–19.

Sternberg, Meir. *Hebrews between Cultures: Group Portraits and National Literature.* Bloomington: Indiana UP, 1999.

Stevenson, Barbara, and Cynthia Ho, eds. *Crossing the Bridge: Comparative Essays on Medieval European and Heian Japanese Women Writers.* New York: St. Martin's P, 2000.

Stiennon, Jacques. "Réflexions sur l'étude comparée des arts plastiques et littéraires." *Approches de l'art. Mélanges d'esthétique et de sciences de l'art.* Ed. Philippe Minguet. Bruxelles: La Renaissance du Livre, 1973. 115–24.

Stokes, Melvyn, et al., eds. *Identifying Hollywood's Audiences: Cultural Identity and the Movies.* London: British Film Institute, 2000.

Storey, John, ed. *What is Cultural Studies?: A Reader.* New York: Arnold, 1996.

Strelka, Joseph. "On German Geistesgeschichte and Its Impact on Comparative Literature." *Aesthetics and the Literature of Ideas.* Ed. François Jost and Melvin J. Friedman. Newark: U of Delaware P, 1990. 44–52.

Strelka, Joseph. "Zu Platz und Methoden der Komparatistik heute." *Neohelicon: Acta Comparationis Litterarum Universarum* 24.2 (1997): 51–70.

Strich, Fritz. "Weltliteratur und vergleichende Literaturgeschichte." *Philosophie der Literaturwissenschaft.* Ed. Emil Ermatinger. Berlin: Junker und Dünnhaupt, 1930. 422–41.

Strich, Fritz. *Goethe und die Weltliteratur.* 1946. Bern: Francke, 1957.

Struve, Gleb. "Comparative Literature in the Soviet Union, Today and Yesterday." *Yearbook of Comparative and General Literature* 4 (1955): 1–21.

Struve, Gleb. "Comparative Literature in the Soviet Union: Two Postscripts." *Yearbook of Comparative and General Literature* 6 (1957): 7–10.

Struve, Gleb. "More about Comparative Literature Studies in the Soviet Union." *Yearbook of Comparative and General Literature* 8 (1959): 13–18.

Sucur, Slobodan. "Theory, Period Styles, and Comparative Literature as Discipline." *Comparative Literature and Comparative Cultural Studies.* Ed. Steven Tötösy de Zepetnek. West Lafayette: Purdue UP, 2002. 152–82.

Sun, Cecile Chu-chin. "Problems of Perspective in Chinese-Western Comparative Literature Studies." *Canadian Review of Comparative Literature / Revue Canadienne de Littérature Comparée* 13.4 (1986): 531–47.

Sun, Jingyao. "The Name of the Game: The Term 'Comparative' and Its Equivalents in the Context of Chinese Literary History." *Yearbook of Comparative and General Literature* 33 (1984): 59–62.

Surber, Jere Paul. *Culture and Critique: An Introduction to the Critical Discourses in Cultural Studies*. Boulder: Westview, 1998.

Sussman, Henry. "In Remembrence of Things Past." *The Comparatist: Journal of the Southern Comparative Literature Association* 20 (1996): 21–24.

Suvin, Darko. "La letteratura comparata come prova di magia bianca." *Comparare i comparatismi. La comparatistica letteraria oggi in Europa e nel mondo*. Ed. Armando Gnisci and Franca Sinopoli. Roma: Lithos, 1995. 89–98.

Swiggers, P. "Methodological Innovation in the Comparative Study of Literature." *Canadian Review of Comparative Literature / Revue Canadienne de Littérature Comparée* 9.1 (1982): 19–26.

Swingewood, Alan. *Cultural Theory and the Problem of Modernity*. New York: St. Martin's P, 1998.

Swirski, Peter. "Popular and Highbrow Literature: A Comparative View." *Comparative Literature and Comparative Cultural Studies*. Ed. Steven Tötösy de Zepetnek. West Lafayette: Purdue UP, 2002. 183–205.

Syndram, Karl Ulrich. "Das Problem der nationalen Literaturgeschichtsschreibung als Gegenstand der komparatistischen Imagologie." *Proceedings of the XIIth Congress of the International Comparative Literature Association / Actes du XIIe congres de l'Association Internationale de Littérature Comparée*. Ed. Roger Bauer. München: iudicium, 1990. Vol. 3, 36–42.

Syndram, Karl Ulrich. "*Laboratorium Europa*—Zur kulturwissenschaftlichen Begründung der Komparatistik." *Europa Provincia Mundi: Essays in Comparative Literature and European Studies*. Ed. Joep Leerssen and Karl Ulrich Syndram. Amsterdam: Rodopi, 1992. 83–96.

Szabolcsi, Miklós. "La Renaissance des méthodes historiques et la littérature comparée." *Actes du VIIIe Congres de l'Association Internationale de Littérature Comparée / Proceedings of the VIIIth Congress of the International Comparative Literature Association*. Ed. Béla Köpeczi and György M. Vajda. Stuttgart: Bieber, 1980. Vol. 2, 469–73.

Szegedy-Maszák, Mihály. "Universalism and Cultural Relativism." *The Search for a New Alphabet: Literary Studies in a Changing World*. Ed. Harald Hendrix, Joost Kloek, Sophie Levie, and Will van Peer. Amsterdam: John Benjamins, 1996. 239–44.

Szegedy-Maszák, Mihály. "Comparative Literature in Hungary." *Comparative Literature World Wide: Issues and Methods / La Littérature comparée dans le monde: Questions et méthodes*. Ed. Tânia Franco Carvalhal. Porto Alegre: L&PM Editores, 1997. 173–96.

Sziklay, L. "Einige methodologische Fragen der vergleichenden Literaturgeschichte." *Studia Slavica Academiae Sciantiarum Hungaricae* 9 (1963): 311–35.

Szili, József. "Comparative Poetics: Eastern and Western Literarariness." *Neohelicon: Acta Comparationis Litterarum Universarum* 17.1 (1990): 45–58.

Szili, József. "The Global Comparatist (A Few 'Do It'-s)." *Neohelicon: Acta Comparationis Litterarum Universarum* 24.2 (1997): 71–78.

Tam, Kwok-kan John. "Issues in Reception Theory and Chinese-Western Comparative Literature." *Tamkang Review* 16.4 (1986): 325–41.

Tan, Chung. "The Indian Cultural Factor in the Development of Chinese Fiction." *Comparative Literature: Theory and Practice.* Ed. Amiya Dev and Sisir Kumar Das. Shimla: Indian Institute of Advanced Study, 1989. 159–80.

Tartalja, Ivo. *Poceci istorije opste knjievnosti kod Srba (The First Serbian Works on the History of World Literature).* Beograd: SANU, 1964.

Tatlow, Antony. "Comparatists in Peking." *Hong Kong Comparative Literature Association Newsletter* 1 (1981): 22.

Tatlow, Antony. "Comparative Literature as Textual Anthropology." *Comparative Literature and Comparative Cultural Studies.* Ed. Steven Tötösy de Zepetnek. West Lafayette: Purdue UP, 2002. 206–15.

Teesing, Hubert Paul Hans. "Die Bedeutung der vergleichenden Literaturgeschichte für die literaturhistorische Periodisierung." *Forschungsprobleme der vergleichenden Literaturgeschichte.* Ed. Fritz Ernst and Kurt Wais. Tübingen: Niemeyer, 1958. 13–20.

Texte, Joseph. "Les Etudes de littérature comparée à l'étranger et en France." *Revue internationale de l'enseignement* 25 (1893): 253–68.

Texte, Joseph. "The Comparative History of Literature." 1896. *Comparative Literature: The Early Years.* Ed. Hans-Joachim Schulz and Phillip H. Rhein. Chapel Hill: U of North Carolina P, 1973. 109–12.

Texte, Joseph. "L'Histoire comparée des littératures." *Etudes de littérature européenne.* Paris: A. Colin, 1898. 1–23.

Texte, Joseph. "Introduction." *La Littérature comparée. Essai bibliographique.* Ed. Louis-Paul Betz. Strasbourg: Karl J. Trübner, 1904. xxii–xxviii.

Thompson, Stith. "Comparative Problems in Oral Literature." *Yearbook of Comparative and General Literature* 7 (1958): 6–16.

Thorlby, Anthony. "Comparative Literature." *Yearbook of General and Comparative Literature* 18 (1969): 75–81.

Thornton, William H. "Analyzing East/West Power Politics in Comparative Cultural Studies." *Comparative Literature and Comparative Cultural Studies.* Ed. Steven Tötösy de Zepetnek. West Lafayette: Purdue UP, 2002. 216–34.

Thys, Walter. "Die Pflege der Allgemeinen und Vergleichenden Literaturwissenschaft in Belgien und den Niederlanden." *Germanica Wratislaviensia* 36 (1980): 177–92.

Tiffin, Helen. "Commonwealth Literature and Comparative Methodology." *World Literature Written in English* 23.1 (1984): 26–30.

Torre, Guillermo de. "Goethe y la literatura universal." *Las Metamorfosis de Proteo.* Buenos Aires: Losada, 1956. 278–89.

Toru, Haga, and Eva Kushner, eds. *Dialogues des Cultures / Dialogues of Cultures.* New York: Peter Lang, 2000.

Tötösy de Zepetnek, Steven. "Systemic Approaches to Literature—An Introduction with Selected Bibliographies." *Canadian Review of Comparative Literature / Revue Canadienne de Littérature Comparée* 19.1-2 (1992): 21–93.

Tötösy de Zepetnek, Steven. "Comparative Literature and Systemic / Institutional Approaches to Literature: New Developments." *Systems Research: The Official Journal of the International Federation for Systems Research* 11.2 (1994): 43–57.

Tötösy de Zepetnek, Steven. *Comparative Literature: Theory, Method, Application.* Amsterdam-Atlanta, GA: Rodopi, 1998.

Tötösy de Zepetnek, Steven. "Constructivism and Comparative Cultural Studies." *CLCWeb: Comparative Literature and Culture: A WWWeb Journal (Library)* (2001–): <http://clcwebjournal.lib.purdue.edu/library/totosy(constructivism).html>.

Tötösy de Zepetnek, Steven. "Comparative Cultural Studies and the Study of Translation: Concepts and Terminology." *CLCWeb: Comparative Literature and Culture: A WWWeb Journal (Library)* (2001–): <http://clcwebjournal.lib.purdue.edu/library/translationstudy.html>.

Tötösy de Zepetnek, Steven. "The New Knowledge Management: Online Research and Publishing in the Humanities." *CLCWeb: Comparative Literature and Culture: A WWWeb Journal* 3.1 (2001): <http://clcwebjournal.lib.purdue.edu/clcweb01-1/totosy01.html>.

Tötösy de Zepetnek, Steven. "Comparative Cultural Studies and the Study of Central European Culture." *Comparative Central European Culture.* Ed. Steven Tötösy de Zepetnek West Lafayette: Purdue UP, 2002. 1–32.

Tötösy de Zepetnek, Steven. "From Comparative Literature Today Toward Comparative Cultural Studies." *Comparative Literature and Comparative Cultural Studies.* Ed. Steven Tötösy de Zepetnek. West Lafayette: Purdue UP, 2002. 235–67.

Träger, Claus. "Zum Gegenstand und Integrationsbereich der Allgemeinen und Vergleichenden Literaturwissenschaft." *Weimarer Beiträge* (1969): 90–102.

Triomphe, Robert. "L'URSS et la littérature comparée." *Revue de Littérature Comparée* 34 (1960): 304–310.

Trivedi, Harish, and Richard Allen, eds. *Literature and Nation: Britain and India, 1800 to 1990.* New York: Routledge, 2000.

Trousson, Raymond. *Un Problème de littérature comparée. Les Etudes de thèmes. Essai de méthodologie.* Paris: Lettres Modernes, 1965.

Trousson, Raymond. "Les Etudes des thèmes hier et aujourd'hui." *Actes du VIIIe Congres de l'Association Internationale de Littérature Comparée / Proceedings of the VIIIth Congress of the International Comparative Literature Association.* Ed. Béla Köpeczi and György M. Vajda. Stuttgart: Bieber, 1980. Vol. 2, 499–503.

Tung, Chung hsuan. "When Comparative Literature Ceases to Compare." *Tamkang Review* 17.2 (1986): 109–20.

Turner, Graeme. *British Cultural Studies: An Introduction.* New York: Routledge, 1996.

Tutungi, Gilbert. "Comparative Literature in the Arab World." *Yearbook of Comparative and General Literature* 13 (1964): 64–67.

Tymieniecka, Anna-Teresa, and Marlies Kronegger. *Phenomenology and Aesthetics: Approaches to Comparative Literature and the Other Arts.* Amsterdam: Kluwer, 1991.

Vajda, György M. "Goethes Anregung zur vergleichenden Literaturbetrachtung." *Acta Litteraria Academiae Scientiarum Hungaricae* 10.3-4 (1968): 211–38.

Vajda, György M. "Comparative Literature in Hungary." *Hungarian Survey* 3 (1968): 87–96.

Vajda, György M. "Über die Zukunft der Literaturwissenschaft." *The Future of Literary Scholarship / Die Zukunft der Literaturwissenschaft.* Ed. György M. Vajda and János Riesz. Frankfurt: Peter Lang, 1986. 11–28.

Vajda, György M. "Methodologische Fragen einer Historiographie der Weltliteratur." *Sensus Communis: Contemporary Trends in Comparative Literature / Panorama de la situation actuelle en Littérature Comparée.* Ed. János Riesz, Peter Boerner, and Bernhard Scholz. Tübingen: Gunter Narr, 1986. 193–202.

Valdés, María Elena de. "Ethnocentrism in Feminist Criticism." *Differential Multilogue: Comparative Literrature and National Literatures.* Ed. Gurbhagat Singh. Delhi: Ajanta, 1991. 163–74.

Valdés, Mario J. "Giambattista Vico at the Crossroads between Literary Theory and Comparative Literature." *Sensus Communis: Contemporary Trends in Comparative Literature / Panorama de la situation actuelle en Littérature Comparée.* Ed. János Riesz, Peter Boerner, and Bernhard Scholz. Tübingen: Gunter Narr, 1986. 441–52.

Valdés, Mario J. "Cultural Intertext as an Alternative to the Concept of National Literatures." *Differential Multilogue: Comparative Literrature and National Literatures.* Ed. Gurbhagat Singh. Delhi: Ajanta, 1991. 79–88.

Valdés, Mario J. "Why Comparative Literary History?" *Comparative Literary History as Discourse.* Ed. Mario J. Valdés, Daniel Javitch, and A. Owen Aldridge. Bern: Peter Lang, 1992. 3–20.

Valdés, Mario J. "From Geography to Poetry: A Braudelian Comparative Literary History of Latin America." *La Formation de l'imagination / Constructing the Imagination.* Ed. Mario J. Valdés. *Canadian Review of Comparative Literature / Revue Canadienne de Littérature Comparée* 23.1 (1996): 199–205.

Valdés, Mario J. *Hermeneutics of Poetic Sense: Critical Studies of Literature, Cinema, and Cultural History.* Toronto: U of Toronto P, 1998.

Valdés, Mario J., and Linda Hutcheon. *Rethinking Literary History—Comparatively.* Occasional Paper 27. New York: American Council of Learned Societies, 1994.

Valentine, James, ed. *Black Women Writers Across Cultures: An Analysis of Their Contribution.* Lanham: International Scholars Publications, 2000.

Van Tieghem, Paul. "La Notion de littérature comparée." *La Revue du Mois* 10.3 (1906): 268–91.

Van Tieghem, Paul. "La Synthèse en histoire littéraire: Littérature comparée et littérature générale." *Revue de Synthèse Historique* 31 (1920): 1–27.

Van Tieghem, Paul. "Le Premier Congrès International d'Histoire Littéraire et la crise des méthodes." *Modern Philology* 29.2 (1931): 129–48.

Van Tieghem, Paul. *La Littérature comparée*. 1931. Paris: Colin, 1951.

Van Tieghem, Paul. "La Littérature comparée comme instrument de compréhension internationale." *Revue de Littérature comparée* 22 (1948): 416–19.

Vasile, Marian. "O teorie comparatista." *Luceafarul* 29.30 (26 July 1986): 1–2.

Vega, Maria José, and Neus Carbonell, eds. *Literatura Comparada. Principios y métodos*. Madrid: Gredos, 1998.

Veit, Walter F. "Comparative Literature, Interculturality, and the History of Australian Literature." *Comparative Literature Now: Theories and Practice / La Littérature comparée à l'heure actuelle. Théories et réalisations*. Ed. Steven Tötösy de Zepetnek, Milan V. Dimić, and Irene Sywenky. Paris: Honoré Champion, 1999. 425–37.

Viatte, Auguste. "La Littérature comparée au Canada français." *Revue de Littérature comparée* 21 (1947): 96–97.

Villanueva, Darío. *El polen de ideas. Teoría, crítica, historia y literatura comparada*. Barcelona: PPU, 1991.

Villanueva, Darío. "Pluralismo crítico y recepión literaria." *Avances . . . en teoría de la literatura*. Ed. Darío Villanueva. Santiago de Compostela: U of Santiago de Compostela, 1994. 11–34.

Villanueva, Darío. "Literatura comparada y enseñanza de la literatura." *1616 9* (1995): 97–104.

Voisine, Jacques. "Les Etudes de littérature comparée." *Revue de l'Einseignement Supérieur* 3 (1957): 61–67.

Voisine, Jacques. "Le Comparatisme en Belgique." *Revue de Littérature comparée* 32 (1958): 302–03.

Vosskamp, Wilhelm. "Jenseits der Nationalphilologien: Interdisziplinarität in der Literaturwissenschaft." *Wie international ist die Literaturwissenschaft?* Ed. Lutz Danneberg, Friedrich Vollhardt, Hartmut Böhme, and Jörg Schönert. Stuttgart: Metzler, 1996. 87–98.

Vossler, Karl. "Nationalliteratür und Weltliteratur." *Zeitwende* 4.1 (1928): 193–204.

Vries, D. de. "De vergelijkende literatuurstudie." *Neophilologus* 35 (1935): 170–75, 300–10.

Wais, Kurt. "Zeitgeist und Volksgeist in der vergleichenden Literaturgeschichte." *Germanisch Romanische Monatshefte* 22 (1934): 291–307.

Wang, Ning. *Bijiao wenxüe yu zhongguo dangdai wenxüe (Comparative Literature and Contemporary Chinese Literature)*. Kunming: Yunnan Education P, 1992.

Wang, Ning. "Cultural Relativism and the Future of Comparative Literature." *The Search for a New Alphabet: Literary Studies in a Changing World*. Ed. Harald Hendrix, Joost Kloek, Sophie Levie, and Will van Peer. Amsterdam: John Benjamins, 1996. 290–95.

Wang, Ning. "Toward a New Framework of Comparative Literature." *Comparative Literature: History and Contemporaneity / Littérature Comparée: Histoire et contemporanéité*. Ed. Milan V. Dimić and Steven Tötösy de Zepetnek. *Canadian Review of Comparative Literature / Revue Canadienne de Littérature Comparée* 23.1 (1996): 91–100.

Wang, Ning. "Comparative Aspects of Contemporary Popular Literature in China." *Comparative Literature Now: Theories and Practice / La Littérature comparée à l'heure actuelle. Théories et réalisations*. Ed. Steven Tötösy de Zepetnek, Milan V. Dimić, and Irene Sywenky. Paris: Honoré Champion, 1999. 439–49.

Wang, Ning. *Bijiao wenxüe yu dangdai wenhua piping (Comparative Literature and Cultural Studies during the Tang Dynasty)*. Beijing: Jen min wen hsüeh ch'u pan she, 2000.

Wang, Zhiliang. "Anatomy of Comparative Studies in China." *Proceedings of the XIIth Congress of the International Comparative Literature Association / Actes du XIIe congres de l'Association Internationale de Littérature Comparée*. Ed. Roger Bauer. München: iudicium, 1990. Vol. 5, 245–50.

Warnke, Frank J. "The Comparatist's Canon: Some Observations." *The Comparative Perspective on Literature*. Ed. Clayton Koelb and Susan Noakes. Ithaca: Cornell UP, 1988. 48–56.

Wägenbaur, Thomas. "Comparative Literature as Anti-Racist Ethnocriticism." *Comparative Literature Now: Theories and Practice / La Littérature comparée à l'heure actuelle. Théories et réalisations*. Ed. Steven Tötösy de Zepetnek, Milan V. Dimic, and Irene Sywenky. Paris: Honoré Champion, 1999. 241–49.

Weber, Samuel. "The Foundering of Aesthetics: Thoughts on the Current State of Comparative Literature." *The Comparative Perspective on Literature*. Ed. Clayton Koelb and Susan Noakes. Ithaca: Cornell UP, 1988. 57–72.

Wegner, Hart L. "Film in Comparative Literature: Plowing with Horse and Ox?" *Actes du VIIe Congrès de l'Association Internationale de Littérature Comparée*. Ed. Milan V. Dimić and Eva Kushner. Stuttgart: Kunst und Wissen, 1979. Vol. 2, 415–17.

Wegner, Michael. "Die sozialistische Kultur der DDR—Bestandteil der internationalen Kultur des Sozialismus. Zu einigen methodologischen Problemen der marxistisch-leninistischen vergleichenden Literaturforschung in der DDR." *Kulturwissenschaft und Arbeiterklasse*. Berlin: Dietz, 1971. 106–12.

Wehrli, Max. "Weltliteratur und vergleichende Literaturwissenschaft." *Allgemeine Literaturwissenschaft*. By Max Wehrli. Bern: Francke, 1951. 153–56.

Weimann, Robert. "History and Value in the Comparative Study of Literature." *Neohelicon: Acta Comparationis Litterarum Universarum* 1.1–2 (1973): 27–43.

Weimann, Robert. "Historizität und Wertsetzung. Zur Kritik der Begriffsbildung in der Vergleichenden Literaturwissenschaft (1973–1979)." *Vergleichende Literaturforschung in den sozialistischen Ländern 1963–1979*. Ed. Gerhard R. Kaiser. Stuttgart: Metzler, 1980. 209–21.

Weisgerber, Jean. "Esquisse d'un programme comparatiste ou de quelques châteaux en Espagne." *Sensus Communis: Contemporary Trends in Comparative Literature / Panorama de la situation actuelle en Littérature Comparée*. Ed. János Riesz, Peter Boerner, and Bernhard Scholz. Tübingen: Gunter Narr, 1986. 203–210.

Weisstein, Ulrich. *Einführung in die Vergleichende Literaturwissenschaft*. Stuttgart: Kohlhammer, 1968.

Weisstein, Ulrich. "Komparatistik: Alte Methode oder Neue Wissenschaft? Grundsätzliches aus Anlaß einer italienischen Reise." *Vergleichende Literaturkritik. Drei Essays zur Methodologie der Literaturwissenschaft*. Ed. Joseph Strelka. München: Francke, 1970. 631–56.

Weisstein, Ulrich. *Comparative Literature and Literary Theory: Survey and Introduction*. Trans. William Riggan. Bloomington: Indiana UP, 1973.

Weisstein, Ulrich. "Influences and Parallels: The Place and Function of Analogy Studies in Comparative Literature." *Teilnahme und Spiegelung*. Ed. Beda Allemann and Erwin Koppen. Berlin: de Gruyter, 1975. 593–609.

Weisstein, Ulrich. "Conference: Comparing the Arts." *Yearbook of Comparative and General Literature* 25 (1976): 5–30.

Weisstein, Ulrich. "Die wechselseitige Erhellung von Literatur und Musik. Ein Arbeitsgebiet der Komparatistik?" *Neohelicon: Acta Comparationis Litterarum Universarum* 5.1 (1977): 93–123.

Weisstein, Ulrich. *Vergleichende Literaturwissenschaft. Erster Bericht: 1968–1977*. Bern: Peter Lang, 1981.

Weisstein, Ulrich. "D'où venons-nous? Que sommes-nous? Où allons-nous? The Permanent Crisis of Comparative Literature." *Canadian Review of Comparative Literature / Revue Canadienne de Littérature Comparée* 11.2 (1984): 167–92.

Weisstein, Ulrich. "Assessing the Assessors: An Anatomy of Comparative Literature Handbooks." *Sensus Communis: Contemporary Trends in Comparative Literature / Panorama de la situation actuelle en Littérature Comparée*. Ed. János Riesz, Peter Boerner, and Bernhard Scholz. Tübingen: Gunter Narr, 1986. 97–113.

Weisstein, Ulrich. "Lasciate ogni speranza: Comparative Literature in Search of Lost Definitions." *Yearbook of Comparative and General Literature* 37 (1988): 98–108.

Weisstein, Ulrich. "From Ecstasy to Agony: The Rise and Fall of Comparative Literature." *Neohelicon: Acta Comparationis Litterarum Universarum* 24.2 (1997): 95–118.

Weisstein, Ulrich, ed. *Literatur und bildende Künste. Ein Handbuch zur Theorie und Praxis eines komparatistischen Grenzgebiets*. Berlin: Erich Schmidt, 1992.

Wellek, René. "The Concept of Comparative Literature." *Yearbook of Comparative and General Literature* 2 (1953): 1–5.

Wellek, René. "The Crisis in Comparative Literature." *Concepts of Criticism*. Ed. Stephen G. Nicholas, Jr. New Haven: Yale UP, 1963. 282–95.

Wellek, René. "Comparative Literature Today." *Comparative Literature* 17 (1965): 325–37.

Wellek, René. "Begriff und Idee der Vergleichenden Literaturwissenschaft." *arcadia: Zeitschrift für Vergleichende Literaturwissenschaft* 2 (1967): 229–47.

Wellek, René. "The Name and Nature of Comparative Literature." *Discriminations: Further Concepts of Criticism*. By René Wellek. New Haven: Yale UP, 1970. 1–30.

Wellek, René. "Memories of the Profession." *Building a Profession: Autobiographical Perspectives on the Beginnings of Comparative Literature in the United States*. Ed. Lionel Gossman and Mihai I. Spariosu. Albany: State U of New York P, 1994. 1–11.

Wesling, Donald. "Methodological Implications of the Philosophy of Jacques Derrida for Comparative Literature: The Opposition East-West and Several Other Observations." *Chinese-Western Comparative Literature: Theory and Strategy*. Ed. John J. Deeney. Hong Kong: Chinese UP, 1980. 79–112.

Wetz, Wilhelm. "Über Begriff und Wesen der vergleichenden Litteraturgeschichte." *Shakespeare vom Standpunkt der vergleichenden Litteraturgeschichte*. By Wilhelm Wetz. Worms, 1890. 3–43.

Wheeler, Samuel. *Deconstruction as Analytic Philosophy*. Stanford: Stanford UP, 2000.

Wilkinson, Nick. "Methodology for the Comparative Study of Commonwealth Literature." *The Journal of Commonwealth Literature* 8.3 (1979): 33–42.

Will, Frederic. "Comparative Literature and the Challenge of Modern Criticism." *Yearbook of Comparative and General Literature* 9 (1960): 29–31.

Will, J.S. "Comparative Literature: Its Meaning and Scope." *University of Toronto Quarterly* 8 (1959): 165–179.

Willemart, Philippe. "Déterminisme ou instabilité dans le manuscrit littéraire. Un nouveau modèle pour la littérature comparée?" *Language and Literature Today*. Ed. Neide de Faria. Brasília: U of Brasília, 1996. 1007–13.

Willoughby, L.A. "Stand und Aufgaben der vergleichenden Literaturgeschichte in England." *Forschungsprobleme der vergleichenden Literaturgeschichte*. Ed. Fritz Ernst and Kurt Wais. Tübingen: Niemeyer, 1958. 21–28.

Wilson, Robert Rawdon. "Seeing With a Fly's Eye: Comparative Perspectives in Comparative Literature." *Open Letter: A Canadian Journal of Writing and Theory* 8.2 (1992): 2–27.

Witke, Charles. "Comparative Literature and the Classics: East and West." *Tamkang Review* 2–3 (1971–72): 11–16.

Wittmann, Lívia Z. "Feministische Literaturkritik. Ein Ansatz der Vergleichenden Literaturwissenschaft. *Comparative Literary Studies*. Ed. István Fried, Zoltán Kanyó, and József Pál. Szeged: József Attila U, 1983. 117–28.

Wollman, Slavomír. "Überblick über die Entwicklung der tschechischen vergleichenden Literaturforschung." *Aktuelle Probleme der vergleichenden Literaturforschung.* Ed. Gerhard Ziegengeist. Berlin: Akademie, 1968. 100–17.

Wollman, Slavomír. *Porovnácia metoda v literárnej vede (The Comparative Method in Literary Scholarship).* Bratislava: Tatran, 1988.

Worsely, Peter. *Knowledges: Culture, Counterculture, Subculture.* New York: New P, 1999.

Wrenn, Charles L. *The Idea of Comparative Literature.* London: Modern Languages Humanities Research Association, 1968.

Xie, Tianzhen. "Le tendenze più recenti della comparatistica letteraria cinese (1990–1992)." Trans. Monica Piccioni. *Comparare i comparatismi. La comparatistica letteraria oggi in Europa e nel mondo.* Ed. Armando Gnisci and Franca Sinopoli. Roma: Lithos, 1995. 37–51.

Yamagiwa, Joseph K. "Comparative, General, and World Literature in Japan." *Yearbook of Comparative and General Literature* 2 (1953): 28–39.

Yano, Hojin. *Hikaku Bungaku (Comparative Literature).* Tokyo: Nan-un do, 1956.

Yegenoglu, Meyda. *Colonial Fantasies: Towards a Feminist Reading of Orientalism.* Cambridge: Cambridge UP, 1998.

Yip, Wai-lim. "The Use of 'Models' in East-West Comparative Literature." *Tamkang Review* 6–7 (1975–76): 109–26.

Yokota-Murakami, Takayuki. *Don Juan East/West: On the Problematics of Comparative Literature.* New York: State U of New York P, 1998.

Yu, Anthony C. "Problems and Prospects in Chinese-Western Literary Relations." *Yearbook of Comparative and General Literature* 23 (1974): 47–53.

Yu, Pauline. "Alienation Effects: Comparative Literature and the Chinese Tradition." *The Comparative Perspective on Literature: Approaches to Theory and Practice.* Ed. Clayton Koelb and Susan Noakes. Ithaca: Cornell UP, 1988. 162–75.

Yuan, Heh-hsiang. "East-West Comparative Literature: An Inquiry into Possibilities." *Chinese-Western Comparative Literature Theory and Strategy.* Ed. John J. Deeney. Hong-Kong: The Chinese UP, 1980. 1–24.

Yuan, Haoyi. "Survey of Current Developments in the Comparative Literature of China." *Cowrie: A Chinese Journal of Comparative Literature* 1 (1983): 81–125.

Yuan, Haoyi. "New Stimuli: Review of Developments in Chinese Comparative Literature from 1984–1985." *Cowrie: A Chinese Journal of Comparative Literature* 3 (1986): 117–23.

Yuan, Heh-Hsiang. "From Cultural Relativism to Cultural Respect." *The Search for a New Alphabet: Literary Studies in a Changing World.* Ed. Harald Hendrix, Joost Kloek, Sophie Levie, and Will van Peer. Amsterdam: John Benjamins, 1996. 311–15.

Yue, Daiyun. "Teaching Literary History in China and the Canon of Comparative Literature." *Yearbook of Comparative and General Literature* 31 (1982): 126–30.

Yue, Daiyun. *Bijiao wenxüe yuanli (Theory of Comparative Literature)*. Changsha: Hunan Literature and Art P, 1988.

Yue, Daiyun. "Prospects of Chinese Comparative literature." *Comparative Literature: Theory and Practice*. Ed. Amiya Dev and Sisir Kumar Das. Shimla: Indian Institute of Advanced Study, 1989. 37–70.

Yue, Daiyun. "Cultural Differences and Cultural Misreadings." *New Perspectives: A Comparative Literature Yearbook* 1 (1995): 13–19.

Yue, Daiyun. "Comparative Literature in China." *Comparative Literature World Wide: Issues and Methods / La Littérature comparée dans le monde: Questions et méthodes*. Ed. Tânia Franco Carvalhal. Porto Alegre: L&PM Editores, 1997. 259–72.

Yue, Daiyun and Wang Ning, eds. *Chao xueke bijiao wenxüe yanjiu (Interdisciplinary Studies of Comparative Literature)*. Beijing: China Social Sciences Publishing House, 1989.

Zaleski, Z.L. "La Littérature comparée en Pologne." *Yearbook of Comparative and General Literature* 2 (1953): 14–19.

Zelenka, Milos. "Wellkova teorie djin literatury v kontextu ceské literární komparatistiky. Strukturální estetika a základy srovnávací metody" (The Basis of Wellek's Comparative Method in Connection with Structural Aesthetics). *René Wellek a meziválecné Ceskoslovensko (René Wellek between the Two World Wars in Czechoslovakia)*. Ed. Ivo Pospísil and Milos Zelenka. Brno: Masarykova univerzita, 1996. 65–79.

Zhou, Xiaoyi, and Q.S. Tong. "Comparative Literature in China." *Comparative Literature and Comparative Cultural Studies*. Ed. Steven Tötösy de Zepetnek. West Lafayette: Purdue UP, 2002. 268–84.

Zima, Peter V. "Die Komparatistik zwischen Ästhetik und Textsoziologie." *Sprachkunst* 16 (1985): 113–40.

Zima, Peter V. *Komparatistik. Einführung in die Vergleichende Literaturwissenschaft*. Tübingen: Francke, 1992.

Zima, Peter V. "Komparatistik als Metatheorie. Zu interkulturellen und interdisziplinären Perspektiven der Vergleichenden Literaturwissenschaft." *Wie international ist die Literaturwissenschaft?* Ed. Lutz Danneberg, Friedrich Vollhardt, Hartmut Böhme, and Jörg Schönert. Stuttgart: Metzler, 1996. 532–49.

Zima, Peter V. "Thesen zur Literaturwissenschaft." *Neohelicon: Acta Comparationis Litterarum Universarum* 24.2 (1997): 119–23.

Zima, Peter V. *The Philosophy of Modern Literary Theory*. London: Athlone, 1999.

Zirmunskij, Viktor M. *Problemy sravnitel'noj filologii (Problems of Comparative Philology)*. Moskva: Akademija nauk, 1964.

Zirmunskij, Viktor M. "Methodologische Probleme der marxistisch historisch-vergleichenden Literaturforschung." *Aktulle Probleme der vergleichenden Literaturforschung.* Ed. Gerhard Ziegengeist. Berlin: Akademie, 1968. 1–16.

Zirmunskij, Viktor M. "On the Study of Comparative Literature." *Oxford Slavonic Papers* 13 (1968): 1–13.

Zirmunskij, Viktor M. *Sravnitel'noe literaturovedenie. Vostok i zapad (Izbrannye trudy) (Comparative Literature: East and West).* Leningrad: Nauka, 1979.

Zirmunskij, Viktor M. "Über das Fach Vergleichende Literaturwissenschaft." 1967. *Vergleichende Literaturforschung in den sozialistischen Ländern 1963–1979.* Ed. Gerhard R. Kaiser. Stuttgart: Metzler, 1980. 77–89.

Contributors

Steven Aoun works in comparative literature and critical and hermeneutic theory at Monash University. In 2001 he published "Everything's Relative, or, The Sopranos as a Sign of The (New York) Times" in *Metro*, the film quarterly. He is co-founder of the Australian Association of Philosophical Counselling <http://www.aaphcl.net/> and he is editorial assistant with *CLCWeb: Comparative Literature and Culture: A WWWeb Journal* at <http://clcwebjournal.lib.purdue.edu/>. Aoun's curriculum vitae is at <http://www.users.bigpond.com/bonnee8/cv.html>.

Kwaku Asante-Darko teaches African literature, literary theory, and poetry at the National University of Lesotho. His recent publications include "The Co-Centrality of Racial Conciliation in Negritude Literature" in *Research in African Literatures* (2000) and "The Flora and Fauna of Negritude Poetry: An Eco-critical Re-Reading" in *Mots Pluriels* (1999). He also writes poetry dealing with the political chaos in post-independence Africa. His forthcoming novel, *The Beast in Man*, deals with the armed conflicts in independent Africa.

Hendrik Birus teaches comparative literature at the University of München. His interests and numerous publications are in the fields of hermeneutics, comparative literature and German literature, particularly Goethe, Lessing, Celan, and Adorno. Birus is editor, among others, of *Hermeneutische Positionen* (1998), of *Germanistik und Komparatistik* (1995), of Goethe's *West-östlicher Divan* (1994) and of the recently published six volume series, *Johann Wolfgang Goethe. Werke* (1999).

343

Amiya Dev has taught comparative literature at Jadavpur University for over three decades, with frequent visiting professorships in North America, Europe, and China, and he served 1990–2000 as Vice-Chancellor of Vidyasagar University. His numerous publications include *The Idea of Comparative Literature in India* (1984), *The Renewal of Song: Renovation in Lyric Conception and Practice* (1999), and he edited with Sisir Kumar Das *Comparative Literature: Theory and Practice* (1998). Dev is now retired and lives in Calcutta.

Marián Gálik works in Sinology, comparative literature, and intellectual history at the Institute of Oriental and African Studies of Slovakia and at Comenius University. He is author of numerous books and papers, published mostly in English and Mandarin, including *The Genesis of Modern Chinese Literary Criticism, 1917–1930* (1980), *Milestones in Sino-Western Literary Confrontation, 1898–1979* (1986), "East-West Interliterariness: A Theoretical Sketch and a Historical Overview" in *Comparative Literature: Theory and Practice* (1989), and "Comparative Literature in Slovakia" in the *Canadian Review of Comparative Literature* (1996).

Ernst Grabovszki works in theory of comparative literature and the social history of literature at the University of Vienna. His recent publications include articles in the *Encyclopedia of Contemporary German Culture* (1999), *Makers of Western Culture, 1800–1914: A Biographical Dictionary of Literary Influences* (2000), and in the *Biographical Dictionary of Literary Influences: The Twentieth Century* (2002). His books are *Methoden und Modelle der deutschen, französischen und amerikanischen Sozialgeschichte als Herausforderung für die Vergleichende Literaturwissenschaft (2002) and Ein Sammelpunkt der europäischen Avantgarde. Jiddische und amerikanische Literatur im Paul Zsolnay Verlag der Zwischenkriegszeit (*2002).

Jan Walsh Hokenson teaches French and comparative literature at Florida Atlantic University. She has published numerous articles on modern French and European writers, including "Intercultural Autobiography" in *A/B Auto/Biography Studies* (1995), "Proust's *japonisme*: Contrastive Aesthetics" in *Modern Language Studies* (1999), "Public Lives: Dominique Desanti and the French Autobiographical Tradition" in *Dalhousie French Studies* (2000), and "Fool: The Learning of Laughter" *The Iron Mountain Review* (2001). Hokenson's next book is *The Woodblocks of Modernism: A History of* japonisme *in French Literature, 1865–2000.*

Marko Juvan teaches Slovenian literature, comparative literature, and literary theory at the University of Ljubljana and he is with the Scientific Research Center of the Slovenian Academy of Sciences and Art. His numerous publications include *Intertekstualnost (Intertextuality)* (2000), *Vezi besedila (Textual Ties)* (2000), "Transgressing the Romantic Legacy? Baptism at the Savica as a Key-Text of Slovene Literature in Modernism and Postmodernism" in *Postmodernism in Literature and Culture of Central and Eastern Europe* (1996), "Introduction" in *Bakhtin and the Humanities* (1997), and "The Sonnet, Self-Referentiality, and Parodicity in Slovenian Literature" in *Die Welt der Slaven* (1997).

Karl S.Y. Kao teaches Chinese fiction and rhetoric, China-West comparative literature, and epistemology at the Hong Kong University of Science and Technology. Previously, he has taught at the universities of Wisconsin, Yale, Alberta, and Tsing Hua. He has published articles and books in Mandarin and in English, including "Self-reflexivity, Epistemology, and Rhetorical Figures" in *Chinese Literature: Essays, Articles, Reviews* 19 (1997) and, in Mandarin, *Rhetoric and the Reading of Literary Texts* (1997).

Krištof Jacek Kozak teaches comparative literature at the University of Alberta. His interests include literary theory and the theory of drama, modernist conceptions of art and culture, critical theory and the philosophy of art, and he has published articles and books in these areas including *Estetski in idejni vplivi na predvojno dramsko in gledališko kritiko Josipa Vidmarja (Aesthetic and Intellectual Influences on Josip Vimdar's pre-World War II Drama and Theatre Criticism)* (1998) and his translation of Szondi's *Theorie des modernen Dramas* into Slovenian appeared in 2000 as *Teorija sodobne drame.*

Manuela Mourão teaches nineteenth-century British literature, women writers, and critical theory at Old Dominion University. Her recent publications include *Altered Habits: Reconsidering the Nun in Fiction* (2002), "Delicate Balances: Gender and Power in Anne Thackeray Ritchie's Non-Fiction" in *Women's Writing* (1997), and "The Representation of Female Desire in Early

Modern Pornographic Texts" in *Signs: A Journal of Women in Culture and Society* (1999).

Wendy C. Nielsen teaches in the Writing Program of the University of California Santa Barbara. In 2001 she earned a Ph.D. in comparative literature at the University of California Davis. In her dissertation, *Female Acts of Violence: French Revolutionary Theater in British and German Romantic Drama*, Nielsen analyzes how violence in the French Revolution was translated into dramatic productions on stage and in print. Nielsen is book review editor with *CLCWeb: Comparative Literature and Culture: A WWWeb Journal* at <http://clcwebjournal.lib.pudue.edu/>

Jola Škulj teaches comparative literature and literary theory at the Research Center of the Slovene Academy of Sciences and Arts. Her recent publications include "The Modern Novel: The Concept of Spatialization (Frank) and the Dialogic Principle (Bakhtin)" in *Space and Boundaries* (1990), "Dialogism as a Non-Finalized Concept of Truth" in *Bakhtin and the Humanities* (1997), "Modernist Features in Lyrical, Narrative, and Dramatic Form" in *Primerjalna književnost* (1998), and "Literature as Repository of Historical Consciousness: Reinterpreted Tales of Mnemosyne" in *Methods for the Study of Literature as Cultural Memory* (2000). She is now completing a book on modernism.

Slobodan Sucur earned his Ph.D. in comparative literature from the University of Alberta in 2000. The published version of his dissertation, his first book is *Poe, Odoyevsky, and Purloined Letters: Questions of Theory and Period Style Analysis* (2001), in which he draws on his interests in Romanticism, Gothic literature, the fantastic, the Doppelgänger, Neoclassicism, literary history and theory, Lacan, and Derrida. He has published papers on Habermas and periodization in literary history in *CLCWeb: Comparative Literature and Culture: A WWWeb Journal* at <http://clcwebjournal.lib.purdue.edu/>. He lives in Edmonton.

Peter Swirski teaches popular culture and comparative literature at the University of Alberta. He is author of *A Stanislaw Lem Reader* (1997) and *Between Literature and Science: Poe, Lem and Explorations in Aesthetics, Cognitive Science and Literary Knowledge* (2000) and he has published papers in the fields of comparative and American literatures, aesthetics, pragmatics, narratology, and interdisciplinary studies in journals such as the *MLA, Orbis Litterarum, SubStance, Criticism, Reader,* and *Contemporary Literature,* in Beacham's *Encyclopedia of Popular Fiction* (1998) and in Scribner's *Science Fiction Writers* (1999).

Antony Tatlow teaches cultural theory at the University of Dublin (previously, he taught at the University of Hong Kong 1965–96). Tatlow's interests are in comparative literature, German and Chinese literature including drama, and the other arts, and his numerous publications include *Brechts chinesische Gedichte* (1973), *The Mask of Evil: Brecht's Response to the Poetry, Theatre and Thought of China and Japan* (1977), *Benwen renleixue (Textual Anthropology: A Practice of Reading)* (1996), *Brechts Ostasien. Ein Parallog* (1998), and *Shakespeare, Brecht and the Intercultural Sign* (2001).

William H. Thornton teaches literary and culture theory at National Cheng Kung University in Tainan. His recent publications include *Cultural Prosaics: The Second Postmodern Turn* (1998), *Fire on the Rim: The Cultural Dynamics of East/West Power Politics (*2002), "Reactionary Globalization: Local, Regional, and Global Implications of the New 'Japan Problem'" (2001) and "Back to Basics: Human Rights and Power Politics in the New Moral Realism" (2000) *in International Politics, Culture and Society,* "Selling Democratic Teleology: The Case of the Chinese Fortune-Tellers" in *International Politics: A Journal of Transnational Issues and Global Problems* (2000), and "Mapping the 'Glocal' Village: The Political Limits of 'Glocalization'" in *Continuum: Journal of Media and Cultural Studies* (2000).

Q.S. Tong teaches English at the University of Hong Kong. His recent publications include *Reconstructing Romanticism: Organic Theory Revisited* (1997), "The Bathos of a Universalism: I.A. Richards and His Basic English" in *Tokens of Exchange: The Problem of Translation in Global Circulation* (1999), and "Reinventing China: The Use of Orientalist Views on the Chinese Language" in *Interventions: International Journal of Post-Colonial Studies* (2000). He has also co-edited, with Douglas Kerr, *Cross-Cultural Communications: Literature, Language, Ideas,* a thematic issue of the *Journal of Asian Pacific Communication* (1999).

Steven Tötösy de Zepetnek's publications are in the humanities and social sciences in the fields of comparative culture and literature, media and communication studies, diaspora, exile, and ethnic minority writing, postcolonial studies, literature and film, European (English, French, German, Central European), US, Canadian cultures and literatures, history, bibliographies, new media scholarship and knowledge management, and editing. From 1984 to 2000 he taught at the University of Alberta, since 2000 he resides in Boston, and he is professor of comparative media studies at Martin Luther University Halle-Wittenberg, Germany. He is author, editor, and co-editor of twenty books and author of over one-hundred-fifty articles, book chapters, bibliographies, and encyclopedia entries. His next book is *Comparative Media Studies* (Purdue UP, 2003).

Xiaoyi Zhou teaches English and comparative literature at Peking University. He received his PhD from Lancaster University in 1993 and was Research Fellow at the University of Hong Kong between 1997 and 2000. He is the author of *Beyond Aestheticism: Oscar Wilde and Consumer Society* (1996). His recent articles include "Oscar Wilde's Orientalism and Late Nineteenth-Century European Consumer Culture" in *ARIEL: A Review of International English Literature* (1997), "Oscar Wilde: An Image of Artistic Self-Fashioning in Modern China: 1909–1949" in *Images of Westerners in Chinese and Japanese Literature* (2000), "Beardsley, the Chinese Decadents and Commodity Culture in Shanghai During the 1930s" in *Journal of the Oriental Society of Australia* (2001), and "The Ideological Function of Western Aesthetics in 1980's China" in *Literary Research / Recherche Littéraire* (2001).

Index